SUING THE PRESS

SUING THE PRESS

Rodney A. Smolla

New York   Oxford
OXFORD UNIVERSITY PRESS
1986

Oxford University Press

Oxford   New York   Toronto
Delhi   Bombay   Calcutta   Madras   Karachi
Petaling Jaya   Singapore   Hong Kong   Tokyo
Nairobi   Dar es Salaam   Cape Town
Melbourne   Auckland

and associated companies in
Beirut   Berlin   Ibadan   Nicosia

Copyright © 1986 by Oxford University Press, Inc.

Published by Oxford University Press, Inc.,
200 Madison Avenue, New York, New York 10016

Oxford is a registered trademark of Oxford University Press

Library of Congress Cataloging-in-Publication Data
Smolla, Rodney A.
Suing the press.
Bibliography: p.   Includes index.
Contents: The thinning American skin—The trials of Martin Luther King:
the New York Times case—From chasing Communists to fighting Lillian Hellman:
the libel suit as guerilla warfare—[etc.]
1. Libel and slander—United States—Cases.   2. Press law
—United States—Cases.   I. Title.
KF1266.A7S46   1986   346.7303′4
ISBN 0-19-503901-7   347.30634   86-812

Printing (last digit): 9 8 7 6 5 4 3 2 1

Printed in the United States of America

TO LINDA

Contents

SUING THE PRESS

1

The Thinning American Skin

It is disgusting, and it is a pack of lies. I—it hurts. It hurts, because words, once they are printed, they've got a life of their own. Words, once spoken, have a life of their own. How was I going to explain to my kids, my family, the people I care about?

Carol Burnett, testifying in
Burnett v. National Enquirer

But he that filches from me my good name
Robs me of that which not enriches him
And makes me poor indeed.
Shakespeare, *Othello* (III, iii, 160–162)

CAROL BURNETT TOOK the witness stand. With her voice slightly trembling and with tears in her eyes, she explained to the jury why she sued the *National Enquirer*.[1] Her testimony was reported live by the Cable News Network, and the highlights were repeated on the three major network evening news broadcasts:

Q. (Burnett's Attorney): When was the first time you had any knowledge of that article or the contents of that article?

A. (Carol Burnett): I believe that it was the day that it came out . . . .

Q. What was your reaction?

A. Well, I was absolutely—I was stunned. . . . I felt very, very angry. I started to cry. I started to shake.

William Westmoreland, retired commander of American forces in Vietnam, approached the microphones at the Navy Club in Washington, D.C., to announce that he was commencing a $120 million libel suit against CBS News. A documentary broadcast by CBS and narrated by Mike Wallace entitled *The Untold Story: A Vietnam Deception* had accused Westmoreland of complicity in a conspiracy to doctor intelligence estimates on the strength of enemy forces in Vietnam.[2] As in Carol Burnett's case, the General's remarks were controlled but emotional, seeping with retributive bitterness:

> I am an old soldier who loves his country and have had enough of war. It was my fate to serve for over four years as senior American commander in the most unpopular war this country ever fought. I have been reviled, burned in effigy, spat upon. Neither I nor my wife nor my family want me to go to battle once again.
>
> But all my life I have valued "duty, honor, country" above all else. Even as my friends and family urged me to ignore CBS and leave the field, I reflected on those Americans who had died in service in Vietnam. Even as I considered the enormous wealth and power that make CBS so formidable an adversary, I thought too of the troops I had commanded and sent to battle, and those who never returned.
>
> It is, therefore, with the very greatest reluctance, and consciousness of the long and bitter legal battle I am about to engage in, that I have advised my attorneys, the Capital Legal Foundation, to bring suit in South Carolina, my home state, against CBS for libel. At this moment, correspondent counsel in South Carolina is filing our complaint against CBS requesting damages for libel. There is no way left for me to clear my name, my honor, and the honor of the military . . .
>
> The only question is whether CBS had an obligation to be accurate in its facts before it attempted to destroy a man's character, the work of his lifetime. I trust the American judicial system and an American jury will fairly evaluate what I and those in positions of responsibility said and did, and I am pleased to put my reputation and honor in their custody.[3]

William Tavoulareas, the fiesty, iconoclast president of the Mobil Oil Corporation, did not appreciate a story by the *Washington Post* stating that he had "set up" his son Peter in business. The story strongly implied that Tavoulareas had acted in violation of ethical business standards, and perhaps even federal securities law. Tavoulareas tried for a frustrating year to get the *Post* to retract its story, but ultimately felt forced to take the *Post* into court for libel. Tavoulareas stated:

> I tried to get them to admit their mistakes. But they're so damned arrogant. I kept telling them I'd sue. But they said I wouldn't because they'd drag me through the mud in discovery. Well, I know my reputation and my integrity, and I knew they'd get nothing on me. I said, "you don't know me. I'm gonna sue."[4]

A comedienne, a general, a corporate executive, each a classic American self-made success story, each wounded by the media, and each striking back, through courtroom attacks that became a cause célèbre, taking on meanings much larger than the lawsuits themselves. They are among the most visible symbols of an astonishing cultural movement. America is in the midst of an explosion of litigation aimed against the media. Americans who feel that their reputations have been impugned or their privacy invaded by the broadcast or print media have increasingly resorted to litigation for vindication. Much of this litigation in recent years has been launched by well known cultural figures, many seeking staggering sums of money. Burnett, Tavoulareas, Westmoreland, Woody Allen, Clint Eastwood, Mohammed Ali, Paul Laxalt, Ralph Nader, Norman Mailer, Wayne Newton, Elizabeth Taylor, Jerry Falwell, E. Howard Hunt, Shirley Jones, Lillian Hellman, Johnny Carson: the list of famous Americans who have taken to suing publishers, broadcasters, reporters, writers, and advertisers in recent years reads as if it were randomly generated from *Who's Who*.[5] The media has been in the uneasy position of continuously reporting about itself as victim, as the lawsuit for libel or invasion of privacy has become one of America's newest growth industries.[6]

Every week a new suit against the media seems to appear, many of the suits brought by politicians, entertainers, sports stars, writers, corporate executives, and other prominent social figures who have themselves previously profited from media attention. And plaintiffs today have no shyness about asking for staggering sums in their complaints. William Westmoreland's complaint against CBS sought $120 million, but there are countless other impressive demands. Former Israeli Defense Minister Ariel Sharon claimed $50 million in his libel suit against *Time* magazine, at one point claiming that *Time* had committed a "blood libel" in a story which implied that testimony before the Israeli investigatory commission into the Phalangist massacres at the Sabra and Shatilla concentration camps in Lebanon in 1982 had put at least part of the responsibility for the massacres on Sharon.[7] Carol Burnett asked for $10 million in her suit against the *National Enquirer*. Beverly Hills physician Robert Fader filed suit for $20 million against *Washington Post* editor Bob Woodward for statements made in Woodward's book on John Belushi, *Wired—The Short Life and Fast Times of John Belushi*, in which Woodward wrote that Dr. Fader prescribed drugs to Belushi and other patients for no valid medical reasons and without regard to his patients' welfare. Norman Mailer sought $7 million in his suit against the *New York Post*, claiming that the newspaper defamed him in reports about the trial of prisoner/writer Jack Henry Abbott. Senator Paul Laxalt sought $250 million against the *Sacramento Bee* for stories linking him to a grand jury investigation of casino operations in Nevada. Former Philadelphia Mayor William J. Green sought $5.1 million from a CBS television station for reporting that he was under federal criminal investigation. Lillian Hellman sought $2.25 million against fellow writer Mary McCarthy after McCarthy said on the Dick Cavett Show that Hellman was "terribly overrated, a bad writer and a dishonest writer," and that "every word she writes is a lie, including 'and' and 'the'." Feminist attorney Gloria Alfred filed a $10 million suit against a California State Senator because of a press release that characterized Alfred as a "slick butch lawyeress." Former Governor Edward J. King of Massachusetts filed a $3.6 million suit against the *Boston Globe* for articles, editorials, and political cartoons that King alleged implied he was unfit and incapable as governor. Governor William J. Janklow of South Dakota filed a $10 million suit against *Newsweek* for an article allegedly implying that he had raped an Indian girl. Actress Shirley Jones and her husband, actor Marty Ingels, sought $20 million from the *National Enquirer* for a story alleging that Jones had severe drinking problems. Nathaniel Davis, former United States ambassador to Chile, and two of his ex-assistants filed a $150 million suit against the makers of the movie *Missing*, alleging that the 1982 film implied that the American embassy was connected with the killing of an American freelance writer during the 1973 coup d'etat in Chile. The owners of the Rancho LaCosta resort in California sought a record breaking $552 million from *Penthouse* magazine for an article claiming that the resort was a hangout for mobsters. And in what may be "the most unkindest cut of all," a group of justices from the Pennsylvania Supreme Court have sued the *Philadelphia Inquirer* for libels allegedly arising from *Inquirer* stories critical of the justices' judicial conduct!

The million dollar libel suit has become the newest American status symbol. It seems at times that everybody who's anybody has a libel suit going on the side. The awards many juries are willing to return indicate that the American public is not shocked by the size of the judgments these plaintiffs are seeking. A Washington, D.C. jury awarded Mobil Oil president William Tavoulareas $2 million in his suit against the *Washington Post*; writer Jackie Collins was awarded $40 million against a Larry Flynt distributing company; Kimerli Jane Pring, Miss Wyoming of 1978, was awarded $26 million by a Wyoming federal court jury in a suit against *Penthouse* magazine; and even E. Howard Hunt of Watergate infamy managed to win a $650,000 damage award from a federal jury in Miami against a weekly newspaper called the *Spotlight*, for a story that linked Hunt to the assassination of John F. Kennedy.[8] Most of these jury awards ultimately get reduced or eliminated altogether by the trial judge or on appeal, but the uninhibited willingness of juries to shower plaintiffs with gigantic awards indicates that something very new has infiltrated the popular mood, and the mere *threat* that one of these huge awards will make it through the legal maze untouched hangs like a litigation time bomb over writers, publishers, and broadcasters of every variety from *Penthouse* to the *New York Times*.[9]

The newfound national fascination with libel and privacy suits is worth studying for what it reveals about current American culture, and for what it reveals about the influences of cultural trends on the fabric and workings of the American legal system. The libel litigation explosion provides an unusually revealing glimpse into the relationship between changes in American law and larger patterns of national life. The new invigoration of the law of defamation and invasion of privacy is in part the result of changes in legal doctrine, but it is even more a reflection of changes in the attitudes and frustrations of contemporary Americans.

The current explosion of litigation against the media poses a long list of intriguing questions. Why do plaintiffs sue the press? Is it money they seek? Vengeance? Restoration of honor? How important is the protection of reputation in our society, and how important should it be?[10] Are libel suits a manifestation of a growing recognition of a new form of "civil right," a manifestation of concern for human dignity that is primarily directed at protecting emotional and mental tranquillity? Or are libel suits a sign of a new national narcissism, a narcissism that provokes violent responses to excessive media criticism of individuals and national institutions? Is the libel litigation explosion a symptom of a society that has grown emotionally flabby and plastic; a society that has developed a slavish and prudish devotion to decorum and self-image? Is there anything unhealthy in too much preoccupation with protecting reputation? Is America becoming too concerned with image, too thin-skinned, too removed from the rough and ready individualism that once would have regarded a libel suit as a wimpish response to criticism?[11] Or is the media's trouble in court primarily of its own making? Has the press grown too powerful, too arrogant, too oracular in tone? When the press makes errors that injure reputations, are the errors usually innocent, or are they often the result of careless or even reckless work? How often are press errors the consequence of conscious, malicious, evil deception? What do our recent experiences with major libel suits tell us about the American judicial system? How does the legal system determine the "truth" in a libel suit? How often is what purports to be a battle over "truth" really a battle of competing ideologies? Are some libel suits really less concerned with errors of fact than with a desire to punish those with opposing political, moral, or religious viewpoints? Have libel suits become a way of striking out against the fringe elements of the media? Do they provide a vehicle for a sort of puritanical backlash against *Penthouse* or the *National Enquirer*, a backlash that later comes to subtly infiltrate attitudes towards the *Washington Post* or CBS News? Are some disputes over "truth" not appropriate for litigation? Are juries able to follow the law as judges instruct them to in libel litigation, or do they apply their own version of justice? ("Their own" version of justice, of course, may well reflect values shared by many Americans, even if they are not the "approved" values of the legal system.)

What sorts of emerging cultural attitudes, biases, and perceptions are shaping jury verdicts? What is the social cost, in terms of court time, legal fees, and other "societal overhead" of libel litigation? Are the social costs worth the social benefits? What is the toll that anti-media litigation takes on First Amendment values? To what extent does it diminish the courage and the ardour of writers, publishers, or broadcasters? On the other hand, to what extent does it encourage greater accuracy, and greater fairness in news reporting, serving the strong societal interest in providing a "check and balance" on the fourth estate that might not otherwise exist? What alternatives, if any, exist to the present legal process for arbitrating conflicts between individual privacy and free expression?

These are the questions this book explores, by examining a large sampling of recent suits brought against the media. The defendant in a contemporary libel or invasion of privacy suit may be a pillar of mainstream media respectability—the *New York Times* or CBS News—or a media outlet that is on the fringe of the orthodoxy spectrum—the *National Enquirer* or *Hustler*. The defendant may be a small town daily newspaper—*The Alton Telegraph*—or an individual writer—Mary McCarthy, or Andrew Greeley. The issues litigated may range from disputes of serious national debate— the conduct of the Vietnam War or the events surrounding the disappearance of a young American writer during the overthrow of Salvador Allende Gossens in Chile. Or the disputes may be of less historical moment— whether fantasies about the sexual life of a fictional beauty queen were meant to refer to a real beauty pageant contestant. But to the plaintiffs who bring these suits, and the lawyers who try them, all of the issues are likely to seem quite serious. More significant for all of us, these suits express the escalating conflict in our increasingly mediatized society between the right of the people to know all and the right of persons to be let alone.

In examining the provocative episodes of media litigation in the chapters that follow, it is worth asking repeatedly how important the protection of reputation and privacy really is, and on the other hand how important to American society is a media so free of the threat of litigation that it can participate in the most wide-open, robust, and uninhibited discussion of issues important, or simply of interest, to the nation as a whole. Abstract discussion of these conflicts easily degenerates into the recitation of pat clichés and reflexive biases. Some find no value more sacred in the constellation of American liberties than free speech, and they react with instant hostility to any hint of censorship. Others dislike the press with all the intensity of Richard Nixon. To some the libel explosion is one of the greatest threats to civil liberties in America today. To others the sight of the pretentious, self-appointed guardians of truth forced by suits to explain why they wrote what they did is a welcome swing in the pendulum of justice. When the focus is shifted from the abstract to the particular, however, there is some hope of dissolving these clichés and prejudices in a bath of more careful and critical examination. An important element of that examination is a willingness to look at modern libel litigation from perspectives that go beyond an examination of the methods of the media. Although the media's behavior is an enormously important component in the whole story (and it receives substantial attention in this book), there are other components as well, components that deal more with the victims of libel, and with the changing cultural perceptions held by each of us as voracious consumers of the media's output.

Today, perhaps more than ever, Americans just don't trust the press. Statistics tell at least part of the story. A recent Harris survey indicated that only about 20% of those polled responded affirmatively to the question of whether they have a great deal of confidence in people running the media. A *Newsweek* poll in October 1984 revealed that television journalism ranked at the bottom of the confidence pile among Americans, with a 26% rating that placed it behind organized religion (which topped the list at 64%), the military (58%), banks, the Supreme Court, public schools, Congress, big businesses, and organized labor. Newspapers fared better; their 34% confidence rating managed to just top Congress, big business, and labor. Seven in ten Americans, however, believe that the nation's most influential papers are biased. And this statistical portrait reveals only part of the national mood.[12]

In the aftermath of Vietnam and Watergate, the American press grew in glamour, power, and profitability, but not in heartfelt esteem. College students flocked to journalism departments in hopes of becoming new Bob Woodwards or Carl Bernsteins, new Leslie Stahls or Tom Brokaws. But somehow, the growing power, glamour, and influence of the media has also been matched by growing suspicion. The evidence indicates that Americans have grown more distrustful of the media, more suspicious of the media's neutrality, and more alert to the possibility that the media may at times be influencing the course of national agendas rather than merely recording and reporting events. Americans have witnessed the power of the media, and are at once attracted to and wary of it.

In recent years highly publicized and embarrassing mistakes have plagued even the most estimable of media outlets. Perhaps the best known is the debacle at the *Washington Post*, in which Janet Cooke won the 1980 Pulitzer Prize for stories published in the *Post* about an 8-year-old heroin addict, stories presented as factual reportage that were later uncovered as inventions of Janet Cooke's imagination. The incident prompted *Washing-*

ton Post editor, Ben Bradlee, to ask "How are you going to protect yourself against pathological liars?"—a question of some irony, for it is this question many libel plaintiffs in effect claim to have asked themselves before bringing suit against news organizations. There are many other recent examples of such mistakes.

Newsweek in 1983 printed Hitler's "diaries" as a cover story one week, writing that "genuine or not, it almost doesn't matter in the end," and two weeks later admitted in embarrassment that they were frauds. The story of the fraud perpetrated on the American and European presses over the fake diaries became as big a story as the diaries themselves. In 1981, Associated Press reporter Gloria Ohland resigned over misattributed quotes and material lifted from a California magazine account of a 200 mile-per-hour "banzai" car ride down a freeway in the heart of Los Angeles. The *New York Times Magazine* ran a story in 1981 about Khmer Rouge guerrillas by Christopher Jones, a 24-year-old freelancer who faked a trip (expenses and all) from Spain to Cambodia. After Jones was caught because he had lifted material virtually verbatim from an André Malraux novel, *Times* Executive Editor A.M. Rosenthal said his newspaper had suffered a "lapse" in its "procedures." And in an incident that seemed to drive home the public suspicion that getting a good story sometimes obsesses the press to the point of inhumanity, a reporter and cameraman in Jacksonville, Alabama filmed away for a full 37 seconds as a man set himself on fire with the camera rolling. They were the only witnesses to the gruesome scene, and they got the story before they tried to save him. Although the press is usually criticized for being too emotionally involved in the stories they report, in this case the public outcry was against what seemed to be a callous detachment.[13]

These examples are nothing new—the press has been making mistakes from its earliest days, and like any human enterprise, always will. But the mistakes grate against the public sensibilities more than they once did, perhaps because of the sense these days that the establishment press takes itself so seriously.

Our image of reporters is different than it used to be. Reporters once wore hats with greasy bands like Indiana Jones; their sports jackets were rumpled, they drank a lot and they didn't get paid much. As Walter Cronkite has nicely put it, "we knew Archie Bunker better than the bankers," and the new "better class of reporters" has taken its toll in "the loss of the common touch." Reporters for the *New York Times* or the *Washington Post* may make $60,000 a year, and television network journalists routinely pull down incomes in six figures. Back in the days when journalism was a seedier business, Americans knew to take the news as we used to take our french fries—with heavy doses of salt. One of the sacred cultural clichés was "Don't believe what you read in the papers." Back in the heyday of yellow journalism reporting was surely much worse than it is today, but it was also less harmful, because there was no presumption, or pretension, of accuracy. Americans understood that the newspapers of William Randolph Hearst were largely an extension of his personality, and so they took that into account. Why believe the *New York World* when it might be flatly contradicted by the *Herald-Tribune*? Prominent Americans could afford to let libels against them slide in those more rough and tumble times, for the press itself never attained complete respectability. Reporters tended to be less well-educated and more raffish, and could thus be regarded by prominent citizens as unworthy adversaries —who cared what a scoundrel said about you?

But today, newspapers, magazines, broadcasters, advertisers, and book publishers are often extremely profitable corporate enterprises that can afford to hire from the ranks of the college-educated, upper middle class. Although the vast majority of reporters working across the nation do not earn particularly high incomes, the most visible reporters and correspondents are paid quite handsomely, and, as an industry, the media today fares substantially better than most other American businesses in terms of returns on equity. Television news is a particularly profitable oligopoly. Dan Rather, Peter Jennings, and Tom Brokaw may or may not be elitists, but they are surely elite. When someone with their style, status, and substance tells bad tales about a person it really hurts, largely because of who it is that is doing the telling. If Walter Cronkite came to be the American personification of avuncular wisdom, what could be worse than to have *him* defame you? The press has accordingly come to attain a more oracular tone: the media today at times seems to dispense not merely news but Truth, and juries may be reflecting a general public backlash against that oracular role.

A related phenomenon that has contributed to the lower esteem in which the press is held is a trend toward a general blurring of the line between the informing and the entertaining functions of broadcasts and publications. News is increasingly packaged as if it were entertainment and entertainment as if it were news. For both broadcast and print media, the post-Watergate mystique of investigative reporting has dusted much current reportage with a touch of glamour. Although *60 Minutes* undoubtedly is seen as elevating the general quality of network programming, and although it quite understandably holds itself to be above its more glittery showbiz clones—*Real People, Entertainment Tonight,* and *That's Incredible*— the fact remains that *60 Minutes* is still at bottom a television series, replete both with stars and reruns. As television critic John Weisman has noted, the roles of Harry Reasoner, Morely Safer, Ed Bradley, Diane Sawyer, and

Mike Wallace "are no less well-defined, no less honed and crafted, than *Hill Street's* Captain Frank Furrilo, *Dallas'* J.R., or *M*A*S*H's* Hawkeye Pierce." Though no major television network has approached the circus atmosphere of the nightly news telecasts in Paddy Chayevsky's movie *Network*, there are easily observable elements of pure show business in much contemporary journalism, and those elements make money. *60 Minutes* reportedly makes a profit contribution of over $60 million a year to CBS, a contribution that can make a big difference to a network's overall profit picture at the end of the season.[14]

And working from the opposite direction toward the same middle ground, much of our prime time and best-selling entertainment purports to be either news or history: the docudrama is a permanent fixture of television life, while Norman Mailer wins the National Book Award for fiction by painstakingly documenting the events surrounding the execution of Gary Gilmore. As fact and fiction merge, as the function of informing becomes inseparable from the function of entertaining, and as showing corporate profit becomes increasingly perceived as the ultimate goal behind all media effort, whatever its label, it is perfectly predictable that the legal system's response would be to generally devalue protestations of First Amendment privilege and treat compensation for those whose reputations have been injured as part of the cost of doing business.

Sometimes the spectacle of a major libel suit itself becomes a form of television news packaged almost as entertainment. When CBS anchorman Dan Rather took the witness stand recently in a $30 million libel suit brought against Rather and CBS's *60 Minutes*, the testimony became a major event. Dr. Carl A. Galloway sued Rather and CBS, charging that he had been defamed in a 1979 segment of *60 Minutes* that portrayed Galloway as the linchpin of a fraudulent auto insurance scheme. With the credibility of CBS News symbolically on the line, Rather's ordeal on the stand was excellent press; excerpts from his testimony made the network evening news broadcasts, and most of his testimony was carried live by the Cable News Network. The televised Galloway trial was as good an afternoon television draw as any soap opera, a high-brow version of Judge Wampler's *People's Court*.

Ironically, to some degree the lowered esteem of the media is part of a broader distrust in some quarters of virtually all things corporate, a distrust that the press in recent years has itself helped foster. CBS News or *Newsweek* may be lumped together in some segments of the public mind with DuPont or General Motors, as embodiments of impersonal corporate wealth that have lost their concern for individuals. As Americans are able to glimpse more of the business side of the press, they may begin to find it harder and harder to distinguish between the corporate press and any other corporate enterprise. Most American corporations are expected to pay their freight by compensating the victims injured by corporate activity. Manufacturers of defective products pay for the injuries their products cause, with no requirement that the claimant prove corporate malice, and American juries may be beginning to perceive the injuries caused by "defective news" that is manufactured by corporate media enterprises as indistinguishable from the more palpable injuries caused by any other defective product. In the public mind the question that seems to be emerging is "why should the media get a special break for its mistakes, when no other American industry does?"

Juries today are simply becoming notorious for their free and easy attitude in awarding gargantuan sums in libel suits. This pattern is more likely to reflect the growing sense among juries that "it is only fair" that the media pay for the damages it causes, no less than Ford or Union Carbide, and the First Amendment be damned. As Henry Kaufman, General Counsel of the Libel Defense Resource Center, an information clearinghouse for libel cases, notes, "When a libel case gets to a jury, the First Amendment kind of drops to the wayside." This observation is consistent with the advice offered in a recent professional book on libel litigation, which counselled defense attorneys not to "overuse the First Amendment theme" because "judges and juries are not necessarily sympathetic to claims of the media that they have a special privilege to run roughshod over their fellow citizens." Judging from juries' behavior, the current reinvigoration of libel law seems to be part of a grass roots response by jurors and the society they represent to the perceived threat posed by an increasingly powerful media.

The mainstream corporate press is now the establishment and is reaping what it has sown. If juries are the legal system's best barometer of social trends, the willingness of juries to sting media defendants with gigantic damages awards almost cavalierly indicates that the incursions of the media have joined other invasions of modern life, like air pollution and radiation, that individuals feel powerless to control. In a libel decision involving William F. Buckley and the *New York Post*, a prominent federal judge, Henry Friendly, remarked that "Newspapers, magazines, and broadcasting companies are businesses conducted for a profit and often make very large ones. Like other enterprises that inflict damage in the course of performing a service highly useful to the public, such as providers of food or shelter or manufacturers of drugs designed to ease or prolong life, they must pay the freight."[15]

For the average Americans who sit on juries, major media outlets appear as powerful and impersonal forces. Few of us have the resourcefulness of the Paul Newman character in the movie *Absence of Malice*; our only outlet for compensation or retribution is litigation. And so it is quite possible that juries (and perhaps, more and more, many judges), moved by this perception of imbalance, are unconsciously applying standards of strict accountability against the media, while all the time adhering "in principle" to First Amendment standards.[16] Plaintiffs' lawyers certainly attempt to exploit this perception of imbalance by constantly trying to associate the harm caused by the media to harm caused by other manufacturers, capitalizing on the view that the information that is spewn forth by modern media outlets is a form of "product," essentially indistinguishable from soap or hairspray, to which civil liability should attach whenever it is "defective" and causes injury. This identification is to some degree invited by the media itself: the daily vocabulary of media insiders has come to include "product" and "market."[17]

Changes in the structure of news organizations, for example, have changed the role of editors. At a recent American Society of Newspaper Editors meeting, one editor asked, "What will be the effects if, increasingly, the position of the editor is less an end in itself and more just another rung on the ladder of top corporate management?" The editor's role now is often partly defined by participation in such corporate functions as strategic planning and marketing; the nostalgic picture of the crusty editor in rolled-up sleeves commanding a shabby newsroom of battered typewriters and overflowing ashtrays has been largely displaced by pristine offices bearing corporate titles. As *New York Times* reporter Alex Jones recently observed, as "newspapers have been consolidated into chains and the chains have grown into communications conglomerates, editors have increasingly become key executives in a corporate structure whose product is news."[18] Events such as the takeover of ABC by Capital Cities Communications, or the purchase of the *Des Moines Register* by the Gannett newspaper chain, or the acquisition of the *New Yorker* by Advance Publications, all large corporate takeovers, reinforce the perception "in the hustings" that many modern media voices are not the independent family owned enterprises of old—media outlets that seemed to have individual personalities with individual claims to their own free speech—but are instead impersonal cogs in centralized corporate conglomerates.

"Investigative journalism," which with Watergate came into its own as part of the American system of checks and balances, seems to have contributed to a growing public perception of mainstream media outlets as centers of power, wielding great influence but totally isolated from accountability to the public or any of the other centers of power. One is struck by how frequently investigative reporting has precipitated libel actions. *60 Minutes* has been sued over 150 times since the show began. In recent years the ABC news show *20/20* and its reporter Geraldo Rivera

have been veritable lightning rods for attracting libel suits, finding themselves sued for everything from a segment on an alleged arson-for-profit
conspiracy in Chicago, to a segment on the Justice Department's witness
program, to a piece that accused the Kaiser Aluminum Company of knowingly selling dangerous products, to a story that claimed that a prostitute
had had sex with a judge in Ohio in exchange for a lighter sentence.[19]

Networks and newspapers are now sued with regularity for their investigative efforts; the more dramatic the underlying events, the more prone
reportage of those events is to attract a libel suit. An emotionally charged
story, like the death of a cultural idol like John Belushi, is likely to send
libel and invasion of privacy suits spinning off in all directions. Bob Woodward's book on Belushi, *Wired*, drew litigation from Belushi's wife, from
his doctor, and from the hotel in which he died. Woodward's role as an
editor for the *Washington Post*, in turn, formed some of the most critical
testimony in William Tavoulareas' suit against the *Post*. In the courtroom,
at least, the investigative journalist, idolized and glamourized by portrayals
such as the movie *All The President's Men*, has become a popular target for
attack. There is growing evidence that American juries and judges are
venting their suspicions concerning the fairness of "muckraking" journalism through decisions adverse to the media in libel litigation. In William
Tavoulareas' suit against the *Washington Post*, for example, a federal
appeals court wrote, in affirming Mr. Tavoulareas' $2.05 million verdict
against the *Post*, that the "*Post* is a newspaper which seeks, among other
things, hard-hitting investigative stories," and that "whether one chooses
to characterize this policy as conducive to 'hard-hitting investigative journalism,' or . . . 'sophisticated muckraking,' it certainly is relevant to the
inquiry of whether a newspaper's employees acted in reckless disregard of
whether a statement is false or not." Plaintiffs' lawyers are obviously sen-
sing the mood of juries, encouraging their clients to pursue anti-media
claims, and the more often juries return large verdicts, the more other
plaintiffs are attracted to such suits.

Most discussions of the recent plight of the media in the courts have
centered around the two most visible institutional components of the litigation, the media and the legal system. But anti-media litigation is not
merely influenced by the behavior of the press and the behavior of lawyers;
it may also reflect changes in the sensitivity of the media's victims. Legal
and cultural critics may have paid too much attention to the more visible
parts of the pyramid, overlooking the possibility that the current anti-
media mood may be caused largely by a general increase in the sensitivity
of the media's victims.

This victim's response is what might be labeled "the general thinning of the American skin." As a culture we have grown more sensitive to the harm that words can do to an individual's emotional and mental tranquillity, and this increased sensitivity has translated into a willingness to use the court system against the media, which is perceived by many as one of the principal invaders of, if you will, "psychic space." Through the actions of the legal system's most democratic barometer of social attitudes—the American jury—libel law today reflects and reinforces emerging attitudes about the importance of "psychic integrity"—the growing need of Americans to nurture and protect both self-image and public image. The anti-media litigation explosion is in part the result of deeply felt cultural attitudes about the importance of protecting psychic well-being, attitudes that have flourished since the Vietnam War in counterpoint to interests in public expression. In the surge of litigation against the media there is also a hidden current of unconscious psychological biases against the technological capabilities of the communications age. The technological power of major American institutions, like the government, banks, credit agencies, advertisers, and the media, to "invade" the inner sanctums of private individuals has for years been slowly raising Americans' sensitivity to threats to their privacy. The media's power to expose secrets, playing havoc with self-image and public image, is yet another modern erosion of the sanctity of individual human dignity, and the sympathy of American juries toward libel and invasion of privacy plaintiffs is a sort of grass roots response to that erosion.

The current state of libel and privacy litigation parallels shifts in American attitudes about the importance of preserving personal tranquillity, and the pertinence of one's public image in that battle for preservation. Libel litigation was once regarded as almost un-American; Rudyard Kipling may have suffered more in reputation among his new American neighbors for having sued than he had as a consequence of the suit-provoking libel. In the tumultuous early days of the Republic, Thomas Jefferson received more than his share of criticism in the press. The *New York Commercial Advertiser*, for example, accused Jefferson of being "a spendthrift, a libertine . . . and an Atheist," while the *New England Palladium* called Jefferson "a coward, a calumniator, a plagiarist," and "a tame, spiritless animal." Yet in his second inaugural address, Jefferson accepted the press's hostility with relative aplomb. "These abuses might have been corrected by the wholesome punishments provided by the laws," he told the young nation. "But public duties more urgent press on the time of public servants, and the offenders have therefore been left to find their punishment in the public indignation."

Of course, Jefferson had more extreme legal means than libel litigation with which to harass his enemies; for instance, after the damaging item appeared in the *Palladium*, the president's allies in the Massachusetts legislature tried to revoke the editors' printing contract. (Richard Nixon, a president with a sense of history, would later attempt to imitate Jefferson; on the Watergate tapes he is heard telling John Erlichman that in retaliation for a *Post* story, the newspaper would have a damnable time getting a FCC license renewed for one of its radio stations.)[20] But Jefferson nonetheless seemed to believe that lawsuits against the press really were not the best use of his time. This Jeffersonian notion persisted in American culture well into this century. In 1947, Zechariah Chafee, an esteemed First Amendment scholar, wrote that "a libeled American prefers to vindicate his reputation by steadily pushing forward his career, and not by hiring a lawyer to talk in a courtroom."[21] Another legal scholar, David Reisman, wrote in 1942 that affording legal protection for one's reputation is intrinsically unimportant in America's capitalist society:

> The American attitude towards reputation is unique. In Europe, where precapitalist concepts of honor, family, and privacy survive, reputation is a weighty matter not only for the remnants of the nobility who still fight duels to protect it, but for all the middle groups who flood the courts with petty slander litigations as we flood ours with automobile and other negligence actions. But where the tradition is capitalistic rather than feudalistic, reputation is only an asset, "good will," not an attribute to be sought after for its intrinsic value. And in the United States these business attitudes have colored social relations. The law of libel is consequently unimportant.[22]

A toughening of the mental hide was thought of as a better protection against the frictions and clashings incident to a robust and open society than the law could ever be.

Americans, however, have quite obviously changed. It is evident that as a culture we have begun to abandon the rough and tumble sentiments of the past and have begun taking that which is said about us more seriously. This (perhaps somewhat idyllic) past in which actions spoke louder and more directly than words bears little resemblance to the world of today, perhaps, ironically, because of the ubiquitous presence of words that the modern media (particularly television) has created. John Wayne, Humphrey Bogart, and Gary Cooper punched their insulters in the nose; but Americans of the 1980's call their lawyers. (In today's litigious climate, of course, if the victim of a media story punched the reporter in the nose, the victim's plight would only be exacerbated: he'd find himself a defendant in a personal injury suit by the reporter, and his already "bad press" would grow even worse.) Rather than employ other instinctual defenses to abuse, such as humor, hide-toughening indifference, or cathartic counter-attack, Americans have increasingly begun to seek the refuge and vindi-cation of litigation. Words published by the media no longer roll over us without penetrating; instead they sink in through the skin and work inner damage, and a consensus appears to be emerging that this psychic damage is serious and must be paid for.

How important is the protection of honor, reputation, and privacy in American society today, and how well do libel suits provide for that pro-tection? Is there anything unhealthy about a society that places too much emphasis on protecting reputation? In talking to *TV Guide* reporters about CBS's documentary *Uncounted Enemy,* William Westmoreland made it quite clear that his own feelings about the value of reputation ran deep.

Westmoreland told the interviewers, "When I returned from Vietnam, I was belittled, I was burned in effigy. I could accept that. I knew I had done the job in Vietnam the president had asked me to do. I was reviled, I was disparaged, but I could accept that. At least my children could hold their head high. Knowing that, right or wrong, I was an honorable man, doing his duty for his country. But now Mike Wallace has gone on national television and accused me of being a liar—or worse, a traitor. How can my children live with that?" Westmoreland then poignantly added, "What CBS was saying was that I have the blood of American soldiers on my hands."

Westmoreland's remarks sounded one of the oldest and most persistent themes in the Anglo-American cultural tradition. In Shakespeare's *Othello,* Iago describes the sanctity of reputation in words that are well-known:

> Good name in man and woman, dear my lord,
> Is the immediate jewel of their souls.
> Who steals my purse steals trash—'tis something, nothing;
> 'Twas mine, 'tis his, and has been slave to thousands;
> But he that filches from me my good name
> Robs me of that which not enriches him
> And makes me poor indeed. (III, iii, 155–162)

As often as these famous lines are held up as evidence of the high regard for reputation that is our cultural tradition, however, other less-famous words, also spoken by Iago, are usually ignored:

> As I am an honest man, I thought you had received
> some bodily wound. There is more sense in that than in
> reputation. Reputation is an idle and most false imposi-
> tion; oft got without merit and lost without deserving.
> You have lost no reputation at all unless you repute your-
> self such a loser. (II, iii, 256–261)

Iago, of course, is a duplicitous character who does not hesitate to utter whatever contradictory sentiments suit his needs of the moment. But the two conflicting views that Iago voices about the importance of reputation are more than merely the self-serving statements of a fickle scheming Shakespearean character; they reflect a deeper dissonance in the culture concerning the value of reputation, a dissonance that is in turn apparent in sharp contradictions within the law of defamation. Like Iago, all of American society has slipped from the insouciant treatment of reputation as "an idle and most false imposition," to a reverence for reputation as the "jewel of the soul."

As Americans spend more and more of the gross national product on narcissistic self improvement, as increasing effort and expense is spent on first finding and then nurturing the inner self, one might expect greater umbrage to be taken when that self is damaged. One does not pay thousands of dollars to an analyst to resurrect a self-image, and then sit idly by as that work is publicly undone by *60 Minutes* or the *National Enquirer*.

Since the end of the Vietnam War, America has turned from outward expression to inward fulfillment. American culture from the mid-1960's to the early 1970's was dominated by collective political statement, first through the Civil Rights movement, and later through anti-war protest. The first unified push in decades for greater equality for women, symbolized by the early success of the Equal Rights Amendment, was also part of this robust period of social activism. Opposition to the Vietnam War vulcanized disparate surges of countercultural energy into a monolithic movement of anti-war dissent. The drives for racial and sexual equality and for an end to the war were mutually reinforcing. It was a time of vigorous self-expression, a throwing off of the conformist yoke of the 1950's, and this celebration of freedom was always collective and communal. Although some turned-on, tuned-in, and dropped-out, this was not the most distinctive ethos of those leading the movement for change: the music, the dress, and the political statements were directed outward, they were directed toward reform. The Woodstock music festival was special not because there were so many people or so many port-o-sans, but because it expressed a cultural identity so totally shared—the experience was communal; the music almost tribal.

When the Vietnam War ended, the anti-establishment energy generated by the anti-war and Civil Rights movements disintegrated into a potpourri of less directed fads and causes, many of them preoccupied with the discovery and nourishment of various formulations of the individual self. Mass movement gave way to me-movement; the country turned from marching with placards to jogging with Sony Walkmans, from chanting slogans to chanting mantras. Jane Fonda switched from sit-ins to sit-ups. The

Age of Aquarius gave way to the the Age of Analysis. Radical leaders were displaced by gurus of selfhood, while Bob Dylan and Eldridge Cleaver became born-again Christians. As Tom Wolfe put it, "Many members of the New Left communes of the 1960's began to turn up in *Me* movements in the 1970's . . . . It is entirely possible that in the long run historians will regard the entire New Left experience as not so much a political as a religious episode wrapped in semi-military gear and guerilla talk." Today when rock musicians come together to raise money for Ethiopia, they do it out of a wonderful sense of charity and altruism, and they indeed perform a very tangible service for the African poor, but the experience is not the same as the experience of Woodstock, for the role of the audience today is essentially passive; the listeners are no longer participants in the scene; the audience is no longer part of a communal experience; its role is rather that of consumer and charitable contributor. Today Woodstock would be a series of video spots on MTV. In a metamorphosis exactly the opposite of the communal consciousness that 1960's activists espoused, the last ten years have witnessed a transformation of the national character, in which deification of one's self and preoccupation with one's feelings have tended to displace emphasis on political activity. The whole change in mood is captured beautifully in movies like *The Big Chill* or *The Return of the Secaucus Seven*; the children of the 60's are reunited years later, but something is lost; everyone has a career and a blow dryer to worry about, and everyone wonders whether his or her idealism is gone forever, or has merely altered and matured.

We are at this point too close to these changes to know for sure whether they are good or bad. At its worst, this turning inward is a new brand of narcissism; at its best it is a new sensitivity to human dignity. But however it is characterized, the longing for personal health, well-being, and security is this era's search for salvation, and whether or not that search is quixotic, as a culture we have come to regard interfering with it as a serious offense.

The sympathy of modern juries for those who have had their reputations impugned, however, is neither trite nor superficial, and we ought not dismiss it lightly as mere ignorance of the law or lack of respect for the First Amendment. That we have come to value personal narcissism over an open society's need for robust debate does not ring true as the complete explanation for jurors' growing sympathy for victims of defamation and invasion of privacy; the more self-centered aspects of the "me-generation" will not explain all of the data. For much of today's anti-media litigation comes from persons who were not part of the cultural upheaval. They belong, rather, to that solid, hard-working segment of middle America that was forced to ride through the storm and never quite understood it. Ronald Reagan has returned the country to that group, and that group is going about the business of settling scores. Environmental laws will be relaxed; affirmative action quotas will be eliminated; entitlement programs for welfare abusers will be cut. And the media, which seemed to cause a lot of this upheaval itself, will be brought under control. It is no surprise that Senator Jesse Helms would try to convince conservatives to buy CBS and "become Dan Rather's boss," or that CBS, one of America's giant (and necessarily impersonal) media conglomerates, would find itself under attack from the likes of a maverick American entrepreneur and individualist such as Ted Turner.

People like Carol Burnett, whose comic roles have always played on middle class lifestyles, or William Tavoulareas, a self-made man, or William Westmoreland, a proud and courageous soldier, are the heroes of this middle America. Although as individuals each pursued their suits against the media out of sincere and highly personal motivations, as *cultural symbols* their lawsuits (like it or not) take on a larger significance; they are part of a movement toward the restoration of balance and decorum in national life, a decorum that will only be achieved if the media is made accountable. One simply has a hard time believing that simple narcissism could possibly be the prime motivation of Carol Burnett's suit against the *National Enquirer*, William Tavoulareas' suit against the *Washington Post*, or William Westmoreland's suit against CBS. Carol Burnett is an excellent actress, but her trial testimony was no act; the *Enquirer* article had deeply hurt her, and her emotion came through spontaneously and genuinely on the witness stand. William Tavoulareas' response was more a fiesty, defiant anger, but it was obviously no less genuine; his efforts to vindicate his reputation became a crusade. And finally, Westmoreland's decision to resort to litigation is worth examining for what it reveals about the interaction between very old-fashioned American values—in Westmoreland's mind and heart, they are captured by the West Point motto, "Duty, Honor, Country"— and the values of the Ronald Reagan 1980's.

At Westmoreland's press conference announcing his decision to commence libel litigation, he spoke at length of his motivation in suing CBS. The most interesting element in Westmoreland's statement was his attempt to reduce the issues in the suit, and his own purpose in pursuing these issues, to the narrowest possible grounds. Was the motivation greed? Surely no one seriously thought it was, and Westmoreland removed any shadow of doubt by declaring, "If I am successful in this case, as I believe I will be, I will not retain any monetary award for my personal use but instead will donate it to charity."

Was the motivation vengeance? General Westmoreland declared without equivocation that "the issue here is not money, not vengeance." That declaration is to the General's credit, and he deserves to be presumed sincere if by his proclaimed lack of a desire for "vengeance" he meant that he did not sue CBS out of some dark, brooding need to see Mike Wallace suffer. But no matter how sincere Westmoreland may have been in denying any motive of rancorous reprisal, the litigation was certainly a form of restrained, civilized "vengeance." And when he took the witness stand in New York during the trial of his case, the General's voice crackled with controlled but very powerful emotion.

One of the remarkable things about the General's explanation of his motivation was his astute effort to preempt accusations that he was insensitive to First Amendment values, and even more significant, that he was attempting to use the courtroom to retry the central issues of the American experience in Vietnam. "I have dwelled at length upon the tremendous bulwark of liberty and freedom that is the First Amendment to the Constitution of the United States," Westmoreland stated, concluding that his pursuit of redress from CBS would enhance, rather than detract from the strength of the First Amendment, for he "now feared that public reaction to CBS as the truth came out might lead to weakening of that bulwark through legislated codes of conduct or other attempts to restrain the media." The General was almost doing the media a favor, forcing down medicine that would purge it of its own worst faults.

But wouldn't the litigation contemplated by Westmoreland require the legal system to perform tasks it was never designed to do? Weren't the disputed issues of history raised by *The Uncounted Enemy* beyond the institutional competence of lawyers, judges, and juries? Again, General Westmoreland's instincts were perfect in anticipating and attempting to displace these questions, substituting for them the view that his case would involve the mere workaday stuff of routine litigation: simple scrutiny of the behavior of the defendant—an examination of the conduct and methodology of CBS. Thus, Westmoreland quite presciently declared that "the question before the American people in *Westmoreland v. CBS* is not whether the war in Vietnam was right or wrong but whether in our land a television network can rob an honorable man of his reputation. The question is not whether I was a good general or a bad general. The question is not whether we won or lost the war in Vietnam."

General Westmoreland was totally correct in placing the methodology of CBS in a position of prominence in the litigation; CBS's conduct, it turned out, would be at the legal and factual epicenter of the suit, and much of what would be exposed would not make CBS proud. Despite Westmoreland's sincere protests to the contrary, however, the issues in *Westmoreland v. CBS* would also inevitably become the precise issues he disclaimed. Libel suits by their very nature place the "truth" at issue, and the clash of competing truths arising from *The Uncounted Enemy* documen-

tary went to the very heart of American perceptions about Vietnam. Perhaps there was an unwitting concession of this inevitability in Westmoreland's curious use of the phrase "the question before the *American people*,"
a phrase that seems to acknowledge the suit's true expansiveness. Indeed,
the latitudinal sweep of the lawsuit would be apparent from CBS's own
retrenchment in the face of the litigation: CBS would make every effort to
make it appear that the fate of independent American journalism was at
stake.

What comes through most strongly from Westmoreland's remarks, however, is the obvious sincerity of the General's proclamation that the CBS
documentary did in fact deeply wound him, and his abiding faith that the
legal system could heal the wound. Without attacking for one second the
authenticity of General Westmoreland's feelings, and without meaning to
intimate that they are petty or frivolous, it seems completely fair to point
out that against the backdrop of American history, the General's decision
to sue CBS does reflect a new way of thinking. Perhaps George Patton was
every bit as stung by media portrayals of him during World War II as William Westmoreland ever was, but Patton did not sue anyone. This observation, however, must be balanced against the other reality of modern
times: perhaps American society is more in need today of the "safety
valve" of anti-media litigation, for whatever the media did to George Patton, it was probably powerless to change the outcome of World War II,
while today the media may indeed influence the outcomes of wars—it
undoubtedly influenced the course of events in Vietnam—and with the
media's increased power there arguably has come an increase in the need
of injured victims to sue the media, not just for themselves, but as representatives of society's interest in keeping the power of the media in check.

We should be careful, in short, about embracing the glib conclusion that
all of our skins have become too thin, that we are a society of wimps. For
in a sense, the greater sensitivity to injuries inflicted by the media is a manifestation of the best shared values between those who fought in Vietnam
for "duty, honor, country" and those who lived through the Vietnam era
protesting the war and who emerged later looking for some deeper psychic
peace. What the two groups appear to share is a conviction that human
beings are more than their visible parts, more than the material aggregate
of their bodies, their property, and their bank statements. The heart of the
matter for William Westmoreland, and for sympathetic juries in other libel
suits across the United States, may have been that in some circumstances
the libel suit provides one of the last hopes for vindicating one's dignity,
and for preventing an impersonal corporate media from assuming the big
brother role that Americans so often fear from government. We rely on
the press to uncover corruption in government, but on whom do we rely

to uncover the mistakes of the press? The media's problems in the court today may be to some degree a result of the American public's view that the libel suit is one of the legal system's few useful restraints on the growing concentration of media power. At this juncture the liberal civil libertarian world-view of many fierce defenders of the media ought to provoke a crisis of conscience, for the affirmation of dignity implicit in the civilized, nonviolent forum of the libel suit is arguably just as much a vital "civil liberty" as free expression is.

One clue that these cultural forces may be part of the recent invigoration of the law of libel is that in areas of civil litigation *other* than libel, legal redress for the infliction of "emotional distress" has steadily expanded.[23] Across the legal landscape the boundaries of the concept of "injury" have been redrawn outward to protect mental and emotional tranquillity. One of the most rapidly expanding areas of civil litigation is a new creation known as "infliction of emotional distress." Rules restricting liability for both the negligent and intentional infliction of emotional distress have steadily relaxed in the last decade. At one time a person suing for having been punched in the nose could expect to win an award restricted to the actual damage to his nose. Now such damage would make up a neglible part of the award, and compensation for the "insult" with punitive damages designed to punish the wrongdoer would dominate the damages verdict. Similarly, courts are increasingly receptive to suits based on invasion of privacy, in which protecting individual peace, tranquillity, and solitude is the sole purpose of the litigation. This new respect for emotional well-being has spilled over into the law of libel and slander, and it shows how the niceties of legal theory often diverge quite sharply from the realities of the courtroom.

From a technical legal perspective, the orthodoxy has always been that the law of defamation does not provide compensation for emotional disturbance, but rather remedies a wrongful disruption in the "relational interest" that an individual has in maintaining personal esteem in the eyes of others. "Reputation" is supposedly something distinct from "personal feelings"; reputation is a sort of intangible "asset". Law students are thus taught in their textbooks that the fundamental difference between the right to privacy and the right to freedom from defamation is that the former directly concerns one's own peace of mind, while the latter primarily concerns one's reputation.

Notwithstanding such neat theorizing, however, it seems clear that the bulk of the money paid out in damage awards in defamation suits is to compensate for psychic injury, rather than to compensate for any objectively verifiable damage to one's community standing. In the long run, the *National Enquirer* article about Carol Burnett probably enhanced her reputation more than hurt it, for her crusade made her a heroine among her peers. Whether officially admitted by the legal system or not, juries are simply becoming more openly supportive of compensating injuries to the psyche, and judges are becoming more willing to let juries do so. It has always been true that one of the functions of law is to promote human dignity by discouraging the violation of an individual's personal or psychological integrity. The law of defamation defends individual dignity by providing a forum for an official declaration that the attack on the victim was undeserved, by imposing on the publisher an economic penalty that acts to deter such invasions of privacy, and by providing compensation to the victim for the loss that occurs. In the battle between the recognition of these values and the preservation of First Amendment interests in free speech, modern American juries are obviously finding that the threat to preserving one's peace is greater than that to speaking one's piece.

Although scores of libel and invasion of privacy suits are mentioned in the chapters that follow, this book concentrates on those lawsuits that as a group address the broadest possible range of issues raised by current anti-media litigation. The case studies begin with the grandfather of all modern media litigation, the only case in this book from the 1960's, *New York Times v. Sullivan*. The *New York Times* decision revolutionized the modern law of libel by declaring for the first time that state libel laws were subject to First Amendment restraints. One of the great puzzles of the modern libel explosion is why, twenty years after a Supreme Court decision that was supposedly a great liberating press victory, the media should find itself so embattled. The solution to that puzzle is partly suggested by one of the basic premises of this book: that the evolution of American law is always much more deeply influenced by changing cultural moods than by changes in technical legal doctrine. Despite the ostensible "reforms" in the modern law of libel after the *New York Times* decision, modern media litigation is still prone to being sidetracked on legal arcana worthy of Dickens' *Bleak House*. Libel suits today often seem to revolve around issues more relevant to lawyers than litigants, and often seem to lose sight altogether of the truly significant social issues (such as Israeli policy in Lebanon, or the behavior of American troops in Vietnam, and the role the press played in presenting or misrepresenting both) out of which the lawsuits originally arose. While lawyers try the case in court, the litigants try the case in the newspapers, and very few clear-cut truths ever finally emerge. To make any sense of all this, however, one must begin at the beginning, and the beginning, for the purposes of the modern law of libel, is a case that began with the civil disobedience tactics of Martin Luther King.

2

The Trials of Martin Luther King:
The *New York Times* Case

The growing movement of peaceful mass demonstrations by
Negroes is something new in the South, something understandable. . . . Let Congress heed their rising voices, for they
will be heard.
New York Times editorial, March 19, 1960

Thus we consider this case against the background of a profound national commitment to the principle that debate on
public issues should be uninhibited, robust, and wide open,
and that it may well include vehement, caustic, and sometimes
unpleasantly sharp attacks on government and public officials.
Justice William Brennan, for the Supreme Court in
New York Times v. Sullivan

IT WAS NOVEMBER, 1960. The *New York Times* had been hauled into
a courtroom in Montgomery, Alabama, to defend itself in a $500,000
libel suit brought by the Montgomery police commissioner, L.B. Sullivan.[24]
Sullivan's court papers alleged that an advertisement run in the *Times* eight
months earlier, on March 29, 1960, which spoke passionately of the tempestuous struggles of Martin Luther King and other civil rights workers
for racial justice in the South, had libeled him. The advertisement had
been placed by a group calling itself "The Committee to Defend Martin
Luther King and the Struggle for Freedom in the South."

The courtroom was thick with racial prejudice. Seating was segregated,
lawyers pronounced "negro" as "nigger," and the judge spoke openly of
"white man's justice," calling the Fourteenth Amendment to the Constitution a "pariah and an outcast" in his court. The trial would be a relatively
short one, and when it was over the jury awarded the police commissioner
his $500,000. Other Alabama officials were already lined up with millions
of dollars worth of additional libel suits against the *Times*. It would take
four years for this case to finally reach the United States Supreme Court.[25]

Of the many landmark Supreme Court cases decided in the last several decades, Americans are far more likely to be familiar with *Brown v. The Board of Education*, which abolished racially segregated schools, or *Miranda v. Arizona*, which imposed the now familiar police warnings of one's rights upon criminal arrest, or *Engle v. Vitale*, which banned public school prayer, or *Roe v. Wade*, which denied states the right to enforce laws restricting women's access to abortion on demand in the first two trimesters of pregnancy, or *Regents of the University of California v. Bakke*, which wrestled with the boundaries of constitutionally permissible "affirmative action," than with the libel case *New York Times v. Sullivan*. While the names of these cases may not all be on the tips of every tongue, the principles they established are well known to most Americans; they remain the stuff of national discussion and presidential debate; they are examples of the Supreme Court deeply affecting the fabric of everyday American life. The *New York Times* case, although celebrated among lawyers and those who work in the media, remains unfamiliar to the average American.

Despite its relative obscurity, however, the *Times* case is one of the most important decisions of this century, for it represents not only the starting point for all discussion of modern libel law, but the intersection of three dominant themes in modern American experience: the power of the federal judiciary, the role of the press as an agent for social change, and the slow and painful struggle of black Americans for legal and social equality. The historic events and legal issues that surround the *New York Times* case endure as power-packed symbols of conflicts that still hold center stage in American life.

Times v. Sullivan revolutionized the American law of libel because in one sudden burst of federal judicial power, state libel laws were made subject to the strictures of the First Amendment, and, with that ruling, hundreds of years of evolving state libel laws were rendered obsolete. But *New York Times* was much more than a libel suit. At one level it demonstrated, as much as any decision during the turbulent tenure of Chief Justice Earl Warren, the awesome power of the Supreme Court to abruptly alter and displace the internal law of the states. At a second level, the *Times* case is the greatest exposition in the history of the Court of the central place of freedom of speech in American society. And on a third level, the *Times* decision is a wonderful example of how much the American legal system is inextricably bound up with American history, and with evolving political and moral values. For the *Times* decision can only be understood in light of the historical events that precipitated it, and those events powerfully reveal that the case is not merely about the First Amendment, but about the struggle of black Americans for civil rights. Just as libel litigation in the 1980's is the forum in which Americans fight battles over the legacies of

Vietnam, or the perceived evils of pornography, the *New York Times* case, the great grandfather of all modern media litigation, was a critical battleground in the fight between blacks and whites in the stormy campaign to destroy America's deeply ingrained habits of racism.[26]

In a sense the *Times* case was a fight that the Supreme Court itself had started. In the 1954 school desegregation cases (*Brown* and its progeny) the Court declared that "separate but equal" public schools for black and white students violated the equal protection clause of the Fourteenth Amendment.[27] The years that immediately followed *Brown v. The Board of Education*[28] were filled with a long series of cases in which the Court struck down Jim Crow laws that had institutionalized American racism, declaring racial segregation illegal in airports, public beaches, bathhouses, municipal golf courses, city parks, athletic events, buses, municipal auditoriums, public housing, prisons, and courtroom seating. Resistance in the South to this Civil Rights revolution was fierce, and for a long time, effective. The South was determined to sabotage the legal and moral mandate of *Brown*.[29]

In the 1963–64 school year, a decade after *Brown*, the eleven states of the Confederacy had only 1.17 percent of their black students in schools with white students. As late as 1965, not *one* of the 30,500 black public school teachers in Alabama, Louisiana, and Mississippi served with any of the 65,400 white teachers in those three states. In response to *Brown*, the voters in Arkansas passed a "Resolution of Interposition," stating that the "State has never delegated to the Supreme Court of the United States the power to change the Constitution of the United States," and that the "People of the State of Arkansas assert that the power to operate public schools in the State on a racially separate but substantially equal basis was granted by the people of Arkansas to the government of the State . . . all decisions of the federal courts or any other department of the federal government to the contrary notwithstanding." In an incredible state constitutional amendment, Arkansas voters also approved a provision ordering the state legislature to "take appropriate action and pass laws opposing in every constitutional manner the Un-Constitutional desegregation decisions of May 17, 1954, and May 31, 1955 of the United States Supreme Court." Throughout the region, southern obstructionism was often ugly, brutal, and violent. Beatings, knifings, shootings, whippings, lynchings, and bombings were often the methods of resistance, and the weaponry was wielded not only by mobs and gangs, but by city police, county sheriffs, state troopers, national guardsmen, and by the highest officials of the political power structure.

The *New York Times* case arose out of racial attacks in Alabama; but it might as easily have arisen anywhere else in the South, in Virginia, or Mississippi, or Texas. On February 29, 1960, Dr. Martin Luther King, Jr. was arrested on trumped-up charges for two counts of perjury in connection with the filing of his Alabama state income tax return. (King was ultimately acquitted on the charges, which were a rather transparent attempt to punish King for his civil rights activities in Alabama.) On March 19, 1960, three weeks after King's arrest, the *New York Times* ran an editorial in support of King's efforts, praising the efforts of blacks in the South to resist racism, and admonishing Congress to "heed their rising voices, for they will be heard." The editorial phrase would later get picked up by a newly formed "Committee to Defend Martin Luther King," which on March 29, 1960, published a full page advertisement entitled "Heed Their Rising Voices." The ad began by proclaiming that, "as the whole world knows" black students in the South were "engaged in widespread non-violent demonstrations in positive affirmation of the right to live in human dignity as guaranteed by the United States Constitution and the Bill of Rights," and the efforts of those students were "being met by an unprecedented wave of terror." The ad quite clearly was intended as a manifesto applicable to the entire South, for it read that in "Tallahassee, Atlanta, Nashville, Savannah, Greensboro, Memphis, Richmond, Charlotte, and a host of other cities in the South, young American teenagers, in face of the entire weight of the official state apparatus and police power, have boldly stepped forth as protagonists of democracy."

The ad claimed that 400 students had been ejected from lunch counters in South Carolina and tear-gassed, soaked to the skin with fire hoses in freezing weather, and arrested *en masse*. According to the ad, after students in Montgomery, Alabama sang "My Country 'Tis of Thee" on the state capitol steps, "their leaders were expelled from school, and truckloads of police armed with shotguns and tear-gas ringed the Alabama State College Campus." When the student body at Alabama State protested to state authorities by refusing to re-register, the ad alleged, their dining hall "was padlocked in an attempt to starve them into submission." The ad lauded the efforts of the students, praising them as "rising to glory." It stated that certain "Southern violators" had repeatedly answered Dr. King's peaceful protests with intimidation and violence. "They have bombed his home, almost killing his wife and child," it stated. "They have assaulted his person. They have arrested him seven times—for speeding, loitering, and similar offenses." The ad then alleged that "now they have charged him with perjury—a *felony* under which they could imprison him for *ten years*." According to the advertisement, it was obvious "that their real purpose is to remove him physically as the leader to whom the students and millions of others . . . look for guidance and support, and thereby to intimidate *all* leaders who may rise in the South." The ad ended with a plea for funds to assist in the civil rights struggle and the defense of King, stating that "We urge you to join hands with our fellow Americans in the South by supporting, with your dollars, this combined appeal for all three needs—the defense of Martin Luther King—the support of the embattled students—and the struggle for the right-to-vote." At the bottom of the ad were the names of a number of prominent Americans comprising the "The Committee to Defend Martin Luther King and the Struggle for Freedom in the South." Among them were Harry Belafonte, Maureen Stapleton, Nat King Cole, Diahann Carroll, Sammy Davis, Jr., Anthony Franciosa, Nat Hentoff, Mahalia Jackson, Rabbi Edward Klein, Langston Hughes, Bayard Rustin, Sidney Poitier, Jackie Robinson, Shelly Winters, Eleanor Roosevelt, and Marlon Brando.

The *New York Times* was paid a little over $4,800 for running the advertisement. The total circulation of the issue was about 650,000, but only 394 copies of the *Times* were sent to Alabama newsdealers, and only 35 copies found their way into Montgomery County, Alabama. The *Times* ad stirred up a whirlwind of bitter reaction from white Alabamans, and soon after its publication a number of Alabama politicians commenced libel suits, including John Patterson, the Governor of Alabama; a former Montgomery City Commissioner; and three incumbent Montgomery Commissioners. Governor Patterson sent a letter to the *Times* claiming that the paper had accused him of "grave misconduct and of improper actions as Governor of Alabama" and demanding a retraction. The *Times* did print a retraction in response to Patterson's letter. (When asked to explain why the *Times* had printed a retraction for the Governor but not for L.B. Sullivan, a spokesman for the *Times* testified: "We did that because we didn't want anything that was published by the *Times* to be a reflection on the State of Alabama and the Governor was, as far as we could see, the embodiment of the State of Alabama and the proper representative of the State and, furthermore, we had by that time learned more of the actual facts which the ad purported to recite and, finally, the ad did refer to the action of the State authorities and the Board of Education presumably of which the Governor is the ex officio chairman.")

A similar demand for a retraction was made by one of the incumbent Montgomery City Commissioners, Mr. L.B. Sullivan, who as Commissioner of Public Affairs was supervisor of the Montgomery departments of scales, cemeteries, fire, and police. The *Times* wrote back to Sullivan and told him that it had investigated the matter and was "somewhat puzzled as to how you think the statements in anyway reflect on you." Without answering the letter, Sullivan sued the *Times* for libel in Montgomery County, seeking $500,000 in damages. Sullivan also sued four Alabama ministers connected with the ad, the Reverends Fred Shuttlesworth, S.S. Seay, Sr., J.E. Lowrey, and Ralph D. Abernathy.

One of the most remarkable aspects of Sullivan's lawsuit was that the *Times* advertisement did not anywhere mention Sullivan by name, and much of the ad referred to events entirely outside Alabama. Sullivan's contention was that the word "police" in the paragraph concerning Montgomery would be understood as referring to Sullivan, because Sullivan was the Montgomery Commissioner who supervised the Police Department. He thus argued that the ad imputed to him the "ringing" of the Alabama State campus with police, and the padlocking of the dining hall to starve students into submission. Sullivan further reasoned that since arrests are ordinarily made by the police, the statement "They have arrested [Dr. King] seven times" would be read as referring to Sullivan, and that the "they" who did the arresting would be equated with the "they" who committed the other described acts of the "Southern violators," thereby effectively accusing Sullivan himself of complicity in bombing Martin Luther King's home, assaulting his person, and charging him with perjury.

As it turns out, some of the statements in the advertisement were inaccurate. Most of the errors were technical and picayune. For example, although black students in Montgomery did stage a demonstration on the capitol steps, the song they sang was not "My Country, 'Tis of Thee," but the national anthem. Further, although nine black students had been expelled from college, they were not expelled for leading the demonstration on the capitol steps, but for demanding service at a lunch counter inside the Montgomery County Courthouse. Not the entire student body, but only most of it, had protested the expulsions, and not by refusing to register for classes, but by boycotting classes on a single day. In addition, the dining hall was never literally padlocked, although some students who had neither registered nor obtained temporary meal tickets were barred from it. Although police were called to the Alabama State campus in large numbers because of race-related protests on three occasions, the police never physically "ringed" the campus, and they had never actually been deployed in connection with the state capitol demonstration. Dr. King had not been arrested seven times, but only four; and although King claimed to have been physically assaulted by a Montgomery police officer in connection with an arrest for loitering outside a courtroom, one of the arresting officers denied that an assault had occurred. Dr. King's home was in fact bombed twice when his wife and child were there, but both bombings took place prior to Commissioner Sullivan's tenure. The police were never implicated in the bombings, and had actually made efforts to apprehend those who were. Three of King's four arrests antedated Sullivan's period as commissioner; and Sullivan was not personally involved in procuring the perjury indictments brought against King.

Sullivan's lawyers developed an ingenious sleight-of-hand argument: through a series of "house that Jack built" steps they were able to turn an ad that did not mention Sullivan and largely had nothing to do with him, into an ad "imputing" the bad conduct to Sullivan. They then turned around and used the same fact that many of the events had nothing to do with Sullivan to prove that the statements "imputing" improper conduct to him were false!

The trial began on November 1, 1960, and was over in only three days. The local press in Montgomery was viciously hostile to its New York counterparts. In an article in the *Montgomery Advertiser*, for example, entitled "The Abolitionist Hellmouths," the *Advertiser* claimed that "The Commonwealth of Alabama with its three million people has been painfully and savagefully injured by the *New York Times*." Montgomery papers also prominently carried the names and photographs of the jurors, and the jurors were followed to the very jury room door by rolling television cameras.

The atmosphere of racial hatred that surrounded the trial was so pervasive and intimidating that the *Times* had great difficulty even finding an Alabama lawyer who would represent it in the trial. Most of the prestigious Birmingham law firms would not touch the case. The *Times* finally retained T. Eric Embry of Birmingham, a lawyer who had previously shown his mettle by having the courage to take on blacks as clients. When the *Times*' regular New York City attorney, Louis Loeb, flew down to Montgomery to monitor the case, animosity against the paper was so intense that Embry took the precaution of getting Loeb a motel room under an assumed name.

The trial judge was Walter B. Jones, who had earlier published a document entitled "The Confederate Creed," in which he proclaimed that "with unfaltering trust in God of my fathers, I believe, as a Confederate, in obedience to Him; it is my duty to respect the laws and ancient ways of my people, and to stand up for the right of my state to determine what is good for its people in all local affairs." Judge Jones had declared from the courtroom bench that "in keeping with the common law of Alabama, and observing the wise, time-honored customs and usages of our people, . . . there will be no integrated seating in this courtroom." Spectators, the Judge declared, "will be seated in this courtroom according to their race, and this for the orderly administration of justice and the good of all people coming here lawfully." Judge Jones always addressed the white male lawyers for both the plaintiff, Mr. Sullivan, and for the *New York Times* as "Mister." When referring to the black lawyers representing the four black

ministers, however, Judge Jones conspiciously dropped "Mister" and used
the appellations "Lawyer Crawford, Lawyer Gray, and Lawyer Seay." Sullivan's attorneys also exploited the racially charged atmosphere in Montgomery. One of them repeatedly mispronounced the word "negro" as
"nigger," for example, forcing a defense lawyer at one point to object:

> Your Honor, we would like to object to the reading of that ad unless
> the counsel who reads it will read what is said and as I recall from
> reading that ad there is nothing on there that is spelled n-i-g-g-e-r-s. It
> is spelled n-e-g-r-o and I am sure he is well aware of it.

Later on, in his closing argument, one of Sullivan's attorneys would tell
the jury: "In other words, all of these things that happened did not happen
in Russia where the police run everything, they did not happen in the
Congo *where they still eat them*, they happened in Montgomery, Alabama, a
law abiding community."

Judge Jones was not about to let the racism that pervaded his courtroom
be thwarted by the niceties of federal constitutional law. In fact, Judge
Jones seemed to accept neither the outcome of the Civil War nor the passage of the Fourteenth Amendment as binding on the sovereign state of
Alabama. Judge Jones defiantly announced in preliminary remarks that the
Fourteenth Amendment "has no standing whatever in this Court, it is a
pariah and an outcast." In an obvious dig at the United States Supreme
Court, Judge Jones noted that while "it is quite the fashion in high judicial
places to work the XIV Amendment overtime," he would "continue with
the trial of this case under the laws of the State of Alabama, and not under
the XIV Amendment, and in the belief and knowledge *that the white man's
justice*, . . . will give the parties at the Bar of this Court regardless of race
or color, equal justice under law."

Commissioner Sullivan's case consisted primarily of his arguments why
the article referred to him, and why it had damaged his reputation. Sullivan himself testified that he felt that the statements referring to "police
activities" or "police action" impugned his "ability and integrity" and
reflected adversely upon him "as an individual." Six witnesses testified for
Sullivan that they had associated the offending passages in the advertisement with Sullivan. None of the six stated that he or she *believed* the allegations, however, and five of the six stated affirmatively that they did not
believe them.

In defense, the four black ministers claimed that they had neither composed nor authorized the ad, nor had they consented to the use of their
names in connection with the ad and therefore could not be held legally
responsible for it. The names of the Reverends Abernathy, Shuttlesworth,
Seay, and Lowrey were part of a list of twenty ministers in the South whose

names in the ad were printed apart from the names of the better known entertainers, writers, sports figures, and political leaders who were listed as members of the "Committee to Defend Martin Luther King." Unlike the other individuals whose names appeared on the advertisement, the names of the ministers had been added to the copy of the ad without their individual consent. Bayard Rustin, the Executive Director of the Committee to Defend Dr. King, had decided that it was unnecessary to obtain each minister's consent, since they were all members of the Southern Christian Leadership Conference, and the SCLC had endorsed the work of the Committee.

The defense used by the *New York Times* was that the advertisement had not referred to Sullivan or charged him with misconduct in office. As a secondary line of defense, the *Times* argued that at the time it printed the ad, it relied on the good reputation of those who were associated with it, and did not know that anything in the ad was false. At it turns out, the *Times* did have information in its news files that contradicted some of the factual details set forth in the advertisement, and had it checked each detail very carefully, it would have uncovered several of the discrepancies. Although the *Times* arguably was negligent in not checking its files— though not checking news files before taking a paid political advertisement hardly seems too unreasonable—this omission could at most be negligent; it certainly did not qualify as reckless or malicious misconduct. The *Times* thus argued to the jury that it did not act maliciously, and it asked the jury, if it should find against the *Times*, to take that into account in reducing damages.

Unmoved by these defenses, the jury expeditiously returned a verdict for Sullivan of half a million dollars against the *Times* and the four Alabama ministers. Just as threatening to the *Times* was the fact that a whole string of libel suits similar to Sullivan's were popping up around Alabama. An article by *Times* reporter Harrison E. Salisbury on conditions in Birmingham had generated $3,150,000 worth of libel claims against the paper, and another $1.5 million against Salisbury.

It is not difficult to account for the ease with which the jury found the *Times* guilty of libel, an ease made all the more menacing to the *Times* by the prospect of a virtual guerilla war of libel attacks forming against it in Alabama. Obviously, a large part of the verdict was the product of the jury's prejudice against what was perceived as a liberal New York newspaper's officious meddling in the traditional regime of white supremacy in Alabama. One of the most important aspects of the *Times* case, however, is that the jury could legitimately vent its rage against the *Times* without much warping of either the letter or spirit of Alabama's libel laws. Unlike some examples of institutional public racism, which required twisted and strained interpretations of local laws to prop them up, the jury could quite validly find against the *Times* under a fairly straightforward application of Alabama libel law as it existed in 1960. Furthermore, Alabama's law of libel was not much different from the libel rules applied by the vast majority of American states at the time.

It is precisely because the law of libel, even when *neutrally* applied, carried with it the potential for penalizing the exercise of unpopular types of free expression that the jury's decision in the *Times* case carries so powerful a lesson. The half a million dollar award contained a double constitutional whammy, attacking two precious amendments for the price of one. For to the extent that the jury suppressed speech merely by the neutral application of traditional libel rules, it severely threatened the First Amendment; and to the extent that the verdict represented the special antipathy that the community of Montgomery, Alabama felt for aggressive blacks and their Yankee fellow travelers, it threatened to cripple the Fourteenth Amendment's guarantee of equal protection under the laws.

And therein, as forcefully as in any legal case in American history, was presented both the glory and the unique fragility of the First Amendment. Freedom of speech is always both a means and an end in itself; free speech is a means by which other goals are accomplished, as well as an expression of individuality that rests on its own bottom. And the dangerous mirror image of this truth is that suppression of free speech always carries the potential of double evil for the speaker, for it both inhibits the accomplishment of the speaker's underlying goals (such as the elimination of Jim Crow laws), and it diminishes the speaker's dignity, individuality and autonomy.

Not until *New York Times* did the legal world perceive just how profoundly the ordinary rules of libel and slander might compromise the ever vulnerable values of the First Amendment. To appreciate the depth of the conflicts posed by the *Times* case, and to understand why in the mid-1980's those conflicts still remain largely unresolved, it is useful to look at exactly how the traditional rules of libel law operated, for without this, it is difficult to understand how cultural and legal trends converge.

The law of libel is part of the law of "torts." Tort law is one of the basic building block subjects that all law students take in their first year of law school.[30] It is the collection of principles and rules that govern civil liability between one person and another ("person," in this context, includes corporations, and even governmental entities) arising from accidental or intentional wrongs. This somewhat formal, stilted definition, however, masks the salt-of-the-earth simplicity of tort law. Tort suits are the bread and butter of everyday civil litigation, arising when one driver sues another for damages from a car accident, when a customer slips on a banana peel in the store and sues the grocer, when the patient sues the doctor for malpractice for leaving a sponge in the abdomen after surgery, when the consumer sues the auto manufacturer because a defect in the gas tank caused the car to explode, when the apartment dweller sues the peeping tom with a telephoto lens for invasion of privacy, and when the local police commissioner sues a newspaper for defamation because the paper claims that the commissioner abused his official duties. Tort suits, in fact, encompass just about every claim of civil liability of one person against another except those that arise from breaches of contract. Some legal textbooks actually treat the definition of "tort" just that broadly; when one person sues another, and no contract is involved, it is a matter for the law of torts—a classification scheme somewhat like that in the statement of Ulysses S. Grant: "I know two tunes. One is Yankee Doodle, the other is not Yankee Doodle."

Are there any unifying principles that bring together this jumble of very different kinds of wrongs? Why do lawyers treat them as part of one body of law that they label "torts"? And what does the fact that "libel is a tort" tell us about libel suits in general, or *New York Times v. Sullivan* in particular? There are some unifying elements. Tort suits are all "civil suits." They are suits between persons in which the typical remedy sought is money damages. Other remedies are also sometimes sought: if someone steals my valuable painting and I sue him in a tort suit for "conversion" (the word in tort law for what is basically theft), I may not want money damages (it may be almost impossible to place a monetary value on my particular attachment to the painting), I may want the painting itself back. The relief in this case would be an injunction, or court order, to return the painting. This point is especially relevant in considering possible alternatives to the traditional tort suit. Is there some way that a court could issue an injunction that would, for example, order CBS News to return what it allegedly "stole" from General William Westmoreland—his reputation—which, like my painting, may be impossible to value in monetary terms?

The fact that a particular incident in the real world may trigger tort liability in the legal world does not mean that tort liability is the exclusive legal consequence. A tort may also be a crime, and criminal proceedings may be brought against the perpetrator at the same time that the victim sues the perpetrator for damages. If Mike Wallace were to punch William Westmoreland in the nose, the local prosecutor could have Wallace arrested, and he could be criminally tried for battery. There is also a tort known as "battery," and in a civil suit completely independent of the criminal case Westmoreland could sue Mike Wallace "in tort" for damages.

Traditionally, most states have had a crime known as "criminal libel." Alabama had such a criminal libel provision in 1960, and the *New York Times* conceivably could have been prosecuted under it. The maximum fine for criminal libel in Alabama was $500; the jury award in Commissioner Sullivan's case was thus one thousand times the *maximum* criminal penalty.

The fact that the same act may result in both criminal and tort liability is significant, in that it highlights what are in theory the different essential missions of criminal and civil litigation. The purpose of criminal law is to punish the wrongdoer, to accomplish social goals of deterrence, restraint, retribution, and rehabilitation. But the main mission of tort law has not been punishment, but compensation. In theory at least, if not in practice, the damages sought by Commissioner Sullivan were supposed to "make him whole" rather than simply punish the *New York Times*. Quite obviously, however, the jury's verdict in the *Times* case was highly punitive (to the point, perhaps, of "cruel and unusual" punishment).

What sort of conduct is tortious? Is a tort committed every time one person harms another? At this point the law of torts begins to get more complicated, especially when applied to that branch of tort law involving libel and slander. As all first-year law students come to learn, there are three different types of tortious conduct: "intentional torts," "negligence torts," and "strict liability torts." All three are relevant to an understanding of the legal issues in modern libel cases.

Intentional torts are the oldest form of tort liability and are cousins of crimes in the criminal law. To be liable for an intentional tort one must intend to commit the forbidden act; many of the classic intentional torts have names identical to their criminal law counterparts: assault, battery, or trespass, for example. Although law students typically spend a substantial amount of time learning about intentional torts, in practice there is very little intentional tort litigation. For one thing, not that many clearly intentional wrongs resulting in injury to others are committed, even in American society, at least when compared to the hundreds of thousands of accidental mishaps that result in injuries each year. Secondly, even when a serious intentional tort is committed, like a shooting or a rape, the perpetrator will often have no money. Very few civil suits are worth bringing if the defendant has no assets, no large income, or no insurance from which a money judgment can be paid. Lawyers refer to a defendant without enough money to be worth suing as "judgment-proof," and many of the intentional torts that would otherwise be worth pursuing are committed by judgment-proof defendants. When was the last time you read in the newspapers of a rape victim recovering huge money damages from the rapist?

Since intentional misconduct is quite difficult to prove, both the criminal law and tort law sometimes permit liability to be predicated on behavior that is quite reprehensible (considerably worse, that is, than run of the mill negligence), but not technically "intentional." This behavior is usually described as "recklessness." As will be seen, the use of recklessness as a substitute for pure intent plays a prominent role in modern libel litigation, and has emerged as the critical legal standard in most current libel cases. Before looking at the mechanics of the recklessness standard in contemporary libel suits, however, it is worth asking why some lesser standard should not apply.

For most of this century, negligence torts have been the backbone of tort law, and negligence torts today still account for the majority of tort litigation. Most of the serious harm that most of us will ever inflict on others is accidental. When an accident occurs, and someone is hurt, whether from a discarded banana peel or a car out of control, the injured party may obtain recovery from the other party involved only "if it was the other guy's fault"—if, in the parlance of tort law, the defendant was "negligent." "Negligence" is a common-sense term; it is simply the failure to act as an ordinary, reasonable person would be expected to act under the circumstances. In a jury trial, the existence or nonexistence of negligence becomes an issue that the jury determines using its own good sense sequestered in the jury room. Negligence is thus an elastic, constantly changing standard that roughly embodies the community's evolving notions of what is reasonable behavior, with the jury as the barometer of that community spirit. Traditionally, judges try to give the jury a common-sense handle on the negligence standard by instructing them to first ask themselves what an ordinary, reasonable person would have done in the particular circumstances, and then to compare that conduct to what the defendant actually did. The ordinary, reasonable person is a mythical norm, neither extraordinarily bright nor stupid, neither especially graceful nor clumsy, neither particularly strong nor weak, neither unusually meek nor hot-tempered—a sort of legal Ward Cleaver, the always temperate father from *Leave it to Beaver*.

If the libel claim in *New York Times v. Sullivan* had been tried as a negligence tort, the jury in Montgomery would have been instructed that even if the *New York Times* did not know that what it printed in the advertisement was false, the *Times* would nonetheless be liable if the falsities of the ad would have been discovered had the *Times* behaved like an ordinary, reasonable person under the circumstances. If the *Times* *should* have known that facts presented in the advertisement were false, but failed to discover the truth because of its own failure to investigate reasonably, then the *Times* would be negligent.

"Strict liability" torts are the third prong of modern tort law. Strict liability has become an increasingly large and important component of tort litigation. Normally there can be no recovery in tort for accidents that "just happen," or that are "nobody's fault." If a deer darts across the road without warning and a car hits it and then bounces into a car in the next lane, the accident would be "nobody's fault"; no negligence would exist, and neither party could sue the other for the damages caused by the accident. Some activities, however, have come to be deemed by the law as inherently fraught with unusual risk, and because of their higher danger level, the law treats them with unique harshness. Activities that are judged as "ultrahazardous," or "abnormally dangerous" are not governed by the negligence standard, but rather by strict liability, which essentially means that if those activities cause someone injury, the victim may recover from the defendant, even when it is "nobody's fault." Blasting with dynamite is the textbook example of an abnormally dangerous activity. If the blaster is absolutely irreproachable in handling the dynamite, in clearing the blast area, and in putting up proper warnings; if in every conceivable way the blaster is cautious and reasonable; and yet somehow, inexplicably, a piece of rock is thrown off by the blast in some unforseen way and injures a stranger, the stranger is still entitled to recovery.

For a long time the law recognized very few activities as abnormally dangerous, and so negligence suits dwarfed strict liability cases. In the last two decades, however, the law of torts has undergone a revolution. Beginning in the early 1960's, states began, through legislation or judicial decision or both, to treat the manufacture of products as the sort of activity to which strict liability would apply. Some products are defective and cause injury, even though the manufacturer's conduct is careful and reasonable. No matter how safety-conscious the soft-drink bottler is, occasionally a bottle of soda will explode in someone's hand because of a latent defect in the glass that no reasonable inspection would reveal. At first, strict liability was applied only to products that were exceptionally dangerous, but today in every state in the United States a manufacturer is strictly liable to the injured victim when any defectively manufactured product causes injury, even if the defect was not caused by any act of negligence by the manufacturer.

This revolution in the law of torts was brought on by the theory that public policy demands that when there may be hazards to life and health inherent in defective products that reach the market, the responsibility for resulting injuries must be fixed wherever it will most effectively reduce the hazards. Although economists and legal theorists continue to argue the matter, the prevailing thinking is that manufacturers can anticipate some hazards and guard against the recurrence of others, in ways that the public cannot. Obviously it is socially desirable to discourage the marketing of products which have defects that are a menace to the public. When such products nevertheless find their way into the market, the law of torts today places the responsibility for whatever injury they may cause upon the manufacturer, who, even if not negligent in the manufacture of the product, is responsible for and profits from its reaching the market. However intermittently such injuries may occur and however haphazardly they may strike, their occurrence is nonetheless a constant risk. The dominant view today is that there should be general protection against such risks, and manufacturers are best situated to afford such protection.

Further, those who suffer from a defective product are too often unprepared to meet its consequences. Modern products liability theory presumes that the cost of an injury and the loss of time or health may be an overwhelming misfortune to the person injured, and a needless one, for the risk of injury can be insured by the manufacturer and as a cost of doing business be distributed among the public at large.

The law of libel, as it existed in 1960 in Alabama, and as it had existed in virtually every state in the country for a hundred years, was a strict liability tort. As a practical matter, the law of libel as it stood before the *Times* case is analogous to product liability law in the 1980's. The jury was told in effect to treat a defamatory publication as we now treat a defectively manufactured product. If the newspaper "product" proved to be defective (that is, contained false statements of fact) then the publisher was strictly liable for the injuries it caused, just as if the publisher were a present-day auto manufacturer that had put out a defective car.

Prior to the *Times* case, no Supreme Court opinion had ever held that the legal rules governing libel were subject to First Amendment restrictions. A publication was deemed "libelous per se" if the words tended to subject the plaintiff to public contempt, or were such as to injure him in his public office. Commissioner Sullivan, of course, claimed that the *Times* advertisement did both. Once the talismanic "libel per se" label was affixed to the *Times* ad, doors magically opened to Commissioner Sullivan. His only significant burden was to convince the jury that the publication was "of and concerning" him. Because Sullivan was a public official, this finding could be supported merely by demonstrating that his *place of control within the governmental hierarchy* had been libeled. Sullivan thus paraded his six witnesses in front of the jury, each of whom dutifully testified that they understood the ad's references to the police to mean, among others, Sullivan.

Though the truth of the statements was available as a defense, relatively minor deviations from the literal truth were sufficient to support the libel action, as long as the jury found that the ad was not "substantially true," a highly malleable standard. Thus, even though the general tenor of the "Heed Their Rising Voices" ad accurately captured what was going on in the South, the errors of detail (once the jury decided the ad was about Sullivan) were enough to make the ad legally libelous. And perhaps most devastating of all, according to the state of the law, damages were automatically "presumed" once falsity was established. Presumed damages made the law of libel even more potent than other strict liability torts, for not only could the speaker be liable without being negligent, he or she could be forced to pay a large money judgment without any actual proof that the plaintiff had suffered any demonstrable harm—the law *presumed* that serious harm flowed from lies, even when, as in Sullivan's case, very few Alabamans actually believed the story. (In fact, Supreme Court Justice Hugo Black, a former United States Senator from Alabama before he was appointed to the Court by Franklin Roosevelt, candidly observed that "Viewed realistically, this record lends support to an inference that instead of being damaged, Commissioner Sullivan's political, social, and financial prestige has likely been enhanced by the *Times* publication.") For Sullivan to be libeled by "outside agitators" like the *Times* was a badge of pride, not infamy.

These traditional libel rules operated with inexorable force against the *Times*. Good motives or belief in the truth did not prevent liability. Although the common law of Alabama did have a highly circumscribed set of "privileges" that a defendant could invoke in limited situations, these privileges, for the most part, did not extend generally to shelter criticism of the actions of public officials when the criticism contained factual inaccuracies. Libel law was, in short, strict liability, with the extra added kick of huge potential damages that could be levied without any real evidence of true injury.

If these were the legal consequences of the Alabama libel rules, the societal consequences in terms of the bitter war against Jim Crow were even more severe. For the driving tactic of Martin Luther King in the American South was the tactic of Mahatma Gandhi in British India, the use of civil disobedience to expose the immorality of existing law. The success of civil disobedience, however, was dependent upon the protestors' ability to appeal to the moral conscience of society, and that appeal was in turn dependent upon achieving widespread publicity for the protestors' action and the oppressive regime's reaction. For Gandhi, civil disobedience was powerful because it transcended the tools of mere rational persuasion, substituting for argument symbolic behavior that more immediately and viscerally moved the hearts of those he hoped to influence. Gandhi perceived that the effectiveness of civil disobedience largely turned on the existence of a moral conscience on the part of the oppressor; the civil-disobedient influences the oppressor not with physical force but psychological force. Gandhi was a master at heightening psychological pressure, first by appealing to the conscience of the British government, and second by appealing to a larger world opinion, thereby tightening the screws of guilt. To quote him, "If Europe but realized that heroic as it undoubtedly is for a handful of people to offer armed resistance in the face of superior numbers, it is far more heroic to stand up against overwhelming numbers without any arms at all, it would save itself and blaze a trail for the world."

America already had its own philosopher of civil disobedience in Henry David Thoreau, who wrote that "Under a government which imprisons any unjustly, the true place for a just man is also a prison." The modern civil rights movement was launched in the 1950's by Martin Luther King with the philosophy of Gandhi and Thoreau as its guide. It was in Montgomery, in 1955, that Mrs. Rosa Parks, a black woman, refused to give up her seat at the front of a city bus to a white man. She was arrested, convicted of violating the segregation law, and fined. The incident was followed by a bus boycott, organized by the Montgomery Improvement Association under the leadership of King, a boycott that would set the pattern of passive resistance by blacks and sympathetic whites for the next decade. The movement reached one of its profoundest moments in 1963 when Dr. King wrote his famous letter from the Birmingham city jail, urging the disobedience of segregation laws on the grounds that they were morally wrong.

This movement needed the *New York Times*, it needed the infant news broadcasts of CBS, NBC, and ABC, it needed the constant, virile, unsuppressed attention of a national press, in order to appeal to a national conscience. And the national press, quite clearly, could have an effect. When Arkansas Governor Orval Faubus dispatched the Arkansas National Guard to prevent the desegregation of Little Rock Central High School, Faubus's defiance of a federal court order was swiftly condemned by the Supreme Court, in the 1958 decision *Cooper v. Aaron*. To add force to the *Cooper* decision, the Court took the extraordinary step of having all nine justices individually sign the Court's opinion—the only time before or since that that has happened on the Court. President Eisenhower ordered federal troops to Little Rock to enforce the federal court's order. But none of this drama was as important to the Civil Rights movement as what the American people read of Little Rock in the newspapers, and most important of all, saw of Little Rock on television. The chilling sight of a small group of black children walking down a corridor cleared by troops to the high school doors, their ears filled with the insults of a mob of angry adults, began to marshal opinion outside the South.

The momentum continued. The more the South flailed against black children who demanded their rightful places in high schools and colleges, the more it pressed its stubborn resistance against blacks at lunch counters, buses, swimming pools, and parks, the more it bombed black churches, and scourged freedom fighters, the more it revealed to a whole nation the moral untenability of its white supremacy claims.

And thus the last desperate reaction of a clinging Jim Crow regime was to try to suppress the message itself, using whatever pretextual legal devices were at hand, including the law of libel. In almost every state in the South efforts were made to undermine the various organizations that were orchestrating these efforts of high-visibility resistance. For instance, Arkansas made it illegal for any member of the National Association for the Advancement of Colored People (NAACP) to be employed by the state government, or any of its subdivisions; Louisiana required groups like the NAACP to file affidavits of nonsubversion (and let there be no doubt that in Louisiana, any such affidavit filed by the NAACP in the year 1960 would have been deemed perjurious by the state); Virginia attempted to make the NAACP's courtroom efforts the illegal practice of law; Alabama sought to oust the NAACP from doing business within the state because its civil rights efforts had caused the state "irreparable injury." The reported opinions of the Supreme Court in the late 1950's and early 1960's were punctuated with case after case striking down these heavy-handed efforts at "legal" retaliation.

And so the strategy of the South was ultimately pushed to its logical end: if one could not stop the marches, one might at least keep the marches off television and out of the newspapers. In Jackson, Mississippi, the local television station engaged in an ingenious systematic blackout of all national coverage of civil rights unrest. Whenever the national news feed would show a journalist reporting from the South about a school integration dispute or a sit-in at a lunch counter, or rocks and molotov cocktails being thrown at freedom marchers, the station would suddenly experience "technical difficulties." Many years later, after litigation that progressed at a glacial pace, the station ultimately lost its FCC license because of its blatantly biased operation—the only television station ever to so lose its license.

No strategy for squelching the media's portrayal of conditions in the South, however, carried more potential for success than the creative use of the law of libel. Certainly, jury after jury could be counted upon to deliver gigantic verdicts against the likes of the *New York Times*. No national media outlet could endure a succession of such verdicts, mounting up to millions of dollars of liability. By the time the *New York Times* case reached the Supreme Court, there were eleven suits pending against it in Alabama, seeking $5,600,000, and five more Alabama suits had been brought against CBS News, seeking $1,700,000.

The strategy nearly worked, even against a newspaper as estimable and respected as the *New York Times*. The *Times*, after all, did back down in a sense by honoring the request of Alabama Governor John Patterson for a retraction. The "Heed Their Rising Voices" advertisement had not mentioned Governor Patterson any more than it had mentioned Sullivan; it was almost as if the *Times* were apologizing to the whole people of Alabama, with the Governor acting as their representative. The *Times* also came perilously close to an ignominious retreat in the Sullivan case itself. Just how close was revealed by a November 1984 article in the *New Yorker* by Anthony Lewis. The Supreme Court of Alabama had affirmed the $500,000 verdict on appeal. The *Times* had hired Professor Herbert Wechsler of the Columbia University Law School to assist in the appeal. After the *Times* defeat in the Alabama Supreme Court, Wechsler was invited to a meeting of the *Times* executives to decide whether to pursue an appeal in the United States Supreme Court. Wechsler found himself on the defensive in the meeting; the *Times* leadership was inclined to confess it had made a mistake and pay up—even though at the time the paper was barely making a profit, and even though the *Times* had already been hit with a second-half-million dollar libel award in a suit by the Mayor of Montgomery, Earl James. Wechsler had to summon his considerable powers of legal persuasion to convince the *Times* to prosecute the appeal. Had Orvil Dryfoos, the *Times* publisher (who sadly did not live to see the outcome of the case, dying of a heart condition in May of 1963), not elected to proceed, the history of the First Amendment and the effectiveness of the Civil Rights movement might both have been forever altered.

Looking back at the *New York Times* case today, and viewing it as an extension of the Civil Rights movement, the final result in the Supreme Court seems far more inevitable than it could have appeared to the *Times* management in 1964. From the perspective of the 1980's it is clear that the Supreme Court could no more permit southern juries in libel trials to punish those who were seeking to snuff out the yet unfulfilled promise of *Brown v. The Board of Education*, than it could permit southern legislation to outlaw or cripple the NAACP. The case was arguably more the product of a *due process* deficiency than a First Amendment concern, for against the backdrop of the period the problem was really one of litigation fairness: four black preachers and a New York newspaper simply could not get a fair trial in Alabama in 1960 in a case concerning civil rights issues. Had the events surrounding the Sullivan lawsuit not been so patently racist, in fact, it is doubtful that the Supreme Court would have bothered to hear just another libel suit at all. What was not foreordained, however, was that in aid of the civil disobedience tactics of Martin Luther King and his followers, the Supreme Court would write an opinion that would forever influence the way American law treated freedom of speech.

Despite the ample lip service that American society had always paid to freedom of speech, the fact is that before the *Times* case, no branch of American government, including the Supreme Court itself, had ever done much to protect it. As a culture we might better realize just how vulnerable freedom of speech is, if we took more time to reflect what a long time coming it has been. No decision of the United States Supreme Court ever declared any law void for violating the First Amendment's guarantee of free speech until 1927, over one hundred and thirty years after the First Amendment was adopted. One of the darkest episodes in that first one hundred and thirty years came shortly after the adoption of the Constitution, during the presidency of John Adams. The Federalist Congress and Adams, the last Federalist President, passed the Sedition Act of 1798, an act that could not have been more inimical to free speech:

> . . . If any person shall write, print, utter or publish . . . any false scandalous and malicious writings against the government of the United States or either house of Congress of the United States or the President of the United States with intent to defame the said government, or either house of the said Congress, or the said President or to bring them or either of them into contempt, or disrepute; or to excite against them or either of any of them the hatred of the good people of the United States . . . then such person being convicted shall be punished by a fine not exceeding $2,000 and by imprisonment not exceeding two years.

The act was an Americanized version of the old English crime of "seditious libel," or slander against the King. Every closed society in the history of civilized government has had some version of seditious libel as its cornerstone in the edifice of state suppression. The crime of slander against the state is the most vital weapon in the arsenal of despotic government, the weapon that silences the Solzhenitsyns and Sakarovs who dare dissent.

The Sedition Act expired by its own terms after two years. At the beginning of his term, the new president, Thomas Jefferson, immediately pardoned everyone who had been convicted under the act. James Madison, the primary author of the Bill of Rights, had eloquently renounced the Sedition Act, rhetorically asking whether but for freedom of speech, "Might not the United States have been languishing at this day, under the infirmaties of a sickly confederation? Might they not, possibly, be miserable colonies, groaning under a foreign yoke?" Because of its short duration, and the pardons granted by Jefferson, no test of the Sedition Act ever reached the Supreme Court.

The First Amendment's next great period of trial came during the "isolationists'" protests over World War I. Again, the Supreme Court failed miserably to protect freedom of speech, as one protestor after another had his conviction affirmed by the Court. Perhaps the lowest ebb came with the Supreme Court's decision in 1919 affirming the conviction of Eugene Debs.[31] The facts of Debs' case are well worth considering for the light they shed on the *Times* case. They illustrate how easy it is for the government to punish free speech inimical to the official party line, and they demonstrate how such punishment can come even at the hand of one of the nation's great spokesmen of free expression, Oliver Wendell Holmes.

Debs came to national prominence as a labor leader in the 1890's, when he led a successful strike for higher wages against the Great Northern Railroad in 1894, and drew sympathy and support from workers across the nation after being sentenced to a six-month jail term for his role in the infamous Chicago Pullman strike. Debs was a warm, compassionate leader; he campaigned for William Jennings Bryan for president in 1896, and then went on to found the Socialist Party of America. Debs was the Socialist Party's candidate for the presidency four times between 1900 and 1920. His highest popular vote total was 915,000, which he received while in prison for having publicly criticized the prosecutions of others who had opposed America's entry into World War I.

On June 16, 1918, Debs was speaking in Canton, Ohio. The main topics of his address were the future of American socialism, and the immorality of the United States' involvement in World War I. Debs said in the speech that he had just returned from a visit to three comrades who were paying the penalty for their devotion to the working class, having been convicted of aiding and abetting resistance to the draft. He stated that he "was proud of them." Speaking of the war, Debs stated that "the master class has always declared the war and the subject class has always fought the battles, . . . the subject class has had nothing to gain and all to lose, including their lives," and "the working class, who furnish the corpses, have never yet had a voice in declaring war and have never yet had a voice in declaring peace." Debs exhorted, "you need to know that you are fit for something better than slavery and cannon fodder."

For this speech, Debs was brought to trial under the Espionage Act of 1917. He addressed the jury himself, and while contending vigorously that his speech did not warrant the charges against him, he nonetheless courageously proclaimed, "I have been accused of obstructing the war. I admit it. Gentlemen, I abhor war. I would oppose the war if I stood alone."

Debs was found guilty, and sentenced to two concurrent ten-year terms of imprisonment.

When Debs' case reached the Supreme Court, Justice Holmes, writing for a unanimous Court, affirmed Debs' conviction, without the slightest hint of reservation or remorse that Debs was being sent to jail for having expressed political opinions. Justice Holmes stated matter of factly that "one purpose of the speech, whether incidental or not does not matter, was to oppose not only war in general but this war," and that the opposition was so expressed "that its natural and intended effect would be to obstruct recruiting." Debs went to prison. He was released by presidential order in 1921, but his citizenship was never restored.

The only bright light in this history came in the mysterious metamorphosis that shortly took place in the views of Oliver Wendell Holmes. Holmes had sent Debs to jail with characteristic dispatch, but shortly after the *Debs* case, Holmes's thinking seemed to undergo a deep change. As the next group of World War I protest cases reached the Court, Holmes defected from the consensus on the Court that such convictions were valid, and began to write eloquently in dissent. His masterpiece was his dissent in *Abrams v. United States*,[32] in which he wrote words so haunting and powerful that they have become part of the literature of the nation. The case involved five Russian immigrants, who had printed up 5,000 leaflets written in English and Yiddish, protesting the combination of "German militarism" and "allied capitalism" to "crush the Russian revolution." The leaflets were distributed by tossing them out the upper-story window of the building in which one of the defendants worked in New York. For this the defendants were convicted under the Espionage Act and sentenced to twenty years in prison. As in all of the other cases from this period, the Supreme Court expeditiously affirmed. But for the first time there were voices calling out from the Court in protest, in the figures of Oliver Wendell Holmes and Louis Brandeis. Over the next decade Holmes and Brandeis would become famous for their dissents in First Amendment cases, but the philosophy expressed in those opinions would not truly be embraced by the Court for five decades, and never in a more important case than *New York Times*. In *Abrams*, Holmes almost seemed to have undergone a conversion; his eyes saw what they could not see in the Debs case, that the defendants were being punished not for any real threat their words posed to the nation, for not enough could be squeezed from their "poor and puny anonymities to turn the color of legal litmus paper" to justify *twenty years* worth of prison time. No, they were being transparently persecuted for the unpopularity of their creed, for the fear and loathing felt by a jury of New Yorkers in 1918 for the radical philosophy of five Russian troublemakers. Holmes thus wrote the most famous paragraph of his life, a passage that (whether one accepts its viewpoint or not) deserves to be required reading in every high school curriculum:

> But when men have realized that time has upset many fighting faiths, they may come to believe even more than they believe the very foundations of their own conduct that the ultimate good desired is better reached by free trade in ideas—that the best test of truth is the power of the thought to get itself accepted in the competition of the market, and that truth is the only ground upon which their wishes safely can be carried out. That at any rate is the theory of our Constitution. It is an experiment, as all life is an experiment. Every year if not every day we have to wager our salvation upon some prophecy based upon imperfect knowledge. While that experiment is part of our system I think that we should be eternally vigilant against attempts to check the expression of opinions that we loathe and believe to be fraught with death, unless they so imminently threaten immediate interference with the lawful and pressing purposes of the law that an immediate check is required to save the country. I wholly disagree with the argument of the Government that the First Amendment left the common law as to seditious libel in force. History seems to me against the notion. I have conceived that the United States through so many years had shown its repentance for the Sedition Act of 1798, by repaying fines that it imposed. Only the emergency that makes it immediately dangerous to leave the correction of evil counsels to time warrants making any exception to the sweeping command, "Congress shall make no law . . . abridging the freedom of speech."

Against this backdrop of eloquent words but impotent holdings, the Supreme Court decided *New York Times v. Sullivan*, a case that put the future vigor of the American civil rights movement and the fate of American free expression in the Court's hands.

The *New York Times* opinion of the Supreme Court was written by Justice William Brennan. Brennan began by stating that even though a libel suit is a civil suit between two private parties, the suit is nonetheless subject to the restrictions of the First Amendment, because the government, through its libel laws, gives the civil judgment its coercive force. The jury, in effect, acts as a sort of after-the-fact censor, and the jury acts as a branch of the government. Justice Brennan then declared that the First Amendment's protection of the *New York Times* advertisement should not be diluted merely because the ad was part of a paid commercial advertisement. Even though the *Times* was paid for running the ad, and in one sense the ad's primary purpose was to solicit money (donations for the defense of Dr. King and other civil rights workers), the underlying message was a political and social statement.

Turning to the first major argument put forward by the state of Alabama, Brennan rejected the notion that any speech that is labeled with the epithet "libel" is automatically outside the First Amendment's protective umbrella. All of us have a tendency at times to use labels as a substitute for reasoning, and human nature being what it is there is a great temptation to avoid hard issues about freedom of speech by simply lavishing grand praise upon the First Amendment, and then mechanically disqualifying certain kinds of speech altogether, as if they were not "speech" at all. If we wish to ban dirty books, we call the books obscene, and declare obscenity something other than speech; if we wish to banish Eugene Debs, we call his oratory insurrection, and declare insurrection outside of the Constitution's protective cloak; if we wish to punish the *New York Times* for publishing material about civil rights in Alabama, we depict the material as libelous, and assert that libel was never meant to be sheltered by the Constitution.

Justice Brennan argued that freedom of speech is too precious to be defeated by the facile manipulation of labels. After recalling the legacy of Holmes and Brandeis, Brennan stated that the Court had chosen to analyze the *Times* verdict "against the background of a profound national commitment to the principle that debate on public issues should be uninhibited, robust, and wide open, and that it may well include vehement, caustic, and sometimes unpleasantly sharp attacks on government and public officials." Quoting James Madison, Brennan noted that "Some degree of abuse is inseparable from the proper use of everything; and in no instance is this more true than in that of the press." Brennan then sounded the central theme of his entire opinion: that in a free and open society, "bad speech" will inevitably be intertwined with "good speech," and that in order to give the "good speech" enough breathing space to prosper, society must be willing to tolerate some of the bad. Drawing on the writing of John Stuart Mill, Brennan emphasized that it is in the very nature of vigorous debate to get overheated, that debaters inevitably resort, often unconsciously, to exaggeration, villification, and misrepresentation.

No significant social or political debate in American history has been without its share of name calling, fraudulent argument, and self-serving lies tossed about in all directions by those most deeply moved by the controversy. Part of the genius of American civilization has been the license to blow off steam on public issues in an uncivilized manner. This robust tradition would be sorely crippled if we were to subject passionate political statement to a jury's cold and painstaking after-the-fact dissection.

The evils that might come from putting an iron lid on America's tradition of tempestuous debate would be multiplied many times over when the objects of criticism were government officials. For to penalize such criticism as libelous does more than choke off the breathing space that political speech requires; it puts the government itself in the role of silencing points of view that are out of step with the prevailing government line. Recalling the foul history of the Sedition Act of 1798, Justice Brennan echoed the remark of Oliver Wendell Holmes, that although the act was never tested in the Supreme Court, "the attack upon its validity has carried the day in the court of history."

But how should these ringing proclamations of our values be put into concrete legal rules? Since Alabama libel law did recognize "truth" as a defense to libel, one alternative would have been to change nothing, on the theory that no speaker will be punished for those parts of his or her speech that are deserving of First Amendment protection, but only for the lies. This alternative, however, could not live side by side with the recognition that some falsity will inevitably find itself mixed in with the truth, particularly when, as was the case in 1960, the "truth" in the hearts and minds of Alabama whites may not be the same as the "truth" in the hearts and minds of Alabama blacks. The traditional Alabama law of strict liability for libel made one subject to devastating money judgments *any time* some falsity crept in, even if the mistakes were unintentional.

At the opposite extreme, one might simply outlaw the entire law of libel, at least when the party claiming injury is a public official who has been criticized for misconduct in office. Three members of the Supreme Court, Justices Black, Douglas, and Goldberg, argued in favor of this sort of absolute immunity from libel prosecution by government officials.

Led by Justice Brennan, however, the majority (six Justices) of the Court refused either of these two polar alternatives, and opted instead for a compromise position. The courts and the culture are still, twenty years later, in the midst of working through the details of the compromise. In order for a libeled *public official* to recover, the Court held, he or she must prove that the defendant published the information with *knowledge of its falsity*, or out of *reckless disregard* for whether it was true or false. Furthermore, the proof of such knowing or reckless falsehood had to be "of clear and convincing clarity." Unfortunately, the Court referred to this new test as an "actual malice" standard, a very poor choice of words, for the standard has nothing to do with "malice" in the accepted sense of ill will or spite. This has caused no end of confusion before judges and juries—a prime example, as will be seen, is the Carol Burnett case—and it is a good lesson in the perils of using a word whose legal sense clashes with the meaning that the word is commonly understood to have in everyday speech.

Yet after all of this, why wouldn't the *Times* still be guilty of libel, since it had in its own files information that would have contradicted some of the statements in the ad? Justice Brennan's answer to this question is what truly gave the *Times* case its practical bite, for it drove home the fact that the "compromise" in the case was a compromise quite heavily weighted in favor of the media. By "knowing" or "reckless" misbehavior, the Supreme Court meant behavior that was worse than mere negligence, worse than mere lack of enterprise or diligence in checking a story out. As Justice Brennan saw it:

> The mere presence of the stories in the files does not, of course, establish that the *Times* "knew" the advertisement was false, since the state of mind required for actual malice would have to be brought home to the persons in the *Times'* organization having responsibility for the publication of the advertisement. With respect to the failure of those persons to make the check, the record shows that they relied upon their knowledge of the good reputation of many of those whose names were listed as sponsors of the advertisement, and upon the letter from A. Philip Randolph, known to them as a responsible individual, certifying that the use of the names was authorized. There was testimony that the persons handling the advertisement saw nothing in it that would render it unacceptable under the *Times'* policy of rejecting advertisements containing "attacks of a personal character"; their failure to reject it on this ground was not unreasonable. We think the evidence against the *Times* supports at most a finding of negligence in failing to discover the misstatements, and is constitutionally insufficient to show the recklessness that is required for a finding of actual malice.

A lot of ink has been spilled by judges, lawyers, and law professors to explain precisely what the "knowing or reckless" standard in the *Times* case really means, and that debate is indeed still the main battleground for much of the current anti-media litigation that fills the daily headlines. But for a moment, at least, in 1964, a great dual victory for civil rights and free expression had been scored. For stripped of all its legalese, the Court seemed to be saying that only the real *lie*, in the basic sense of the elemental moral principle of the Eighth Commandment, that "Thou shalt not bear false witness against thy neighbor," would be the grounds for a libel suit by an officer of the government. This may help explain the introduction of the word "malice" in the Court's newly articulated standard; the newspaper must be more than negligent to be punished, it must trangress virtually to the point of being *sinful*; it must deliberately lie, or try to cause others to believe something it itself does not believe to be true.

The *Times* case was indeed a thrilling historical moment, preserving the vitality of a vigorous and open culture; it was, in the words of the great law professor Harry Kalven, an occasion for dancing in the streets. And the victors were not merely the *New York Times*, or CBS News, or Harrison Salisbury, or Dan Rather. Nor were the victors merely the NAACP, or the SCLC, or Ralph Abernathy, or Martin Luther King. The victors included all Alabamans, and all Southerners everywhere, for it helped usher in the cleansing light of a larger moral conscience—a conscience that Gandhi and Thoreau and King knew was the world's most powerful agent of change. As very far as the whole nation still needs to go, the South in the last twenty years has come an amazingly long way toward eradicating most officially sanctioned racism. School desegregation in the South is now an everyday reality, and is, in fact, statistically much farther along than in the North. And T. Eric Embry, the Birmingham lawyer who stood out as brave enough to defend the *Times* in an Alabama court, the lawyer who had to book hotel rooms in Montgomery for the *Times* New York counsel under an assumed name, is now a Justice on the Supreme Court of Alabama. The progress of the South in civil rights today is the most powerful argument of all for the genius of free expression as classically articulated by Holmes and Brandeis. In Brandeis's words, the lesson is "that it is hazardous to discourage thought, hope and imagination; that fear breeds repression; that repression breeds hate; that hate menaces stable government; that the path of safety lies in the opportunity to discuss freely supposed grievances and proposed remedies; and that the fitting remedy for evil counsels is good ones."[33]

3

From Chasing Communists to Fighting Lillian Hellman: The Libel Suit as Guerilla Warfare

Don't get the impression that you arouse my anger. You see,
one can only be angry with those he respects.
Richard Nixon, addressing the White House press corps
on October 26, 1973

Every word she writes is a lie. . .
Mary McCarthy, discussing Lillian Hellman
on the *Dick Cavett Show*

IN THE YEARS that immediately followed the *New York Times* case, American culture went through one of the most tumultuous periods since the Civil War, a period that was characterized as much as any other in our history by the sort of "uninhibited, robust, and wide open" debate that Justice Brennan had encouraged in the *Times* decision. The Supreme Court rode the crest of this cultural upheaval by expanding on its original decision in the case; the law of libel in the twenty years following the *Times* ruling was dominated by a series of developments that substantially altered the practical application of the *Times* doctrine. First, the scope of the *Times* case was expanded to cover "public figures" as well as public officials, but lower courts struggled with the problem of how to decide who qualified as a "public figure." Second, the ancient distinction between libelous statements of "fact" and statements of mere "opinion" was reaffirmed and placed on a constitutional footing—"opinions," no matter how derogatory, could not be the basis of a libel suit, because the First Amendment recognized no such thing as a "false idea." This protection of "opinion," however, was qualified by a willingness on the part of many judges to treat many statements that are ostensibly opinion as factual, thus subjecting those who express such statements to possible liability. Third, plaintiffs in libel suits were permitted to undertake an investigation of the media's internal decision-making process in order to attempt to establish proof of knowledge of falsity or reckless disregard for the truth, a development that brought the public inside the journalistic process, exposing both the media's power and its susceptibility to bias and normal human error. Fourth, the costs of defending libel suits, and the attendant costs of obtaining liability insurance, dramatically escalated, choking off much of the "breathing space" for free speech that the *Times* case sought to provide.

The first major development following the *Times* decision was the change in the scope of cases subject to the special "knowing or reckless disregard for the truth" standard. In two 1967 cases the Supreme Court first broadened the standard to cover suits brought by plaintiffs who were outside the government, but who were nonetheless "public figures." The first case grew out of an article in the *Saturday Evening Post* that claimed that Georgia football coach Wally Butts had conspired to fix a college football game with the opposing coach, Bear Bryant. The second case involved Edwin Walker, a retired army general, who challenged an Associated Press report that he had led a violent crowd at the University of Mississippi to oppose the enforcement of a desegregation order. The Court declared that both Butts and Walker would have to satisfy the *New York Times* rule to prevail in their libel suits. (The two cases actually involved a collection of opinions from various justices suggesting a variety of different approaches to libel suits brought by public figures, but the "lowest common denominator" among the various opinions was that the *New York Times* standard would apply to public figure cases as well as cases by public officials.) The Court reasoned that in the United States the lines between government and the private sector are often blurred and that public figures often play as influential a role in shaping society as government officials; the First Amendment, the Court thus reasoned, should not differentiate between libel suits brought by government officials and libel suits brought by famous or "public" persons.[34]

The Supreme Court's next expansion of media protection came in a case in which the plaintiffs who sued the press were represented by none other than the man who ultimately came to be the greatest antagonist to the media in American history, the man who the press would one day seem to conclude was the very personification of the dark side of the force: Richard Nixon. Nixon was practicing law at the time in New York City prior to his successful run for presidency. The case, *Time, Inc. v. Hill,*[35] arose out of an incident in 1952, in which James Hill and his wife and five children were held hostage for nineteen hours by three escaped convicts in their suburban home in Whitemarsh, Pennsylvania. The family members were released unharmed, and the family stressed to news reporters after the ordeal that they had not been molested or abused, and were in fact treated courteously. The family moved to Connecticut after the incident and tried to avoid the public spotlight. In the spring of 1953, James Hayes published a novel entitled *The Desperate Hours*, which depicted the ordeal of a family of four held hostage by three escaped convicts in a suburban home. In Hayes' novel the convicts were violent and abusive, and engaged in verbal sexual assaults against the daughter. Hayes' novel was "triggered" by the Hill news story, but Hayes had collected news stories about other similar incidents and based his novel on composite impressions from various episodes. The Hills apparently never took exception to the novel.

The novel was subsequently made into a play, also entitled *The Desperate Hours*. In its February, 1955 issue, *Life* magazine ran a picture story about the opening of the play, directly linking *The Desperate Hours* to the Hill family. The brief text that accompanied the pictures announced that the play was based on the novel, and that the novel was in turn inspired by the Hill family's ordeal. "The play," *Life* stated, "is a heart-stopping account of how a family rose to heroism in a crisis." The real message of the *Life* story came, however, in the photos, which showed the play's cast enacting scenes from the play, including a picture of the son being "roughed up" by one of the convicts (captioned "brutish convict") a picture of the daughter biting the hand of a convict to make him drop a gun (captioned "daring daughter"), and one of the father throwing his gun through the door after a "brave try" to save his family was foiled.

The Hills' complaint was that the *Life* story placed them in a false light in the public eye, by giving the false impression that the sensationalized events portrayed in the photographs mirrored the family's actual experiences. During the trial, it was disclosed that the text of the article had originally stated that the play was a "somewhat fictionalized" account of the incident and that in the final editing process these words were cut. The jury found in favor of the Hills, originally awarding them $75,000 in damages, which was subsequently reduced by the judge to $30,000.

Life appealed the damages award all the way to the Supreme Court. *Life* took the position that the "knowing or reckless disregard for the truth" *New York Times* standard should apply to any story involving a matter of "public interest." *Life* magazine further stressed that its view of the "public interest" standard required by the First Amendment was not limited to political or governmental questions, but rather it embraced an extremely broad definition of "public interest" that translated roughly into "anything the public is interested in." The Supreme Court, despite lawyer Richard Nixon's efforts on behalf of the Hills, agreed with *Life*, holding that "constitutional protection is not limited to utterances that might enhance the resolution of political or governmental questions." The Supreme

Court stated that there was no indication that this magazine review would contribute to the "resolution of any serious social or governmental problems, or advance the arts." Rather, the key seemed to be that it was a matter of "public interest," and that fact was sufficient to trigger the special constitutional standard of *New York Times*. The Hill case was a powerful victory for the media, and it is arguable that it swung the pendulum of the First Amendment too far: for here was a family of private citizens dragged haplessly into the news by events beyond their control, and several years later swept back into the public eye by *Life's* sloppy handling of a story concerning a play not truly based on the Hills' experiences at all. The Hills' grievance concerning *Life's* poor journalism was not, it should be pointed out, among the most grabbing, for by depicting the family's heroism in a crisis the story actually made them look good—but it was nonetheless a false depiction involving events that the Hills clearly did not want exposed yet again to national attention.[36]

The highwater mark for this approach to First Amendment protection for the media came toward the very end of the cultural activism that characterized the Vietnam and civil rights protest eras, in a 1971 Supreme Court decision entitled *Rosenbloom v. Metromedia, Inc.*[37] The case involved a suit brought by George Rosenbloom, an alleged distributor of pornographic magazines in the Philadelphia area, against the operators of radio station WIP in Philadelphia. Following Rosenbloom's arrest during a police crackdown on the distribution of allegedly obscene books and newspapers, WIP broadcast a series of news stories describing Rosenbloom's arrest and the seizure of pornographic books and magazines from his home and a local warehouse. Rosenbloom sued the radio station. The station claimed that it was entitled to invoke the *New York Times* actual malice standard as a defense. The judgment of the Supreme Court was announced in another opinion written by Justice Brennan, who phrased the issue before the Court as "whether the *New York Times'* knowing-or-reckless-falsity standard applies in a state civil libel action brought not by a 'public official' or a 'public figure' but by a private individual for a defamatory falsehood uttered in a news broadcast by a radio station about the individual's involvement in an event of public or general interest." The opinion of Justice Brennan held that the *New York Times* standard applied to any defamatory speech involving matters of "public or general interest." Justice Brennan's analysis, like the analysis of the Court in *Hill*, shifted the focus of the *New York Times* standard from the status of the defamation victim to the status of the speech itself. "If a matter is a subject of public or general interest," Brennan wrote, "it cannot suddenly become less so merely because a private individual is involved, or because in some sense the individual did not 'voluntarily' choose to become involved."

Rather, Brennan wrote, the public's primary interest is in the *event*; the public's natural attention is on the content, effect, context, and importance of the conduct and actions of the participants in newsworthy events, not the participants' prior anonymity, notoriety or fame. The Court thus extended the coverage of *New York Times* "to all discussion and communication involving matters of public or general concern, without regard to whether the persons involved are famous or anonymous."

It was at this juncture in history that the Supreme Court's protection of the media seemed so broad that the law of libel appeared headed for extinction. Law professors and lawyers around the country were declaring that the Court had emasculated the law of libel to the point where it was essentially powerless. What no one could see, however, was that the entire nation was at a cultural break point. With the second coming of Richard Nixon, and Watergate yet to appear, the momentum of the 1960's was about to be broken, giving way to a new conservatism that would slowly overtake the nation, coming to triumph with the election of Ronald Reagan. That same shift in national mood would have a major impact on attitudes toward the media and free expression. The legal system quickly began to reflect a new distrust of the press and devaluation of the First Amendment. The new attitudes would be visible both at the grass roots level, in the responses of American juries, and at the highest level, the Supreme Court.

In 1974, the Supreme Court first began to back away from its earlier friendliness to the press. The case, *Gertz v. Robert Welch, Inc.*,[38] overruled the *Rosenbloom* decision, and set the tone for the anti-media mood that would gather increasing steam over the next ten years. The case was brought by Elmer Gertz, a well-known Chicago attorney and law professor, against the publisher of the monthly magazine *American Opinion*, an organ of the John Birch Society. Gertz had been retained as co-counsel by the family of a seventeen-year-old Chicago boy named Ronald Nelson, who was shot and killed by a Chicago police officer named Richard Nuccio. Nuccio ultimately was convicted of Nelson's murder. Gertz played no role in Nuccio's criminal prosecution; he was retained by the Nelson family only to pursue civil damages against Nuccio. Shortly after Nuccio's conviction, an article appeared in *American Opinion* entitled "Frame-Up—Richard Nuccio and the War on Police." The article alleged that Nuccio was being "railroaded" as part of a communist conspiracy to undermine local police so as to pave the way for a national police force which would support and enforce a communist dictatorship. The article named Elmer Gertz as one of the members of this conspiracy. He was identified as the lawyer for the Nelson family and one of the leaders of the attack on Nuccio. Gertz was further described, among other things, as a "Communist-fronter," a "Leninist" and a "Marxist."

The *Gertz* case ultimately reached the United States Supreme Court, and the Court used it to begin to reverse the expansion of First Amendment protection that the Court had achieved in a series of rulings since the *Times* case. The *Gertz* decision was a judicial compromise that attempted to accommodate the competing values of "uninhibited, robust, and wide open" debate of public issues with society's need to protect reputation. The *Gertz* Court reiterated the unsuitability in a free society of the traditional rule of strict liability for defamation, since compelling a speaker to "guarantee the accuracy of his factual assertions may lead to intolerable self-censorship." The need to avoid self-censorship, however, was not the only societal value recognized by the Court; to give absolute protection to the news media would completely neglect the competing social concerns underlying the law of defamation.

Gertz attempted to resolve the inherent friction between freedom of speech and protection of reputation by announcing a series of rules that set forth the minimum constitutional requirements for compensating injury to reputation. First, suits brought by public officials and public figures, at least when they involve issues of public concern, must always meet the *New York Times* actual malice test. Second, defamation suits brought by private individuals which involve issues of public concern must, at the minimum, be based upon proof of negligence. Third, "presumed damages" would no longer be permitted unless one could satisfy the *Times* "knowing or reckless disregard" standard; if the *Times* standard for malice was not met damages could not be awarded without proof of injury, though the scope of injury and the nature of the evidence required remained broad. Fourth, any award of punitive damages would always require a showing of *Times* "knowing or reckless disregard for the truth."

The *Gertz* opinion stated that it was unwise for the Supreme Court itself to proceed on a case-by-case basis in attempting to balance the constitutional claims of the press against individual claims for compensation, and the Court invited state courts to develop for themselves the proper standard of liability in suits brought by private plaintiffs. Thus, the Court stated that as long as the states did not dip below the negligence standard, they should "retain substantial latitude in their efforts to enforce a legal remedy for defamatory falsehood injurious to the reputation of a private individual."

The *Gertz* compromise was grounded on two rationales reflecting the Supreme Court's perceptions about the differences between public and private figures. Public officials and figures, the Court reasoned, are more likely to have effective opportunities for self-help when they are defamed.

Given the fact that public officials and public figures generally enjoy significantly greater access to channels of effective communication, the Court assumed that, as a class, they have a more realistic opportunity to contradict the lie or correct the error than do private individuals. The second rationale of the Court was more normative, largely reflecting the homespun moral that one who seeks the public arena must accept the heat of the fire as the price for entering the kitchen. People who voluntarily attain public figure status often have assumed roles of special prominence in social affairs, and they can in all fairness be required to accept greater public scrutiny and greater exposure to defamation as part of the cost of such fame. Some public figures occupy positions of such great power and influence that they are public figures for all purposes. Johnny Carson or Mohammed Ali might be considered "universal" public figures. Most public figures, however, are "limited public figures," persons who have "thrust themselves to the forefront of particular controversies in order to influence the resolution of the issues involved." Such limited public figures are subject to the *New York Times* standard when they are defamed in connection with issues about which they have invited attention, but in all other aspects of their lives they remain private figures, for whom states are free to create compensation on a lesser showing of simple negligence. Applying these new rules, Elmer Gertz, the court decided, was simply a private figure.[39]

The Supreme Court sent the *Gertz* litigation back to federal district court in Chicago to be tried under its newly established rules. Gertz won the retrial and in 1982, eight years after the historic Supreme Court decision, the Federal Court of Appeals in Chicago decided an appeal in favor of Gertz. In the retrial, Gertz was able to prove both negligence and knowing or reckless disregard of the truth, and the appellate court affirmed a jury award of compensatory damages in the amount of $100,000 and punitive damages of $300,000. At the retrial the court noted that the managing editor of *American Opinion* had pre-conceived a story line, solicited a writer with a known and unreasonable propensity to label persons or organizations as communist to write the article, and after the article was submitted, made virtually no effort to check the validity of statements that were defamatory of Gertz, and in fact added further defamatory material based on the editors' own views. There was more than enough evidence, the court stated, for the jury to conclude that the article was published with utter disregard for the truth or falsity of the statements it contained.

Although the *Gertz* decision was a defeat for the press, most media lawyers and First Amendment scholars actually praised the decision. Perhaps much of the praise came from the sympathy that many of them had for hapless Elmer Gertz, a respected lawyer and professor dragged into the mud by the extremist John Birch Society. The "respectable press," after all, could hardly endorse what the editor of *American Opinion* had done—it looked like a case of deliberate character assassination. But despite the distance that those who work for *Time* magazine or CBS News might like to put between their brand of journalism and the journalism of the John Birch Society, there were anti-media themes in *Gertz* that would come back to haunt the establishment press as it moved into the 1980's.[40] The basic *Gertz* distinction between public officials and figures and private figures continues to dominate the law of libel. (As discussed in the final chapter of this book, however, the Supreme Court in the summer of 1985 handed down a case entitled *Dun & Bradstreet v. Greenmoss Builders, Inc.*, which cut back substantially on the *Gertz* ruling, by holding that the First Amendment protections in *Gertz* apply only when the speech involves matters of public interest.)

The second major development after the *Times* case involved an issue also posed by the *Gertz* litigation, the distinction between false statements of fact that injure a plaintiff's reputation, and statements of mere opinion, which are not, at least in theory, ever actionable as libels.[41] The distinction between "fact" and "opinion," however, is easier to state than to apply; the neat lawyer's reality suggested by the two terms is not matched by any corresponding neatness in the daily use of language. As Oliver Wendell Holmes once observed: "A word is not a crystal, transparent and unchanged; it is the skin of a living thought and may vary greatly in color and content according to the circumstances and the time in which it is used."[42] Depending on the context, for example, the statement "Dr. Jones is a murderer" may be either a straightforward statement of fact or an opinion. If the statement is written on a placard protesting the fact that Dr. Jones performs abortions, it is obviously not a literal statement of fact, but rather an ideological (or moral) judgment that abortion is murder. (The term "ideological," in this sense is used very broadly, to encompass any moral, religious, philosophical, artistic, or political opinion that is not capable of empirical proof or disproof.) Such a statement, in this context, would be labeled "opinion" and could not form the basis of a libel suit. Similarly, it would be "opinion" if an article stated, "Doctor Jones drew her gun to shoot and kill an assailant who accosted the doctor and her husband with a knife in a dark alley—Dr. Jones is a murderer." In this situation the reasonable reader would understand the statement "Dr. Jones is a murderer" as the irrational conclusion of the writer, and pre-sumably, because the reader is able to draw his or her own conclusion from the disclosed facts, would understand that the words "Dr. Jones is a mur-derer" express the mere opinion of the author. Imagine, however, that the article merely stated, "Dr. Jones shot John Doe in a dark alley—Dr. Jones is a murderer." Here, the omission of the crucial mitigating fact that the shooting was in self-defense, and the lack of any ideological content in the statement, make it appropriate for the reasonable reader to conclude that the author intends the words "Dr. Jones is a murderer" to be understood as fact, thus rendering the statement proper grounds for a libel suit.[43]

In *Gertz*, the Supreme Court *in principle* gave its imprimatur to the rule that opinion is not actionable, by stating in ringing language:

> Under the First Amendment there is no such thing as a false idea. However pernicious an opinion may seem, we depend for its correction not on the conscience of judges and juries but on the competition of other ideas.

This eloquent statement, however, was qualifed by a caveat that left misstatements of fact out in the constitutional cold:

> But there is no constitutional value in false statements of fact. Neither the intentional lie nor the careless error materially advances society's interest in "uninhibited, robust, and wide-open debate on the public issues."

The relatively mechanical division between fact and opinion suggested by this language from *Gertz* is often not sufficiently flexible to take into account what might be called the problem of "ideological fact"—statements couched in factual form that are in substance born of ideological predispositions that are either not susceptible of proof or disproof, or that are so ideologically biased that no reasonable reader or listener truly understands them as serious statements of fact. The problem is well illustrated by the "ideological history" of the *Gertz* case itself.

To put the charges against Elmer Gertz in perspective, one needs to reflect on where exactly the *American Opinion* magazine and its publisher Robert Welch, were coming from. Robert Welch, who died in 1985 at the age of 85, was a Harvard Law School graduate, a former Massachusetts politician, a successful businessman, and founder of the ultra-conservative John Birch Society. Welch was the sort of person who saw communists everywhere. Like a bizarre character from *Dr. Strangelove*, Welch seemed to see life as a continuous communist plot, floridating our water and polluting our precious bodily fluids. Welch once even called *Dwight Eisenhower* "a dedicated conscious agent of the Communist conspiracy," and maintained that all Americans fell into four categories: "Communists, Communist dupes or sympathizers, the uninformed who have yet to be awakened to the Communist danger, and the ignorant." In 1950 Welch started his own magazine, *One Man's Opinion*, which later changed its title to *American Opinion*.

Elmer Gertz, in short, had not exactly been labeled a communist by NBC News or the *Washington Post*. The attack came from the right-wing fringe, and one might have thought that Gertz would take a certain pride in it. Gertz, as a lawyer active in civil rights, might have taken vilification by the John Birch Society as a sign that he had arrived, and worn the attack as a badge of honor.

For certainly, Elmer Gertz himself did not believe anything he read in *American Opinion* magazine, nor is it likely he would have had much respect for anyone who did. The likelihood in fact was that no real threat to Elmer Gertz' reputation was posed by the John Birch Society's wild-eyed accusations. To be called a communist by the likes of Robert Welch was less to be victimized by a false and libelous "fact" than it was to be identified as an ideological opponent. Although the accusation was a lie, it was an ideological lie, a lie born of a mind-set that could see Dwight Eisenhower as a communist agent.

And perhaps more fundamentally, why should it be considered libelous to call someone a communist anyway? In this country a person has a constitutional right to be a communist, as much as a John Bircher, a Democrat, or a Republican. Would an enlightened and tolerant person think any less of Elmer Gertz because someone had labeled him communist? Perhaps not, but the law of libel has always taken the position that it is irrelevant what the "enlightened and tolerant" or "right-thinking" segment of the public would think. The test, rather, is whether one's reputation has been impugned in the eyes of a substantial group. Cases that have tested the point under this standard have concluded that it is indeed defamatory to be called a communist. Does this mean that in the deep south in the 1950's one might have sued for having been labeled a "nigger-lover," even though the idea behind the slur was in fact one that ought to have been thought laudatory—that one is sympathetic to the plight of blacks victimized by racism? The answer, apparently, is that such a suit could be brought; we know, at least, that prior to 1954 in Mississippi, South Carolina, Alabama, Virginia, and Louisiana there were cases holding that it was defamatory just for a white person to be called a black. Perhaps these cases would not hold up in the 1980's—at some point the law regards the group that has been unfavorably influenced by the accusation as too negligible and anti-social to be counted—but it is clear that exception is narrowly construed, and that for Elmer Gertz, at least, to be called a commie in Chicago was good enough to support a suit.

The threat to free expression posed by the inflexible application of the fact/opinion distinction is perhaps illustrated best by a bizarre case involving two American writers, a case containing grudge match overtones that stretch back decades. The case, *Hellman v. McCarthy*,[44] began with a literary wisecrack on the *Dick Cavett Show*.

Dick Cavett was at his best, good-naturedly tweaking his guest to say something both literary and outrageous. His guest was writer Mary McCarthy, and during the course of Cavett's January 1980 interview the topic turned to "overrated" authors. In an impishly provocative dialogue with Cavett, McCarthy proceeded to name John Steinbeck and Lillian Hellman as two nominees for overratedness. In one of the better exchanges of zapping lines one is ever going to hear on a television talk show, McCarthy then went for the literary jugular:

Dick Cavett: We don't have the overphrased writer any more?

Mary McCarthy: At least I'm not aware of it. The only one I can think of is a holdover like Lillian Hellman, who I think is tremendously overrated, a bad writer, and dishonest writer, but she really belongs to the past, to the Steinbeck past, not that she is a writer like Steinbeck.

Dick Cavett: What is dishonest about her?

Mary McCarthy: Everything. But I said once in some interview that every word she writes is a lie, including 'and' and 'the'.

Cavett's studio audience erupted in laughter, but Lillian Hellman, to her eternal discredit, did not. Instead of laughing it off, or topping Mary McCarthy with a sniping crack of her own, Lillian Hellman sued McCarthy, Dick Cavett, and the Educational Broadcasting Corporation for libel, to the tune of $2,250,000. A New York judge upheld Hellman's right to take her case to trial, and Mary McCarthy would still be embroiled in expensive litigation had not Lillian Hellman died before the trial could begin.[45]

What was it in Mary McCarthy's remarks that hurt Lillian Hellman? Surely not the "factual" errors (if any) in McCarthy's statement that Hellman was "dishonest," in the sense of misrepresenting the events and characters from which Hellman's writings were drawn. Rather, the real sting of the remark appears to have been in its literary slam—that Hellman's writings in a larger sense did not ring true, either as philosophical statements, or as inquiries into human nature. That slam is sheer opinion, and to force McCarthy to go to trial over such an expression of opinion is to permit the court system to be used as a tool to harass someone who expresses an unpopular idea. A New York judge, however, ruled that a jury could find that McCarthy's statements were to be taken literally, and that McCarthy would thus have to stand trial on the issue of whether her statements were fact or opinion. Had the case gone to trial and then to a jury, there is an excellent chance in today's legal climate that Lillian Hellman would have won a substantial jury award. And whether or not the award would have been affirmed on appeal, it would have cost Mary McCarthy a small fortune in legal fees.

The libel litigation between Hellman and McCarthy is a particularly sad indictment of the current state of libel law in American culture, for it transparently placed deep philosophical, political, and literary conflicts in the ridiculous arena of a civil trial. Mary McCarthy's statement, however meanly and brutally it may have wounded Hellman, should have been recognized by the judge as the pure stuff of literary invective, beyond the censorship of the libel laws.[46]

Mary McCarthy, in essays, book reviews, drama criticism, and through characters in novels, has assailed most major literary figures of her time, usually with direct and acrid humor. Among those criticized by McCarthy over the years were Tennessee Williams, J.D. Salinger, Virginia Woolf, Ernest Hemingway, and Grahame Green. Of Salinger, for example, she wrote that he "suffers from this terrible sort of metropolitan sentimentality, and it's so narcissistic, so false, so calculated, combining the plain man with an absolutely megalomaniac egoism." McCarthy has voiced displeasure with most American playwrights, and with most women writers. Her unflattering critiques of Lillian Hellman date back several decades. In a 1946 piece in the *Partisan Review*, for example, she derided in passing the "oily virtuosity" of Hellman; in a 1956 review of Hellman's adaptation of *Candide*, McCarthy called it "a sad fizzle which is more like a high school pageant than a social satire," elaborating that a "bowdlerized *Candide*, a *Candide* that cannot afford to be candid, is a contradiction in terms." Ironically, in a 1976 interview she attacked Hellman for allegedly having defamed John Dos Passos in an episode at Sarah Lawrence College in 1948. Her criticisms of Hellman over the years, however, were by McCarthy's standard neither unusually frequent nor unusually harsh—it was McCarthy being McCarthy.[47]

Lillian Hellman, by the same token, also accumulated a long series of feuds and quarrels of varying intensity during her rich and often tumultuous life, including several with other women literary or theatrical figures, including Claire Booth Luce, Dorothy Thompson, Tallulah Bankhead, and from time to time, Mary McCarthy. Hellman once said of McCarthy that she is "often brilliant and sometimes even sound."

The background of the McCarthy/Hellman litigation also includes their divergent reactions to the political events of the 1930's, 40's, and 50's. Lillian Hellman, it has been noted before, was during that period called a communist almost as often as a playwright, and she was one of the most visible and courageous American figures to stand up in the witch-hunting era of Senator Joseph McCarthy. Hellman was blacklisted during the period, and her stand at that time forms a significant part of her public persona. One of her great moments came in 1952 when she published a defiant open letter to the chairman of the House Un-American Activities

Committee, in response to the Committee's subpoena. She told the Committee, in words far braver than those of most other artists at the time, "I will not cut my conscience to fit the fashions of our time."

Mary McCarthy, on the other hand, after some early fringe and highly tentative contacts with the communist movement, gradually became identified as a liberal anti-communist. In 1936 she became embroiled, somewhat unwittingly, in the internecine battles of left-wing politics, finding herself under attack from Communist Party members because she had joined the "Committee for the Defense of Leon Trotsky." By her own account, McCarthy's politics never reached the intensity of Hellman's; she said in 1963 that politically she "was more or less passive," getting "involved with politics because the men I was with were involved in politics." Her attitude toward the Communist Party, she said, was "not hostile but merely unserious." In the spring of 1949, Mary McCarthy and several other literary and intellectual figures infiltrated a Peace Conference at the Waldorf Hotel in New York, which was backed by the Communist Party, and attempted to disrupt the conference with fiery anti-communist speeches.

And so the special poignancy and tragedy of the lawsuit *Hellman v. McCarthy*: two brilliant American writers and visible cultural figures working through a feud laden with political and philosophical crosscurrents in the unseemly forum of a libel trial, when the only sure consequence is less freedom and literary honesty for all writers. The suit prompted an open plea in the *New York Times Book Review* to both writers by Norman Mailer.[48] No one familiar with their respective writings, Mailer observed, would be surprised that they would clash, their differences are profound and capable of producing mortal insults. To say what McCarthy said of a fellow writer, Mailer wrote, "was a barbarity and a brutality," and Hellman struck back by filing suit, perhaps because she felt it was the only way that she any longer could. Mailer wrote: "Lillian is not a mature woman in the full command of her powers, eager to defend herself; she is an honorable and much-damaged warrior who could not raise a pistol since she can no longer see."

No writer, Mailer observed, is ever honest except in the rarest of moments—not Hellman, not McCarthy, not Mailer or Bellow or Cheever or Updike or James. McCarthy's statement, Mailer wrote, was "a stupid remark to utter on television and best left unsaid." (Perhaps Mailer overstates that point, for if McCarthy chooses to be a harsh critic of another writer's perception of "truth," so be it—no reasonable viewer could not but discount the remark with the knowledge that Mary McCarthy has no more of a monopoly on that rare comodity than Hellman or Dick Cavett. Mailer, himself, in once reviewing McCarthy's book *The Group*, wrote that she suffered from "the accumulated vanity of being over-praised through the years for too little and so being pleased with herself for too little.") In a moving conclusion to his essay, Mailer pleaded with Hellman to drop the suit, for it could bring "censorship and self-censorship on writers." And then, speaking to the essential sadness of the whole episode, Mailer ended: "I have learned so much about writing from each of you that your quarrel is as painful to me—and to many others, I expect—as a quarrel between the nearest and best of one's relatives, one's dearest, one's friends."

But Norman Mailer's plea went unfulfilled, and before she died Lillian Hellman managed to force Mary McCarthy to spend thousands in legal fees defending herself for a talk-show comment that was obviously an expression of opinion. Why was the legal process triggered by this remark so costly and intimidating? The answer has more to do with the litigation process itself, and with the enormously high legal fees generated by that process, than the legal principles established in *New York Times* and *Gertz*. To appreciate how the *Times* doctrine works today in actual practice one must first understand something of how lawyers go about puttting together the nuts and bolts of a libel suit. In a modern trial of a libel case lawyers spend a considerable amount of time probing the inner decision-making process of the publisher or broadcaster being sued, a process that makes for very expensive legal fees, but also contributes greatly to media accountability. This dissecting of the media's internal procedures, which received much attention during the William Westmoreland trial, was given its greatest boost by the Supreme Court in a decision several years before the Westmoreland case, a decision that, ironically, also involved CBS, Mike Wallace, and the Vietnam War.

The third major development in the aftermath of *New York Times* was the exposure of the media's decision-making processes to the scrutiny of plaintiffs and their lawyers. If *Gertz* began the media's downhill slide in First Amendment decisions from the Supreme Court, the case that more than any other seemed to seal the media's declining fortunes would come five years later, in a decision entitled *Herbert v. Lando*.[49] The case presaged the suit that William Westmoreland would later bring against CBS News, for it, like the Westmoreland case, involved a CBS report by Mike Wallace, and a soldier from Vietnam. Most significantly, however, the case effectively turned the tables on the media, by opening up its procedures to the same sort of painstaking investigation that the media, when it is at its best, applies to others.

In novels and movies lawyers always have tricks up their sleeves: secret witnesses produced at the last second to stun the other side, a telltale letter unveiled at the last instant to save the day, a torn piece of clothing pulled up from behind the defense attorney's table that establishes the defendant's innocence. Clever use of the element of surprise is part of the romantic vision of the American trial lawyer, the stuff of Jimmy Stewart battling George C. Scott in *Anatomy of a Murder*. Although some room for surprise evidence still exists in criminal trials, in civil cases such as libel suits the law has for the most part abolished surprise evidence. Instead, both sides go through a long pretrial process (in a complicated case it may last years) known as the "discovery" period. During the discovery period each side in effect must lay its cards on the table for the other to see and evaluate. Each party must turn over to the other any documents or other evidence in its possession that is relevant to the dispute that the opponent requests. Each side is entitled to examine the other side's witnesses by taking their depositions. (A deposition is a sort of dress rehearsal examination of a witness, with lawyers from both sides permitted to conduct direct and cross examination, just as in a real trial. A court reporter is present, and the witness is under oath. No judge is present at the deposition, which is usually conducted in the offices of one side's attorney, but if a dispute arises concerning the testimony that cannot be resolved by the lawyers on the spot—if a witness, for example, claims that he or she need not answer a question—then the lawyers may temporarily adjourn the deposition and appear before the trial judge to have him or her rule on the dispute.)

One of the primary preoccupations of the discovery process in a major libel suit is the investigation into whether the media defendant acted with knowledge of a story's falsity or in reckless disregard of the truth— whether the media defendant, in short, violated the *New York Times* privilege. In a 1968 case the Supreme Court held that in applying the "recklessness" half of the *New York Times* standard, the mere failure to investigate a story before publishing it, when a reasonably prudent publisher would have so investigated it, is not reckless for First Amendment purposes. In that case, *St. Amant v. Thompson*, the court stated that instead there must "be sufficient evidence to permit the conclusion that the defendant in fact entertained serious doubts as to the truth of his publication." The Court also made it clear, however, that although *Time* magazine may say it sincerely believed its story about Ariel Sharon, or CBS may say that it sincerely believed its story about Westmoreland, the jury does not have to believe it. Mere protestations by the defendant that it subjectively believed a story was true do not insulate the defendant from liability; the trier of fact must still find the protestations believable. The Court noted that professions of good faith will not be persuasive when the story is fabricated or a product of the defendant's imagination, or is based wholly on an unverified, anonymous tip. More important, the Court recognized that claims of subjective innocence will not be convincing "when the publisher's allegations are so inherently improbable that only a reckless man would have put them in circulation . . . [or] where there are obvious reasons to doubt the veracity of the informant on the accuracy of his reports."

For a period after the *New York Times* decision, many media defendants resisted efforts by plaintiffs to plumb the editorial thought processes that led to the publication or broadcast of a story, on the theory that the very act of reexamining and second-guessing those editorial processes would chill First Amendment press freedoms. In its 1979 decision in *Herbert v. Lando*, the Supreme Court rejected any such special First Amendment privilege to avoid the usual discovery process. The significance of *Herbert v. Lando* cannot be overstated, for it subjected the American media to the same sort of scrutiny that the media had so often visited upon others. The Supreme Court in *Herbert* gave plaintiffs the power to investigate the internal thought processes of a media defendant. It was the *Herbert* decision that truly opened the door to the sort of inquiry into outtakes (film footage not used in the final broadcast), reporters' notes, the veracity of sources, discussions among editors, and inquiries into the mental state of reporters that is the centerpoint of modern libel litigation in suits such as William Westmoreland's or Ariel Sharon's. *Herbert v. Lando* gave to the plaintiff's lawyer the right to try to out-Mike-Wallace Mike Wallace and is one of the great examples of how an idealistic legal rule (the rule in *New York Times v. Sullivan*) can become substantially transformed in practice when ingenious lawyers get hold of it.

The plaintiff in the case, Colonel Anthony Herbert, sued CBS producer Barry Lando, reporter Mike Wallace, and the CBS network, for remarks on the television program *60 Minutes* about his behavior while in the military service in Vietnam. Colonel Herbert, a decorated war hero (he was awarded 22 medals in Korea), emerged as a major critic of the military hierarchy in Vietnam, gaining tremendous media attention for his charges that his superiors had covered up war crimes and atrocities in Vietnam. Herbert claimed, for example, that he witnessed a South Vietnamese soldier slit a young Vietnamese girl's throat, while one of her children clung screaming to her legs. Herbert became a media hero, receiving glowing reports for his courageous whistle-blowing. Among the media outlets that jumped on Herbert's bandwagon were the *New York Times* and the *CBS Evening News*.

In the course of only fifty-eight days as a battalion commander in Vietnam, Herbert won the Silver Star and three Bronze Stars. Suddenly in 1969, he was relieved of his command. According to Herbert his command was taken away because his superiors wanted him to keep quiet about atrocities, while Herbert continued to press for investigation. Following close upon the trial of William Calley for the My Lai massacre, the press leaped at Herbert's story, and he became a media cult figure on Vietnam. His book *Soldier*, which elaborated on his charges about war crimes and cover-ups in Vietnam, emerged as a national bestseller. (*Soldier* was published by Holt, Rinehart and Winston, which ironically is owned by CBS, and is the premier publishing house in the CBS conglomerate's publishing operation.)

60 Minutes set out to do a story on Herbert, a story that was originally conceived as a tribute to Herbert's book. But as *60 Minutes* delved into the merits of the accusations made by Herbert, doubts about Herbert's veracity emerged in the mind of Barry Lando, the CBS producer in charge of the story. Herbert's superiors steadfastly denied his accusations about atrocities—denials one would have expected—but denials also came from other quarters, from persons with no obvious axes to grind. The army lawyer who investigated Herbert's accusations, Ken Rosenblum, who had left the army and was working as an assistant district attorney in New York, made a convincing case that the army investigation had been evenhanded and thorough, and had turned up nothing. A second witness, Major Jim Grimshaw, a subordinate of Herbert's who admired the Colonel, and whom Herbert lavishly praised in *Soldier* for heroism, contradicted Herbert's account of an incident in which Grimshaw had allegedly rescued a Vietnamese baby from a Viet Cong cave. Grimshaw claimed no such incident had ever occurred. In a dramatic interview, Mike Wallace brought Herbert and Grimshaw together face to face in front of the rolling cameras, and Grimshaw told his former superior Herbert that Herbert had lied.

In the aftermath of this interview, Herbert and Lando had a bitter quarrel; Herbert accused Lando of setting out to get him because Herbert had chosen another collaborator to write *Soldier*. (Lando and Herbert had once briefly discussed such a possible collaboration.) In the actual running of the *60 Minutes* segment in February, 1973, a segment entitled "The Selling of Colonel Herbert," CBS juxtaposed Herbert's account with the contradictory accounts of other witnesses, and concluded with summations by Mike Wallace and Ken Rosenblum, the army lawyer who had investigated Herbert's charges:

> *Wallace*: The deeper we got into this investigation, the more we felt that the way in which the media—including CBS News—reacted to Herbert's allegations was almost as interesting as Herbert's story itself. Several reporters did make an effort to check out Herbert's story, found his case was far from clear-cut and made that obvious in their reports. But many others did not. The *New York Times* did more, probably, to publicize Tony Herbert's story than any other paper. When Herbert passed a lie-dector test on whether or not he had reported

war crimes to Franklin, the *Times* gave it a big play. But when the army said Colonel Franklin—the man Herbert had accused—had also passed a lie-detector test, other papers reported it, but there was not one word about it in the *Times*.

Attorney Ken Rosenblum, the former army lawyer who investigated many of Herbert's charges, says the attitude of the media towards Herbert was understandable.

Rosenblum: Well, he's highly decorated and a respected soldier, and he makes these charges and he gets alot of newspaper coverage about it. Because of the temper of the times and what the country wanted to hear, perhaps, or because the media was looking for another hero, they tended to accept these allegations uncritically.

CBS's indictment of the media's uncritical acceptance of Herbert's story would later become the same charge leveled against CBS itself by General Westmoreland—that CBS uncritically accepted the accusations of Westmoreland's critics. And the trial in the Westmoreland case would be profoundly influenced by the Supreme Court's ruling in the *Herbert* litigation—for Herbert made essentially the same sort of allegations against CBS that Westmoreland would later make, that CBS did not broadcast interviews that CBS had gathered that were favorable to Herbert, but had edited the broadcast in a one-sided manner to further Lando's vendetta against him.

During his deposition in the discovery portion of the suit, Lando responded to most questions, but he refused to answer some questions about why he made certain investigations and not others. Lando similarly refused to discuss what he concluded about the honesty of certain people he interviewed for the program. Finally, Lando would not reveal the substance of his conversations with Mike Wallace during the preparation of the program segment. Lando contended that these thought processes and internal editorial discussions were protected from disclosure by the First Amendment. The Supreme Court disagreed, in a 6–3 decision. Justice White, the author of the decision, began by observing that liability for defamation was "well established in the common law when the First Amendment was adopted," and the framers had no intention of abolishing it. During the period before the historic *New York Times* case, mental processes and attitudes were often explored in libel trials, and defendants often testified to their good faith in writing a story. "Courts have traditionally admitted any direct or indirect evidence relevant to the state of mind of the defendant" in libel suits, White wrote.

CBS argued that "the defendant's reckless disregard of truth, a critical element, could not be shown by direct evidence through inquiry into the thoughts, opinions and conclusions of the publisher but could be proved only by objective evidence from which the ultimate fact could be inferred."

But Justice White found that this would be too substantial a barrier to plaintiffs, "particularly when defendants themselves are prone to assert their good-faith belief in the truth of their publications, and libel plaintiffs are required to prove knowing or reckless falsehood with 'convincing clarity'."

Justice White concluded that permitting plaintiffs "to prove their cases by direct as well as indirect evidence is consistent with the balance struck by our prior decisions." He found it "difficult to believe that error avoiding procedures will be terminated or stifled simply because there is liability for culpable error and because the editorial process will itself be examined in the tiny percentage of instances in which error is claimed and litigation ensues."[50]

In the *Herbert v. Lando* litigation, Barry Lando's deposition alone continued intermittently for a year, and consumed *over 3,000 pages of transcript.*[51] This huge expenditure of money and effort, however, would come to be dwarfed by the discovery process in cases such as those later brought by Ariel Sharon and William Westmoreland. The discovery process in suits like Sharon's or Westmoreland's may cost many millions of dollars before they are completed. In *Westmoreland v. CBS* the attorneys for both sides examined over 300,000 documents, and interviewed hundreds of witnesses all over the globe.

It is important to note that the use of discovery as a weapon for intimidation is not limited to those who sue the press; it also may be used by the press itself, to scare off would-be plaintiffs. Once sued, the media defendant will use discovery to probe every aspect of the plaintiff's existence that might have any relevance to the issues being tried. The plaintiff will be under court order, under pain of contempt of or dismissal of the suit, to comply. For many plaintiffs, the prospects of turning over secret files to a newspaper to comb over is enough to deter bringing suit. According to Mobil Oil President William Tavoulareas, for example, the management of the *Washington Post* thought he would never sue them for a story alleging he had set up his son in business "because they'd drag me though the mud in discovery." As it turns out, the attitude only spurred Tavoulareas on all the more.

The plaintiff need not have skeletons in the closet to be intimidated by press discovery. Even the scrupulously honest plaintiff may have secrets that are legitimately private. But the plaintiff who wants vindication in court must take the bitter with the sweet, and must turn over all relevant evidence in its possession. In recent years, parties in libel suits have increasingly sought to turn over evidence with a string attached: that the evidence be used only within the confines of the case, and not be disseminated publicly. In the *Tavoulareas v. Washington Post* litigation, Mobil Oil for a long time managed successfully to get a "protective order" from the court suppressing the public disclosure of depositions and documents Mobil was forced to release to the *Post* during the litigation. The *Post* thus had access to Mobil's records for the purpose of defending itself at trial, but it could not turn around and publish them in the paper.

In spite of press protests that such "protective orders" act as a prior restraint on free expression and corrode the substantial social interest in open and public trials, the Supreme Court held in May of 1984 that such protective orders were permissible if in the trial judge's discretion there appeared to be "good cause" for their issuance. The Supreme Court's decision grew out of a lawsuit for libel brought by a religious group in the state of Washington known as the Aquarian Foundation, against the *Seattle Times* and the *Walla Walla Union-Bulletin*. The Aquarian Foundation, which has about 1,000 members, is led by a man named Keith Milton Rhinehart.[52] Aquarians believe in life after death and the ability to communicate with the dead through a medium, Rhinehart being the main medium. During the seventies both the *Union-Bulletin* and the *Times* ran a number of exposés on Rhinehart's group. The articles included descriptions of seances conducted by Rhinehart in which people paid him to put them in touch with deceased relatives and friends, and descriptions of sales by Rhinehart of magical "stones" that had been "expelled" from his body. One article described Rhinehart's conviction, later vacated, for sodomy; other articles described an "extravaganza" sponsored by Rhinehart at the Walla Walla State Penitentiary, which allegedly included give-aways of cash prizes and chorus lines of girls in bikinis. Two articles discussed a purported connection between Rhinehart and television actor Lou Ferrigno, the "Incredible Hulk."

Claiming the articles were "fictional and untrue" and that they tended to impeach his "honesty, integrity, virtue, religious philosophy, reputation as a person and in his profession as a spiritual leader," Rhinehart sued the two newspapers for over $14 million. Early in the discovery process the papers asked Rhinehart to produce extensive information relating to the financial affairs of Rhinehart and the Aquarian Foundation, including such information as the identity of the Foundation's donors over the last ten years, and a list of all Aquarian Foundation members for the same time period. Rhinehart and the Foundation claimed that if such information were made public, Rhinehart and his followers might be subjected to embarrassment, annoyance, harassment, and even physical violence, all as a penalty for exercising *their* First Amendment right to the free exercise of religion. Persuaded by these concerns, the Supreme Court upheld a ruling by the Washington courts that barred any public disclosure of the financial records and membership lists that were produced during discovery. Thus media outlets that Rhinehart claimed had defamed him could not use the threat of further intimidating dissemination to force Rhinehart to back away from his right to go to court, before his claims were ever heard on the merits. This precedent was subsequently relied upon by Mobil in support of its suppression efforts in the *Tavoulareas v. Washington Post* litigation.[53]

The fourth major development in the law of libel since *New York Times* is the growing expense and energy now consumed by such litigation. Given the huge legal fees attendant to modern libel suits, and the tendency of each side in such cases to wage total warfare against the other through the discovery process, the main fact of life in modern libel litigation is that it is lengthy and costly. It is not at all clear whether anyone (other than lawyers) has benefited from the twists and turns that the law of libel has taken since the *New York Times* case.

One of the most revealing statistics about modern libel suits is the plaintiff's success rate in front of juries. Whereas in most other areas of tort litigation, plaintiffs tend to recover in roughly one-third to one half of all cases tried to juries, in the libel area the success rate in front of juries in recent years has ranged in different studies from roughly 55% to 85%. (In product liability and medical malpractice cases, by contrast, plaintiffs prevail only 30% to 40% of the time.) And unlike other forms of personal injury litigation, in which the award of damages is tied at least to some degree to quantifiably measurable forms of loss—medical bills, lost wages, or diminished future earnings power—the lawsuit for libel or invasion of privacy is one of the most unusual creatures known to the legal world. The wrong inflicted on the victim is a subjective loss of reputation or privacy triggered solely by the spoken or written word; on the mere basis of what has been said about a victim, a jury is instructed to employ a sort of alchemy to transform the intangible "damage to reputation" or "invasion of privacy" into cold dollars and cents. Unrestrained by any mechanical standard of measurement, juries will do such things as award writer Jackie Collins $40 million because a magazine misidentified a woman in a nude scene from the movie *The World Is Full of Married Men* as being Collins, or award Miss Wyoming of 1978 $26 million because they believed that a *Penthouse* fantasy story referred to her. (Appeals courts later wiped out both gigantic jury awards.)

Litigation dollars in media cases have been flying recently, and as is always the case in high-powered litigation, many of the dollars are flying into the pockets of lawyers. It is not unusual for a jury award in a libel suit today to be measured in millions of dollars. Prior to 1980, only one libel award of over $1 million was returned by a jury. In 1982, however, nineteen percent of the awards exceeded $1 million, and by 1984 and 1985, one third of all the jury awards in libel cases were over $1 million. Litigation survey data compiled in studies in 1982 indicated that thirty out of forty-seven recent damage awards included awards of "punitive" damages—damages levied by the jury explicity to punish the media defendant rather than simply compensate the victim—and seven of those punitive damages awards were for $1 million or more. More recent survey data indicate that punitive damages awards have now become even more common and have reached an astronomical average of almost $3 million per award. Punitive damages awards cannot be awarded unless a showing of *New York Times* actual malice is made; but juries are quite obviously not at all intimidated by the actual malice standard, and stupendous punitive damages awards are becoming almost routine.

To an individual writer like Mary McCarthy, or to a small media outlet without great assets, the threat of a huge libel judgment can be psychologically chilling; they must defend libel actions under the peril of bankruptcy or shutdown if they lose. In a case involving the *Alton Telegraph*, a small daily paper from Alton, Illinois with a circulation of 38,000, the paper was faced with a $9.2 million jury judgment because of a memorandum written by two of its reporters, a memorandum never published in the paper, but simply sent to a federal investigator.[54] The newspaper was forced to file for bankruptcy to avoid having to sell all its assets. The *Alton Telegraph* finally managed to reach a settlement that allowed it to stay in business, but its near-demise was a chilling lesson: however painful a successful libel action may be to CBS or the *National Enquirer*, it can be fatal to a small media outlet.[55]

As the *Alton Telegraph* example suggests, large judgments have also increased the cost of settling cases. Although public announcements of settlement results are rare, because the media defendant will often make the payment of the settlement conditional on the plaintiff's promise not to disclose the amount, the current jury climate in media cases assures that many settlements will be impressive. The *New York Post* recently disclosed that it had settled a libel suit for $470,000. The ABC television network reportedly settled a suit brought against it by Synanon, a California communal organization, for $1.25 million, and Synanon reportedly received another $600,000 in settlement of a suit against the *San Francisco Examiner*. Philadelphia Mayor Green's settlement with CBS was reported in the *New York Times* as between $250,000 and $400,000.[56]

Whether a suit is settled, won, or lost, the legal fees alone can be chilling. From the media's perspective, the "big chill" in libel litigation comes more from legal fees than from jury verdicts—for most jury verdicts are overturned on appeal, while the legal bills come anyway. In the United States parties to a civil action generally pay their own legal fees. Other than in certain kinds of civil suits, the practice is that win, lose, or draw, the plaintiff's legal fees come out of the money the plaintiff recovers, if any, and the defendant similarly pays his or her own lawyer. In the United States one can hurt someone dearly by suing him, for even if one loses, the opponent still must pay his legal bill. Hundreds of thousands, and even millions of dollars can be spent paying lawyers to defend a single case, and the ongoing costs for counseling on libel matters and for liability insurance escalate as the media perceives the threat of successful libel actions with increasing fear. Legal fees comprise 80% of the aggregate costs of defending suits against the press, with the remaining 20% covering all actual jury awards, settlements, and incidental expenses. ABC reportedly spent $7 million in defending a libel suit brought against it by Synanon before the suit was finally settled; *Time* magazine reportedly spent $2 million in a suit that was dismissed before trial; and CBS reportedly spent between $3 and $4 million in defending the suit (still in progress) brought against it by Colonel Anthony Herbert. The legal bill for CBS in the protracted Westmoreland case was reportedly piling up at a rate in excess of $100,000 a month, with estimates for totals between $5 and $10 million. Exact figures on legal fees are hard to come by, but it is clear that for most major media outlets today substantial legal fees must be treated as an unavoidable cost of doing business. The McClatchy Newspaper chain based in California, for example, has publicly stated that its legal fees now run over $1 million per year.

Lawyers on both sides seem to profit (perhaps more than anyone else) from much libel litigation. Lawyers may be paid on an hourly basis for their time (in larger cities such as New York or Washington, D.C., the hourly billing rate may be $200 to $250 an hour), or, in the case of plaintiff's lawyers, they may take the suit on a "contingency fee" basis, in which the lawyer in effect finances the suit out of his or her own pocket, in exchange for a percentage of the recovery if the suit is successful. The typical contingency fee percentage is between 30% and 40% of the damages award. The plaintiff's lawyer may also work out a combination payment system, involving a reduced hourly rate plus some percentage of the recovery if the suit is successful. In recent years, wealthy and famous litigants have been opting for more expensive lawyers, most of whom get paid on an hourly basis. In Mobil Oil President William Tavoulareas's suit against the *Washington Post*, for example, Tavoulareas's legal costs were $1.8 million (which was essentially "covered" by the $2.05 million Tavoulareas received from the jury), and in a suit pitting *Penthouse* against a California resort complex that *Penthouse* alleged to be a hangout for mobsters, both the plaintiff's lawyers (led by Louis Nizer) and the defense law-

yers (led by *Penthouse's* usual attorney, Roy Grutman), reportedly generated multiple millions in legal fees.

The fees paid to defense lawyers who defend libel actions get more publicity than the fees paid to plaintiff's attorneys who bring them, because
the media to some degree gains by emphasizing defense costs. If a newspaper spends a million dollars to defend a suit and is successful in that
defense, it may have won the case, but it is still out a million dollars. By
emphasizing such defense cost, the media draws attention to the chilling
effect that the very bringing of libel and invasion of privacy suits may have
on the newspaper's exercise of First Amendment rights. (Sometimes the
defense costs are so high, however, that the media defendant seems almost
embarrassed to discuss them. CBS, for example, has not yet disclosed its
defense costs in the Westmoreland case, despite reports placing them in
the $5 to $10 million range.)

What is clear from this financial portrait is that if the plaintiff's primary
motive is vindication through punishment of the media defendant, it is not
necessary to win in order to win. If the suit can be prolonged sufficiently
the mere ticking away of the defense lawyer's clock will be enough to
extract the pound of flesh.

This form of litigation guerilla warfare is constantly cited by many in the
media to support the position that libel and invasion of privacy actions
should be abolished altogether. The argument is that official censorship is
replaced in anti-media litigation by a more subtle but equally damaging
form of self-censorship. Why run a controversial story, a story that is a
prime candidate for precipitating a libel suit, when a safer, duller story will
fill space just as well, without the risks attendant to the bolder story? If
reporters uncover information suggesting that the mayor may have taken
a bribe, will the rewards of running the story outweigh the costs if the
mayor sues? It might be thought that the responsible editor's concern in
this situation would simply be whether the paper would ultimately win or
lose the ensuing libel action. If the reporter's facts are strong enough to
warrant running the story in a respectable and cautious newspaper in the
first place, they would presumably be strong enough to later convince a
libel jury that the paper was legally innocent, and so the editor would not
"self-censor," and the story would be run. But the editor's decision is not
in fact so simple. His or her concern in an economic sense is not whether
or not the litigation war would ultimately be won, but whether or not the
casualty toll along the way would make the costs of victory prohibitive.

From this perspective the legal system is intimidating, and may well chill
editorial ardour. The legal standards applicable to most libel and invasion
of privacy suits are exceptionally complex, and tend to turn on the subjective state of mind of the defendant. This means that early termination of

an anti-media suit is difficult; the plaintiff normally has a relatively good chance of getting his or her case in front of a jury. Stringing a case out to the point of jury deliberation is in itself a powerful form of anti-media harassment, for in most of the United States the time lapse from the commencement of a civil suit until the end of the trial is at minimum a year, and more typically several years.

Although many media outlets have libel insurance to help defray defense costs (though, it should be pointed out, a number of prominent media outlets, such as the *New York Times,* carry no such insurance), the premiums for libel insurance have now become almost prohibitive for many media outlets, and for more controversial publications, not available at all. Insurance companies must pay defense costs even if the litigation ends in a defense victory, and insurance companies are well able to see that the media is now one of America's most popular litigation targets. The chilling effect of modern libel litigation on free speech is perhaps nowhere more clearly observable than in insurance markets, where today media outlets must often scramble to purchase insurance at all, and then at premium rates that are escalating precipitously.

The cold reality that the editor must face, therefore, is that if the paper runs the controversial story, and the story triggers a libel suit, the statistics indicate that after a protracted trial a jury is very likely to find against the newspaper for a substantial sum. Of course, the newspaper will almost certainly appeal the jury award, and here the statistics heavily favor the media. Two-thirds of the jury judgments awarded to plaintiffs get reversed on appeal. The First Amendment works its protective legal magic in front of appellate judges, not in the minds of juries. But is this high appellate defense success rate likely to be of much comfort to the pragmatic editor? How could it be? The appellate victory comes after years (most certainly two, more likely three to five) of litigation, in which legal fees, and time lost by reporters and editors conferring with lawyers, filling out documents, and testifying at depositions and trials is as much punishment as the plaintiff's award would have been had the plaintiff simply been paid off the day after the story was run. And in the cold-blooded accounting of insurance companies, it matters not whether the newspaper was ultimately successful in winning the suit, for the suit itself represents an insurance loss; so the paper can expect its premiums to rise, and perhaps even its policy to be cancelled. Finally, there is always the possibility that the paper will be among the hapless statistical minority which, after all the expense and effort, still lose.

The libel or invasion of privacy suit thus carries an inherently extortionate undertone. Justice Thurgood Marshall of the United States Supreme Court has observed that "many self-perceived victims of defamation are animated by something more than a rational calculus of their chances of recovery. Given the circumstances under which libel actions arise, plaintiffs' pretrial maneuvers may be fashioned more with an eye to deterrence or retaliation than to unearthing germane material." It has been estimated by a number of libel attorneys that as many as half of all libel cases are purely "nuisance" cases, in the sense that there is no realistic prospect of final victory on the merits.

Perhaps the threat of debilitating nuisance suits will not dissuade the more courageous media outlets from running risky stories. We like to think of our American news editors as fiesty, hard-boiled Lou Grants who work long hours with their shirt sleeves rolled up, and with whom the First Amendment is secure; the Lou Grant's of the world will not be intimidated. But as much as we can be sure that there are some publishers and broadcasters who have never been deterred from running a story because of the threat of subsequent legal harassment, the more common (and surely more human) reaction is to avoid excessive risk. Very few media outlets in the country feature in-depth investigative reporting as a stock in trade. Over the long haul there is enough risk-free news to keep readers and viewers satisfied; the correlation between being the first to break a scandal and being the first in circulation or market share or advertising revenue is likely to be too faint to merit much adventurism. Very few media market areas have extensive newspaper competition, and although competition among various types of print and electronic media may be fierce in certain areas of the country, that competition is as likely to turn on the cleverness of the happy talk patter between the news anchor and the weatherman as it is upon who first uncovers corruption in city hall. Particularly when the media outlet is relatively small, like the daily newspaper with only a handful of permanent editorial staff members, or the low-power FM radio station with a one person news department ("this is Les Nesmith reporting for WKRP in Cinncinati"), the threat of libel or invasion of privacy litigation may be severely crippling to the exercise of First Amendment rights. Such small outlets are not only financially unable to sustain the costs of litigation, the physical process of mounting a defense may consume so much manpower that the publication or broadcast of news literally stops. One small monthly paper, the *Milkweed*, with a circulation of 1,300, was twice forced to combine issues because the editor-publisher had to spend time in a distant city helping his attorneys prepare the defense in a libel suit in which the plaintiff was seeking $20 million.

The litigation chill caused by these small local media outlets is no frivolous matter. The *Alton Telegraph* or the *Milkweed* are not going to break the latest events from Lebanon, or be the first to print the Pentagon Papers, but it would be elitist in the extreme to deny that within the confines of their small-town markets they serve First Amendment interests as vital as those advanced by the *New York Times* or the *Washington Post*. For most Americans, reportage about the local sheriff who is on the take, or a sweetheart land deal arranged by a member of the town zoning board, or physical abuse of children by a public school teacher, or any of a thousand other possible stories central to the life of the community are as vital as the CBS Evening News' latest report on the national debt or the sale of missiles to Saudi Arabia.

The recent explosion of law suits against the media is thus more than a mere amusing curiosity. It is a phenomenon with a substantial social cost. The time, energy, and money consumed is enormous, and its tendency to reduce the aggressiveness and courage of the media in pursuing significant issues of public concern is very real. Yet the cost alone ought not seduce one into prejudging matters. The First Amendment's protection of free speech is a wonderful thing, but there are a lot of other wonderful things in this world—among them love, productivity, food, shelter, drink, and sex—and it is not at all obvious that free speech deserves special preeminence in the priority list of social values.[57] America in recent years seems to have been growing increasingly convinced that freedom of speech does not deserve the level of preeminence that the *New York Times* case suggested. One of the more fascinating indications of how these changing cultural attitudes have come to be reflected in adjustments to the law of libel comes from a case involving a non-American plaintiff, in *Sharon v. Time, Inc.*, a libel suit that, like so much in America today, was imported.

4

Ariel Sharon v. Time Magazine: The Libel Suit as Political Forum, International Style

When you read now *Time* magazine reports that were written in the past 30 years, you cannot but find an attempt to libel Israel, to attack Israel, to write untrue stories about Israel. The difference was that in this case they accused me with murder. That is the most terrible thing that a human being could have accepted.

Ariel Sharon, former Defense Minister of Israel, on *This Week with David Brinkley*, January 27, 1985

This libel suit is over, *Time* has won it. *Time* feels strongly that the case should never have reached an American courtroom. It was brought by a foreign politician attempting to recoup his political fortunes. He could not sue Israel's Kahan Commission, which had found him guilty of indirect responsibilities for the massacres at Sabra and Shatila and recommended his ouster as Defense Minister. So he sued *Time*. This caused a long, expensive, and inappropriate legal action.

From *Time's* "victory statement" following the jury's verdict in *Sharon v. Time, Inc.*

THE LIBEL SUIT as political battleground recently took on an international flair in *Sharon v. Time, Inc.*[58] The plaintiff, General Ariel Sharon, former Minister of Defense of Israel, charged that *Time* magazine had libeled him in a February, 1983 article involving the "Kahan Commission Report," a report describing the final findings of Israel's commission of inquiry into the events surrounding the massacre of Palestinians at the Sabra and Shatila refugee camps in West Beirut.

The case grew out of events surrounding the 1982 Israeli invasion of Lebanon. On September 14, 1982, Lebanese President-elect Bashir Gemayel was assassinated by unknown assailants. General Sharon the next day paid a "condolence call" on members of the Gemayel family. Two days after Bashir Gemayel's assassination, Israeli occupation forces permitted the grieving and armed Christian Phalangist followers of Gemayel to enter two Palestinian refugee camps at Sabra and Shatila—ostensibly to look for Palestinian terrorists hiding in the camps. What followed instead was a massacre of horrible proportions, with the Phalangist forces murdering hundreds of unarmed refugee men, women, and children. Israel found itself bearing the brunt of the international furor over the tragedy, as many around the world accused Israel of everything from gross negligence to complicity in the massacres for having permitted them to take place. At the heart of the storm was the hard-line defense minister, Ariel Sharon. The Israeli government convened a special commission to inquire into the tragedy, headed by an esteemed President of the Israeli Supreme Court, Yitzhak Kahan. When the Kahan Commission Report was released in 1983, *Time* made the report its cover story.[59]

The report strongly criticized General Sharon's behavior concerning the massacres. *Time* quoted several statements about Sharon contained in the report, including the statement that "[it] was the duty of the Defense Minister to take into account . . . that the Phalangists were liable to commit atrocities and that it was necessary to forestall this possibility as a humanitarian obligation and also to prevent the political damage it would entail. . . . [We] know that this consideration did not concern him in the least," and that his "blunders constitute nonfulfillment of the duty with which [he] was charged." (Sharon himself would testify at trial that the commission had put "the mark of Cain" on him—though, he said, the phrase was figurative and certainly did not mean he was a murderer.) *Time* also reported General Sharon's difficulties within the Israeli Cabinet, including two acrimonious exchanges in which other ministers criticized Sharon's behavior.

The bottom line was that Sharon was assigned by the commission report, and by other Israelis, *indirect* responsibility for the massacres, and *Time* accurately reported that bottom line. But then *Time* seemed to take the story one critical step further. *Time* spoke of a part of the Kahan Report that had been kept secret from the public, and then stated "*Time has learned*" what was in the secret section:

> One section of the report, known as Appendix B, was not published at all, mainly for security reasons. That section contains the names of several intelligence agents referred to elsewhere in the report. *Time* has learned that it also contains further details about Sharon's visit to the Gemayel family on the day after Bashir Gemayal's assassination. Sharon reportedly told the Gemayels that the Israeli army would be moving into West Beirut and that he expected the Christian forces to go into the Palestinian refugee camps. Sharon also reportedly discussed with the Gemayels the need for the Phalangists to take revenge

for the assassination of Bashir, but the details of the conversation are
not known.

This one paragraph, dealing with what was supposedly in "Appendix B,"
outraged Sharon. In Sharon's reading of the paragraph the statement that
during his "condolence visit" to the Gemayel family he "discussed with the
Gemayels the need for the Phalangists to take revenge for the assassination" was in effect a statement that Sharon either knew of the likelihood
of the massacre in advance, or possibly even encouraged it outright.
Sharon blasted *Time* for having committed "blood libel." Sharon alleged
in his $50 million suit that this statement was false and defamatory in two
respects: first, that it depicted him as having "encouraged" the Phalangists
to massacre the Palestinians, and second, that it stated that the Commission had made a secret finding that he had encouraged or condoned the
massacre.

Sharon's deliberate and repeated use of the phrase "blood libel" in his
statements concerning *Time* illustrates the degree to which his lawsuit was
as much a political statement by Sharon as a simple libel trial. The phrase
"blood libel" is historically associated in Western consciousness with Christians' attacks on Jews. The "blood libel" specifically refers to pogroms in
which the irrational attacks on Jews were fed by the charges that Jews had
kidnapped Christian children to use their blood in religious and medicinal
rites involving ritualistic murders. Before the Holocaust, blood libel
against Jews was one of the most devastating tools of anti-Semitism, and
for Sharon to repeatedly invoke the phrase was to emotionally exploit the
term's association with the historic suffering of the Jewish people. For
Sharon to charge that *Time* committed blood libel against him was thus to
ally himself with the victims of centuries of Jewish persecution in a manner
that would surely raise the emotional pitch of the trial.

As would be the case in William Westmoreland's suit against CBS, the
parties in the Sharon case were fortunate to draw (through random selection) an exceptionally able federal trial judge, Abraham Sofaer, who just
happened to possess a number of attributes that seemed to make him
peculiarly well-equipped to preside over the case. Sofaer, who had been a
law professor at Columbia before going to the federal bench, once
described himself as "a Jew who is unambivalently proud of his Arab heritage." Sofaer speaks some Arabic and some Hebrew, vacations frequently
in Jerusalem, was editor-in-chief of the *New York University Law Review*,
and had clerked for both Federal Court of Appeals Judge J. Skelly Wright
and Supreme Court Justice William Brennan, two of the country's most
esteemed members of the federal bench. As a law professor and as a judge,
Sofaer had spoken out on the importance of free expression, but he

proved throughout the trial to be meticulously evenhanded toward both Sharon and *Time*. Given the worldwide attention and emotive frenzy generated by the case, the random-draw choice of the judge could not have been more fortunate: a scholarly judge with impeccable credentials and ethnic ties to and an understanding of the Middle East.

In a lengthy trial, the jury of six New Yorkers in the Sharon case was essentially put in the bizarre position of acting as yet another court of inquiry into the Israeli invasion of Lebanon and the massacres at Sabra and Shatila. During the course of the trial the jury heard a mini-biography of Sharon, learning of his childhood in an agricultural village in Palestine in the 1930's, of his "never remembering his mother having shoes," and of his military and political career. The jury was educated on recent Middle East history, on the entangled and chaotic political and religious factions in Lebanon, on the decision-making process surrounding the Israeli invasion of Lebanon, and on the precise events surrounding the massacres. During the trial, Sharon talked of his army's crossing of the Suez canal in 1973 as "maybe the most terrible battle that I have seen," recalling "hundreds of our soldiers lying dead, together with hundreds of Egyptian soldiers." He talked of Anwar Sadat, calling him "a great man of vision" and noting that "President Sadat himself was assassinated by Arab terrorists."

All of this was romantic and powerful stuff, and it made wonderful news copy from the *New York Times* to *Entertainment Tonight*—but was it what the law of libel was really supposed to be about? Judge Sofaer seemed to sense that Sharon's testimony was stretching the normal boundaries of a trial when he broke the courtroom up into laughter by filling a pause in Sharon's testimony with the crack that Sharon's statements had reached the point where "you just finished grade school in the village."

Illustrative of the hair-splitting tasks the poor jurors in the Sharon case were asked to perform was the testimony of one of the final witnesses in the trial, a Hebrew language expert who testified for one and a half hours on the meaning of the Hebrew word "etslenu." *Time's* article stated that on the eve of the massacres, Sharon had "discussed" the need to avenge the slaying of the Phalangist commander, Lebanese President-elect Bashir Gemayel. Before the Kahan Commission in Israel, Sharon had testified in Hebrew, stating that he had discussed the issue of revenge "etslenu." The word "etslenu" can be translated into English as either "among us" or "by us." Sharon said he used the word to mean "among us"—that he used "etslenu" in the context of a discussion with other Israelis. *Time's* Jerusalem correspondent apparently interpreted the word to mean that Sharon had discussed revenge with the Christian Phalangist leaders. The nuance in translation was important, because if Sharon meant to say that he had discussed the possibility of revenge prior to the massacre, that testimony would be strong evidence that Sharon shared moral and legal responsibility for the atrocities.

These sorts of details, no less than the details during Watergate that helped answer the question "What did the President know, and when did he know it?" are certainly important. They are important to the citizens and governments of Israel and Lebanon; they are important under international law; they are important to Americans concerned about the Middle East and with United States foreign policy. But once again, is this sort of political and historical debate what libel suits were meant for? And more fundamentally, do we increase our understanding of these sorts of world events by holding the threat of $50 million in damages over magazines and newspapers that dare to delve beneath official explanations to try to determine the "truth" for themselves? The gist of the harm caused by the *Time* article was really stated between the lines—that the Kahan Commission in its heart thought that Sharon's behavior was more reprehensible than the Commission's public report had let on. This was an interpretation by an organ of the press in one country of the real motives and beliefs of an organ of the government of another country. Although the lawyers for Sharon, as good legal technicians, were able to paint the suit in the colors of a raw factual misstatement, in truth it was just as much a matter of political judgment. As sincere as Ariel Sharon may have been in wanting vindication for "blood libel," there is no escaping the fact that his trial took on overtones of a mini-plebiscite on his political judgment.

None of this is to say that *Time* magazine's journalism in the Sharon story was exactly above reproach. *Time's* journalism, in fact, was in many ways egregiously wanting; it was precisely the sort of journalism that has led many to believe that the First Amendment now gives the media too much shelter. The *Time* story originated with a *Time* reporter in Jerusalem, David Halevy. Halevy was an Israeli, who had served as an Israeli military officer, commanding an armoured battalion. He was a lieutenant colonel in the Israeli reserves. Halevy described himself at the trial as "a low ranking reporter, who sits and tells some other people what he saw, what he evaluated, what is the color, what is the smell."

On December 6, 1982, Halevy filed a report with *Time* based on a "highly reliable" confidential source, claiming that at the condolence meeting between Sharon and the Gemayels, Sharon "had given the Gemayels the feeling" that he understood the necessity for the Gemayels to take revenge, and that the Israeli army would not hinder them or try to stop them. Two months later, in February 1983, the Kahan Commission report was released. Harry Kelly, *Time's* Jerusalem bureau chief, wanted to know if the secret Appendix B would substantiate Halevy's prior report.

Halevy testifed that he told Kelly that "there is a case against General Sharon or Minister Sharon between the lines" of the Kahan Report and that "it is probably in Appendix B." Halevy went to his confidential source to find out.

However, the confidential source, named "source C," *never confirmed* Halevy's suspicions. Although at the trial *Time's* lawyer equated its confidential source to the famous "Deep Throat" in the Watergate scandal, unlike Deep Throat, source C did not deliver the goods. Source C told Halevy that Appendix B was a "reference book and index" of names, sources, and intelligence agents used by the Commission. Source C also confirmed that certain intelligence agents of the crack Israeli Mossad Secret Service were mentioned in Appendix B, *including* an agent who was present at the meeting between Sharon and the Gemayels. *But Halevy never asked his source if in fact Appendix B stated that Sharon had discussed revenge with the Gemayels.* As Judge Sofaer ruled, "A jury could find that Halevy chose not to ask source C the ultimate question because he knew or suspected that source C's answer would undermine his hypothesis."

How then, did Halvey "confirm" his story? He went back to the *public* portions of the Kahan Report, and attempted to extrapolate through a sort of intuitive process what he thought must have been in the secret appendix. In his trial testimony Halevy stated, "I went back to the public report. I mean, the report I had in my hands. And correctly so, if you read it very carefully. Intelligence officer A. Intelligence officer that. Intelligence officer this. You got a very clear feeling that we are talking about the same people."

How did Halevy communicate his conclusions about the contents of Appendix B to his Jerusalem bureau chief, Harry Kelly? Did Kelly and Halevy thrash it out, sifting piece by piece through the evidence, measuring the information from the confidential source to see how far it would go? The amazing answer is quite the contrary. Halevy testified that he simply "went into Kelly's office and raised my thumb to the kind of 'Okay, all cleared.'" And so on the basis of a thumbs up, the bureau chief accepted a reporter's reassurance that he had received confirmation from a confidential source as to what was in the secret appendix, although neither the bureau chief nor the reporter had seen the appendix, nor even asked the confidential source the blunt question of whether the appendix supported the accusation against Sharon they were in the process of formulating. The most important link in the chain of evidence was thus never truly verified, and was communicated in an almost offhand, haphazard way. "I kind of told Mr. Kelly in substance, not in words," Halevy stated, "that the information which we discussed earlier, previously is confirmed."

Judge Sofaer honed in on this point on several occasions. During Halevy's testimony Sofaer asked Halevy point blank if source C had told him that there was testimony about the Sharon meeting with the Gemayels in the appendix. Halevy did not immediately answer, and so Sofaer then prompted him: "So you inferred that?," he asked. "Yes, I would say so," Halevy admitted. He then elaborated: "Yes, that is the way I read it. It's my evaluation, my analysis based on my knowledge of forty-three years living in Israel and going through a lot of coverage of governmental official matters." This was a remarkable piece of testimony, for it made it unequivocally clear that at rock bottom the phrase in the *Time* story that said "*Time* has *learned*" what was in Appendix B rested on nothing more than Halevy's inference—in essence, his guess.[60]

Furthermore, the evidentiary puzzle was strewn with clues that should have alerted someone in the *Time* hierarchy that Halevy's guess might be fatally flawed. Although *Time's* Jerusalem chief Harry Kelly testified that it was his impression that Halevy had seen the notes of the confidential source (the Mossad agent who was at the condolence call meeting), Halevy himself testified that he had never actually seen any notes. Halevy's surmise as to what was in the appendix, therefore, was really based primarily on his analysis of the parts of the Kahan Report that were published. However, as Judge Sofaer pointed out, although the published report referred frequently to Appendix B in discussions of other aspects of the events surrounding the massacres, Appendix B was never mentioned in connection with any aspect of the condolence meeting. Halevy's guess, therefore, was not even a particularly educated one.

A second flaw in *Time's* procedure was that the person who actually wrote the story changed the wording of the information Halevy had supplied to make it more sensational and damaging to Sharon. The actual writer of the story was William Smith, a *Time* writer headquartered in New York. Halevy had used the deliberately vague phraseology that Sharon "gave them the feeling after the Gemayel's questioning, that he understood their need to take revenge." Halevy said in his deposition that he chose these words because he had been told by his source that Sharon had *not* said anything, but had communicated through "body language." Smith changed this wording to the far more definitive wording of the article as it finally appeared, that Sharon had actually "discussed with the Gemayels the need for the Phalangists to take revenge."[61]

A third problem with *Time's* methodology was that *Time* discounted apparently credible information it received at the last minute that squarely contradicted its theory. Days before the issue would actually appear, *Time* sent out a public relations press release previewing its story, under the headline "Sharon Said to Have Urged Lebanese to Send Phalangists into

Camps." The inflamatory press release went well beyond even *Time's* own story, by using the word "urged." After this release reached Jerusalem, and word of it spread through the city, *Time's* bureau chief ran into a member of the Israeli Knesset, Ehud Olmert, who was not a Sharon supporter. Olmert said that he had read Appendix B, and that it did not contain the material that *Time* said was in it. Kelly asked Olmert to double check his information, and Olmert did, emphatically reporting back to Kelly, "there is nothing in this that resembles your story." Thus, although bureau chief Kelly had given great weight to the wispiest of undisclosed source "evidence" supplied by Halevy, he essentially ignored the information from Olmert, information that Olmert claimed he had just double checked.

At the very least, one would have thought that Olmert's information, coming as it did from a Knesset member who was not a Sharon supporter, would have triggered some doubt in the *Time* heirarchy—at least enough doubt to examine Halevy more rigorously.

Halevy, it turns out, had been involved before in erroneous reporting for *Time* concerning Israel. In 1979 he reported that Prime Minister Menachem Begin was in extremely poor health and had been told to work only three hours a day by doctors. The report, which was published by *Time*, turned out to be wrong. *Time's* own internal investigation of the error was highly critical of Halevy, stating that he was either "inexcusably shoddy in his reporting," or that Halevy had "intentionally misled" *Time*, or was "the victim of an incredibly well orchestrated disinformation plot." *Time* placed Halevy on probation for a year because of the foul-up with the Begin story.

Halevy, whose testimony took seven days, turned out to be an intriguing figure. Much of the basic factual background for the events in Lebanon was supplied by Halevy, who used a yellow pencil as a pointer to show the jury key points on a large map. Halevy's prolonged testimony at one point made Judge Sofaer restless, and he asked "Do we really need so many details?" But he let the testimony go on. It became obvious that Halevy had gotten emotionally involved in his coverage of Israel's invasion of Lebanon. Calling Sharon a "boyhood hero," Halevy told the jury that his opinion of Sharon changed with Israel's "bombardment of Beruit," stating that Sharon is "a ruthless leader" who "is causing tremendous damage to the State of Israel." Halevy had been present in Beruit on the day Bashir Gemayel was killed. An explosion had destroyed the headquarters of the Phalange, the dominant Christian group in Lebanon. "The building, which was a three story building, was cut in the middle," he said. "Actually the second floor collapsed on the first one. The building was open to the sky."

"The picture was a picture of chaos, of total destruction," he continued, adding that Phalangists were shouting, screaming and identifying bodies.

Sharon's lawyer objected that the emotive testimony of Halevy was not relevant to the case. But Judge Sofaer, who said to Halevy, "This all had a profound effect on your mind," ruled that it was relevant to understanding Halevy's motivation and thought process.

Replying to questions by *Time's* attorney, Halevy testifed about the Gemayel funeral in the Phalangist village of Bikfaya, the day after the assassination. In the main street, he said, there was a "very emotional" scene of Phalangists chanting "revenge, revenge." Amin Gemayel, Bashir's brother and now President of Lebanon, spoke at the funeral. Halevy quoted him as proclaiming, "We will avenge you, my brother, Bashir."

What was Halevy's attitude toward Sharon? Halevy evidently thought that unlike reporters, generals and politicians should not be given a second chance after they make mistakes. Halevy said that Ariel Sharon "should have quit politics" after the massacres. "The Kahan Commission practically fired him," Halevy said. "I think a public figure, once there is a verdict on a public figure, that public figure should hide, should stay away from politics."

Halevy also displayed deep convictions about what he called "the Jewish terror network," referring to attacks on Palestinians by settlers of the Isreali-occupied West Bank. Halevy said, "the occupation of the West Bank is corrupting my country, is corrupting my society. I am a great believer that occupation means corruption."

Time's editors and reporters all sounded the same essential positions at trial, positions that often seemed internally contradictory. *Time* officials seemed too insulated from the grass roots efforts of reporters like Halevy to pick up either nuances or trouble signs in their reports from the field. *Time* seemed to have a faith in Halevy out of proportion to his evidence, a faith that often seemed to transcend mere loyalty to become self-righteous certitude. *Time* seemed incapable of even entertaining the possibility that it might be wrong. Managing Editor Ray Cave captured the *Time* party line best. Did Cave still believe in the story? "You are asking me," Mr. Cave said, "if I believe this story then and now? Absolutely."

Judge Sofaer asked whether Cave believed that the Kahan Commission knew that Sharon had discussed revenge with the Phalangists.

"Yes, sir," Cave replied. "I believed that then and now."

"I do believe that the commission had that information at the time," he continued.

"On what," Sharon's lawyer asked, "do you base that belief, sir?" "I base the belief," Cave responded, "on the reporting supporting this story."

Did this mean that *Time* really felt that Sharon encouraged the massacres? Not exactly. Cave made it clear that he and *Time* believed that Sharon bore responsibility for the massacres. "Revenge was in the air," he said, and "a prudent defense minister, general or anybody else, might take steps to ameliorate the degree of that revenge." But Cave, like all the other *Time* employees, never would say that he thought Sharon had actually antici- pated the atrocities, and he denied that the article ever said or implied as much. Thus, when Sharon's lawyer asked Cave whether Sharon had "any reason to anticipate that there would be a massacre," Cave said: "Unequiv- ocally not and I have said that," adding that he did not believe that Sharon had "the slightest idea that there would be a massacre."

"I think if he had had it," Cave continued, "it would have horrified him and he would have prevented it on the spot." Sharon's attorney then quite naturally suggested that *Time* readers could interpret the article as saying that Mr. Sharon's reported discussion of revenge with the Phalangists was connected with the massacre by the Phalangists. (Hadn't *Time's* own press release, after all, talked about how Sharon "urged" the Phalangists?) But Cave insisted to the contrary: *Time* readers would not believe that *Time* was saying that Sharon's discussion with the Gemayels about "revenge" was connected to the massacre.

An exactly parallel line was taken by the actual writer of the story, Wil- liam Smith. Saying that Sharon had "an obsession," Smith claimed that Sharon had "allowed the Phalangists to go into the camps, and the result of that action was the murder of 700 or 800 unarmed civilians while these people were looking for terrorists whom they never found."

Sharon's lawyer asked Smith if he understood that the commission had found Mr. Sharon "indirectly responsible" for the massacre?

"Yes, sir, I believe I do," Mr. Smith answered.

"Did you understand," the attorney asked, "that your article accused him of direct responsibility?"

"I assure you, sir, I did not," Mr. Smith replied, "and I do not believe so to this day."

Asked why he trusted Halevy's information, Smith answered, "I had worked with David Halevy's files week after week for a number of years and I had been impressed, even dazzled, by the quality of his reporting."

In short, the image that *Time* projected at the trial was the very image of the media that those who most love to hate it have long nutured. Rich- ard Nixon or Spiro Agnew could not have orchestrated the testimony more effectively: *Time's* journalism seemed shoddy and haphazard, infiltrated with biases from Jerusalem to New York, top heavy in assumptions and woefully empty of hard data. And on top of it all, *Time* almost contuma- ciously ascended the high horse, defiantly standing by its story.[62]

As bad as *Time's* journalistic techniques seemed to be, however, the case for the longest time seemed doomed to deadlock, for there was no way to

know, really, whether or not the infamous Appendix B contained what
Time said it contained. Maybe *Time* was arrogant, but Sharon quite clearly
was no meek spirit—he was just enough of a hardbitten warrior for Israel
to make it *just possible* that he had encouraged the Gemayels to seek an eye
for an eye and a tooth for a tooth. Maybe *Time*, however much it based its
story on inference and analysis, had still got it right. Maybe the Kahan
Commission was hinting to the world that Sharon had acted from much
darker motives than it let on; maybe the cosmic truth reported by *Time* was
really in Appendix B.

The real break in the deadlock of evidence came late in the trial. Until
the closing days of the trial, Israel would not release Appendix B to *Time*,
citing national security justifications. *Time* strenuously objected that it could
not adequately defend itself if it could not see the secret document in
order to determine once and for all what was in the appendix. Through
the good offices of Judge Sofaer's negotiations with the government of
Israel, a compromise agreement was reached at the last moment. The
agreement provided that the Israeli lawyers for *Time* and Sharon would
read the appendix, in the presence of the former Israeli Chief Justice Yitzhak Kahan, who had headed the commission. Kahan would then answer
yes or no to the three questions considered crucial to the case:

Did the appendix say that Sharon held a conversation with the Gemayel
family or any other Phalangist in which he discussed the need to avenge
the death of Bashir Gemayal? Did the appendix state that any Phalangist
mentioned the need for revenge in the presence of Sharon? And, did the
document say whether Mr. Sharon knew in advance that Phalangists would
massacre civilians if they entered the refugee camps unaccompanied by
Israeli troops?

The agreement provided that both sides would accept Justice Kahan's
answers as evidence in the case to be presented to the jury, but that the
lawyers must not reveal the contents of the appendix to the general public
or even to their American associates. Justice Kahan's answers were
emphatic on all three questions. Appendix B simply did not contain the
information that *Time* had said it had.

"In none of the documents or testimony, Justice Kahan wrote, "is there
any evidence or suggestion that Minister Sharon had a discussion with the
Gemayel family or with any other Phalangist, at Bikfaya or elsewhere, in
which Minister Sharon discussed the need to avenge the death of Bashir
Gemayel."

"In none of the documents or testimony," he added in reply to the second question, "is there any evidence or suggestion that Minister Sharon
had any discussion with a Phalangist in which either person mentioned the
need for revenge."

Finally, Justice Kahan stated in response to the question about whether Sharon knew in advance about the possibility of the massacres that there was "no mention in the said documents or testimony" that Sharon knew in advance of the possibility of a massacre if Phalangists were allowed to enter the camps unaccompanied by Israeli troops.

"The conclusions to be drawn from the documents," he added, "with regard to Minister Sharon's knowledge of the massacre—in the sense of foreseeing in advance that such an occurrence was liable to happen—were considered in detail in the published report of the commission."

The trial thus ended with all the momentum in Sharon's favor. In his summation for the jury, Sharon's lawyer asked: "Why don't they come out in the open and say 'we told a lie, we are sorry, we shouldn't have done it'." He said to the jury that the decision to allow the Phalangists into the camps was "a tragic mistake," a mistake that threatened to leave "an indelible scar on the reputation of a great soldier."

"Your verdict will determine whether he will go down in history as a great man, a great soldier," he stated, or "whether he will go down as a kind of monster, another Herod, a man who ordered a massacre of women and children," arguing that the article "put the stamp of a mass murderer" on Sharon.

The jury's deliberations lasted eleven days. In a stroke that heightened the suspense of the deliberations, Judge Sofaer gave the jury three questions to answer, one at a time, with the jury to return each answer before going on to the next issue. First, Judge Sofaer told the jury that it must answer if Sharon had "proved by a preponderance of the evidence" that the disputed paragraph defamed him by indicating that he "consciously intended" or "actively encouraged" the killing of civilians. The jury returned with a decision that *Time's* statement about the intent of Sharon was defamatory. Second, the judge asked the jury if Sharon "proved by clear and convincing evidence" that he did not discuss the need for the Phalangists to take revenge for the assassination of their leader. Again, the jury answered that *Time* had been wrong, and that Sharon had not discussed the revenge issue. Third, the judge asked if Sharon had also "proved by clear and convincing evidence" that someone at *Time* had "serious doubts" about the truth of the false and defamatory statement when it was published?[63]

After struggling with the final issue in the case, the *New York Times* "knowing or reckless disregard" standard, the jury came back with its decision. *Time*, the jury said, did not act with knowledge of falsity or out of reckless disregard of the truth.[64] But in a highly unusual statement accompanying the verdict, the jury foreman Richard Zug said that the jury found that "certain *Time* employees, particularly correspondent David Halevy, acted negligently and carelessly in reporting and verifying the information which ultimately found its way into the published paragraph." After the jury's verdict and announcement were read, Judge Sofaer asked everyone in the courtroom to stand as they filed out, in tribute to the jury's wisdom.[65]

Neither *Time* nor Sharon were particularly gracious in victory or defeat. They did not agree, in fact, on who was the victor and who was the vanquished. Despite the clear statement by the jury that *Time* had gotten the story wrong, and had acted negligently and carelessly, *Time* to this day has never shown the slightest hint of heartfelt regret about the whole incident. When it became clear that Appendix B did not support *Time's* story, the magazine printed a quasi-retraction that was in fact every bit as critical of Sharon as its original story: "Almost two years after Minister Sharon began litigation against *Time* over this paragraph, the Israeli government has permitted an Israeli attorney representing *Time* to examine this secret appendix. Based upon this examination last week, *Time* now issues a correction: Appendix B does not contain further details about Sharon's visits to the Gemayel family. *Time* regrets that error."[66]

Time, however, stood by the substance of the paragraph in question: "that Sharon also reportedly discussed with the Gemayels the need for the Phalangists to take revenge for the assassination of Bashir, but the details of the conversation are not known."

Time was obviously damning with faint retraction—in effect saying, "okay, so we made a picayune error about a stupid appendix; that doesn't change the fact that Sharon still did what we said he did." Sharon's lawyer called the dubious "correction" "an outrage," adding that, "It's the most arrogant thing I have ever seen—they stand on their story." Working for *Time*, it seemed, means never having to say you're sorry.

After the jury verdict, *Time* clothed itself in the royal garments of the First Amendment and attacked Sharon for what it perceived as his transparent political motives in bringing the suit. *Time's* Managing Editor Ray Cave reiterated "we remain confident the story is true and in due course it will be shown that it was true." Thomas Barr, *Time's* attorney, could not forgo military analogies: "A lawsuit is very much like a war," he said. "Who wins the battle is not particularly important. The war is over and we won." Barr also impugned Sharon's motives in bringing the suit, claiming that Sharon had told another Israeli official that he was using his suit against *Time* "to wash my hands clean of this terrible mess."

Sharon, for his part, claimed "a great moral victory." The case had established, Sharon said, that "*Time's* allegations were false." Sharon further proclaimed, "We were able to prove that *Time* magazine did lie and that they were negligent and careless . . . It is very important for men and women around the world. We hope it will prevent *Time* magazine from libeling in the future."

What began in politics thus ended in politics, with nothing very clearly resolved.[67] The fact that the Sharon trial was in reality a forum for doing political battle was even more obvious in Israel than in the United States. The Israeli press carried extensive daily coverage and analysis of the trial. At the time of the trial many in Israel remained enormously bitter over what they perceived to be biased American media coverage of the Israeli invasion of Lebanon in 1982. The Sharon trial was seen by many in Israel as the chance to get even. Sharon's enemies in Israel—and Sharon had many—often seemed to hate *Time* magazine even more than they did Sharon. Zeev Chafetz, an author and a former head of the Israeli Government Press Office, told a *New York Times* reporter that "*Time* is so disliked here that it has the capacity to make people who despise Sharon want him to win." Although some of Sharon's staunchest enemies made it clear that they would not mind seeing Sharon defeated by *Time*, the prevailing sentiment among Sharon's enemies and supporters alike was that it was in the best interests of Israel for Sharon to win. And indeed, for most Israelis, Sharon did win—the jury's first two verdicts, declaring that *Time* had been in error and had libeled Sharon, were what really mattered—that technical niceties of American First Amendment law had caused the third verdict to fail were inconsequential.

In the coverage by the *Jerusalem Post*, Sharon was assured of "a hero's welcome" on his return to Israel. Quoting "Sharon admirers," the *Post* wrote that "Sharon will be presented as the man who finally gave the lie to Israel's media enemies abroad and saved Israel's honor. He will be met at the airport by supporters planning to greet him in much the same manner as victorious sports teams are saluted. There will be placards, flowers, singing and dancing, organizers promise."

The newspaper further noted that a congratulatory telegram to Sharon from former Prime Minister Menachem Begin after the first of the jury's verdicts was returned had given added momentum to plans for Sharon's hero's welcome. Begin had been portrayed by many as a man who was misled by Sharon during the war in Lebanon and ultimately destroyed by the results of the war and the Sabra and Shatila massacres. Begin's telegram was thus a sort of dispensation and certification of honor from the former Prime Minister.

Perhaps the Sharon case was "a testament to the system," as a leading First Amendment expert, Floyd Abrams, put it. "Sharon has won a public relations battle and can go home to Israel with a good deal of benefit in his career," said Abrams. "*Time*, at least, can take solace in the fact that the jury found that it did not publish anything that it knew was false."[68]

But in the last analysis, what did the Sharon case prove, and was it all worth it? One get's the feeling, for example, that Judge Sofaer had reservations throughout the process as to whether the tenacity on both sides was worth the huge expenditure of public time and effort necessary to complete the litigation.

In a pretrial opinion denying *Time's* motion to have the case thrown out, Sofaer was exceptionally candid about *Time's* litigation behavior. Both Sharon and *Time* would throughout the trial seem to want to widen the issues being litigated to a referendum on Israeli foreign policy and Sharon's political judgments. Sofaer noted that, at least on *Time's* part, this tendency began early in the litigation:

"*Time* seeks to litigate the entire history of the Lebanese civil wars, the Israeli invasion of Lebanon, and the relationship of Israel and the Phalangists," Sofaer wrote in his pretrial opinion. "These contents are far removed from the legitimate issues. They would be important if *Time* had merely stated in the article at issue that it thought that the Commission was incorrect in finding Minister Sharon not 'directly' responsible—an opinion for which *Time* in any event would have been immune from suit. But the jury may find that *Time* said something very different by reporting that the Commission knew, and withheld from the public, details which could reasonably suggest that Minister Sharon condoned or encouraged the massacre as a measure of revenge."

And in a paragraph harsh in its tone, Judge Sofaer strongly intimated that *Time's* litigation strategy had been unduly contentious, arrogant, and perhaps even socially wasteful:

> *Time* has refused to issue any correction or to print plaintiff's denial. *Only through the litigation process has plaintiff been able to uncover and publish the evidence from which Time claimed to have learned the contents of the Commission's secret appendix. And only through this avenue has he been able to bring to light the process by which the allegedly offending statement came to be written, including evidence of the possible motivations and truthfulness of its author.* That this process has proved enormously expensive, and painfully contentious, is as much the product of *Time's* all-out litigation strategy as of any plan by plaintiff to intimidate the press. Despite the fact that every single *Time* witness claims to have had no evidence that plaintiff knew in adance that the massacre would occur, *Time* has chosen to pour enormous resources into proving precisely that. *Time* may be entitled to enhance through such tactics the risks plaintiff faces in suing for defamation. *But it would be pure fantasy to treat Time in this case like some struggling champion of free expression, defending at great risk to itself the right to publish its view of the truth.* [emphasis added]

In the emphasized portions of this quote from Judge Sofaer, one sees the emergence of a social issue that is quite clearly coming to the forefront of American consciousness: that the "public's right to know" *includes the right to know how critical media decisions are made*. Indeed, the "public's right to know" in the traditional usage of that phrase—the right to information about important political and social events—is meaningless unless the public also has "a right to know" about the process through which the principal mainstream gatherers and disseminators of that information go about their business. The public cannot intelligently evaluate the news unless it can intelligently evaluate the newsroom. Judge Sofaer's words made explicit the mood that has undoubtedly influenced many other media trials around the nation: the press is jealously secretive about its own methods, to the point where those methods must be dragged out into the open bit by bit through expensive litigation; if this slow and costly litigation is damaging to the media, that is too bad, for it is the media's own arrogant secretiveness that makes it so. The press, in short, cannot have it both ways—if society is to be open to the press, the press must be open to society.

What, after all is said and done, do we as a society "know" now about the facts of the Sharon case? We know now that Appendix B to the Kahan Commission Report did not say that Ariel Sharon had encouraged the massacres or even that he had discussed them with the Gemayels. This "we know" because an Israeli Supreme Court Justice, Mr. Kahan, has told us that it is so, and because *Time's* lawyer was permitted to read the report in Kahan's presence. *Time* printed a correction admitting that Appendix B did not say what *Time* had said it said, and presumably *Time* would not have printed that correction if *Time's* lawyer knew that Kahan was lying.

But who really cares about Appendix B anyway? Almost no one in either the United States or Israel had ever heard of it until the trial. It is not what is in the appendix, but the underlying historical reality that is truly important: *did* Sharon foresee the possibility of the massacres; did Sharon "discuss" revenge with the Gemayels; did Sharon, worst of all, either verbally or with "body language" encourage revenge? Only Sharon, the Gemayels, and others present at their meeting really know. On the basis of the evidence presented at the trial, six New Yorkers concluded that Sharon did not discuss or encourage revenge against civilians.

But Sharon could be lying and the jury could have been fooled. Perhaps *Time* really did have an Israeli secret agent who had given *Time's* reporter the real essence of the Sharon-Gemayels meeting. Perhaps, on the other hand, *Time* was lying, or at least, had itself been duped. After millions of dollars in legal expenses and the devotion of enormous social resources to the inquiry, *Time* magazine steadfastly insisted that the real truth is that Sharon did discuss revenge, and Sharon insisted every bit as resolutely that the jury verdict proves that *Time* "lied."

If the Sharon trial has failed ultimately to clearly affix the level of responsibility Ariel Sharon should bear for the massacres at Sabra and Shatila—if it failed, in short, to clarify how much of "the mark of Cain" Sharon can validly be charged to bear, the results of the trial were no less ambiguous in their judgment of whether the current interpretation of the First Amendment protects the media too much, or not enough.

For many, what came out in the Sharon case was eloquent testimony why the media, and perhaps *Time* especially, are so easy to hate. As much as any American publication, *Time*, with its giant size, wealth, and aura of respectability, seems to hold itself out as a dispenser of real truth. We may not in our hearts expect to be getting the genuine "facts" out of *Penthouse* or *The Nation* or *The Village Voice* or the *National Enquirer* or the John Birch Society's *American Opinion*; we expect those publications to have a point of view, we come to think of them, in fact, as points on a political/cultural spectrum, we know in advance that the "news" we read in those publications has been filtered through certain world-views. But somehow *Time* is supposed to be a kind of *Cliff Notes Summary* of hard-core reality; *Time* is supposed to contain actual facts; *Time* deals not in interpretation, but in hard data.

And therein is the jolt of the Sharon trial: the testimony made it clear that *Time*, like everybody else, has a point of view, and that for all its trappings of objectivity, what *Time* portrays as fact may only be intrepretation. *Time* told its readers that *it had learned* that something was in a secret report, when in fact it had guessed. The reaction of many is that that is a lie, pure and simple, and if the *New York Times* standard will protect this sort of behavior, it will protect anything.

There is, however, an opposite lesson that one might extract. What the Sharon case may show is the inherent subjectivity of investigative reporting, particularly when the investigation concerns a government's activities that are conducted in secret. Reporters can either accept the official pronouncements of the government as accurate, or they can dig around to try to uncover the truth themselves. We want the reporters to dig, for if they do not dig none of us will ever know what our governments are really doing. The problem in the *Time* case is that *Time*'s reporters really did not dig, but then told us that they had. Inevitably, the digging process will entail judgment calls. Is the Mossad agent telling the reporter the truth, or is he lying? Is the Commission saying something between the lines, or is its report to be read literally? Reporters every day make judgments that are not truly concrete "facts." When the media is careful to tell us simply that a source has stated a particular thing (naming the source, preferably), or that in the reporter's *opinion* a particular fact is true, no real problem exists—for the public is not being mislead into believing that the truth has been independently "confirmed." But when the story we read presents reportorial judgments as "facts," we are being lied to. What *Sharon v. Time* reveals is that contrary to the typical expectations of much of the public, what we often get from the press is an admixture of the objective and the subjective, without being alerted where the hard data ends and speculation begins.

Perhaps, the most natural human response to this problem is to concede that reporters and editors may guess, speculate, and summarize all they want, but if they turn out to be wrong, then they by-God ought to have to pay for the damage they cause. Our natural human impulse is to say that if *Time* wants to strut around so cocksure of itself and make us think it is giving us hard data even when it is not, then *Time* will just have to fess up and pay when it guesses wrong.

The *New York Times* rule works directly against this psychological impulse. The First Amendment burden of proof is quite different from the natural "psychological" burden of proof. For under the *New York Times* rule, as long as *Time* believes in the guesses it makes, it is entitled to make them, and need not pay if it is wrong.

And that, perhaps, is why, at the end of the trial, Judge Sofaer had everyone in the courtroom stand in tribute to the jury's wisdom. For contrary to the impression that most media lawyers have come to form of jury behavior in libel cases, the Sharon jury clearly seemed sensitive to the distinction between the ingrained human burden of proof and the burden as cast by *New York Times*. One of the clearest impressions that came through in the Sharon trial was that *Time's* reporters and editors were prejudiced. What the jury apparently perceived was that the First Amendment shelters such prejudice, as long as it is sincere. The psychology of the key man in the picture for *Time*, reporter David Halevy, was of an Israeli whose faith in his own government and in Ariel Sharon was shaken; a man who had witnessed the assassination of Bashir Gemayel, and felt the emotion of the funeral; a man stunned and disillusioned by the massacres; a man ready to believe the worst about what might have taken place in the meeting between Sharon and the Gemayel family. It is true that *Time's* statement that it had "learned" what was in Appendix B was in one sense a lie, since *Time* had only "conjectured"; but in another sense *Time* believed it indeed had "learned" what was in the appendix. Halevy believed he knew the truth, then and now, and *Time* apparently shares Halevy's conviction. The social lesson of the Sharon case is not that we want to encourage reporters like Halevy to keep quiet about these sorts of half-hard-facts-half-convictions, for we don't necessarily want them to keep their mouths shut until they really "know," but rather, that we want them to clearly delineate between certainty and surmise.

Even those who would be inclined to go back to the pre-*New York Times* days, and reimpose the risk of error on the media, should ask themselves whether any greater attention to factual accuracy that might result would be worth the huge social cost these trials would exact. The "social cost" of the Sharon trial includes many, many millions of dollars that are not all that clearly visible on the balance sheet but that nonetheless are real.[69] In addition to the millions of dollars worth of legal fees involved, there is the enormous time and money spent by all who peripherally surround the spectacle. The court personnel, the witnesses, the armies of reporters, photographers, camera crews from around the world, all cost money. Think of all the Israeli bonds that could have been purchased, think of all the donations that could have been made to Palestinian relief organizations, with the money spent by Sharon trying to destroy *Time* and by *Time* trying to destroy Sharon.

Finally, in today's climate the costly courtroom production that was *Sharon v. Time* may find itself recycled as a production of a different sort. What network will be able to resist a docudrama depicting the Sharon trial—a docudrama, of course, that will itself be "tainted" by subjective judgments. (Why was a dashing actor picked to play one character and make him appealing; why was one character portrayed as cunning and cold; why did the docudrama include one part of Sharon's testimony, but not another?) Fantasizing with other reporters toward the end of the trial, Arnold Lubasch of the *New York Times* wrote that the journalists had been casting the actors who ought to perform in a movie version of the case, choosing Rod Steiger as Ariel Sharon, Elizabeth Taylor as Sharon's wife, Richard Dreyfus as David Halevy, and Dustin Hoffman as Judge Sofaer. Lubasch then wryly noted that "such a film would cost a lot to produce— perhaps $50 million."

The real Sharon case actually did seem to become one of New York city's entertainments for the winter, with Mayor Koch presiding over the festivities as if it were the opening run of a blockbuster Broadway musical. Sharon and his wife Lili, both of whom had attended the entire trial, celebrated Chanukah with Mayor Koch at Gracie Mansion. Ray Cave, *Time's* managing editor and, like Sharon, a longstanding friend of Koch's, had dinner with the Mayor the day before Sharon's visit. Even Judge Sofaer had dinner with the Mayor, a week after Cave and Sharon. Whether one's daily coverage of the trial came via *Entertainment Tonight* or the *New York Times*, there was usually something spicy to hear about from the case—it was news, but it was also a curiosity, an extravaganza.

If, in fact, there is one bottom line that can be stated with confidence, it is that the spectacle of *Sharon v. Time* was great entertainment, entertainment that someone at some point may find worth replaying. And given the current inclinations of the law of libel, one of the main amusements of the legal system today is recycled libel litigation—libel litigation brought by persons who do not claim to be libeled in the immediate "hard news" coverage of a particular event, but in the documentaries, fictionalizations, docudramas, parodies, and satires that follow it. To what extent is a person, having achieved celebrity status, or having played a crucial role in major historical events, simply "fair game?" The next several chapters explore that issue, beginning with the "celebrity case" that seemed to launch much of the current hostility against the media, the suit of Carol Burnett against the *National Enquirer*.

5

"I Read It in the *Enquirer* . . . Carol Burnett and Henry Kissinger!" —The Carol Burnett Case

> I want to go on record right here in front of the American public, because this is the only forum I have. They have this publication and I have this show. This is absolutely, completely, one-hundred-percent falsehoods. It's untrue, for openers. So I'm going to call the *National Enquirer* and the people who wrote this liars. Now, that's slander—or they can sue me for slander. You know where I am, gentlemen.
>
> Johnny Carson, on the Tonight Show

> They didn't give a darn about my rights as a human being. I didn't do a thing to the *National Enquirer*; they did it to themselves.
>
> Carol Burnett, after the $1.6 million
jury verdict in her favor

ON MARCH 2, 1976, the *National Enquirer* published a brief four-sentence item concerning actress/comedienne Carol Burnett, as part of a gossip column written under the name of *Enquirer* columnist Steve Tinney. The headline of the column stated: "Carol Burnett and Henry K. in Row." The item read, in its entirety:

> In a Washington restaurant, a boisterous Carol Burnett had a loud argument with another diner, Henry Kissinger. Then she traipsed around the place offering everyone a bite of her dessert. But Carol really raised eyebrows when she accidently knocked a glass of wine over one diner and started giggling instead of apologizing. The guy wasn't amused and 'accidently' spilled a glass of water over Carol's dress.

The actual events out of which the *Enquirer* story arose took place on the evening of January 29, 1976, some five weeks before the gossip column item was published. Burnett and her husband were dining with three friends at the Rive Gauche restaurant in the Georgetown section of Wash-

ington, D.C. Burnett was in Washington to honor an invitation to be a
performing guest at the White House. Burnett did have "two or three"
glasses of wine with dinner, but she was not inebriated. Andrew and Charlotte Wiessner, a young couple, were seated at a table next to Burnett's;
they were at the restaurant celebrating a birthday. Burnett engaged in
friendly conversation with the couple, and eventually, in response to the
couple's curiosity about Burnett's chocolate soufflé, passed small tastes of
the soufflé to them on plates they had passed to her. The exchange was
made by waiters. A family at another table seated near Burnett, having
witnessed the gesture, in turn offered some of their baked alaska for a taste
of Burnett's soufflé, and a similar friendly exchange was made. Later in
the evening, when Burnett was leaving the restaurant, she was introduced
by a friend to Henry Kissinger, who also happened to be dining at Rive
Gauche that night. After a brief exchange of pleasantries, Burnett and her
party left the restaurant. According to Kissinger's testimony, he and Burnett were politely introduced, they "exchanged a few words," spoke in a
"perfectly civilized manner" with "no commotion of any kind."

The *Enquirer* article was riddled with false statements and misleading
innuendos. Burnett was never intoxicated, as was strongly implied by the
Enquirer's use of such words and phrases as "boisterous," "loud argument," "traipsed," "raised eyebrows" and "giggling." In fact she never
"traipsed around the place offering everyone a bite of her dessert," nor
did she spill wine on anyone, nor did anyone spill water on her, nor did
she have any occasion to start "giggling instead of apologizing." Her conversation with Henry Kissinger was not a "row"; there was in fact no argument at all between the two, and their short conversation was neither
"loud" nor "boisterous."

The *Enquirer's* interest in the story commenced with a tip from a paid
"freelance tipster" named Court Hays, who was paid by the *Enquirer* for
information that he supplied from time to time, if the information was
ultimately published. Hays's tip, communicated to *Enquirer* writer Brian
Walker, was that Hays had been told that Burnett had taken her soufflé
around the restaurant and flamboyantly given bits of it to other patrons.
Hays also claimed to have "unverified" information about a wine-spilling
incident, but according to Hays's sources, Burnett was "specifically,
emphatically" not drunk. Hays's tip made no mention whatsoever of any
incident with Henry Kissinger. Walker passed Hays's information on to
Steve Tinney, under whose name the *Enquirer* gossip column is written.
Walker expressed doubts about whether Hays could be trusted, which Tinney shared. Walker then asked another *Enquirer* reporter, Gregory Lyon,
to attempt to verify the story. Lyon was able to confirm only that Burnett

had shared some of her dessert with others. Lyon also learned, however, that Burnett and Kissinger had had a brief and good-natured conversation at the restaurant.

Despite the fact that no evidence at all had surfaced of any argument with Henry Kissinger, that no verification of any wine-spilling incident had been made, that no details concerning Burnett sharing her dessert had been adduced, and that the sources had uniformly and quite emphatically made it clear that Burnett was not intoxicated, Walker composed the four-sentence item that was ultimately published as part of the Tinney column, appearing under the "Carol Burnett and Henry K. in Row" headline.

The *Enquirer*, in short, had flat-out lied. Out of a scintilla of evidence about Carol Burnett graciously sharing a dessert, the *Enquirer* manufactured a story that made Burnett appear as a drunk. The implication of drunkenness was particularly offensive to Carol Burnett, because both of her parents died at the age of 46 from complications arising from alcohol abuse.

To her great credit, however, Burnett did not attempt to exaggerate her emotional pain in her libel suit against the *Enquirer*. At the trial, Burnett testified that she had managed to put aside her distress and was able to function as an actress and comedienne. Although she said that occasionally she felt a little paranoid about talking too loudly in restaurants, her anxiety over the article did not have deep residual effects. Burnett never felt the need to seek the services of a psychiatrist, psychologist, or counselor as a result of the article.

The trial judge, Peter Smith, found it commendable that Burnett had not "sought the unnecessary services of some 'phoney build-up-artist' in order to inflate her damages." She did not, the judge was saying, look for a psychiatrist who could be paraded in front of the jury to try to impress it with "expert testimony" of Burnett's lasting psychological scars. Remarking that she should "not be penalized for self-treating," Judge Smith stated that Burnett was "a highly credible witness who did not exaggerate her complaints."[70]

The trial, much of which was carried live by the Cable News Network, boiled down to a few dramatic minutes at the heart of Burnett's testimony on the stand. The critical moments in that testimony, even when read from the cold transcript, speak forcefully for themselves:

Q. When was the first time you had any knowledge of that article or the contents of that article?

A. I believe it was the day that it came out. . . .

Q. What was your reaction?

A. Well, I was absolutely—I was stunned. . . . I felt very, very angry. I started to cry. I started to shake.

Q. Why such a reaction to this?

A. Well, it portrays me as being drunk. It portrays me as being rude. It portrays me as being uncaring. It portrays me as being physically abusive. It is disgusting, and it is a pack of lies. I—It hurts. It hurts, because words, once they are printed, they've got a life of their own. Words, once spoken, have a life of their own. How was I going to explain to my kids, my family, the people I care about? How am I going to go talk to do things . . . against alcoholism? . . .

Q. . . . You mentioned something about work against alcoholism. What is that?

A. It didn't start out as any kind of a crusade at all. I think I must have spoken about it many years ago, first maybe in a magazine article for *McCall's* or *Redbook* or *Ladies' Home Journal*, or something like that, when, in a sense, I came out of the closet about my parents. I told about my background. . . . Then I was asked about it on a few talk shows, and then I started getting requests to do various public service things relating to abuse of alcohol, which I was very happy to do.

Q. Now, when you first heard about this article, when you first heard what the article said, I take it, from what you said, that you at least interpreted the language of the article as inferring that you were intoxicated?

A. I think anyone who can read would.

Q. And your reaction—one of the reactions you had—we are not talking about now, but at the time you heard about this article, one of the reactions you had was, as you described it, related to this work that you had been doing, the—let's say image, for lack of a better word, the image that you have in respect to this working against abuse of alcohol?

A. Yes. I mean, it hurts. If you think you are going to get up there and talk to somebody and say, 'Hey, you know, there is a way, there is a cure for this, and people have been cured' —If I get up and talk about that and somebody having read that or heard about it says, 'Who is she to get up there and tell me what to do, she runs around having fights with people and throws wine on them,' I mean, what—You see what I'm getting at? I tell you what really hurts is that I know—I really know that most people believe what they read. And that hurts.

Q. What did you—And I preface this by saying, and obviously you know it already, that we have to describe the feelings that you had, both physical and mental, at the time you found out about this article. What did you feel like physically, if anything different than usual?

A. Well, I don't think I would be different from anybody else, if anyone in here just put their name on that. Some people might get a headache. My stomach just went back and forth, and did flip flops. My stomach did flip flops. I cried. When you cry and your stomach does that, your heart pounds real fast. You shake. You cry. You calm down, you cry; you calm down, then you start thinking about all the ramifications, about, 'Oh, my God, should I call my kids? Are they going to hear about this in school or should I talk to them about it and say, 'Hey, it didn't happen'? Should I call my relatives? What should I do? Should I ignore anything that anybody is going to say to me today? But what am I going to do tomorrow? . . . .

Q. Was the article that had been read to you still on your mind as you were walking to rehearsal?

A. Yes.

Q. Did anything unusual happen to you during the time you were walking?

A. I was crossing the street and a cab driver yelled out at me and said, 'Hey, Carol, I didn't know you liked to get into fights.'

Q. This, apparently, obviously, was a person that you did not know?

A. No. It was a cab driver. . . .

Q. Does this article still concern you?

A. Yes.

Q. Why is that? . . .

A. When I am dead and gone, it's going to be in my files. My kids, my grandchildren, great-grandchildren, whatever—everybody's got a file on people, library, if you will—they can look that up. And unless—it's always going to be with me.''

Burnett's testimony seemed to put into simple, understandable, and believable words the growing sentiments of many Americans about the media's power to really hurt people with words. Among other celebrities, the testimony became a rallying point, vulcanizing resentment and bitterness toward the *Enquirer* that had obviously been seething for some time.

Statements made by Johnny Carson on the *Tonight Show* during the trial of the case, in fact, almost forced the trial to be scuttled and started over, with a new jury. In the midst of the Burnett furor, the *Enquirer*, with incredibly bad timing, printed a story trumpeting rumors of an impending divorce between Carson and his third wife, Joanna. (As it ultimately turned out, a divorce between Johnny Carson and Joanna Carson did eventually occur.) The *Enquirer* story visibly angered Carson, and in an uncharacteristically serious mood on the *Tonight Show* he lambasted the *Enquirer*, calling the story a "one-hundred percent falsehood," and stating that "the *National Enquirer* and the people who wrote this are liars," and ending dramatically by stating that his remarks were slander, and that if they wanted, the people at the *Enquirer* could sue him, stating: "You know where I am, gentlemen." The studio audience errupted in applause, and Carson's statements were heavily reported the next day in the national press. Carol Burnett for her part stated, "I thought he was wonderful. I think he had a right to use his platform to talk about how he felt."

Unfortunately, at least two members of the Carol Burnett jury were watching late night television and were tuned into the *Tonight Show* broadcast for Carson's statements. The next morning, William Masterson, the *Enquirer's* attorney, asked Judge Smith for a mistrial, arguing that Carson's remarks were highly prejudicial to the *Enquirer* and had tainted the jury. Judge Smith interviewed each juror about the incident, and was satisfied that Carson's statements had interfered with the impartiality of only two of them. The judge dismissed those two jurors, instated the one available alternate juror who had been monitoring the case, and ordered that the trial proceed with only eleven jurors. (The procedure was later affirmed on appeal.)[71]

And thus, as in the Ariel Sharon case, the Burnett trial wound to a close with sentiment heavily in the plaintiff's favor. The *Enquirer* did what it could to stem the tide by referring to the First Amendment. In his closing argument for the *Enquirer*, the paper's attorney William Masterson stated "I speak not only for a client but also for a principle, and that is the freedom of the press—your right to know." But however much "enquiring minds want to know" (a line the publication uses in its advertising campaign), the jury was not much impressed with the *Enquirer's* efforts to protect itself in the hallowed cloak of freedom of speech.

The jury, after hearing all the evidence and argument, deliberated for two days before returning with a unanimous verdict, handing a resounding victory to Burnett. The jury awarded Burnett $300,000 in "compensatory" damages and $1.3 million in "punitive" damages. The verdict, the first libel judgment ever against the *Enquirer*, received lavish nationwide publicity. Although Burnett's original complaint had sought $10 million in damages, at trial Burnett's lawyers had cut their demand to $1.5 million. The jury thus actually gave Burnett $100,000 more than she asked for. In an interview later with one of the jurors, Anthony Brown, it was disclosed that the jury believed that the *Enquirer* had not sufficiently checked the truthfulness of the news. Burnett, who broke into a smile and then tears at the announcement of the verdict, said she would donate the money to charity.

The trial judge, however, has the power in California to reduce jury awards, and although the judge in Burnett's case was generally in agreement with the jury's disposition, he reduced the judgment to $50,000 in compensatory damages, and $750,000 in punitive damages. The trial judge thus cut the total award in half, though it still remained a hefty $800,000. After the verdict, *Enquirer* attorney Masterson said that the high jury verdict was excessive, and "almost the equivalent of capital punishment for a corporation."

Hollywood celebrities were predictably ecstatic with the jury verdict. Johnny Carson said "I'm not only delighted for Carol but for all of us in the public eye." Marty Ingels, who with his wife, Shirley Jones, was also suing the *Enquirer*, captured the celebrity mood more colorfully, stating that "It is about time that we got in there and scraped out some of the abhorrent leeches that are hiding in the great broad shadow of the First Amendment."

Conventional mainstream media journalists did not rally around the *Enquirer*. As long as the public sentiment was highly sympathetic to Burnett, and to the jury's treatment of the *Enquirer*, the institutional press was not disposed to buck the trend. Instead the mainstream media sought to distance itself from the *Enquirer* and its methods. Nes Murphy, the editor of the *San Francisco Examiner*, for example, called the *Enquirer* "a disgrace to journalism" that was not worthy of being defended because it "has not played with the same rules with everybody else in the country." As Jonathan Friendly wrote for the *New York Times*, many journalists "cannot be comfortable riding in the same First Amendment boat with the *Enquirer*."

The reaction of the "respectable press" toward the *Enquirer* verdict had traces of elitism and shortsightedness. Maybe the *Enquirer* did not play by "the same set of rules" as more orthodox media outlets—and yet again maybe it did. The *Enquirer* had never lost a court judgment for libel prior to the Burnett case (though settlements and retractions had preempted some prior disputes that might have led to defeats). And according to statistics from a libel insurance pool program sponsored by the American Newspaper Publishers Association, the *Enquirer* had proportionately fewer cases filed against it than the average for the pool.

Statistics aside, the attempt by some in the mainstream to assert the difference between the methods of the *Enquirer* and the methods of the conventional press would, in the aftermath of the surge of libel litigation that followed the Burnett case, begin to ring hollow. Mistakes by the "respectable press" in the 1980's in some instances looked just as bad as or worse than the *Enquirer's* treatment of Burnett. *Newsweek* would get caught printing bogus "Hitler's Diaries," for example, and the *Washington Post* would have to admit that a Pulitzer Prize winning story by Janet Cooke was phony. Perhaps the most striking parallel, however, would be *Time's* coverage of Sharon's involvement in the Lebanese massacres. Given the far more devastating insinuations in the *Time* piece, *Time's* behavior was arguably much worse than the *Enquirer's*. It is one thing to be wrongly accused of traipsing around drunk in a restaurant, and quite another to be accused of complicity in the murder of eight hundred refugees. Both *Time* and the *Enquirer* had printed stories purportedly based on "confidential sources," when in fact the sources had never confirmed what was at the heart of the allegations. In its defense, however, it can be said that *Time* at least had apparently been sincere in believing the inferences it drew; the *Enquirer* fabrication was a far more cold-blooded exercise in manufacturing sensationalism.

Of the issues raised by the Burnett case, probably the most interesting is the question "what is a reputation worth?" When the media is caught in a bare-faced lie, what remedies are appropriate? Why, in fact, should we award money damages at all? Wouldn't the best remedy be a legal device designed to force the media outlet to retract or correct its story?

In the Burnett case there was an intruiging byplay involving that very issue—the printing of a retraction. Burnett's lawyers had demanded a retraction the day after the *Enquirer* piece first appeared. On the day the *Enquirer* piece was published, Burnett's attorney sent the *Enquirer* a telegram (followed by a letter), claiming that the article was entirely false and libelous, and demanding a correction or retraction. Burnett's attorney further indicated that if the *Enquirer* failed to retract its errors, suit would be brought. On April 6, 1976, a little over a month after the Burnett item had been published, the *Enquirer*, in response to Burnett's demands, actually did publish a retraction, which also appeared as an item in the gossip column. The retraction read:

> An item in this column on March 2 erroneously reported that Carol Burnett had an argument with Henry Kissinger at a Washington restaurant and became boisterous, disturbing other guests. We understand those events did not occur and we are sorry for any embarrassment our report may have caused Miss Burnett.

The state of California has a "retraction statute" that permits a "newspaper" or "radio broadcasting station" to substantially limit its exposure to liability for libel if the newspaper or radio station publishes or broadcasts a correction of the offending defamation.[73] The victim of the allegedly libelous statement must make a written demand for a correction within twenty days of the publication or broadcast. The newspaper or station then has three weeks to publish or broadcast its correction, which must be in a "regular issue or broadcast," and must be placed in the newspaper layout or radio programming in "substantially as conspicuous a manner" as the prior statement that was claimed to be libelous. If the newspaper or radio station complies with these correction requirements, the victim may still sue the newspaper or radio station for libel, but the damages that may be recovered in such a suit are severely limited to only actual pecuniary losses to the plaintiff's "property, business, trade, profession or occupation." In Carol Burnett's case, for example, she would have had to prove some tangible monetary loss, like being turned down for a part in a movie or a television series.

When damages are limited to real out-of-pocket loss (lawyers refer to these types of damages in libel suits as "special damages"), libel suits are seldom worth bringing, at least if the sole purpose of the suit is to obtain money. For in most libel litigation the real sting of the libelous statements has nothing to do with money; the real damage is of a more intangible nature—the humiliation, shame, injured feelings, and sense of personal invasion that comes from a well-publicized lie. This is not, of course, to say that defamatory statements never result in direct monetary losses. A false statement that a doctor is a quack may lead to a collapse of her practice. Similarly, no one can doubt the combined financial and emotional losses accompanying the ruined or interrupted careers of writers and entertainers blacklisted in the heyday of the Joe McCarthy era because of false or misleading accusations that they were communists. But in most modern libel cases the major component of jury awards is not compensation for pecuniary loss, but rather compensation for the victim's injured reputation and feelings (usually called by lawyers "general damages"). In many cases today, there is additionally an award of "punitive damages," designed to punish the defendant for particularly deplorable conduct and to set a deterring example to others.

Although it is theoretically conceivable that someone like Carol Burnett could suffer actual financial losses because of an article like the one in *Enquirer*, the likelihood is that such losses will usually be either minor or nonexistent, and certainly extremely difficult to document in court. In Burnett's actual case there were no apparent direct financial losses. Burnett's chances for punishing the *Enquirer* thus hinged on her eligibility for general non-pecuniary compensatory damages, and perhaps most of all, punitive damages. But how could she receive such damages under California law, in light of the fact that the *Enquirer* had ostensibly complied with the retraction statute by printing its later correction?

The answer is that the California courts essentially disqualified the *Enquirer* from making use of the retraction device. Judge Peter Smith found the *Enquirer's* retraction to be "half-hearted" and evasive, possibly adding to the damage rather than reducing it. (It is worth remembering that this is the same reaction Ariel Sharon had to the even more half-hearted "correction" by *Time* magazine in his case.) While the original article had been highlighted by the "Carol Burnett and Henry K. in Row" headline, and had been placed on the page near an eye-catching photograph of Barbara Walters, the retraction carried no headline, was buried at the bottom of the column, and was not placed near a photograph of a celebrity. The copy of the retraction was approved by both Ian Calder, the President of the *Enquirer*, and Generoso Pope, the Chairman of the Board and sole stockholder. Judge Smith noted that even though Calder knew that none of the libelous material could be substantiated, Calder insisted on placing the modifying words "we understand" at the beginning of the story, inviting the reader to see the retraction as if it were made with a winking eye, by implying that the events *could* have occurred. Judge Smith contrasted the waffling Burnett retraction with an unequivocal retraction the *Enquirer* had published in 1976 for a gossip column item that had falsely accused Steve Allen of smashing a glass door at the William Morris Agency. It was not as if the *Enquirer* did not know how to write an effective retraction when it wanted to.

The California court that reviewed the Burnett case on appeal took the retraction issue even farther, holding that the *Enquirer* was not covered by the California retraction statute at all, because the *Enquirer* is a "magazine" rather than a "newspaper" or "radio broadcasting station," the only two types of media outlets literally mentioned in the statute. But how could the court say with a straight face that the *Enquirer* did not qualify as a newspaper, and how can California even justify discriminating between "newspapers" and "magazines" in the first place?

The masthead of the *Enquirer* proudly proclaims it as having the "Largest Circulation of Any Paper in America." The *Enquirer* is a member of the American Newspaper Publishers Association. The *Enquirer* does not subscribe to the news services of the Associated Press or United Press International, but it does subscribe to the Reuters News Service. The *Enquirer* is described as a "newspaper" for insurance and tax purposes, and it is classified as a "newspaper" by the United States Department of Labor.

The court, however, emphasized the *Enquirer's* content in deciding that it did not legally qualify as a newspaper. To be a newspaper, the court seemed to be saying, you must print "the news," and the *Enquirer* just doesn't. The *Enquirer* does not provide contemporaneous coverage of politics, business, or sports; its content consists primarily of stories about celebrities, personal improvement stories, "how to" stories, and miscellaneous other topics of the medical, "believe it or not", or gossip variety. The court was heavily influenced by what it saw as the special time demands on "real" newspapers, who must of necessity publish "news while it is new." The policy of the retraction statute, the court reasoned, was to protect news outlets who make mistakes while acting in good faith because of the pressure of deadlines. A newspaper or a broadcaster cannot protect itself completely against such inadvertent errors, particularly in light of the far-flung activities of the news services upon which they must rely. By contrast, the court reasoned, the *National Enquirer* had no similar deadline pressures. The normal "lead time" for an *Enquirer* story, that period of time between the completion of an article and its publication, was between one and three weeks. Conventional newspapers, on the other hand, generate

many stories on a day-to-day basis, and often measure lead times for articles in terms of hours, rather than days or weeks.

From a cultural perspective, the court's decision that the *Enquirer* did
not qualify for the protection of the retraction statute has some worrisome
overtones, the same overtones of elitism that existed in much of the mainstream media's reaction to Burnett's huge jury victory. It is not at all clear
that when the California legislature passed its retraction statute decades
ago, the legislature meant to use the words "newspaper" or "radio broadcasting station" in a hyper-technical sense; the words may simply have been
loosely meant to cover the field of all periodicals and broadcasters. If the
court were strictly literal, for example, it would bring "radio" within the
compass of the statute, but not necessarily "television." Given the fact that
television has eclipsed radio as the primary source of mainstream news for
most Americans—the average American is more likely to get his or her
daily diet of national broadcast news from Peter Jennings, Tom Brokaw,
or Dan Rather than from network radio, and is similarly more likely to
listen to thirty or sixty minutes of local evening television news than radio
news—it would be perverse to interpret the term "radio" as excluding
television.

Prior to the Carol Burnett case, California courts had given the word
"newspaper" an expansive reading.[73] The retraction statute had previously
been applied to magazines, including the *Reader's Digest*, which in form,
purpose, and content is far less like a conventional newspaper than the
National Enquirer. In drawing a sharp distinction between newspapers and
magazines the court made stereotypic assumptions that are simply not
always accurate. Not all newspaper stories are written under deadline pressure; some feature and investigative reporting stories may be weeks or
months in the making. Not all magazine stories have the luxury of extensive lead times. If *The Nation*, or *Atlantic Monthly*, learns of some major
scandal and cover-up in the White House six weeks before an impending
presidential election, it may decide to put together and publish that information immediately, so as to at least open up matters for debate and
inquiry. If *Time*, *Newsweek*, or *U.S. News & World Report* wish to cover a
major story that breaks at the last moment in their weekly publication
cycles for the current weekly issues, their time pressures may in some cases
be far more severe than those of the *Los Angeles Times* or *Washington Post*.
The distinction the court drew between newspapers and magazines just did
not wash on its own terms. Could the court have had some other motivation for its ruling?

The tone of the court opinion in the Burnett case makes one suspicious
that its ruling that the California statute was meant to distinguish between

magazines and newspapers was simply legally expedient, a thin rationalization masking what was in fact open judicial antagonism for the *Enquirer*.[74] If since 1964 there has been a branch of specialized *"New York Times* law," the Burnett case may mark the start of a subspeciality of *"National Enquirer* law." For the *National Enquirer*, one gets the feeling, is a second-class First Amendment citizen, unworthy of the special legal treatment afforded "serious" news outlets.

The trial judge, in language that the appellate court endorsed, blasted the *Enquirer's* conduct in handling the Burnett story, and its general mode of operation. He labeled the *Enquirer's* conduct as "highly reprehensible," amounting to "fabrication and reckless disregard" of the truth. The court found that the failure "by top management to publish an adequate correction is substantial evidence of malice and bad faith." The *Enquirer*, the court said, "has absolutely no remorse for its misdeeds." The court stated that "it is the policy of the *National Enquirer* to publish two or three unflattering articles about celebrities every week." This amounts, the court said, to "a form of legalized pandering designed to appeal to the reader's morbid sense of curiousity," a "style of journalism [that] has been enormously profitable." In a nutshell, the California courts seemed to be saying that what the *Enquirer* puts out is gossip rather than news, and gossip is beneath the dignity of the First Amendment and other protections afforded "real" newspapers.

Having decided that the *National Enquirer* was a magazine and not a newspaper, and that magazines were not within the ambit of the California retraction statute, Carol Burnett was eligible for both compensatory and punitive damages. The issue then became, how much? As already noted, the trial judge had already lowered Burnett's compensatory damages from $300,000 to $50,000, and her punitive damages from $1.3 million to $750,000, thus reducing the total original judgment in half, from $1.6 million to $800,000. The appellate court affirmed the new $50,000 compensatory damages award, but further reduced the punitive damages to $150,000, slashing the total award to $200,000. Why did the appellate court cut the award?

Carol Burnett said after the jury verdict, "If they'd given me one dollar plus car fare, I'd have been happy, because it was the principle." But the way trials in libel suits actually work, "the principle" cannot always be so neatly separated from the amount of damages awarded. The profitability of the *Enquirer*, and the impact of a million-dollar-range libel judgment upon it, were subject to some debate. The trial judge found that the *Enquirer's* net worth was $2,600,000, a figure that seems quite low in view of the 16 million weekly circulation of the paper. The trial court also found that the *Enquirer's* earnings *after* taxes for only the *ten months* prior to the trial were $1,300,000, an income figure that, contrary to the net worth figure, makes the *Enquirer* look enormously profitable.

How badly would the jury's $1,600,000 verdict have hurt the *Enquirer*? Looking at net worth alone, it seems severely damaging, for it would constitute over fifty percent of that figure. But net worth figures in this context may be deceptive. If a substantial amount of the *Enquirer's* income is paid out as earnings to stockholders (the *National Enquirer's* sole stockholder, and Chairman of the Board, was Generoso Pope), the net worth figure will appear low. Looking at the income stream of the *Enquirer*, however, it would take less than a year's worth of after-tax profit to pay the jury's award. This would certainly hurt—the disgorging of a year's worth of earnings is no slap on the wrist—but then again, isn't a punitive damages award *supposed* to hurt? After all, the first $1,300,000 of the award was punitive. The appellate court's ultimate reduction of punitive damages to $150,000 could be paid by the *Enquirer* out of about *one month's* profits, an award that seems hardly punitive at all.

More fundamentally, there is a certain failure of conviction in the reduction of the Burnett award, for if the *Enquirer's* conduct was really that reprehensible, and if the damage to Carol Burnett was truly severe, why should the legal system care how badly the *Enquirer* is damaged? Somebody is making a great deal of money from the *National Enquirer*. There are a lot of newspaper owners in the country (both corporate and "family owned") that would relish after-tax earnings of $1,500,000 a year. The officers, owners and employees of the *Enquirer* make their substantial profit largely by using the lives of celebrities as unpaid-for raw material. Carol Burnett, Elizabeth Taylor, Johnny Carson, Michael Landon, Clint Eastwood, and Jacqueline Kennedy Onassis, by their very existence as celebrities, are the grist out of which the *Enquirer's* gossip mill earns its profits. When the *Enquirer* exploits this raw material recklessly and maliciously, causing gratuitous injury to the celebrities from which it has profited, shouldn't the legal system let the punishment fit the crime?

Free-market zealots of the type that now tend to dominate Ronald Reagan's administration argue that corporations should be allowed to die a financial death with dignity when the normal forces of the market force them under. Chrysler, or Braniff Airlines, or the Continental Illinois National Bank should be allowed their natural demise, as the price of their mismanagement or bad luck. The cornerstone of social and economic Darwinism, which is central in the ideology of President Ronald Reagan (though President Reagan, out of politic deference to the sensitivity of some of his constituency to Charles Darwin, would undoubtedly not choose to invoke the biologist's name), is that survival is deserved only by the fittest. The only concession that the free-market advocate would make is that the financial destruction, particularly of a large concern, ought to be orderly and fair to creditors; and so the bankruptcy system is utilized to equitably distribute the leavings.

A newspaper or magazine that cavalierly trods on the legally protected interests of individuals by invading their right to privacy and ruining their reputations is as sorely guilty of mismanagement as the bank that makes bad loans, the airline that extravagantly overexpands, or the auto manufacturer that makes unpopular cars. Sympathy for such mismanagement is further diminished when the company goes beyond negligence and into the realm of reckless or malicious behavior that hurts others. If the bank loans are not merely bad but fraudulent, if the airline's practices were not merely imprudent but predatory, if the auto company's cars were not merely unreliable but dangerous, then the thought of involuntary bankruptcy is all the more palatable.

If these values are valid for other profit-making ventures, why should they not apply to the *National Enquirer*? What would be so bad about Carol Burnett putting the *Enquirer* out of business? If Chrysler or Ford or General Motors were to act recklessly and maliciously in manufacturing an automobile that caused great injury, we would not let the victims go without their just awards (compensatory and punitive) merely to insulate the stockholders of those corporations from reduced earnings. It is true, of course, that the legal system is not always deaf to a defendant's cries of financial ruin. Large tort judgments at times do force corporations into bankruptcy, and it may sometimes be socially desirable to use the bankruptcy laws to strike a compromise between the social interest in paying victims and the usefulness of resurrecting the offending defendant in a new financial form. The Johns-Manville Corporation, plagued with potentially astronomical tort judgments against it in cases involving the disease asbestosis, has sought the refuge of bankruptcy to try to prevent the complete dissolution of the corporation as a going concern. Perhaps it is not irrational for the legal system to make some accommodation to the company in such a situation, if for no other reason than that many workers' jobs depend on the continued existence of the company. The *Enquirer*, however, was escaping almost scot-free.

In the publishing context, there is a precedent for permitting a libel suit to force the publisher to the brink of ruin. The *Alton Telegraph* newspaper was forced into bankruptcy by a multi-million dollar libel judgment because it did not have even the financial ability to bring an appeal. The result of the bankruptcy was a settlement in which plaintiffs took less money, and the paper, financially reorganized, was given a second life. The essential point, however, is that the *Telegraph* was actually forced all the way to the drastic step of bankruptcy before any financial lenience was permitted. If the damages award is otherwise legitimate, the tort system does not normally let the defendant off the hook because the award will render it insolvent. When the system does let the defendant off the hook, it is merely transferring wealth from deserving victims to stockholders. In effect, a decision to excuse the *National Enquirer* from paying the damages awards that it would otherwise be responsible for, soley on the basis of the financial grief paying the award would cause the *Enquirer*, is to permit the *Enquirer* to exercise a sort of right of eminent domain over the personalities of the celebrities it writes about. The reputation of Carol Burnett is in effect condemned and appropriated for use by the *Enquirer*, which is later forced to pay only a fraction of its "fair market value."

Carol Burnett's case similarly demonstrated that the rules that currently govern damages awards in libel suits are ridiculously confusing. Very few judges and lawyers can keep them straight, let alone hope to translate them into intelligible guides for a jury. The Burnett case is a classic example of the chaos surrounding these rules. Because Burnett was a public figure, under the First Amendment requirements from the *Gertz* case, she had to establish that the *Enquirer* printed the false elements of the story about her with knowledge of falsity or out of reckless disregard for the truth, in order to receive any recovery at all. The Supreme Court in *Gertz*, however, left the states free to decide what rules they would apply to determine when to award punitive damages, as long as the threshold intentional or reckless disregard of the truth standard was first met. In California, in order to establish punitive damages, a public figure like Burnett must establish two different kinds of malice. She must first prove the existence of *New York Times* "knowing or reckless" malice, and then, over and above that, she must show malice of a more personal quality, malice in the sense of real ill-will, spite, or fraudulent or evil motive. The first type—*New York Times* malice—must be proven by "clear and convincing evidence"; the second type—ill-will malice—can be established by a mere "preponderance of the evidence." To get a sense for just how confusing these rules can be, it is worth sampling verbatim some of the court's opinion from the appeal in the Burnett case. Relying on precedent from prior cases, the court observed:

> These aspects of the *New York Times* rule having been related, we observe additionally that, as will hereinafter be seen, the reference in the rule to 'actual malice' may prove confusing when juxtaposed to similar terms commonly employed in the law relating to libel, where, as in a case like the one before us, those terms are involved with the question of punitive damages.
>   . . . it is necessary only to define two of the several terms . . . , namely malice in law and malice in fact, the former being understood as:

> . . . that malice which the law presumes (either conclusively or
> disputably) to exist upon the production of certain desig-
> nated evidence, which malice may be fictional and construc-
> tive merely, and which, arising, as it usually does, from what
> is conceived to be the necessity of proof following a pleading,
> which in turn follows a definition, is to be always distin-
> guished from true malice or malice in fact.

and the latter referring to:

> . . . a state of mind arising from hatred or ill-will, evidencing
> a willingness to vex, harass, annoy, or injure another person.

or to:

> the motive and willingness to vex, harrass, annoy, or injure,

that is to say:

> *malus animus*—indicating that the party was actuated either
> by spite or ill will towards an individual, or by indirect or
> improper motives, though these may be wholly unconnected
> with any uncharitable feeling towards anybody.

> And while in the cases this malice, the existence of which we have
> declared to be essential to a recovery in punitive damages, is sometimes
> called express malice, sometimes actual malice, and sometimes real
> malice, and sometimes true malice, it is always in its analysis malice of
> the one kind, the malice of the evil motive.[75]

The law of California has got more kinds of malice than there are deadly
sins. This sounds like Groucho, Harpo, and Chico go to court. ("You got
yer malice of da first part, you got yer malice of da second part. . .") If
Carol Burnett herself had set out to write a parody of legal gobbledygook
for a comedy sketch, she could hardly have done better. Lawyers have
failed the public when million dollar lawsuits turn on the doubletalk of
distinguishing among various shades of meaning of a single word. Is it any
wonder that a jury will be moved to slice through this jumble of lawyer-
talk and simply apply its own homespun justice? Only a handful of the
nation's new law school graduates, crammed with knowledge on the day of
their bar exams, would be able to give clear explanations of the differences
(if any) between "malus animus," "actual malice," "implied malice,"
"express malice," "real malice," "true malice," "malice-in-law," and "mal-
ice-in-fact." Legal terminology this complex has lost its tie to human
nature; there just aren't that many ways to *be* malicious.

One can have all the respect in the world for the intelligence, common
sense, and integrity of juries, and still conclude that when the law gets this
baffling, it is openly inviting judicial anarchy. The jury in the Burnett case
may well have reached an intelligent and fair verdict, but it did so in spite
of, not because of, the instructions it received. The jury in the Burnett case
was not only required to find two different kinds of malice, it was supposed

to impose different standards of "evidence quality" to each type ("clear and convincing" proof in one instance and "preponderance of the evidence" in another). Not only do individual human beings and human organizations like the *National Enquirer* not act in seven different shades of malice, individual jurors, and the jury as a collective group, in judging their behavior later, do not *think* or *feel* in such compartments.

Finally, the Burnett case highlights the basic hypocrisy in the message that the libel system sends to juries today. To reverse or to lower a jury award of punitive damages, the appellate court must find that the award is so grossly excessive that it raises a presumption that the jury acted out of "passion or prejudice." When the court examines an award of *compensatory* damages, this legal test makes sense, for if the goal of such damages is to fairly compensate the victim for what he or she has lost, we want the calculation to be as coldly objective as possible. The passion or prejudice test in the context of punitive damages, however, poses an incongruity sadly typical of the libel law's tendency to create legal standards that bear no relationship to the normal habits of the human mind. For the jury is quite deliberately instructed that their duty in levying a punitive damages award is to punish particularly despicable and malicious conduct, as a means both of expressing the community's outrage at the behavior, and of deterring similar activity in the future. All of the words used to explain to a jury when punitive damages are appropriate are purposely cast in emotive language—the jury's passions and prejudices are consciously played upon. In the colorful language of one Florida court, punitive damages "are such as not only compensate the wrong done, but also tend to protect all good citizens of the State from like wrongs from the reckless and malicious tongue of such lawless persons as have no regard for the good name of their fellows, or for the name and virtue of the women of the land, but turn themselves loose like ravenous wolves to destroy that which money cannot buy, and that which, when lost, the powers of earth cannot restore." And yet, having in one breath invited the jury to act as nemesis in instances of particularly abominable misconduct, the legal system then reduces the jury's award when their temper seems intemperate—when it is infected with passion or prejudice.

In the end, the Burnett case raised more questions than it answered. Carol Burnett's reputation was restored; in the public mind she was vindicated. But the system used to achieve that vindication was cumbersome, costly, and often arbitrary. The process was tainted by elitist distaste for the likes of the *National Enquirer*, and by legal rules that were Byzantine and baffling. Yet the result in the Burnett case would trigger a new anti-media activism on the part of American celebrities, an activism that would include claims by public personalities to rights in their identities broader than simple freedom from defamation. The Burnett case generated new interest in the broad question of what exactly it means to be a celebrity in America, and the extent to which celebrities surrender their private lives to the public domain.

6

Jackie Onassis, Elizabeth Taylor, Clint Eastwood, and Mohammed Ali— Of Public Personality and Private Property

Jackie Kennedy Onassis is not merely a celebrity, but a legend. Not a legend, but a myth. No, more than a myth. She is now an historic archetype, virtually a demiurge.
Norman Mailer, on "Fifty Who Made the Difference," in *Esquire*, December, 1983

A good name is rather to be chosen than great riches.
Proverbs 22:1

I F NORMAN MAILER is right, and Jacqueline Kennedy Onassis is in fact an American demigodess, a deity assigned to the earthly duty of incarnating America's most glamorous visions of itself, does "Jackie's myth" belong to Jackie, or is her myth something that all America owns? What parts of the lives of Jackie Onassis, or Elizabeth Taylor, or Clint Eastwood, or Mohammed Ali no longer belong to them as individuals, but have ascended and gone to celebrity heaven, to sit at the right hands of the great advertisers, docudrama makers, and gossip journalists in the sky? To what extent is Jackie's life her own, and to what extent does her life now belong to all of us?

Perhaps because she is more an American deity than a mere celebrity, Onassis has been unusually successful in litigation efforts to protect not merely her privacy, but her whole persona. The most interesting of her legal efforts put Onassis against one of the nation's great commercial purveyors of myths, Christian Dior. In a designer label culture, who, after all, could be better associated with one's label than a genuine cultural demigodess? Through the advertising ingenuity of the J. Walter Thompson agency and photographer Richard Avedon, Christian Dior hit upon an advertising campaign for its Christian Dior designer label using a series of

118

ads that would feature three people, to be known as the "Diors." The Diors, one female and two males, were to convey the impression of being suggestively decadent, sporting-set rich, slightly outrageous and aggressively chic. Their ménage à trois became an instant phenomenon within the advertising trade, and soon began to attract more general notice, even drawing the attention of a *Newsweek* article. The trio was putatively inspired by the characters portrayed by Noel Coward, Alfred Lunt, and Lynn Fontanne in Coward's 1933 play *Design for Living*, and were said to be the hottest personae in advertising since Brooke Shields refused to let anything come between her and her Calvins.

The Diors were created to convey an image of Christian Dior products as elegant but unorthodox, elite but unconventional. The Dior consumer (who would never think of himself or herself, of course, as just a "consumer") is sophisticated and chic, but also just a bit outrageous, audacious, and even quirky, in an elegant sort of way. The sexual relationships among the three Diors were purposefully left ambiguous by the campaign, specifying nothing but suggesting everything. The copy for one of the Dior's ads read: "When the Diors got away from it all, they brought with them nothing except 'The Decline of the West' and one toothbrush."

One of the ads in the series depicted a wedding between two of the Diors (though not necessarily intimating the exclusion of the third), with the heading "Christian Dior: Sportswear for Women and Clothing for Men." In the ad the three Diors and a crowd of friends were portrayed ecstatically celebrating the wedding. The copy for the ad sounded the note of chic unorthodoxy typical of the entire campaign: "The wedding of the Diors was everything a wedding should be: no tears, no rice, no in-laws, no smarmy toasts, for once no Mendelssohn. Just a legendary private affair." Surrounding the three Diors in the ad were a number of well-known personalities —actress Ruth Gordon, model Shari Belafonte, and television movie critic Gene Shalit. Also among the celebrities in attendance was a woman who at first glance appeared to be Jacqueline Kennedy Onassis, but who after a slightly longer look was revealed to be someone else made up to appear astonishingly similar to Onassis. That "someone else" was a New York secretary named Barbara Reynolds, who happens to bear a remarkably close resemblance to Jackie Onassis.

The makers of the ad, knowing that the real Jackie Onassis would not pose for a Christian Dior ad no matter what the price (Onassis has steadfastly refused throughout her life to lend her name or likeness to the promotion of commercial products, sparingly permitting the use of her name only in support of certain art, public service, civic, and educational projects), contacted a New York agency known as "Ron Smith Celebrity Look-Alikes" to find someone who looked like Onassis. They supplied Barbara

Reynolds. (The same Ron Smith Celebrity Look-Alikes company would later get into a similar legal brouhahah by furnishing a Woody Allen look-alike to appear on a television ad for a video cassette rental store—the look-alike was shown walking into the rental store to ask for cassettes of two Woody Allen movies.)

The Dior wedding ad was a great success, appearing in the fall of 1983 in publications like the *New Yorker, Esquire, Harpers Bazaar*, and the *New York Times Magazine.*

Onassis filed suit against Christian Dior, and obtained a court order banning any further publications of the ad.[76] In an interesting and provocative opinion, Judge Greenfield of the Supreme Court of New York County upheld Onassis's right to block the use of look-alikes in advertising campaigns, relying on a New York statute that makes it illegal to use "for advertising purposes, or for the purposes of trade, the name, portrait or picture of any living person without having first obtained the written consent of such person."

The purpose of the law, Judge Greenfield stated, is "to protect the *essence of the person*, his or her identity or persona from being unwillingly or unknowingly misappropriated for the profit of another." In a world increasingly dominated by the visual arts—photography, television, motion pictures, and video cassettes—visual image has become an increasingly important means of communicating "personality." In the campaign of 1984, how many votes did Walter Mondale first lose to Gary Hart among voters who prefer the dry look to the greasy kid stuff, and how many votes did he later lose to Ronald Reagan because he was less tanned and more baggy-eyed? In the 1980's if the law wants to accord protection to "the essence of the person," it must jealously guard the appropriation of the person's visual image. "For some people," Judge Greenfield said, "even without their American Express Cards, the face is total identification, more than a signature or a coat of arms." To give visual image the total protection it needs in an image-conscious world, the law must not merely protect the person's "picture," in the literal sense of a photograph before the lens; it must encompass rather a broader protection for the "essence and likeness" of the individual—it must protect "identity" from exploitation, even when the identity is portrayed impressionistically.

Onassis had long been sensitive to the problems of exploitative use of her identity and encroachment on her privacy. Several years prior to the Christian Dior campaign, Ms. Onassis and the Kennedy children were the ongoing preoccupation of a freelance photographer named Donald Galella. Galella fancied himself a "paparazzo," which, translated literally from Italian, means a kind of annoying insect. "Paparazzi" photographers specialize in making themselves as visible to the public and as cloyingly obnoxious to their photographic subjects as possible, creating a publicity mystique about their photographs that is designed to aid the advertisement and wide sale of their works. Galella's paparazzi tactics included such actions as bringing his power boat close to Ms. Onassis while she was swimming; jumping suddenly out of bushes as she was walking past; jumping into the path of John Kennedy, Jr., to photograph him as he was riding his bicycle; and infiltrating the Kennedy children's schools. Gallela even went to the extremes of bribing apartment house, restaurant, and nightclub doormen, and romancing a family servant, to keep him advised of the movements of the family. Onassis sued Galella, seeking not money but a court order getting him to stop his paparazzi tactics. After a trial that ended in favor of Onassis, Galella was ordered by the judge not to keep Onassis or the Kennedy children under surveillance, and was ordered to keep 100 yards away from both Onassis and the children at all times.[77]

On appeal, the court relied on Galella's violation of a New York criminal statute against "harassment" and concluded that it could be invoked in a civil case. In response to Galella's claims that he had a First Amendment right to follow and photograph Onassis and her children because they were "newsworthy" subjects, the court concluded that "Crimes and torts committed in news gathering are not protected. There is no threat to a free press in requiring its agents to act within the law."

Although the appellate court upheld in general the lower court's order, the minimum distances were reduced from 100 yards to 25 or 30 feet. Galella was also enjoined from blocking movement of Onassis or the children in public places, and from "any act foreseeably or reasonably calculated to place the life and safety" of Onassis in jeopardy or that could "reasonably be foreseen to harass, alarm or frighten" her. Similar injunctions were awarded in favor of the Secret Service agents assigned to protect the Kennedy children.

In 1982, Galella was found guilty of twelve violations of the court order, for taking photographs within 25 feet of Ms. Onassis. The judge suspended a fine of $120,000 when Galella agreed to pay the $10,000 in legal fees incurred by Onassis, and never again to photograph her. The judge warned that if Galella should renege on the promise, the judge would revive the fine or impose a six-month jail sentence for each violation.

The Christian Dior situation, however, was quite a bit different from the Galella escapade. Christian Dior had not harassed Onassis in any way, and in fact it had not even used her photograph. Christian Dior's tongue-in cheek use of an Onassis look-alike in a somewhat flippant ad campaign was not all that evil, was it? What harm was done?

In the eyes of Judge Greenfield the harm *was* substantial; as important as any economic damage was the principle of the thing. Judge Greenfield was obviously worried that if he did not rule for Onassis, there would be no stopping clever advertisers from using the arts of illusion to exploit the personalities of others for commercial gain. Where illusion is routinely used to heighten, accent, or alter reality, where all is not what it seems, is the law to be left impotent? For Judge Greenfield, this would be "sanctioning an obvious loophole," by permitting the illusionist to reap the benefits of the creative allusion to a real person, and then later disclaim the very impression he purposefully set out to create. If you can't get Jackie Onassis to endorse your product, you simply hire a double at a fraction of the price and the same effect is achieved. "Let the word go forth," Judge Greenfield announced, "there is no free ride." From now on, the rule would be that the "commercial hitchhiker seeking to travel on the fame of another will have to learn to pay the fare or stand on his own two feet."

But how can a court prevent Barbara Reynolds from using her own face? The judge answered this question by stating that Barbara Reynolds was a mere unknown secretary. The appearance of Barbara Reynolds at the wedding of the Diors would not have made it "legendary." Only the conscious manipulation of Reynold's face to mimic the face of Onassis—the set of the hair, the choice of make-up and accessories, the wardrobe, the distinctive facial expression—made Reynold's face commercially valuable. The effect was then heightened by putting the "counterfeit Jackie" next to the genuine photographs of personalities like Gene Shalit, Shari Belafonte, and Ruth Gordon.

Judge Greenfield qualified this holding, however, by stating that Barbara Reynolds, and the Celebrity Look Alikes agency that markets her, may capitalize on Reynold's similarities to Onassis by charging for Reynold's appearance at parties, television appearances, or dramatic works. Reynolds is free to appear on the Merv Griffin or Phil Donahue shows to be gawked at and interviewed for her striking resemblance to Onassis; she can be hired to play Jackie Onassis's character in a docudrama. But the line is drawn for commercial advertisements, the judge reasoned, because the use of a look-alike in advertisements conveys by implication a deceptive message—that the real Onassis endorses the product.

One of the ironies of the Dior-Onassis dispute is that Christian Dior has itself been plagued constantly with the problem of counterfeit Dior products. Dior has very aggressively policed the market against such counterfeit products, and has used litigation to prevent such fraudulent exploitation of the fruit of Dior's own marketing labors. From the perspective of Christian Dior, however, there was an essential difference between those who counterfeit Dior products and Dior's own "counterfeiting" of Jackie Onassis. Dior argued that the Onassis ads were transparently tongue-in-cheek. On second glance one could see it was not really Jackie in the picture. Onassis' portrayal was a subtle touch of humor; it was part of the clever mystique of the ad, and indeed of the whole "Diors" campaign. The wedding picture, for example, also contained a model resembling the late General Charles DeGaulle. (Though only his nose and chin were visible in the cropped left edge of the picture, and he was less instantly recognizable than Onassis.) Dead men don't attend weddings; the DeGaulle touch added to the ad's overall impression of chic fantasy.

The solicitous protectiveness of New York courts for the "essence of the identity" of Jackie Onassis is part of an historical evolution in the thinking of American courts involving a legal concept that is distinctly American in origin, the "right of privacy." The notion of a distinct branch of tort law designed expressly for the protection of "privacy" was unknown in English common law, and is still not recognized in many other jurisdictions that share a common English legal heritage. To this day, for example, Canadian courts generally do not acknowledge a tort for "invasion of privacy."

Before this century, legal restraints on the media in the United States were limited primarily to the law of libel and slander. But in 1890, Samuel Warren, a Boston lawyer and legal scholar, and Louis Brandeis, later to become a Supreme Court Justice, wrote an enormously influential article in the *Harvard Law Review* entitled *The Right of Privacy*,[78] in which they urged courts to supplement the law of defamation with a new legal right to privacy. Their article was a direct challenge to the press, and has remained remarkably timely. Warren and Brandeis wrote:

> The press is overstepping in every direction the obvious bounds of pro-
> priety and decency. . . .Modern enterprise and invention have,
> through invasions upon [man's] privacy, subjected him to mental pain
> and distress, far greater than could be inflicted by mere bodily injury.

As convincing as their article was, courts at first were reluctant to follow Warren's and Brandeis's suggestion. In 1902, for example, a flour manufacturer used an attractive young woman's picture, without her permission, to adorn 25,000 posters advertising the company's flour. New York's highest court dismissed her lawsuit against the company.

The decision created a public outcry, and in 1903 the New York Legislature passed a law that prohibited the use of any person's "name, portrait, or picture for advertising purposes or for the purposes of trade" without the person's written consent. (This is the statute that would come to be put to such heavy use in the late 1970's and early 1980's by celebrities from Onassis to Elizabeth Taylor to Mohammed Ali.) Gradually, other states began to recognize various similar types of "rights of privacy." From the very beginning, one of the main branches of this developing privacy law concerned rights that were really not primarily of a "privacy" nature in the strict sense, but were rather more of a "property right" in one's own face and name. It was more one's right to control one's own "publicity" than one's privacy that was being protected. Courts around the country became increasingly willing to intervene to prevent the unauthorized commercial appropriation of a person's name or likeness. This branch of privacy law became generally known as the tort of "appropriation," or alternatively, as an invasion of one's "right of publicity." In recent years the development of "privacy" and "publicity" rights by American courts has accelerated alongside the rejuvenation of the law of libel, and suits for invasion of rights to privacy and publicity have become additional vexations for the media.

In the last several years a large number of entertainers and sports figures have gone to court to try to prevent the unauthorized use of their names, pictures, and in a broader sense, their "identity." Cher, for example, successfully sued *Forum* magazine (a *Penthouse* subsidary) and *Star* magazine for printing an unauthorized interview. Johnny Carson successfully sued the makers of "Here's Johnny Portable Toilets" for using the famous *Tonight Show* phrase "Here's Johnny!" to sell toilets. The theory of a protected legal interest in the exploitation of one's name and likeness has been used by personalities as various as Jackie Onassis, Woody Allen, Jerry Falwell, Clint Eastwood, Mohammed Ali, Cary Grant, Jackie Collins, Joe Namath, and Elizabeth Taylor. In some instances the estates of deceased performers have even succeeded in protecting the privacy of public personalities after they are dead; courts have actually enjoined the professional mimicking of both Elvis Presley and Groucho Marx.

In many of these cases, the personality has not merely sought to prevent the unauthorized use of his or her name in connection with the sale of a product, but rather seems to have challenged the unauthorized use of their *identity* in a much broader sense, claiming, if you will, a sort of copyright on their own lives. Celebrities have gone to court to attempt to block unseemly or unwanted attention in dramatic works, gossip columns, and even news articles. Public personalities seem increasingly less willing to accept the notion that much of their activity is newsworthy and fair grist for news reportage, public discussion, critique, and satire. And in recent years some courts have been almost obsequiously protective of the famous, dead or alive.

In a New Jersey case, the estate of Elvis Presley attempted to ban a concert designed to imitate a performance of Elvis. A federal court in New Jersey upheld the suit against the concert. Although the court admitted that the Presley imitation concert did contain an "informational and entertainment element," the court nonetheless decided that "the show serves primarily to commercially exploit the likeness of Elvis Presley without contributing anything of commercial value to society." Well, sez who? Apparently *somebody* thought the Presley imitation was valuable, or they wouldn't have paid to see it. The court seemed to think that a federal judge interpreting the First Amendment ought to function as a rock and roll critic, for he decided that the performance lacked "its own creative component" and lacked "significant value as pure entertainment, sufficient to warrant First Amendment protection from the right-of publicity claim." Well once again, sez who? When an Elvis imitator does "Blue Suede Shoes" in an Elvis-like voice with Elvis-like movements of an Elvis-like pelvis, there's not supposed to be any new "creative component of its own" in the act, is there? The whole point of the act is to look and sound as much as possible like Elvis. The creative component is in the imitation. And obviously for a lot of Americans, the resurrection of Elvis through mimics is very important free expression. Who is a federal judge to disagree with those tastes and decide the mimic's act is not "creative"?

The issue in the Elvis case is closely related to the issue in the Jackie Onassis case; for although their constituencies do not completely overlap, they are both American deities. Can a hero of mythical proportions such as Elvis continue to have a monopoly on his face even after he is dead? No one doubts that any literary property that Elvis owned, such as movie rights and royalties or copyrights in songs, ought to be treated like any other piece of property, and fully descendable to Elvis's heirs. Part of the theory behind copyright laws is that creative expression deserves the added incentive of protected legal status extending beyond an author's own lifetime. If copyright expired with the death of the writer, people might not be sufficiently encouraged to spend their energies doing creative works. But to say that Elvis's heirs may continue to enforce copyrights in his songs is a far cry from saying that they may prevent Elvis imitators who have obtained licenses to use the songs from mimicking Elvis on stage.

The Elvis sound and the Elvis look should be thought of as part of the culture, a part of Elvis that is owned by everyone. Elvis may be more popular in death than in life, an American King Tut for whom millions of fans make periodic quasi-religious pilgrimages to Memphis. It is not exactly as if Elvis's decedents are going broke for want of record sales. The judge just gave the wrong answer to the question of whether there is a creative informational First Amendment value to Elvis Presley imitations—of course there is; to those who attend them they are fun, maybe even cathartic. The better question is whether there is any substantial social interest in banning Elvis imitations. Extending the monopoly on Elvis's life enjoyed by his legal heirs just does not seem very significant.

The Elvis imitation is less intrusive than Christian Dior's use of an imitation Jackie. First, the Elvis mimic is selling only entertainment—not some separate commercial product. Second, there is no potential for being misleading. Perhaps some people who saw the Diors wedding ad mistakenly thought that it was really Onassis, or assumed that even if it wasn't, Onassis endorsed the Dior designer label. But however mawkish and bleary eyed some in the audience might get when an Elvis imitator croons "Love Me Tender" into the microphone, certainly no one ever forgets that Elvis is dead. As Huck Finn said to Aunt Polly when he found out that the story of "Moses in the Bullrushers" involved someone who'd been gone "a considerable long" time: "I don't put no stock in dead people."

A federal judge in New York made a ruling similar to that in the Elvis case in a suit involving an imitation of Groucho Marx. Once again, the court was unwilling to accept the simple proposition that pure imitation may itself be great comedy, and that often the truer the reproduction of the original, the more entertaining. The case involved the Broadway show *A Day in Hollywood/A Night in the Ukraine*. The court "reviewed" the play, and decided, as in the Presley case, that the show did "not really have its own creative component." The court rejected the argument that the show was a parody of the Marx Brothers, stating that the show merely imitated the Marx Brothers' own parody and was not a "parody of their parody." The court commented that "although literary commentary may have been the intent of the playright, any such intent was substantially over-shadowed in the play itself by the wholesale appropriation of the Marx Brothers characters." Maybe the judge was right; maybe the judge should get a job as a critic for the *New Yorker*; but at least since the decision in *New York Times* in 1964, one would not have thought that a play's First Amendment protection could turn on how much a judge likes it—it was the play, not the trial, that was supposed to be set in the Ukraine. If Groucho is looking down somewhere on the judge's decision, I'll bet he's laughing. (The decision in the Groucho Marx case was partially overruled on appeal on unrelated legal grounds, so its precedential value, to the relief of satirists everywhere, is not completely clear.)

The development of these types of lawsuits was encouraged by a 1977 Supreme Court decision entitled *Zacchini v. Scripps-Howard Broadcasting Co.*, otherwise known as "the human cannonball case." The case involved the entertainment act of one Hugo Zacchini. Zacchini's act was pretty good stuff: he would climb into a cannon and get shot through the air two hundred feet into a net. Zacchini was doing his act at an Ohio fair, when a freelance reporter filmed the whole act, which takes about fifteen seconds from entry to blast-off to landing. Zacchini explicitly told the reporter not to film the stunt, but he did so anyway. An Ohio television

station was given the film, and it ran the fifteen-second clip the same evening, along with favorable commentary, on the eleven o'clock news. Zacchini sued the television station for violating his right of publicity, and the
United States Supreme Court sided with him, saying that even though Zacchini's act was not appropriated for advertising, the television station did
nonetheless broadcast Zacchini's entire act, permitting viewers to see for
free an act that Zacchini normally gets paid for.

On a lazy summer night in rural Ohio the sight of a guy named Zacchini
being shot two hundred feet from a cannon was pretty fair news, and the
local television station could certainly have reported Zacchini's feat on its
evening broadcast, with the appropriate accompanying banter between the
anchorwoman, sportscaster and weatherman. But that does not mean that
they had a right to show the whole performance on film—the First Amendment did not give them a right to in effect steal Zacchini's act. As good as
it is, it only takes fifteen seconds, and once you've seen it, even on television, the cat's more or less out of the bag. If people will watch football
games on television rather than pay for tickets and trek to the stadium,
they may just as well be happy enough with the television version of Hugo
Zacchini.

The Zacchini case makes perfect sense, because what the media appropriated in the name of "news" was a creative performance. But cases like
Onassis' suit against Christian Dior, or the suits by the estates of Elvis Presley and Groucho Marx, do not really involve the taking of creative effort,
or even the taking of a name or a likeness. Why should a society permit a
celebrity to bar others from borrowing from their identity through imitation and mimicry, the sincerest forms of flattery? In trying to sort out the
conflicts posed by those types of cases, it is useful to go back to a case of
some vintage, involving Cary Grant, in which a court came up with a subtle
and very persuasive analysis of the problem.

Back in 1946, *Esquire* ran an article about the clothing tastes and habits
of several Hollywood stars, including Cary Grant. The *Esquire* piece was
illustrated with posed pictures of the stars, which had been obtained with
their consent. The caption under Cary Grant's picture read:

> Hollywood Luminary Cary Grant—Cary Grant, always coming up with
> the unexpected in pictures (as witnessed by his roles in films from
> *Gunga Din* to *Notorious* with Ingrid Bergman), leans to conservative
> dress in his private life. Accordingly you see him in his favorite town
> suit of blue-striped unfinished worsted. The jacket, designed with
> slightly extended shoulders, has long rolled lapels which emphasize a
> trim waistline. The shirt, of off-white silk shantung, has a full collar.
> The black and white small-figured tie is typical of his taste in neckwear.
> He designs his own easygoing dress shirts, by the way. Made with a fly

front, they fasten informally with buttons. As a concession to usage, they have studs but the purely decorative devices go only through the flap of the shirt.

Having consented to and posed for the *Esquire* picture, Grant made no bones about the 1946 article.

Twenty-six years later, in 1971, *Esquire* decided to make use of Cary Grant's photograph a second time. In a 1971 issue the magazine republished the same picture of Grant, but with one modification: everything below the collar line had been replaced with the figure of a model clothed in a cardigan sweater-jacket. Under the picture was the following caption:

> To give a proper good riddance to the excesses of the Peacock Revolution we have tried a little trickery. And what better way to show the longevity of tradition than by taking the pictures of six modish men that appeared in *Esquire* in 1946 and garbing the ageless enchantment of these performers in the styles of the Seventies. Above, Cary Grant in a descendant of the classic cardigan, an Orlon double-knit navy, rust, and buff sweater-coat (Forum, $22.50).

Grant did not consent to the use of his photograph the second time, and he sued *Esquire*, under the same New York law that Onassis had invoked, which prohibits anyone from using a person's "name, portrait or picture" for "advertising purposes or for the purposes of trade" without first obtaining that person's written consent.

Esquire's defense to Grant's suit was that it had a right under the First Amendment to use Grant's picture. *Esquire's* reasoning was not frivolous. The original 1946 article was indeed "fashion news," containing information about Grant's habits and lifestyle that would be interesting and informative to *Esquire* readers. *Esquire* argued that the second article was no different. It was designed to make a point about fashion—deriding the "excesses of the Peacock Revolution." The superimposition of Grant's picture from 1946 on a "classic cardigan" from 1971 drove home *Esquire's* point about "the longevity of tradition."

New York federal Judge Whitman Knapp rejected *Esquire's* First Amendment argument, however, in a thoughtful opinon. Judge Knapp argued that there is a critical difference between the use of a person's photograph for its news value, and the use of the photograph for "advertising" or "purposes of trade." *Esquire's* use of Grant's picture was not truly an "advertisement," even though it did have the manufacturer, Forum, and the price, $22.50. But, Knapp reasoned, the photograph was used for "purposes of trade."

To make his point Knapp posed a hypothetical problem involving the English actress and model Leslie Hornby, known to most of us by her professional name "Twiggy." Twiggy has amassed a small fortune by exploiting the publicity of her name, looks, and reputation, and in the process she has become a public personality, and fair game for the media. If Twiggy were to appear at the opera in a Givenchy creation, she could not complain if her photograph appeared in the *New York Times*, the *National Enquirer*, or on *Entertainment Tonight* in connection with a story about the opera, about fashions, or about the life and times of Twiggy herself. It by no means follows, however, that publishers could present an apparently posed picture of Twiggy, and without her consent use it in competition with other pictures for which she had professionally posed, or in competition with (or in substitution for) the professionally posed pictures of other models. Similarly, no magazine could without her consent crop her head off a posed photograph and superimpose it on the torso of another model.

In all of these cases, Twiggy's picture would be used by the publisher or broadcaster to sell something. The difference between the examples is that in the first case what is being "sold" is the news itself. Twiggy, in the first example, *is* the news, and the news is "owned" by no one. The *New York Times*, the *National Enquirer*, or *Entertainment Tonight* may all freely take Twiggy's picture without her consent and use it in connection with bona fide stories. In doing so, they are all in a sense making money from Twiggy's fame, since all three enterprises are in business to make money selling various shadings of "news." But the law has always permitted this sort of "exploitation," because virtually all news is ultimately news about people, and to give individuals property rights in their news value as personalities would make a free press impossible. A free press is dependent on "free" news; those who make the news necessarily surrender part of themselves to the public domain.

Why then wouldn't Cary Grant's picture in *Esquire* be freely usable by the magazine under the First Amendment? The answer is that in the second instance Grant's face was no longer being utilized for its news value, but rather for its performance value. Grant was now being used in effect as a professional model, and was not being paid for it. In the second picture, Grant could not be "news," *because Grant had never worn the sweater—* it was pasted on an old photograph. It can't be news if it didn't happen. If *Esquire* *had* caught Grant strolling through Central Park on a fall day wearing an elegant cardigan it could have printed that photograph in connection with a story about the fashions of the day. But to dress Grant up as a model without his consent is really nothing more than an attempt to get Grant's professional services, as opposed to his newsworthiness, without paying the freight. The manufacturer, Forum, must have been delighted when *Esquire* chose to superimpose Grant's face on its sweater, for it would have cost Forum dearly to coax Grant into modeling for the cardigan (if indeed, Grant would ever have done it). If Forum had itself pasted Cary Grant's picture in its fashion line catalogues wearing Forum products no one would doubt that such a blatant appropriation of Grant's likeness for free advertising would be illegal. Although *Esquire's* situation is arguably different, because *Esquire* doesn't manufacture sweaters, the magazine still seems to have crossed the hazy line between that part of Cary Grant that is public property and that part that is the exclusive property of Cary Grant.

This line between one's news value and one's performance value is not always easy to draw. Take, for example, an incident involving the production of the movie *Woodstock*. An employee of a company that supplied portable latrines to the music fest was filmed going about his latrine-related tasks. The makers of the movie shot pictures of the employee while he was working on the latrines, and also drew him out in conversation about his job, producing some very good comic effects. The latrine scenes and the interview were memorable parts of the movie and were part of the loose documentary "we're all one big family and its far out" technique that made the movie both a popular and critical success. The employee sued the makers of *Woodstock*, however, claiming that he had been drawn out as a performer rather than merely photographed as a participant in a newsworthy event, and a federal court agreed with him, sending to movie producers and publishers the message that the First Amendment does not absolve them of the obligation to pay for their help.

Joe Namath, on the other hand, was unsuccessful in blocking *Sports Illustrated* from using his photograph in advertisements promoting *Sports Illustrated*. Namath's picture had appeared on the cover of the January 20, 1969 issue of *Sports Illustrated*, celebrating his role as the quarterback of the New York Jets in a dramatic Super Bowl victory over the Baltimore Colts the week before. In later advertising, *Sports Illustrated* followed the popular practice of displaying the covers of its own past issues, to attract attention to the sales solicitation. Although this subsequent use of Namath's picture was done sheerly for the magazine's own commercial gain, a New York court held that so long as the reproduction was utilized only to illustrate the quality and content of the periodical, the law did not prohibit its use, even without the consent of the person depicted.

Joe Namath was thus "hot news" after the 1969 Super Bowl, and *Sports Illustrated* could forever rewarm him in connection with its own advertising, on the theory that the replication of the prior content of the magazine was itself "news" in a limited sense, in that it informed would-be readers of the nature of the magazine. As a practical matter the legal "rule" that emerged from the Joe Namath case was eminently easy to apply—a magazine can reproduce its own past covers in advertising for itself, without paying the people that appear on them. In theory, however, the rationale of the Namath decision is teasingly elusive, for it seems clear that the second time around Namath's face was no longer being used for its own real news value, but for its value in selling *other* news—the stories in future issues—and that looks a lot like free advertising. This confusing legal picture has been further blurred by a number of recent cases, including the Jackie Onassis litigation, involving celebrities who have claimed rights in their personalities that go quite beyond the traditionally recognized bounds. At least three such cases have involved claims against the media even more aggressive than that of Jackie Onassis, brought by three other Americans at the very top of American celebritydom: Elizabeth Taylor, Clint Eastwood, and Mohammed Ali.

The most successful of these cases from the celebrity's perspective was Elizabeth Taylor's, for she managed to get the unwanted publicity about her stopped before it was even released. In 1982 the ABC network announced its intention to air an unauthorized biography of Elizabeth Taylor. The plan was to produce a "docudrama" about Taylor's life, along the lines of similar unauthorized docudramas about the likes of Jackie Onassis, Gloria Vanderbilt, Grace Kelly, Jean Harris, Prince Charles, and Lady Diana. A younger, thinner actress would play Taylor (rumors circulated that it would be Christina Ferrare, ex-wife of John DeLorean), as the story would wind through Taylor's successive loves for Conrad Hilton, Michael Wilding, Mike Todd, Eddie Fisher, Richard Burton, Richard Burton again, and John Warner. The formula, from ABC's perspective, was perfect prime time television. America's insatiable *People* magazine voyeurism could be exploited on a superstar personality whose "true story" would need no embellishment to be interesting.

The idea did not seem so wonderful to Elizabeth Taylor, however, and she took an extraordinarily aggressive step: she hired lawyers to sue ABC and the docudrama's production company in federal court in New York to stop production of the docudrama before it got off the ground. Taylor's lawyers had several strategies for blocking the program. The first was that the docudrama would by its very nature be a mixed bag of fact and fiction, and would inevitably, therefore, place Taylor in a false light in the public eye. It is important to understand precisely how aggressive this theory was. Taylor did not claim that the docudrama would misrepresent the underlying historical events of her life. As far as she knew, the historical events—this film role or that divorce—would be portrayed with perfect accuracy. The falseness in the television program would come, it was alleged, not from manipulation of the raw events in her life, but from the dramatic devices used to depict those events. An actress other than Elizabeth Taylor would flutter violet eyes at Eddie Fisher and declare eternal devotion to him. The actual words that that actress would utter, of course, would not truly be Taylor's, but would come from the screenwriter's imagination. Unless the honeymoon suite was bugged and surreptitiously video-taped, no one alive other than Taylor herself knows what happened on the night of her second wedding to Richard Burton. Whatever locked embraces, voice inflections, or raised eyebrows appeared on the ABC screen would be, in a literal sense, invented.

This observation by Taylor was, of course, absolutely correct. But it does not follow that Taylor should be able to ban the ABC production. For Taylor's claim boiled down to an objection to the form, rather than the substance, of the program. If Taylor's objection were valid, no fictionalized portrayal of a public figure's life would ever be permissible without the public figure's consent, since much of the dialogue and physical action necessary to bring the story to dramatic life would necessarily be fictional. This blend of drama and reality is what the "docudrama" is by definition, and Taylor's theory, taken to its logical conclusion, would destroy the unauthorized docudrama as a modern medium.

If ABC had embarked on a libelous misrepresentation of the underlying events in Taylor's life, her grounds for protest would be far more understandable. If the docudrama depicted her as cheating on husband John Warner three days after their wedding, and no such cheating had occurred, and Taylor could demonstrate that the screenwriter deliberately manufactured the incident to make the story more racy and outrageous, then she would have a straightforward case of libel. She would have been defamed by a bare-faced lie, and the fact that the ABC production was labeled a "docudrama" should not insulate ABC. ABC's purpose, in this situation, would have been reprehensible; they would be passing off their show as a truthful biography, when in fact much of the underlying reality was falsified.

But ABC did not propose anything so brazen; it proposed instead to produce a sort of pop biography. If the format were a book, such as the 1981 biography *Elizabeth Taylor, The Last Star*, by Kitty Kelly, then Taylor would have no legal grounds for objection, since the printed words would not include any invented dialogue or physical gestures. ABC could have purchased the rights to Kitty Kelly's book and hired an actor to read the book at a lectern in front of the camera. Such an exercise, of course, would be unimaginably boring—no matter how well-written Kelly's book; it would not be good television. And so the Taylor case illustrates one of the sharpest conflicts in modern media litigation: may the media dramatize real life events and people, even though the process inevitably involves manufacturing certain facts, or should the media be required to adhere strictly to the historical record, without invented dialogue, however boring such a presentation may be?

Like it or not, the docudrama is one of the stock ingredients of modern television, and to prevent dramatized depictions of events that are themselves true is to cut at the roots of an entire genre. On the other hand, perhaps the docudrama is a genre that deserves evisceration; after all, why should society place any value on this modern mixture of fact and fiction— why should the insatiable thirst of pop culture for slicked-up prime time portrayals of reality give producers of the docudrama a license to invent their own truth?

Those who produce docudramas would argue that the test should not be whether the dialogue is technically imaginary, but whether the gist of the dialogue is faithful to real events. If an actress playing Elizabeth Taylor says to an actor playing Eddie Fisher, "You've made me happier than I've ever been in my life, I want to grow old and gray with you," no harm is done, even if Taylor never spoke such words. For in the public record are Taylor's actual words to Fisher, spoken on May 12, 1959: "I have never been happier in my life . . . We will be on our honeymoon for thirty or forty years." Producers of docudramas would thus maintain that the legal system should not mess with trifles; as long as the underlying facts of Taylor's marriage to Fisher and professed feelings at the time are accurately captured, Taylor should have no grounds for complaint when fictional dialogue and facial expressions are invented to flesh out the biographical skeleton to meet the demands of the television format. If Taylor thinks the finished product is tawdry, cheap, and shoddy, then fine—she is entitled to her opinion, and she will have no trouble getting her opinion out in front of the public. The television critics might even agree with her. But as long as the docudrama is historically accurate, as long as it contains no real lies, the defenders of docudramas would argue that there is no strong social interest in granting Taylor veto power over portrayals of her life.

One problem with this defense of the docudrama is that it is reminiscent of the children's game "Telephone." Small liberties in each retelling of a story may lead to gross distortions. Some docudramas take giant steps away from fact, rather than the baby steps of making minor changes in actual dialogue. Nevertheless, if Taylor is permitted to veto such a depiction of her life, then society would in effect be granting her a monopoly on her own biography, at least for the purposes of the television docudrama format. The consequence would be to turn a chunk of cultural history into Taylor's private property. And that, in fact, was exactly what Taylor's lawyers argued in the second prong of their complaint against ABC: that Taylor's life story is not part of the public domain, but rather is a piece of private property that she alone owns, and that she alone may financially exploit. Again, Taylor's theory was bold, and went well beyond traditional notions of private property. Certainly Taylor does have a "property right" in her face or name that prohibits others from appropriating it to sell lingerie or designer jeans. An advertiser could not place a picture of Taylor in an ad with the statement "Use Revel Cologne, I do." Taylor has a right to sell her endorsement to the highest bidder. To take her endorsement without paying for it is to steal her valuable property. Similarly, in a sense Taylor has a property right in her own life story, in that she alone can bestow upon it the hallowed status of "authorized biography." For Kitty Kelley or ABC to pass off these biographies as having Taylor's official imprimatur when in fact they did not would be a fraudulent taking of Taylor's property—the stamp of approval that is hers alone to give.

But it is quite another thing entirely to say that because a celebrity might well profit from selling "my own story," no one else enterprising enough to put the story together may tell it. The basic details of Elizabeth Taylor's life are in the public domain; they are part of history, to be freely picked up and reproduced by anyone. Taylor has, after all, profited immensely from the glittering persona that the media has helped create. Her life story has monetary value not only on the strength of performances in *National Velvet, Cat on a Hot Tin Roof,* or *Who's Afraid of Virginia Woolf?*; her celebrity status is rather every bit as much the product of a highly public private lifestyle. Having profited from the doting curiosity of many Americans for all things glamourous, Taylor must accept the fact that her life has ceased to be exclusively her own. There is, after all, some inherent tension between Taylor's claim, on the one hand, that the docudrama invades her privacy by depicting the "private" events of her life, and the claim, on the other hand, that it appropriates her property by diminishing her own right to sell those secrets. No "secrets," in fact, are really involved; no one pilfered her diary; no one was hidden beneath the hotel suite bed. Taylor's life has largely been an open book, and no one, not even Taylor, has the exclusive copyright. ABC, under pressure, dropped the program.

In its April 13, 1982 edition, the *National Enquirer* ran a picture of Clint Eastwood on its cover, with the caption "Clint Eastwood in Love Triangle with Tanya Tucker." On page 48 of the *Enquirer,* there appeared a 600-word article about Eastwood, headlined "Clint Eastwood in Love Triangle." The article claimed that Eastwood was romantically involved with singer Tanya Tucker and actress Sandra Locke. The article stated that Eastwood loved Tucker, that he was "swept off his feet" and "smitten" by her, that she "made his head spin," "that she used her charms to get what she wanted from Eastwood," and that Eastwood daydreamed about their "enchanted evenings" together. The *Enquirer* reported that Eastwood and

Tucker were constantly seen in public together; that they publicly kissed, hugged, gazed at each other romantically, and "cuddled." To complete the alleged triangle, the article reported that in February 1982 there were serious problems in the romantic relationship between Eastwood and Sandra Locke, that they had had a huge argument over marriage, and that Locke had stormed out on him. Locke and Tucker, the *Enquirer* claimed, were involved in a romantic tug-of-war over Eastwood, and Eastwood was torn between them. At one point, claimed the *Enquirer*, Locke camped on Eastwood's doorstep and on her hands and knees begged Eastwood to "keep her," vowing she wouldn't pressure him into marriage. But Eastwood, the *Enquirer* claimed, acted oblivious to her pleas.

Eastwood sued the *Enquirer*, claiming that the article was false, and that it had been published by the *Enquirer* willfully and maliciously to disgrace him. In addition to his libel claim, however, Eastwood added a bold new theory of recovery. The *Enquirer*, Eastwood claimed, had violated his "right of publicity" by using his name and photograph on the cover of its issue without Eastwood's permission. This commercial exploitation of Eastwood's name and likeness, Eastwood further maintained, was compounded by telecast advertising of the issue, featuring Eastwood's name and photograph, and prominently mentioning the article about him.

In a groundbreaking decision, a California appellate court ruled that Eastwood's right of publicity theory against the *Enquirer* was valid. Eastwood's very picture on the front of the *Enquirer*, the court wrote, could be a commercial appropriation of Eastwood's right of publicity, *if* the underlying story about Eastwood were knowingly or recklessly false. If the story were false and that falsehood were calculated or reckless, the court reasoned, then the *Enquirer* could no longer claim the defense that the picture was used in connection with news—for if the information was false it was not actually news. The Eastwood decision was a radical break with the past, for it turned the issue of commercial appropriation into an inquiry into the bona fides of the underlying news story, as opposed to the manifest character of the article. It was not whether the *Enquirer* thought it was publishing real news, but whether it turned out to be real news in the end, that would determine if it could put Clint Eastwood's picture on its cover.

If there is any American (other than a president of the United States) in this century that truly qualifies as a "world class" public figure, it is Mohammed Ali. If ever an American lived who embodied the reason for the First Amendment, it is Mohammed Ali. Ali was indeed the greatest. The greatest known of any heavyweight champion of the world; the greatest known American athlete of the century; the greatest American symbol of his time: a courageous, proud, defiant, outspoken, deeply committed

black man, who stood up against the stultifying artificial mores of the ath-
letic world, against the subjugation of blacks, against the war in Vietnam.
At the height of his career, in everything he did, Ali *was* free expression.
Of all American figures to strike out against the press in recent years, none
presents a greater paradox in his resort to litigation against the media than
Mohammed Ali.

The story pits Ali against an improbable opponent, *Playgirl* magazine.
In its February 1978 issue, *Playgirl* ran a segment that included an illustration of a nude black man seated in the corner of a boxing ring. The
artistic illustration (it was not a photograph) was captioned "Mystery
Man," and was accompanied by a verse that referred to the illustrated figure as "The Greatest." Ali sued *Playgirl* in New York, claiming that the
nude portrait would be understood by readers as portraying Ali, and that
the magazine had therefore used his "portrait or picture" without his permission, in violation of New York law (the same New York law that was
successfully used by Jackie Onassis, Cary Grant and Elizabeth Taylor).

In one of the most extraordinary rulings ever in the media law area, a
federal judge in New York ruled in favor of Ali, and actually enjoined all
sale and distribution of the February 1978 issue of *Playgirl*, physically
impounding all extant copies. This amazingly drastic remedy—the physical
confiscation of the offending magazine issues —is all the more remarkable
because *Playgirl* neither used Ali's name, nor his picture. *Playgirl* simply
used an Ali-like character as the basis for a drawing of a nude heavyweight
boxer as a vehicle for some lightweight verse involving a sexual fantasy.

The judge was absolutely sure, however, that the man in the *Playgirl*
fantasy drawing was really Ali:

> Even a cursory inspection of the picture which is the subject of this
> action strongly suggests that the facial charateristics of the black boxer
> portrayed are those of Mohammed Ali. The cheekbones, broad nose,
> and wide set eyes, together with the distinctive smile and close cropped
> black hair are recognizable as the·features of the plaintiff, one of the
> most widely known athletes of our time. In addition, the figure
> depicted is seated on a stool in the corner of a boxing ring with both
> hands taped and outstretched resting on the ropes on either side.

As far as the verse accompanying the drawing, the judge dismissed it as "a
plainly fictional and allegedly libelous bit of doggerel."

The *Ali v. Playgirl* case is a legal and cultural puzzle on several levels.
Ali's portrait was not appropriated by *Playgirl* to sell a product. Unlike the
Onassis case, Ali's likeness was not being used to sell aftershave, razor
blades, beer, or gym shoes. Yet the judge almost cavalierly decided that
indeed Ali's portrait "was clearly included in the magazine solely for the
purposes of trade—e.g., merely to attract attention." But how can it be

that the portrait loses its First Amendment protection merely because its purpose is "to attract attention." No photograph or drawing in any publication is included to repulse attention. All expression tries to attract attention. The likeness of *Time* magazine's "Man of the Year" on its cover is there to attract attention, and to sell issues of *Time*. The judge cited as legal support for his proposition the case involving Cary Grant against *Esquire*. In the Grant case, however, Gary Grant's *actual picture* had been used without his permission to call attention to a particular manufacturer's sweater, along with the sweater's price. The appropriation was "for the purposes of trade" in the most basic sense of the phrase, promoting a commerical sales transaction.

Playgirl was using Ali's likeness for a fundamentally different purpose: as part of the actual content of its magazine. If what *Playgirl* did was illegal, then one has to ask how it would be any different for *Time* magazine to place Ali on its cover as "Man of the Year" without Ali's permission, or for *Sports Illustrated*, without Ali's permission, to place Ali on its cover.

Until the recent surge of litigation against the media, it seemed fairly clear that *Time* or *Sports Illustrated* or the *National Enquirer* or *Playgirl* could put just about anyone on the cover they wanted, without getting the permission of or paying the person depicted. The portrait was considered part and parcel of reporting the news. "News," in this sense, was thought of as broad enough to encompass more than politics, and more than the speech preferences of sophisticates and elites—it included information on sports, art, leisure, and entertainment of all kinds from all levels of society. Those who become famous, it was thought, had no right to prevent others from writing about them, and as part of that coverage, there could be pictures. With litigation such as the Onassis, Taylor, Eastwood and Ali cases, however, this freedom appears to be eroding.[79] If Clint Eastwood and Mohammed Ali won't let these frivolous and petty impositions roll over their skins like water off a duck's back, who will? Tough guys don't dance; but they do sue.

7

From *Touching* to *Missing*:
Libel Arising from Fiction and Docudrama

As in the case of Mr. Forsyth's first novel, *The Day of the Jackal*, many characters in *The Odessa File* are real people. Some will be immediately recognized by the reader; others may puzzle the reader as to whether they are true or fictional, and the publishers do not wish to elucidate further because it is in this ability to perplex the reader as to how much is true and how much false that much of the grip of the story lies.

From the "Publisher's Note" to Frederick Forsyth's novel
The Odessa File

I have allowed myself, as to such points, nearly or altogether as much license as if the facts had been entirely of my own invention. What I contest for is the authenticity of the outline.

Nathaniel Hawthorne, *The Scarlet Letter*

W AS THE CHARACTER played by Orson Welles in *Citizen Kane* really William Randolph Hearst? Was Governor Willie Stark in Robert Penn Warren's *All the King's Men* really Governor Huey Long? When Father Andrew Greeley wrote *The Cardinal Sins*, did he have in mind John Cardinal Cody? American writers and filmmakers have always used real people and events, in greater or lesser disguise, as the raw material for their creative works. Art exists to explore, interpret, and expand reality, and many artists draw on real people in their efforts. Some characters in novels, plays, and movies are composites of several real people's traits, but as characters they have lives completely their own. But at times it suits the artist's purpose to draw on reality more directly, to copy characters in total, with little or no disguise. Henry James was once accused of having created his character Miss Birdseye in *The Bostonians* as a vicious caricature of Nathaniel Hawthorne's sister-in-law, Miss Peabody. In a nicely twisted reply, James remarked that the character Miss Birdseye was drawn "entirely from my moral consciousness, *like every other person I have ever known*" [emphasis added].

Fiction is, on a literal level, "knowing falsehood." Someone like Frederick Forsyth in *The Odessa File* can afford to openly flaunt his intertwining of fact and fiction. Forsyth's book was about Nazi war criminals plotting their revenge and reincarnation. Forsyth can libel Nazis to his heart's content, for what Nazi war criminal is going to come out of hiding to sue him? But for most authors and movie-makers today the threat of suit is much more worrisome. In an *Alice in Wonderland* sort of trial, your own fictional characters can turn on you!

Although quite a number of fictional works drawn heavily from real people and events have triggered lawsuits for invasion of privacy or libel, two recent cases are particularly revealing. The first involves the racy subject of a novel about "nude encounter therapy" in Southern California; the second involves the movie *Missing*, which portrayed the murder of an American photographer during the overthrow of Salvador Allende Gossens in Chile in 1973. The two cases highlight in different ways the inadequacy of the law's current treatment of the problem of libel arising from fiction, and the dangers that litigation over fictional works may pose to both political and artistic expression.

Gwen Davis Mitchell, a successful novelist, set out to write a novel about women of the leisure class. She decided to attend a distinctly Californian variety of leisure class activity, a "nude marathon encounter group therapy session." Mitchell approached Paul Bindrim, Ph.D., a licensed clinical psychologist, who held what Bindrim described as "nude marathon" group therapy sessions to help patients shed psychological inhibitions. Mitchell attempted to register for a nude therapy session, but was told that she could not do so if she was enrolling to gather material for a novel. Mitchell assured Bindrim that she had no intention of writing about the nude marathon sessions and that her only purpose was personal therapy. Bindrim showed Mitchell a paragraph in the contractual consent form which she would be required to sign, which stated:

> The participant agrees that he will not take photographs, write articles, or in any manner disclose who has attended the workshop or what has transpired. If he fails to do so he releases all parties from this contract, but remains legally liable for damages sustained by the leaders and participants.

Mitchell again emphasized that she would not write about the session; she paid her fee and the next day signed the contract and attended Bindrim's nude marathon therapy session.

Two months later Mitchell entered into a book contract with the Doubleday publishing company, under which she would receive a $150,000 advance for a novel, to be entitled *Touching*. The novel would depict a nude encounter marathon session in Southern California led by a fictitious therapist named "Dr. Simon Herford, M.D." Mitchell told an executive at Doubleday that she had attended a nude encounter marathon session, and that it was "quite a psychological jolt." Mitchell was cautioned by Doubleday that the characters in *Touching* would have to be totally fictitious, and Mitchell assured the publisher that none of the characters in the novel were capable of being identified as real persons. Doubleday had an editor knowledgeable in the field of libel go over the manuscript.

The hardbound edition of *Touching* was published, and Paul Bindrim quickly asserted that the novel was in fact a libelous portrait of himself. His lawyers sent protests to both Mitchell and Doubleday; nonetheless, nine months later a New American Library edition was published in paperback. Bindrim sued Mitchell and Doubleday for libel and won a $75,000 jury award, which was affirmed on appeal.

The first-person narrator in the novel *Touching* is herself a writer. Early in the book she explains her intention to attend a nude marathon session: "Naturally I intended to protect my journalistic flank—not revealing their names, of course, that would be dishonest and opening the magazine to threats of libel. But if anything occurred that was actually outrageous I fully intended to report it as such and not use Herford's name." This is a fascinating passage—an ironic fictional confession, in which the real writer Gwen Mitchell unveils the *modus operandi* of her fictional narrator, a *modus operandi* that a California jury would later ascribe to Mitchell herself.

Bindrim's suit complained that Mitchell's entire book was libelous, but he zeroed in on a number of segments that he found specifically offensive, placing particularly strong emphasis on a passage in the book describing the therapist's attempt to persuade a minister to get his wife to attend a nude therapy session.[80] Bindrim had tape recordings of his actual therapy sessions, and during the trial the jury was required to compare the offending passage in the book with the tape-recording of the actual session. A comparison of the two illustrates exactly what a suit like Bindrim's is all about. The following two excerpts were introduced side-by-side as evidence at the trial:

Transcript of Dr. Bindrim's Actual Session	*Excerpts from "Touching"*
"I've come a little way,"	
"I'd like to know about your wife. She hasn't been to a marathon?"	The minister was telling us how the experience had gotten him further back to God,
"No."	

"Isn't interested? Has no need?"

"I don't—she did finally say that she would like to go to a standard sensitivity training session somewhere. She would be—I can't imagine her in a nude marathon. She can't imagine it."

"Why?"

"Neither could I when I first came."

"Yeh. She might. I don't know."

"It certainly would be a good idea for two reasons: one, the minor one is that you are involved here, and if she were in the same thing, and you could come to some of the couple ones, it would be helpful to you. But more than that, almost a definite recipe for breaking up a marriage is for one person to go into growth groups and sense change and grow . . ."

"Boy they sure don't want that, and once they're clear they don't need that mate anymore, and they are not very patient."

"But it is true, the more I get open the more the walls are built between us. And it's becoming a fairly intelligent place, a fairly open place, doing moderate sensitivity eyeballing stuff with the kids. I use some of these techniques teaching out class work."

"Becoming more involved?"

"Yeh, involved at the same time that I am more separated from. It's a paradox again, isn't it?"

"Mmm."

And all the time he was getting closer to God, he was being moved further away from his wife, who didn't understand, she didn't realize what was coming out of the sensitivity training sessions he was conducting in the church.

He felt, he, more than felt, he knew, that if she didn't begin coming to the nude marathons and try to grasp what it was all about, the marriage would be over.

"You better bring her to the next marathon," Simon said.

"I've been trying," said the minister. "I only pray she comes."

"You better do better than pray," said Simon. "You better grab her by the cunt and drag her here."

"I can only try."

"You can do more than try, Alex. You can grab her by the cunt."

"A man with that kind of power, whether it comes from God or from his own manly strength, strength he doesn't know he has, can drag his wife here by the fucking cunt."

"I know," Alex said softly. "I know."

Bindrim argued that the passage in the novel involving the minister's wife made him appear vulgar, coarse and domineering, whereas, in the actual session, Bindrim appears to be polite and sensitive in attempting to persuade the minister, and he never resorts to vulgarity.

Bindrim also complained about an incident in the novel in which a patient becomes so distressed after a weekend nude encounter session that as she drives away she crashes her car and is killed, an incident that he claimed had never taken place. Bindrim similarly took offense to passages in the book in which the fictitious Dr. Herford is depicted as "clutching," "ripping," and "pressing" a patient's checks, and "stabbing against a pubic bone," and a statement in the novel in which Hereford cuts off a female patient with the words, "Drop it, bitch."

Gwen Mitchell's character Dr. Herford was in fact created with a number of marked dissimilarities to the real Paul Bindrim. Herford was an M.D., Bindrim a Ph.D.; Herford was a "fat Santa Claus type with long white hair, white sideburns, a cherubic rosy face and furry forearms," Bindrim was clean shaven and had short hair.

The driving incident in Mitchell's book was not manufactured out of whole cloth. The actual tape recordings of Bindrim's sessions reveal that he had worried about his patients driving immediately after the nude therapy sessions. He would admonish his departing patients, saying "you're turned on, that is you're about as turned on as if you've had 50 or 75 gammas of LSD. That's the estimate of what the degree of the turn on is. And it doesn't feel that way, because you've been getting higher a little bit at a time. So don't wait to find out, take my word for it, and drive like you've had three or four martinis. Drive cautiously." Apparently, however, no one actually crashed a car and was killed as a result of a therapy session.

Mitchell also tried to demonstrate that the sexual innuendos in the novel were not completely fantasy. At trial Mitchell's attorneys tried to introduce evidence alleging that Bindrim had had sexual intercourse with a patient from a nude marathon session. The court prohibited the introduction of this evidence, however, reasoning that the allegation against Bindrim was legally irrelevant, since such alleged sexual conduct was not the basis of his suit.

Mitchell's argument would thus be that most of what was portrayed in *Touching* that Bindrim found offensive involved fictitious incidents that everyone admitted never actually took place, which was precisely what made the book "fictional" in the first place. Gwen Mitchell was not trying to write a documentary. Bindrim's attorneys in effect managed to resurrect the clever technique that had supposedly been discredited in *New York Times v. Sullivan*. Contrary to superficial appearances, they convinced the jury that the statements in the novel referred to Bindrim. They then demonstrated that those *same* statements ascribed to Bindrim actions and words that were not his own. Anything in the novel that resembled Bindrim was thus used to prove that the book was actually about him, while anything in the novel that did not resemble him was used to prove that Mitchell's portrayal was a lie. If you can get a court to buy this technique, it is a wonderful way to manufacture a libel verdict against a fiction writer, for once having gotten your foot in the door by demonstrating some resemblance to the fictional character, you then turn around and reap the litigation benefits of all the things the writer did to make the fictional character behave differently from you. Those differences then become the very "lies" you ride to victory. This is nice work if you can get it.

On the other hand, weren't Bindrim's lawyers giving to author Mitchell precisely the treatment that her fictional technique asked for? If, as seems obvious, her novel was in fact essentially based on the real Dr. Bindrim, why should Mitchell be permitted to portray him as vulgar, and as making sexual advances on patients. Should Mitchell be insulated from the normal rules that govern the law of libel simply by making a few cosmetic changes in her character's identity and labeling the book a "novel?"

The problem is more difficult than it seems, for the usual terminology of the law of libel tends to break down when applied to fictional works. The normal legal vocabulary, which speaks of "knowing falsehood," is difficult to apply to a genre in which all is false on one level, in pursuit of truth on other levels.

From Dr. Bindrim's perspective, however, the novel *Touching* is false on two levels. It is false in the literal sense that all novels are false—it is an artistic creation that does not purport to represent any specific reality. What is perhaps the fault in *Touching*, however, is that the novel is *not as false* as the reader was led to believe: in basing her therapist character too closely on the real Dr. Bindrim, Mitchell was false to the reader by not being false enough. Bindrim might thus argue that it is perfectly legitimate for the law of libel to restrain the artistic license of the novelist. The novelist has two choices: either borrow very blatantly from a real person's identity *and* portray that character without significant embellishment (*i.e.*, do not turn the character into someone vulgar or promiscuous), or, borrow only suggestively and modestly from a real person and create a "composite" character that is not reasonably identifiable as an actual person.

To substantiate his claim that the fictional Dr. Herford was in fact him, Bindrim relied on his own testimony and on the testimony of only three witnesses, all of whom had either participated in or observed one of Bindrim's nude therapy sessions. The *only* characteristic of the fictional Dr. Herford that these witnesses claimed identified the character as a disguised Paul Bindrim was the use of nude marathon encounter therapy itself. (This, apparently, included resemblances in techniques and incidents such as the sensationalized conversation with the minister.) There was testimony that about a dozen psychologists were using nude marathon therapy techniques when the novel *Touching* was published (oh, Southern California!). Only those few witnesses who knew Bindrim and had been to his sessions, however, testified and identified the fictional character with Bindrim. One witness, for example, stated that he had attended the same nude marathon as Mitchell and only read *Touching* after being told by Bindrim of the alleged identification and the lawsuit. He looked upon *Touching* as "semi-fictional" and testified that one would have to know Bindrim to recognize him in the book.

The fact that the only people who recognized Herford as Bindrim were people who had actually been to Bindrim's marathon sessions raises another puzzle about the $75,000 victory for Bindrim in the suit: how badly could Bindrim's reputation truly be hurt when the only people who knew the book was about him also knew what his sessions were really like? The only people who knew enough to make the novel potentially damaging to Bindrim also knew enough not to believe what they read—they were, arguably, completely able to separate fact from fiction. The patient who was present when the real Paul Bindrim tried to persuade the minister at the therapy session to bring his wife along the next time knew full well that Bindrim had never told the minister to "grab her by the cunt and drag here here," the vulgar language upon which Bindrim largely based his suit. From Mitchell's viewpoint, the bizarre logic of Bindrim's case is that he allegedly suffered thousands of dollars worth of lost reputation in the minds of patients who were present when the language he did not use was not spoken.

Once again, however, Dr. Bindrim's case is not wholly unsympathetic, for again the problem is that his real identity was in fact close enough to the fictional character that even patients who knew Bindrim from their own sessions might begin to have doubts about his behavior with *other* patients. Might not a patient who had attended a "clean" session with Bindrim nonetheless worry about suggestions that in other sessions the doctor had used vulgar language with a minister, or pressed up against the pubic bone of a woman patient. Dr. Bindrim might reasonably argue that these hints of impropriety, even if never confirmed in a patient's actual experience with him, might nonetheless make his clients insecure and suspicious.

This sort of insecurity would be plausible, however, only if Dr. Bindrim's patients believed that Gwen Davis Mitchell was portraying actual incidents, or facets of Dr. Bindrim's character. If they instead believed that Mitchell had used Bindrim as a prototype, but then had embellished the character for dramatic reasons, never intending to actually reflect on Bindrim, then they would logically think no less of Bindrim, since they would realize that Mitchell was not in fact communicating that her fictional therapist's evil charactistics were shared by the real Dr. Bindrim. All of this comes back to the problem of how to make intelligent use of the words "truth" and "falsity" in the context of a libel suit arising from a fictional work. There may actually be multiples of truth and falsity that shift with the perspectives of the viewer: there is writer's truth and writer's falsity, reader's truth and reader's falsity, and the law's truth and the law's falsity.

The tendency of the law is to apply its own relatively simple formula for when a fiction writer has acted with knowledge of falsity or reckless disregard for the truth. The California court's logic on this point in the *Bin-*

drim case is illustrative. The court first concluded that reasonable readers would identify Herford as Bindrim. Since everybody conceded that Gwen Mitchell "intentionally" made up actions and words for the fictional character Herford, it followed inexorably that Mitchell wrote with "knowledge of falsity."

The common-sense appeal of this approach, however, probably fails to track either the average fiction writer's or the average fiction reader's understanding of what "truth" and "falsity" in fiction mean. To say that fiction writers all write with "knowledge of falsity," to say that what all fiction writers do is lie for a living, is to us the word "lie" in a simplistic, literal sense that ignores the conventions with which writers write and readers read. Authors "make up stories," in order to communicate truth on other levels. As John Irving conveyed the point in *The World According to Garp*, to create is not to lie for a living; one might as well say that Picasso's or El Greco's distortions of human form are lies.

Mitchell's argument would be that the "truth" in *Touching* was in her evaluation of the theraputic validity of nude encounter therapy. She painted a devastating portrait because she wanted to indict what she apparently thought was a worthless and perhaps dangerous form of faddish Southern Californian psychic distraction. Seen from this perspective, Mitchell was punished because she portrayed the whole enterprise of nude marathon encounter therapy in a highly unflattering light. Paul Bindrim, quite understandably, didn't like it—but so what?

No medical professional, from heart surgeon to psychologist, is promised in our society that his or her professional techniques will be immune from attack as quackish, freakish, or worthless. Experimental techniques, whether they be the transplanting of a baboon's heart into the body of an infant, or the group disrobing of patients for marathon therapy, can expect and must accept criticism, criticism that will often be vitriolic, hyperbolic, and irreverent.

Having said all this, however, it does not necessarily follow that Gwen Davis Mitchell deserved to be let off the hook for what she did in *Touching*. Dr. Bindrim might forcefully protest that Mitchell in effect "cheated" in the exercise of her constitutional right to criticize his techniques, by choosing to package as fiction what in substance was intended by the author and understood by readers to be factual reportage. Bindrim attempted to close his sessions to exposure and investigation through the device of the contract he made Mitchell sign, promising she would not write about the sessions. Perhaps the key to the Bindrim case is the possibility that Mitchell chose to use the form of a novel in an attempt to circumvent the contract she had signed.

Had Mitchell decided to simply write a nonfiction book, without embellishment, portraying exactly what the sessions had been like, she would have been immune from suit for libel. Having disclosed all facts accurately, she could then have added whatever personal opinions she had concerning the efficacy or dangers of Bindrim's techniques. But Dr. Bindrim may quite legitimately complain that although he is admittedly fair game for critiques of nude marathon encounter therapy in scholarly professional journals, or nonfiction books by authors such as Mitchell, he certainly is not fair game for being erroneously depicted as using words like "fuck" and "cunt" in sessions with patients.

If Bindrim had written a straight work of nonfiction she would be free of worry about libel but would still have the problem of the contract she signed. Bindrim could sue Mitchell for breach of that contract. In such a scenario, however, it is not necessarily clear that Bindrim would win, for a court might take the position that contractual provisions that attempt to prevent public disclosure of and discussion concerning professional techniques are not enforceable, being "void as against public policy." Although it is rare for a court to strike down a contractual provision on such grounds, very powerful arguments can be marshalled against such provisions when the alternative is to permit fraud or quackery to go undetected. A court might well enforce such a contractual provision in order to protect a professional's legitimate trade secrets, or to protect the privacy of patients (requiring, for example, that names be changed or deleted). But many courts would be reluctant to enforce a wholesale ban on *any* discussion of the techniques of professionals such as doctors, lawyers, or even ministers.

When Mitchell decided to use a fictional format, and to significantly embellish reality, however, she took a gamble with the law of libel. If she had written the novel in a way that identified Bindrim such that readers *who had never been to one of Bindrim's sessions* nonetheless understood the fictional character as Bindrim, and if she intentionally falsified reality by portraying Bindrim using obscene and vulgar language, then Bindrim should have a right to recover damages against her for libel. Mitchell in this case would have gone beyond the expression of negative opinions about the therapy, and into conscious misstatement of fact.

What is worrisome about the result of *Bindrim v. Mitchell*, however, is that although Mitchell came perilously close to the line, the evidence in the case seemed to demonstrate that according to the *average reader's* understanding of truth and falsity, Mitchell did not libel Dr. Bindrim. The evidence in the case was that readers who had never been to Bindrim's sessions would not be able to identify the book as depicting Bindrim. The only people at the trial who were to make the nexus between the fictional

Herford and the real Bindrim already knew what kind of language Bindrim used; for those critical persons (the only persons to whom the book was communicating about *Bindrim*, as opposed to about nude therapy in a *generic* sense), damaging factual misstatements were possible only if they truly believed that Mitchell knew more about the real Dr. Bindrim than the patients knew—and the evidence indicated that in this case that was not so—that instead, as one of the key witnesses testified, the work was understood to be "semi-fictional."

If this interpretation is accurate, it means that the real sting of the novel *Touching* was not a sting that attached to Bindrim personally, but a sting that attached to the whole notion of nude marathon encounter therapy. In that sense, Mitchell probably deserved to win the suit. On the other hand, one is left with a nagging sense that Mitchell treated Bindrim unfairly by not disguising him enough, and if the evidence in the case had more convincingly demonstrated that those who recognized Bindrim did think less of him because of the novel, Bindrim's victory would be justified. Mitchell went to Bindrim's therapy session, drew conclusions about the value of what she saw, and transformed those conclusions into a novel. That is exactly what we expect and want from writers, but not through the device of gratuitous distortions that injure the reputations of real people.

What is so deeply disturbing about this case is the sense one gets from the California court's decision that novels drawn from real people and events are somehow bad *per se*, as if in some sense Dr. Paul Bindrim has a right to control the flow of information about a medical technique that he (and others) practice. Maybe the nude marathon is the greatest therapeutic development since Freud; maybe it is a worthless sham; maybe it is different things to different people. Perhaps Mitchell "did a job" on nude encounter therapy, and perhaps nude encounter therapists don't much like it. But in an open society—a society open enough to tolerate nude marathon therapy as a plausible professional palliative for overly inhibited psyches—one would have thought that such therapy would be fair game for fictionalized critique. No therapist is granted a monopoly on public opinion about nude therapy. The issue of the worth or worthlessness of nude marathon therapy should be no one's private property. If Bindrim is going to try to coax the minister to bring his wife along to disrobe, there's just going to be some public comment on the practice, and Bindrim should expect that his techniques will be within the public domain, to be trod upon through satire, parody, and ridicule by his detractors and praised by his admirers.

If authors such as Mitchell wish to engage in such commentary, however, they must also recognize that the law of libel does not and should not magically cease to operate just because a work is labeled "fiction." If Mitchell had written a nonfiction account of Bindrim's sessions without any attempt at disguise, she certainly could not have thrown in false episodes of vulgarity just to spice up the book. The lesson of *Bindrim v. Mitchell* is that the rules do not suddenly change when the work is fiction. If the writer chooses not to disguise the character, then the writer must either not embellish, or somehow make it clear to the reader that the character's behavior should not be attributed to the real person—a task that may be almost impossible if the resemblances are too strong. The writer's other option is to genuinely create characters that are not reasonably identifiable as actual persons, but that nonetheless communicate the truths about reality that the writer hopes to reveal. We all know that the character Willie Stark in *All the King's Men* was suggested by the real Huey Long, but we also know that Willie Stark is a powerful creation of Robert Penn Warren's imagination, and that his great novel is not to be taken as a Huey Long biography.

The Bindrim case drew substantial criticism from the publishing industry and from many legal commentators.[81] Perhaps it was most frightening to fiction writers, however, for it seemed to challenge the writer who draws heavily from real facts to attempt to portray truth through either perfect accuracy or perfect creation; the imperfect middle ground, where most writers tread most of the time, will require the use of substantial disguise.

If these problems plague fiction writers, they can be even trickier in visual formats, and one of the most interesting examples is the litigation surrounding the blockbuster movie *Missing*.[82]

Charles Horman was a freelance writer and documentary film maker. In 1972, to observe firsthand the development of the new socialist regime of Chilean President Salvador Allende Gossens, the thirty-year-old Horman moved to Santiago with his wife, Joyce. Horman was visiting the seaside resort of Vina del Mar on September 11, 1973, with another American friend, Terry Simon, when Salvador Allende was overthrown by a military coup d'état. (Allende's bullet-ridden body was found the day after the military takeover.) According to the journal Horman was keeping at the time, Horman and Simon spoke to several United States military officers in Vina del Mar, who hinted that the coup had been planned there and that the United States had been involved in it. Horman and Simon quickly returned to Santiago. Two days later, Horman mysteriously disappeared. Neighbors of Horman's in Santiago gave accounts (some of the details conflicting) of Horman having been arrested by Chilean plainclothesmen.

On October 5, 1973, a little over two weeks after the disappearance, Charles' father, Edmund Horman, a New York industrial designer, flew to

Chile to assist in the search for his son. According to Edmund Horman, the American embassy thwarted his investigation to the point that he ultimately came to believe that embassy personnel were involved in his son's disappearance, probably because his son had accidently stumbled across evidence of the United States' complicity in the overthrow of Salvador Allende. Five weeks after the coup, a body identified by finger prints as that of Charles Horman was found in a Santiago city cemetery. According to the government of Chile, Horman was found dead on a Santiago street and taken to a morgue on September 18, 1973.

Edmund Horman spent the years after his son's death attempting to build a case against eleven American government officials, including Henry Kissinger, for the wrongful death of his son. He filed suit in October of 1977 against Kissinger and the other officials allegedly involved. Most of the counts were dismissed on procedural grounds, and Horman eventually dropped the entire suit, largely because he was unable to obtain the release of classified documents he believed were critical to his case. Horman insisted that "if the real story ever came out, its implications would be as serious as Watergate's."

To substantiate his suspicions, Horman has pointed, among other things, to a cable he obtained under a Freedom of Information Act request. The cable was from Ambassador Nathaniel Davis, who served as United States Ambassador to Chile at the time of the Allende overthrow and Charles Horman's death. On October 4, 1973, the day before Charles Horman's father arrived in Santiago to search for his son, Davis cabled Secretary of State Kissinger, recounting neighbors' descriptions of Charles Horman's arrest, as well as an eyewitness report of Horman's detention by the military. Yet when Edmund Horman arrived in Santiago the next day, October 5, he was told by Ambassador Davis that his son was probably in hiding.

In 1978, a book written by New York attorney Thomas Hauser, entitled *The Execution of Charles Horman: An American Sacrifice*, was published in hardcover by Harcourt Brace Jovanovich. The book detailed Edmund Horman's experiences in his search for his son. The book did not receive a great deal of publicity, and evoked little response from government officials. In 1979, Hauser signed an option agreement to sell all movie rights in the book to Warner Brothers, which in turn assigned the option to Universal City Studios. Universal exercised the option in 1981 to produce a movie, entitled *Missing*, directed by Greek filmmaker Constantin Costa-Gavras.

Although Costa-Gavras had both "political" and "nonpolitical" films among his prior credits, his international fame arose from suspenseful "fictionalized documentary" films. Costa-Gavras became an almost heroic figure of the left for his 1969 film Z, an emotionally charged muckraking political detective story attacking the methods of the facist military junta in Greece. A series of films after Z continued Costa-Gavras's technique of making fast-paced, tense entertainment out of elaborations on a recurrent political theme: government officials descending into the realm of thuggery, terrorism, and crime to victimize private citizens who pose a threat to their power.[83] *The Confession*, released in 1970, was an exposé of the 1952 Prague trials with actor Yves Montand as the victim of a witch hunt in Czechoslovakia; the government exposed by Costa-Gavras this time was communist, and *The Confession* was banned in many communist countries. *State of Seige*, in 1973, turned the ideological tables once again, depicting the assassination of an American foreign aid official by Uraguayan rebels. Again the star was Yves Montand, this time as a CIA agent meddling in Uraguayan affairs. *The Special Section*, in 1975, was set in occupied France in 1941, and dealt with the issue of French collaborators participating in trials conducted by a newly created court (the "special section") set up to administer reprisals for the death of a German naval cadet murdered in the Paris Metro.

Missing followed the quasi-documentary approach of Costa-Gavras' prior films. Jack Lemmon portrayed Edmund Horman, Charles Horman's father, Sissy Spacek portrayed Horman's wife Joyce, and John Shea portrayed Charles Horman himself. For the most part the plot of the film was faithful to the narrative of Hauser's book. Edmund and Joyce Horman run through a frustrating gauntlet of American and Chilean officials who profess to be helping in the search, but who appear to the viewer to be subtly sabatoging the search efforts, or at least to be revealing less than they know. Joyce Horman is suspicious of and antagonistic to the embassy officials from the start. Edmund Horman is at first trusting and respectful, but he too gradually comes to believe that the embassy officials are being obstructionist.

Although the movie never made the statement explicitly, the strong suggestion was that Horman was executed by Chilean officials because he knew too much about the background of the coup d'état, having inadvertently discovered clues that the CIA had orchestrated Allende's overthrow. The most damning single moment of dialogue went one step further, suggesting that American embassy officials may themselves have Charles Horman's blood on their hands. Jack Lemmon, as Edmund Horman, states, "I have reason to believe that my son was killed by the military." An American military officer responds to Horman by demanding, "Where did you hear that?"; and Horman replies, "I do not think they would dare do a thing like that unless an American official co-signed a kill order."

Following the release of the movie, a lawsuit was filed by three of the American officials who were stationed in Santiago during the Horman incident: Nathaniel Davis, the Ambassador; Fredrick D. Purdy, Counsel to the Santiago Consulate; and Captain Ray E. Davis, Commander of the United States Military Group and Chief of the United States Navy Mission in Santiago. The suit named as defendants Thomas Hauser, who wrote the book upon which the movie was based; Harcourt Brace Jovanovich, the publisher of the hardbound edition; Universal Studios, the producer of the movie; Costa-Gavras, the director; and the Hearst Corporation, the publishers of the paperback edition of the book. The plaintiffs sought $150 million in damages.

According to Ambassador Davis, "the thrust of the movie essentially is that we were complicit in telling the Chileans to murder Charles Horman." Such an implication, Davis claimed, is "a very corrosive thing to suggest about public service when it's false." Although Edmund Horman is obviously the prime mover behind the troubles that these historical events have brought down on Nathaniel Davis, Davis decided not to bring Horman in as a defendant in the lawsuit. "Horman," Davis stated, is "a little different from people who are making a pile of money on saying things that are false about me and my colleagues and the United States public service . . . . I was sad that this unhappiness and frustration of the family seemed to find its expression in turning on United States public officials who were trying to help them."

The State Department similarly seemed to view *Missing* as a mean-spirited act of ingratitude. In an extraordinary gesture, the Department actually released its own movie review of the film *Missing* on the eve of its premier, in the form of a three page "white paper." To the State Department, at least, something more than a movie was at stake. The white paper declared that after an eight-year investigation "no light was shed upon the circumstances of [Charles Horman's] death and little upon the circumstances of his disappearance. Furthermore, nothing was discovered to support any charges, rumors, or inferences as contained in the complaint against United States government officials." (Perhaps the State Department should go back over other movies released in the past and issue a series of white papers; how else are Americans to know, for example, the proper view to take on *The Ugly American* or *Apocalypse Now?*)

It is testimony to the power and influence in modern American culture of movies such as *Missing* that no lawsuit was filed against Thomas Hauser or his publisher Harcourt Brace Jovanovich when the hardcover book was originally published in 1978; nor was any suit filed when the book came out for the first time in paperback in an Avon Books edition (Avon is a division of Hearst) in 1980. Nor was there any "white paper" or other negative hoopla from the State Department aimed against Hauser's book, even though both the hardcover and first paperback edition bore Hauser's quite devastating original title, *The Execution of Charles Horman: An American Sacrifice.*

The State Department's almost panicky denials, and the lawsuit by the three United States officials, were both precipitated by the movie, and by the re-release, in a new 1982 paperback edition, of the Hauser book, now with its new title, *Missing.* To show the power of a "movie tie-in" for this sort of book, it is worth noting that only 5,813 copies of the original hardbound edition were printed. Avon printed 30,000 paperback copies under the original title in 1980, but two-thirds of them were never sold. Once the tie-in with the movie *Missing* was arranged, Avon actually destroyed the 20,000 paperback copies in its warehouse that bore the original title. Avon then released the new 1982 edition, bearing the movie title *Missing* in the distinctive red-lettered logo of the film, and it did very well, with over 165,000 copies shipped nationwide. Ambassador Davis for his part stated that he had seen "no need to take any action" with respect to Hauser's original book. Davis's belated inclusion of the author and book publisher in his lawsuit were prompted by his fear that the Costa-Gavras film would "portray as truth" the various "theories, conjectures and suppositions" contained in the book.

Davis and the State Department clearly had their finger on an important aspect of modern culture—a suspenseful movie with Jack Lemmon and Sissy Spacek can be a lot more damaging to reputation than a documentary book. Implicit, however, in Ambassador Davis's decision to sue the book publishers along with the movie producers is another point (though whether Davis consciously intended to make it is unclear) that is even more revealing: the release of the movie can do more than cosmetically alter the original book's title—it can alter the *meaning* of the book itself, creating a cinematic gloss on the printed words, a gloss that gives those words a new and more injurious shading because of the preconceived perceptions that the reader brings to the book. Hauser's original book contained raw evidentiary details about the events in Chile, and speculation about the meaning of that raw evidence, but that alone was not seen by either the government or the individual officials as particularly awful. The movie actually contained *less* explicit evidentiary material that was damaging to the defendants. The book, for example, contained some evidence left out of the movie, which purported that at least two embassy members had been told of Horman's murder before his father ever arrived in Santiago. Similarly, the movie contained *less* explicit speculation than the book about who was responsible.

But the medium in this case was indeed much of the message. The immediate visceral reaction that the film produced was something writer Thomas Hauser could not hope to replicate in a documentary book. Having been emotionally charged by viewing a powerful film, well over a hundred thousand readers went out and bought the book, and now the combination of the imagery on the screen and the "hard evidence" of the printed word combined to produce a damning perception of the actions of the American embassy in Chile, a perception far more potent than the sum of the constituent parts.

To Ambassador Davis and the State Department, *Missing* distorted reality to the point of being unpatriotic. The movie paints an unflattering picture of the conduct of the United States in Chile, and the conduct of the responsible Santiago embassy officials. The problem is, maybe this is one of those cases where we ought to be "unpatriotic"; maybe Edmund Horman is right. The dispute over the movie *Missing* is not reducible to simplistic judgments of whose version of "the facts" is correct. It may well be that the "truth" about American involvement in the overthrow of Salvador Allende, and in the death of Charles Horman, can no longer be reliably ascertained. The "truth" about these events has moved from the realm of physical fact to "ideological fact."

The official reality, according to Richard Nixon, Henry Kissinger, CIA directors Richard Helms and William Colby, and Ambassador Nathaniel Davis, is that the United States was not involved in the coup against Allende or in the death of Charles Horman.[84] It is completely possible that Nixon, Kissinger, Helms, Colby, and Davis are telling the whole truth, and not merely the officially sanctioned truth. It is completely possible that the version of reality portrayed by father Edmund Horman, writer Thomas Hauser, and director Constantin Costa-Gavras is based on paranoia, sentimentality, or ideologically tainted conviction.

Yet is is also at least theoretically possible that the likes of Nixon and Kissinger are lying about Chile. It is not as if they have never lied before. Both sides in the debate can point to some specific historical evidence to support their case, but neither side can really come near anything like reliable proof to clinch the issue either way. Belief in either the "Kissinger reality" or the "Costa-Gavras" reality eventually requires a leap of faith and boils down to a question of "whom do you trust?" At this level the dispute becomes wrapped up in political bias and cultural perceptions. An open, robust, and uninhibited airing of the conflicting evidence, political biases, and cultural world-views are the very stuff of a free society, and in the milieu of the United States in the 1980's, these conflicts, if they are to reach a meaningful number of Americans, will inevitably be carried on in movies and paperback books. And therein lies the great potential for evil in Ambassador Davis' lawsuit: a government official is attempting to punish (and $150 million in damages can only be described as punishment) a film-maker because he dares to challenge official reality as the government has decreed it.

The Charles Horman story has become a symbolic battleground over American foreign policy in Latin America. The competing mythologies from the Nixon era that surrounded Allende's overthrow are being repeated again in the Reagan presidency in debates over American foreign policy in Nicarauga, El Salvador, and once again, Chile. A substantial body of Americans (many of them now in power in Washington) believe that surreptitious American activity is necessary and proper in Latin America to undermine the exportation of communism and terrorism in the Western hemisphere. A substantial body of Americans in turn believe that quite the opposite is true, that the United States should not involve itself in the internal affairs of Latin nations, and that the efforts undertaken by the CIA and the military often lead to the assumption of power by brutal right-wing reactionaries. Inextricably wrapped up in the debate over what the United States should do is debate over what we have done and are doing. Did the CIA mine Nicaraguan harbors? Is the CIA planning assassinations of Sandinista leaders? The very fact that these sorts of questions are the constant stuff of editorials and exposés, that they are the fair game of pres-idential debates and congressional inquiries, demonstrates that they have no business being the central issues of a libel suit. The First Amendment is a whimpering and weak guarantee of free speech if high government officials can use the courts to stifle criticism, to the point of fining critics $150 million dollars if they are caught with facts out of place.

It should make no difference whatsoever that Costa-Gavras is able to tell his story in a compelling way, or that Jack Lemmon and Sissy Spacek rather than Ted Koppel or Seymour Hersh are the storytellers. It is arguable, however, that a society that constantly uses the "docudrama" as the vehicle for political exposé and statement need not give the docudrama as much First Amendment leeway as *Nightline* or the *New York Times*, on the theory that any format that consciously presents "quasi news" must take its lumps for the deliberate manipulation of facts. This argument against the docu-drama is relatively forceful when the victim of the creative license is a pri-vate citizen, such as Dr. Bindrim in *Bindrim v. Mitchell*. The argument, however, loses its force when the victims are government officials and when the factual mistakes that are alleged involve areas of official conduct in which the citizen simply does not trust the government's official version of events.

The movie *Missing* should not be embroiled in costly libel litigation merely because an impressive list of American officials do not much care for Costa-Gavras' version of history. Kissinger, writing about Chile in the second volume of his memoirs, *Years of Upheaval*, stated that his chapter on Chile "is a testament to the power of political mythology—for, contrary to anti-American propaganda around the world and revisionist history in the United States, our government had nothing to do with planning his overthrow and no involvement with the plotters." Yet Kissinger does not hide his animosity for the Allende regime, and many Americans just do not believe Kissinger—one man's political mythology is another's political fact.

One of the reasons that "political mythology" about American foreign policy in Latin America exists is that secrecy and deception have prevented the gathering of any hard dependable facts about the United States' conduct there for so long. The official bottom line on Chile, confirmed by Nixon, Helms, and Colby, is that the United States undertook a massive but confused effort to prevent Allende's election, and after his election, to undermine his political support, but always stopped short of plotting his actual overthrow. There is no substantial evidence that these accounts are false. Neither a congressional committee nor the enterprising efforts of investigative reporters like Seymour Hersh has ever uncovered a "smoking gun." On the other hand, it is just possible that the coup in Chile is simply one of the few CIA escapades in which the CIA neither failed nor was caught. We certainly had the motive to overthrow Allende—that is well documented by the main actors themselves. In *The Price of Power*,[85] Seymour Hersh quite aptly entitles the two chapters on Chile, "Hardball" and "Get Rid of Allende," and those chapters reveal Kissinger's and Nixon's unrestrained animosity toward the regime. That animosity is further documented by Kissinger's and Nixon's own memoirs. Judging by the covert CIA activity in Chile that the government has *confessed to*, we certainly had the opportunity and the means to orchestrate the coup and Allende's murder. Helms, for example, "for reasons of national security," perjured himself before Congress in testifying about covert action. Charles Horman's death is a case in which officials caught in lies about small details in "what the embassy knew and when it knew it" precipitate natural suspicion about the possibility of much larger official lies.

Ultimately, the real threat to the State Department posed by *Missing* is not that it might be caught with the blood of an American on its hands. (One can conjure up a State Department official somewhere thinking out loud that Horman was after all a bit of a left-winger—why was he stirring up trouble in Chile in the first place?) Rather, the danger to the government is that *Missing* might begin to unravel the larger version of reality that the State Department prefers to preserve inviolate. Isn't it interesting that Ambassador Davis would choose to use the word "corrosive" to describe the movie? For "corrosive" is exactly what it must seem to the government, corrosive of the view that America never acts as a machismo imperialist power capable of collusion with foreign thugs.[86]

This is precisely the sort of corrosiveness, however, that the First Amendment requires the government to endure. If the corrosive images of *Missing* are based on facts that the government disputes, the government may come forth with its own convincing evidence. But one of the essential points of the First Amendment is that citizens are not required to mutely take the government's word for it. The freedom of Constantin Costa-Gavras, Jack Lemmon, and Sissy Spacek to combine to produce a corrosive political indictment of United States policy is in fact precisely what differentiates the constitutional structures of Chile, indeed of most democracies, from that of the United States.

Nathaniel Davis himself saw firsthand the power of the Chilean government to suppress freedom by attacking the media. Soon after he took office in Santiago, Davis observed that Allende was attempting to consolidate his political position by undermining opposition media voices. Allende seized control of the supply of newsprint and used regulatory devices to economically undermine opponents in the press. Nathaniel Davis wrote:

> [S]piraling inflation produced officially-decreed wage and salary hikes every month. Bills for back taxes were presented under new interpretations of the law. Fire code and other violations were found against opposition newspapers and radios. When leftists seized and illegally operated the University of Chile's TV station, the authorities turned a blind eye. Import licenses and foreign exchange permits to import radio and television tubes and printing equipment were denied. Smaller radios and newspapers did go under—and were brought up by the parties of the government.
>
> As for the parties, their expenses were in large part the costs of their media—newspapers, radios and publications—plus posters, campaign expenses, and of course salaries. They were vulnerable in the same ways the media were.

According to both Davis and Henry Kissinger, in fact, it was the fear that opposition media voices would be silenced that led to the American foreign policy decision to funnel aid to "moderating" groups in Chile. In the words of Kissinger, "small, disciplined groups can have a disproportionate impact; control of the media will not be balanced by the checks and balances of a pluralistic society."

And so the ultimate irony of the *Missing* litigation is that the same American officials who worked to prop up dissident media voices in a foreign country by funneling United States dollars into their coffers now seek to punish America media voices for the free exercise of criticism of perceived excesses of that policy. Ambassador Davis, of course, must claim that his suit has nothing to do with the merits of American foreign policy in Chile, or with the ideological dispositions of Costa-Gavras. Davis's view of the litigation is surely much narrower. He does not sue as the surrogate for the State Department; his lawsuit is not entitled *United States v. Costa-Gavras*; rather he is suing to vindicate his individual outrage at a movie that in effect charged him with complicity to commit murder. From Ambassador Davis's perspective, the First Amendment may entitle Costa-Gavras to say anything he wants about the foreign policy of the United States, but it does not entitle Costa-Gavras to imply that Nathaniel Davis, as an individual, authorized the assassination of a fellow American.

If Nathaniel Davis had nothing to do with Charles Horman's death, then the movie *Missing* has in fact done him wrong. If, on the other hand, Davis was involved in Horman's execution, he deserves any damage the movie has caused him, and much more. We know only the skeletal facts, and will probably *never* know much beyond them. We also know, however, that the father of the dead American, Edmund Horman, fiercely believes that Ambassador Davis is lying, and we know that Mr. Horman's convictions run every bit as deep as Ambassador Davis' protestations of innocence. For better or for worse, Nathaniel Davis, no less than Richard Nixon and Henry Kissinger, *is* the government, at least in his own little corner of the government's activity. The United States government only acts through human beings, and Edmund Horman's sickened and passionate distrust of Nathaniel Davis the human being and Nathaniel Davis the personification of the presence of the United States government in Chile are in the end inseparable.

Ambassador Davis and the other American officials stationed in Santiago at the time of Allende's overthrow and Charles Horman's disappearance have the full power of the United States government to back up their version of reality. Publishers will fight for the right to publish the memoirs of Henry Kissinger and Richard Nixon, who have no trouble, long after they are out of office, continuing to disseminate their versions of reality.

Against this power the flailing efforts of Edmund Horman to tell his side of the story are indeed "poor and puny anonymities," until some louder voice becomes convinced that perhaps the story merits a wider telling. Even a carefully documented book does not, in today's "I'll wait for the movie" culture begin to make a dent in the governmental facade; whether it is *Silkwood* or *China Syndrome* or *Missing*, nothing muckrakes in modern America quite like the half-fiction, half-fact movie.

Constanin Costa-Gavras' films represent the very best modern example available of the intentional blurring of the entertaining, informing, and persuading possibilities in modern cinema. And if one had to nominate a modern filmmaker most likely to draw the lightning of a libel suit by a government official, it would be Costa-Gavras, precisely because of his technique. The very fact that Costa-Gavras' treatment of the "facts" is suggestive and impressionistic, however, is what makes his films so important a medium of emotional political debate. Many great novels, movies, and plays that draw from historical reality make leaps of faith; they bridge gaps of hard fact with impassioned ideas. Obviously, the straight and true documentary, scholarly study, or pure historical research project do in a sense add more to the store of human "knowledge" than a Costa-Gavras film, but the advancement of "knowledge" in a technical and literal sense is not the only or even the primary purpose of freedom of speech. Emotions and ideas are not reducible to verifiable entries in data banks, and the impassioned idea is always an incitement. As Costa-Gavras himself said of his efforts in *Missing*: "I don't try to *prove* the truthfulness or not. But I'm convinced the United States government had something to do with the coup in Chile." For Costa-Gavras, "the most extraordinary part of the story is that it shows how this country has the possibility of criticizing itself. Americans made the movie, not radicals, some very conservative people, and they back it now. It's probably one of the biggest proofs of democracy and freedom in this country."

The current willingness of the legal system to entertain libel actions based on novels, docudramas, and movies threatens to severely dampen the American capacity for self-criticism that a Greek filmmaker like Costa-Gavras finds so admirable. And when a nation shuts off self-critique, particularly by the most creative and impassioned in its midst, it tends to lose its way in the world. A movie like *Missing* takes courage to produce, but that courage, like freedom of speech itself, is a fragile thing. Ambassador Davis calls a movie "corrosive," as if it were a pollutant containing a toxic agent. When measured against the sixties, today's Americans seem increasingly willing to condemn speech condemnatory of government policies or establishment figures for being corrosive, or unseemly, or indecorous, or just not polite. As the nation has grown more conservative, some elements within it have become, in a sense, less American, and more like the upper-crust English at the height of the Empire. Novels like *Touching* abound and are widely read, but if they might be understood to criticize a real doctor—well, maybe that's going too far. *Missing* is exciting movie entertainment, but if Costa-Gavras doesn't have his facts absolutely nailed down—well, maybe it was a bit too exciting. As we begin to circumscribe speech within narrower and narrower bounds of decency, we inevitably begin to punish anyone who dares to take chances, anyone who dares to buck prevailing sensibilities about what is decent and genteel.

There is, of course, a social cost that we pay for taking too much of our self-critique from movies such as *Missing*; the cost is the displacement of the cerebral with the visceral, an abandonment of the academic injunction to stand back and observe with the injunction to jump in and feel. The works of filmmakers such as Costa-Gavras give us an instant injection of political passion, dislodging the inertia of apathy. But they also substitute intuition and speculation for investigation and analysis. This social cost, however, is probably worth paying when the object of the criticism or emotional indictment is the government, as represented by the acts of government officials. For there is nothing evil or unpatriotic about a robust skepticism of the American government's behavior and policies. And as important as it is to try to evaluate one's government by dispassionately examining the facts, it is also important that the emotional spirit that generates society's self-critique, and that gives it the courage to speak freely, often comes from artistic efforts that do not and should not claim accuracy as much as they simply generate concern and further inquiry. That is the vital function that movies such as *Missing* serve, and government officials should not be permitted to censor that function through the law of libel.

8

Of Vanessa Williams and Jerry Falwell: The Contributions of *Penthouse* to the First Amendment

> I can't describe how hurt I was, because as I say something like that involved not only me but my children, particularly. I had four young boys and a little young daughter, . . . three of my five children were still in school and I know how evil school children can be without realizing that they are being evil.
> *Penthouse* publisher Bob Guccione, testifying in a libel suit he brought against *Hustler* publisher Larry Flynt

> Vanessa Williams will prosper like no Miss America before or since. No Miss America has the fame that that girl has at this very moment. She's known all over the world. She's front page news everywhere. She'll get all kinds of film offers. The pageant will prosper, too. Can you imagine the number of people who will be glued to their television sets when the next Miss America pageant comes up? In our society scandal breeds prosperity.
> Bob Guccione, defending his decision to publish nude photographs of Vanessa Williams, Miss America of 1983, in *Penthouse*

WHEN *PENTHOUSE* MAGAZINE ran nine nude photographs of the reigning Miss America, Vanessa Williams, in its September 1984 issue, the magazine found itself in a familiar position: at the center of a cultural firestorm. The September issue (*Penthouse's* 15th Anniversary Issue) was released a month early, and priced at $4.00 a copy. Publisher Bob Guccione estimated that the press run would hit at least 6 million copies, which translates into gross sales of over $24 million. Across the country, newsstands and drugstore counters were sold out the day the issue hit the streets. Secondhand copies were being scalped for upwards of $30 apiece, and in New York the special entrepreneurial pluck of newsstand proprietors led them to post signs offering peeks at single, not-for-sale "library" copies at "$2.00 a look."

160

In response to the publication, Vanessa Williams, the first black Miss America, reluctantly relinquished her title to Suzette Charles, who had been first runner-up. Ms. Williams claimed that she had never authorized *Penthouse*, or anyone else, to publish the photographs. According to Williams the pictures were taken by a photographer named Tom Chiapel in the summer of 1982. The grainy black and white photographs, which included some shots of Williams in sexually suggestive poses with another nude female model, were, Williams insisted, "just for me to see." She said that she "never consented to the use of any photograph by Tom Chiapel, or anyone else."

Penthouse, through its publisher Guccione, and its lawyer, an iconoclastic and bombastic trial attorney named Norman Roy Grutman, told a different story. Grutman, a colorful and often controversial lawyer, said that *Penthouse* had a release signed by Williams, and that her signature had been reliably authenticated. Guccione elaborated, stating that William's signature on the release had been verified by one of the top handwriting experts in the United States. *Penthouse* was reported to have paid photographer Chiapel $100,000 for the photos.

Although the interests of Americans in the *Penthouse* photographs of Williams seemed insatiable, for the most part the initial public reaction was to rally around Williams, and to paint Guccione as a heavy. Guccione was criticized, for example, for not waiting to publish the photographs until Williams' tenure as Miss America was over, which would have been only an additional two month's wait, so as to spare Williams the humiliation of a resignation. "My answer," Guccione responded, "is why didn't the *Washington Post* wait until Nixon was out of office before exposing his fraudulent activities in Watergate?" Guccione added that "she committed a fraud on the pageant. When she signed her contract, she was duty bound to reveal to them anything in her past that could surface and embarrass the pageant and her reign as Miss America." According to Guccione, Williams "knew perfectly well she had done these photographs and that they could have been published, so she really gambled. She gambled that it wouldn't happen while she was Miss America." Guccione rhetorically asked, "Are we the heavies? Are we the bogeyman, the bad guy? No. All that has happened to Vanessa Williams was brought about by Vanessa Williams herself."

Among Guccione's sharpest critics for the Vanessa Williams episode was the publisher of *Playboy*, Hugh Hefner. According to Hefner, *Playboy* had been offered the Williams photos, but turned them down because it was not satisfied that they had actually been shot for publication. Appearing on the *Today Show* in an interview with Bryant Gumbel, Hefner said: "When one is publishing a magazine that has erotic content, if you don't approach the business that you're in with a moral set of values, then we're in a lot of trouble." Guccione responded with low-key urbane restraint, calling Hefner "a moral cripple and a liar." Guccione further observed that *Playboy* had waited until Suzanne Somers was famous before it published nude photos of her that had been taken years earlier and filed away when she was an unknown. In the midst of all the furor, Williams acquitted herself with great dignity and calm. Ultimately, Williams sued photographer Tom Chiapel, but not *Penthouse* directly. (The magazine has nonetheless played a peripheral role in the litigation.)

Penthouse has been sued for libel and invasion of privacy countless times, and has probably been embroiled in as much First Amendment related litigation in recent years as any other publication in America. *Penthouse* and Guccione have also done their share of suing other publications; they appear to have a particular fancy for going after *Hustler*, and its publisher Larry Flynt. *Penthouse*, Guccione, and their lawyer Roy Grutman have probably contributed as much as anyone to the growing body of First Amendment law that has accompanied the libel and privacy litigation explosion, and that contribution has in turn spurred a renewal of a far broader national debate over the unique First Amendment questions posed by pornography, and its effect on perceptions of women, sexual mores, and the general moral fabric of society. The current anti-media movement cannot be thoroughly explored without looking at that side of the national mood that is growing increasingly hostile toward the likes of *Penthouse*, *Hustler* and *Playboy*. Are they in fact cultural heavies? What, if anything, are the contributions of *Penthouse* to the First Amendment?

The Vanessa Williams incident was not the first time that *Penthouse* had crossed swords with the Miss America Pageant. In its August, 1979 issue, *Penthouse* ran an article it described as "humor," entitled "Miss Wyoming Saves the World." The article was set at a Miss America contest in Atlantic City. It depicted the exploits of a fictional beauty queen named "Charlene," who was entered in the contest as Miss Wyoming. Charlene was a baton twirler. In the story Charlene was depicted as about to perform her act in the pageant as a baton twirler, when her thoughts wandered back to an incident from college. She remembered performing fellatio on a Wyoming football player, an act that mystically caused him to levitate. Once on stage, Charlene began to simulate fellatio on her baton, a performance that stopped the orchestra. Charlene did not make it to the finals of the competition, but Charlene nonetheless thought she had a "real talent." While at the edge of the stage watching the finalists answer questions, Charlene's mind again wandered, this time over to how she might answer one of the "poise and intelligence" questions. Charlene fantasized about how she could "save the world" with her real talent, with the "entire Soviet Central Committee," "Marshall Tito," and "Fidel Castro." Charlene would be the ambassador of love and peace. Charlene then began to perform fellatio on her coach at the edge of the stage, as the audience was applauding the new Miss America. This fellatio also caused her coach to levitate. The story ended with the television cameras leaving the image of the new Miss America to focus on Charlene, and the sight of her coach floating in the air.

Despite the obviously fictional nature of this *Penthouse* sexual fantasy, the article drew not one but two separate lawsuits against the magazine, one by Ms. Kimerli Jayne Pring, who was the real Miss Wyoming of 1978, and the other by the Miss America pageant itself. A New Jersey federal judge dismissed the suit brought by the Miss America pageant, but a federal court in Wyoming permitted Ms. Pring to pursue her suit against the magazine for libel.

Pring was represented by the well-known trial lawyer Gerry Spence. (Among other famous cases, Spence was the lawyer for the family of Karen Ann Silkwood in its suit against Kerr-McGee.) At the time the *Penthouse* article was published, Pring was a senior at the University of Wyoming. She had been selected "Miss Wyoming" in 1978, and had attended the Miss America pageant in Atlantic City. She was an accomplished baton twirler, having won the Wyoming baton twirling championship in each of six years, and having won the National Baton Twirling Championship in 1977. She had won the title of Miss Majorette of Wyoming four times, and was runner-up in the 1977 Majorette of America contest. She had been a contestant and participant in numerous other pageants and competitions, including the Miss U.S.A. Beauty pageant, the Wyoming Miss University Contest, and the Miss Black Velvet Contest. She was Miss Wyoming at the 33rd National Sweet Corn Festival.

Ms. Pring claimed that the sexually promiscuous baton twirling Miss Wyoming known as "Charlene" in the *Penthouse* story would be understood by readers as referring to her, and that the "net effect" of the article was to create the impression "throughout the United States, Wyoming and the world," that she committed fellatio on the Wyoming football player and also upon her coach "in the presence of a national television audience at the Miss America pageant." She further alleged that the article also created the impression that she "committed fellatio-like acts upon her baton at the Miss America contest." Kimerli Pring's case was tried before a Wyoming jury, which returned a verdict against *Penthouse* of $1.5 million in actual damages and $25 million in punitive damages, ranking as one of the largest jury verdicts of all time.

The jury award was overturned by a close 2–1 vote in the federal Court of Appeals. *Penthouse* thus came within a single vote of the dubious honor of having been saddled with the largest libel award ever to be affirmed on appeal. Although it handed the magazine a narrow victory, in its general tone the Court of Appeals decision was sharply critical of *Penthouse*, describing the story as "a gross, unpleasant, crude, distorted attempt to ridicule the Miss America contest and contestants." The article, the court concluded, had "no redeeming features whatever." The court stated, however, that "although a story may be repugnant in the extreme to an ordinary reader, and we have encountered no difficulty in placing this story in such a category, the typical standards and doctrines under the First Amendment must nonetheless be applied." And then in one of the more candid and revealing statements that any court has made in such a suit, the court stated that: "The magazine itself should not have been tried for its moral standards." The First Amendment, the court determined, could not tolerate the jury's staggering verdict, because no reasonable reader could have understood the story as anything but fantasy and fiction. Charlene's ability to cause others to levitate through the act of fellatio was obviously fantasy, as was the act of performing simulated fellatio on her baton during the pageant on national television.

The decision exonerating *Penthouse* drew a sharp dissent from one of the three appeals judges. The article, he argued, contained an admixture of fact and fiction: "I consider levitation, dreams, and public performance as fiction. Fellatio is not." The judge then maintained that the jury quite properly punished *Penthouse* for conveying the impression that Ms. Pring engaged in fellatio, stating that it "has long been recognized as an act of sexual deviation or perversion," and that it falls "within the crime of sodomy, which civilized people throughout the world have long condemned."

The Miss Wyoming case highlights a fact of life for *Penthouse*. It will often be sued not so much because of anything inherently evil in a particular issue, but because of a guilt by association concern on the part of people who worry that the public will perceive that they have something to do with the magazine. What probably worried Ms. Pring as much as anything is that some people, reading or learning of the *Penthouse* story, would assume that where there's smoke there's fire.

The best example of this concern is a lawsuit against *Penthouse* brought by Reverend Jerry Falwell, for publishing an interview with Falwell that was in all respects perfectly accurate. In a suit entitled *Falwell v. Penthouse International, Inc.*, Reverend Falwell sued *Penthouse* for publishing the interview, along with Falwell's name and picture, in *Penthouse's* March, 1981 issue. Falwell had granted an interview to two freelance journalists,

who in turn sold the interview to *Penthouse*. In a lawsuit that based its arguments on a potpourri of legal theories stretching from violation of an
alleged copyright interest in his own interview, to invasion of privacy, defamation, and appropriation of his likeness and personality, Falwell sought
to enjoin distribution of the March, 1981 issue, as well as compensatory
and punitive damages. A federal court sitting in Lynchburg, Virginia (Falwell's hometown and the center of his evangelistic broadcasting activities)
found in favor of *Penthouse* on all counts.

The judge in the case quite astutely identified what Falwell was really
after in his suit. Falwell's complaint was not that the interview itself was in
any literal sense "false"—the interview simply reproduced Falwell's own
responses to questions, and Falwell did not claim that there were any mis-
quotes or other inaccuracies in the interview as published by *Penthouse*.
Nor could Falwell seriously maintain that his spoken words were "copyrighted." To be copyrighted, one's work product must normally be embodied in some tangible form. One's spontaneous spoken statements are as
much part of the public domain as exhaled air; the law has never supposed
that the spoken utterances of even the most brilliant among us create valuable property rights. The quips of Winston Churchill, John Kennedy, and
Bernard Shaw are instantly public property, to be repeated by anyone
without the payment of royalties. So too, a celebrity's responses to a
reporter's questions at press conferences or interviews do not "belong" to
the celebrity—they are not the protected product of his or her intellectual
or creative efforts.

Although a celebrity might grant an interview to a journalist with certain
strings attached, such as a contract between the reporter and the interviewee that the interview could only appear in *Esquire*, or the *Christian Science Monitor*, an interview at large—when someone gives an interview to a
freelance reporter with no such strings attached—leaves the reporter free
to sell to the highest bidder. It is even conceivable that in some situations
a reporter might have a legal right to breach the contractual agreement
with the interviewee. Imagine if Richard Nixon were to grant an interview
with a journalist on the condition that Nixon could strike out any questions
and answers prior to publication. If in a heated exchange between the
reporter and the ex-President, Nixon let it slip that he had known of the
bugging of Larry O'Brien's Watergate suite in advance, the reporter might
decide that the contract be damned, she will disclose the revelation. If she
sold the interview to the *Atlantic Monthly* or *Playboy* (either of which might
also conclude that the contract be damned), it is not at all clear that a court
would agree to enforce the contract in favor of Nixon. (This is, of course,
a problem for the law of contracts in the interview context that is analogous to the sort of problem created by Dr. Bindrim's nondisclosure con-

tract in *Bindrim v. Mitchell*, discussed in Chapter Seven.) Sometimes disclosure of an uncovered fact may be of such vital public interest that it might override legitimate contractual provisions or confidential relationships. To use an analogy, courts have held that a psychiatrist who finds out that a patient has an insane, irresistible desire to murder a specific person may in some circumstances have a legal duty to notify the police, or to warn the victim. Basing his suit on this theory, former White House Press Secretary James Brady sought recovery against the Colorado psychiatrist of John Hinkley, Jr., who allegedly had information about Hinkley's notion of trying to demonstrate his love for the actress Jody Foster through a dramatic act of violence against President Reagan. Just as larger social interests in public safety might at times obligate a psychiatrist to divulge information originally obtained in confidence, a reporter might at times have a pubic obligation to report a story originally gathered in confidence.

No such block-buster revelations were made in Falwell's interview, however, and he claimed that the freelance journalists violated an oral agreement they had with Falwell in selling the interview to *Penthouse*. But Falwell was able to point to no tangible evidence to support his claim, it was just his word against the reporters. The court thus held that Falwell could not claim any legal "ownership" in the interview.

If the interview was true and accurate, and if it did not in any demonstrable legal sense "belong" to Falwell, why was he complaining? Indeed, if the great mission of a dedicated evangelist is to spread the "good news" to *sinners*, what better audience for the cost-free dissemination of Jerry Falwell's gospel could the Reverend claim than the readers of *Penthouse*? From Falwell's perspective, who could be more in need of conversion? Why did he object?

Well only Reverend Falwell knows for sure, but it is clear that federal Judge James Turk in Lynchburg had his own suspicions. In his decision the judge observed that "Stated succinctly, Reverend Falwell does not approve of *Penthouse* magazine. He contends that the appearance of the interview was inconsistent with his ministry." What Falwell objected to was not the substance of the interview (which was, after all, his), but the mere fact that it appeared in *Penthouse*. Falwell was worried that the interview might give rise to the mistaken implication that Falwell approved of *Penthouse*, or was willing to lend his name to *Penthouse's* sales. Just as in Miss America's case, there is a certain commercial scandal value in the juxtaposition of the pure and the prurient.

Although the judge acknowledged (and there was no reason not to) that Falwell was sincere in his belief, all of his legal theories were ultimately aimed at attempting "to redress what is really his personal dissatisfaction with the particular magazine in which the interview was published." But,

Judge Turk said, the mere fact that Falwell "may not approve of publications such as *Penthouse*, or may not desire *Penthouse* to discuss his activities or publish his spoken words, does not give rise to an action cognizable under the law. The First Amendment freedoms of speech and press are too precious to be eroded or undermined by the likes and dislikes of persons who invite attention and publicity by their own voluntary actions." Score one for *Penthouse's* constitutional right to exhibit bad taste (at least as Reverend Falwell would define it).

Despite the victory in the Falwell case, *Penthouse* has not always been successful in suits arising from the publication of unauthorized interviews with public figures. Cher, for example, sued *Penthouse* and its subsidary publication, *Forum*, for printing an interview with *Cher* in the March, 1981 issue of *Forum*. Cher had agreed to do an interview with a reporter of *Us* magazine, to be used by *Us* in conjunction with a cover story on Cher. *Us* hired a freelance reporter to act as *Us's* interviewer, and the reporter conducted a tape-recorded interview with Cher. Following the interview, Cher decided that she did not like the way it had turned out, and she requested a second interview. *Us* obliged her, and a new substitute interview was conducted by a second interviewer. The first freelance reporter hired by *Us* was told that his interview would not be published. The freelance reporter then turned around and sold the interview to *Forum*, which published it, accompanied by heavy advance broadcast and print advertising, using Cher's name and likeness to help sell the issue.

In the suit by Cher against *Forum* and *Penthouse*, the court found the ingredients that had been missing in the Falwell suit. *Forum* changed the text so that *Forum*, not the reporter, appeared as the poser of questions. *Forum* falsely proclaimed in its advertising that Cher "tells *Forum*" things that she "would never tell *Us*." The court emphasized that "Cher had intended to 'tell' the rival magazine, *Us*, the very words in the interview, and had not 'told' *Forum* anything." Unlike Falwell, who surrendered any interests he had in his words by talking to "freelance" reporters and not protecting himself in writing in advance, Cher could point to the fact that in her case *Forum* had done more than merely print her interview: it had falsely created and exploited the impression that Cher had granted *Forum* an exclusive interview, and further exploited Cher's celebrity status to imply that she endorsed *Forum*. An award in favor of Cher of over $200,000 was affirmed on appeal, with the court remarking that "this kind of mendacity is not protected by the First Amendment."

Penthouse and its usual trial lawyer Roy Grutman are not always on the defense. Publisher Bob Guccione, and attorney Grutman have been on the offensive in a number of libel and privacy suits.

In one of the great turnabouts in litigation history, Jerry Falwell hired Roy Grutman, the very lawyer Bob Guccione had used to defend Falwell's suit against *Penthouse*, and retained Grutman as his own lawyer in a suit against Larry Flynt and *Hustler* magazine. Falwell's suit against *Hustler*, tried in front of Judge James Turk, the same federal judge in Lynchburg who had dismissed Falwell's suit against *Penthouse*, arose from a viciously satirical mock ad that appeared twice in *Hustler*. The fake ad was a parody of a Campari Liqueur advertisement that quoted Falwell as saying that he drank, and had sex with his mother. No one ever accused Larry Flynt of oversensivity.

One of the intriguing ironies of Falwell's suit against *Hustler* was that Falwell's lawyer, Roy Grutman, was in the position of making the very same accusations against *Hustler* and Larry Flynt that Grutman is constantly fending off on behalf of his other clients, *Penthouse* and Bob Guccione. In Falwell's $45 million suit against Flynt and *Hustler*, the attorney for *Hustler* magazine told the jury that Roy Grutman "wants you to judge this lawsuit based on your taste . . . he wants you to find *Hustler* magazine in poor taste." The issue, *Hustler's* lawyer said (in language that could have been taken verbatim from Grutman's many defenses of *Penthouse*) "is whether or not a reasonable person would read [the ad] and believe it to be true. That's what the law says. You can say things as long as they are not a statement of fact."

For his part, Grutman claimed that the jury had seen two Larry Flynts: one a cursing publisher who said in a deposition that he was out to assassinate Jerry Falwell's reputation, and the other a well-dressed, soft-spoken man who testified live in front of the jury. "That man is a Dr. Jekyll and Mr. Hyde," Grutman said. "That man is exactly what his magazine is called, a hustler. The leopard doesn't change his spots. The three-piece suit isn't going to conceal the blackrot that comes out of his magazine."

According to *Hustler's* attorney, the satiric ad had actually aided Falwell's ministry, by creating a rallying point for Falwell to use with his moral majority constituency—sort of like the football coach posting the opposition coach's derogatory remarks about his team on the bulletin board to fire up the boys. He told the jury that Falwell had used the ad to raise more than $500,000 for the Moral Majority and his Old Time Gospel Hour television program by enclosing copies with fundraising letters. Grutman's counterattack included the claim, reminiscent of the claim that Kimerli Pring had made about *Penthouse's* Miss Wyoming beauty queen parody, that *Hustler* had used Falwell's name and likeness, and had despoiled the memory of his mother, "because Larry Flynt thinks its funny."

In the end, the Falwell suit against *Hustler* resulted in a jury verdict that on its surface seemed a compromise. The jury found that the article was not libelous, apparently thinking that the ad was not taken as literally true by anyone—the very outrageousness of the ad's portrayal of Falwell carried with it its own implicit disclaimer. But in an ominous development from the media's perspective, the jury nonetheless awarded Falwell $100,000 on a separate legal theory—the intentional infliction of emotional distress. What made the award worrisome from the media's perspective was not the amount of the verdict, but the principle underlying it: that even if the story was not libelous (because nobody took it seriously as purported "truth"), it could still be the subject of a suit for damages, *purely because it made Falwell feel bad*. This completely divorced parodies such as the irreverent ad run by *Hustler* from all the checks and balances built into the law of libel, for it permitted recovery merely because the butt of the "joke" found it offensive.

This jury award was subsequently overturned by the trial judge, on the logical grounds that the ad was so completely outrageous that no one could take it seriously. Although precious few people thought that *Hustler's* crude satire was particularly amusing, no one really believed Falwell was an incestuous drunk. If no one accepted the ad at face value, then to award Falwell damages is to say that he cannot be joked about, at least when the jokes are in "bad taste." The Falwell jury award was truly an award for being thin-skinned, pure and simple. For if the jury did not believe that anyone who saw the ad truly took it as signifying that Falwell was a drunk who had sex with his mother, than its decision to still go ahead and award damages meant that the jury felt it legitimate to find against *Hustler* purely for the fantastic joking suggestion of these obviously spurious "facts." *Hustler* was punished by the jury, in short, for bad taste, the very punishment one would have thought repugnant to an attorney like Grutman, who is constantly defending *Penthouse* from the same sort of persecution.

On another occasion, Roy Grutman found himself going against Larry Flynt's empire in a more oblique way, suing Flynt's business for a magazine piece that it did not publish, but merely distributed. In its May 1980 issue, a relatively obscure publication called *Adelina* magazine proclaimed on its cover: "In the Nude from the *Playmen* Archives . . . Jackie Collins." Inside the magazine there were two photographs printed from the movie *The World Is Full of Married Men*, based on the book of the same title by Collins. One of the photos showed a topless woman; the other showed the same woman in a nude orgy scene. The caption accompanying the photos identified the woman as writer Jackie Collins, with a short article commenting on the increasing willingness of "serious" actresses to appear nude in films.

Jackie Collins wrote the book *The World Is Full of Married Men,* and she wrote the screenplay for the movie, which was directed by her husband Oscar Lerman. Jackie Collins, however, did not appear in the movie, clothed or unclothed, and she has never appeared nude in public. The magazine had mistakenly identified the anonymous actress who appeared nude in the photos as Collins, when it was not her at all.

Jackie Collins sued the publishers and distributors of the magazine, including Larry Flynt's distributing company. And for her lawyer Collins chose, like Jerry Falwell, none other than *Penthouse* lawyer Roy Grutman, who seemed to be developing litigation against Larry Flynt as a subspeciality. Collins claimed that the use of her name and the false identification of her as the nude actress in the photographs violated her rights of publicity and privacy. Collins claimed that there was nothing newsworthy in the magazine's coverage of her, and that the magazine was thus not entitled to a First Amendment defense.

After a relatively short trial in New York federal court, a jury returned a verdict in favor of Jackie Collins for a whopping $40 million in damages—$7 million in compensatory and $33 million in punitive damages. In analyzing her claim on appeal, the Federal Court of Appeals pointed out that Collins had achieved substantial fame as the author of nine novels. Her books, the court noted, were controversial because of their emphasis on a recurring theme—that there is ubiquitous inequality in the treatment of woman relative to men, an inequality that is particularly pronounced in sexual mores. Collins points to the fact, for example, that women appear naked in films and magazines more frequently than men, a phenomenon that she regards as unfair because men have more opportunity to view unclad women than women have to view unclad men. Collins advocates "equal nudes for all."

Collins' books are racy and sensual; they are laden with four-letter words and sex, and they sell in the millions. One of her books, *Hollywood Wives,* has made the lucrative crossover to prime time television. Some of Collins' works have been banned in Australia, an honor not unlike being banned in Boston. Her novels have been translated into 32 languages. She is a frequent television guest, she grants many media interviews, and her general persona as an outspoken critic of sexual double standards obviously contributes to her success as a writer. In light of all of this the court held that Collins had purposefully surrendered part of what would otherwise have been her protected privacy rights, at least in matters bearing some relationship to her media appearances, books, and screenplays. The court ruled that the magazine piece fell into the category of newsworthy commentary about Collins, and that she could thus recover against the defendants only upon clear and convincing proof of recklessness. Such proof, the appeals court said, was lacking. The court then chastized the jury for its gargantuan damages award, stating that: "Putting aside First Amendment implications of 'mega-verdicts' frequently imposed by juries in media cases, the compensatory damages awarded shock the conscience of this Court." The damages, the court went on, were "grossly excessive and obviously a product of plaintiff's counsel's appeals to the passion and prejudice of the jury." Jackie Collins' lacerated feelings, the court remarked, could not be "worth anything close to $7 million." However sordid and obscure the magazine *Adelina* may seem to Collins, it had only a modest circulation. And in words that will surely be unenthusiastically received among celebrities, the court ended its discussion by stating that "given the number of famous persons portrayed in this fashion, one wonders whether such pictures are even capable of producing genuine reputational harm. Even assuming the word would get around to those whose esteem of plaintiff would be diminished, the main source of publicity for the pictures came not from the magazine's publication but from [Ms. Collins'] lawsuit and statements to the press." Score one against Roy Grutman.

The battles between Bob Guccione and Larry Flynt have at times erupted into direct confrontation. In its June 1979 issue, *Hustler* depicted Guccione engaged in an act of anal intercourse, with the caption, "Bob Guccione Discovers Vaseline." A photograph of Guccione's head purchased from U.P.I. was superimposed on the body of another man performing the act. In a wild trial, both sides ranged far and wide in their attacks. In Guccione's testimony, he suggested that Larry Flynt might do anything to him, including future libels on his daughter and mother. Guccione's laywer, Grutman, put the invitation to stop Larry Flynt more bluntly:

> The law, you will learn, says that it is not Mr. Guccione's need which is relevant, but the necessity, the imperative crying necessity to put an end and stop to this kind of calumny.
> What would stop Larry Flynt? The lawyer's letter? He paid it no mind. The lawsuit, which was originally commenced, he laughed at. . . .
> Ladies and gentlemen, this man knows nothing except that he will go on doing what he willfully wants to do unless you stop him, and the only way in which he can be stopped, and that is in his pocketbook. Those are why punitive damages are essential.
> If you award a verdict against Larry Flynt of several hundred thousand dollars above the several hundred thousand dollars of lawyers' fees already expended to make Mr. Guccione whole, do you think that would stop Larry Flynt, a man who has a cash flow that he admits is more than a million-and-a-half dollars a week? Now, these are sums, I

know, astronomical, and outside of the experience of almost all of you, all of us, but that is the reality of the bloated Larry Flynt, a man heaped up on his own ill-gotten success. A modest verdict, he will rear back and roar at you, and will have gotten away with it, and what will happen next month or the month after to Mr. Guccione, to his mother, to Ms. Keeton, to his children, to President Carter? . . .

. . . To anyone whom he may elect to vent his spiteful, vicious ire upon. That is the focus. How to you stop that man? How do you stop him. I have calculated from the figures which the Flynt organization provided to us that of the magazines which were involved in the publicatons of the specific evils against Mr. Guccione, Mr. Flynt probably made over $10 million, and I could ask you rationally, as a matter of punitive damages, to stop Mr. Flynt by making him pay back the money that he made on this vile pile of swill.

The jury clearly took this invitation to heart, for it returned with an award calculated to put *Hustler* and Flynt out of business: $1.5 million in compensatory damages and $11 million in punitive damages against *Hustler*, and $26 million in compensatory damages against Flynt. But like the $26 million that a Wyoming jury had returned against *Penthouse* in the Miss Wyoming case, Guccione's award against *Hustler* and Flynt was reversed on appeal, on the grounds that the jury had been motivated by passion and prejudice against Flynt.

This litigation between Bob Guccione and Larry Flynt may seem ultimately unimportant to many in the "respectable" media. The mainstream press is often quite anxious to distance itself as far as possible from the likes of *Penthouse* or *Hustler*, and it may be content to write off their litigation struggles with the shrugging judgment that Flynt and Guccione deserve each other.

But these fights between the powers behind *Penthouse* and *Hustler* extract their toll on First Amendment values in a more generalized way. A victory for Roy Grutman against *Hustler* may create a legal precedent that at some future date will haunt the *New York Times* or *The Reader's Digest*, or for that matter, *Penthouse* itself. A good illustration of this possibility is the case *Keeton v. Hustler*, involving a libel suit by Kathy Keeton, the vice chairman of *Penthouse*, against *Hustler* and Larry Flynt. Roy Grutman was Keeton's lawyer in the litigation, which went all the way to the United States Supreme Court.

Keeton claimed that she was libeled in five separate issues of *Hustler*, published between September 1975, and May 1976. She first filed suit against *Hustler* and Flynt in Ohio, where *Hustler* is incorporated, but the Ohio courts ruled that her suit had expired because she had failed to commence it before the Ohio statute of limitations had run out. Keeton's lawyers looked around for another jurisdiction in which to bring the lawsuit, and were discouraged to discover that the statute of limitations had run out in every state in the United States except one, New Hampshire. New Hampshire stood alone because it had a six-year limitations period for libel suits, which was very unusually long.

Could Keeton, who lived in New York, sue *Hustler*—a publication incorporated in Ohio and based in California—in New Hampshire, a state that seemed at first blush to have little, if anything, to do with the dispute? The usual rule in civil litigation is that a state must have a sufficient level of what courts call "minimum contacts" with a company in order to force it into its courts. Did *Hustler* have sufficient contacts with New Hampshire to be subject to that state's jurisdiction?

Hustler, it turned out, was not exactly what you would call a big seller in New Hampshire. *Hustler* had no offices, employees, bank accounts, or real property in the state. *Hustler's only* contact with New Hampshire was that its magazine was available for sale there—but sales were relatively miniscule. New Hampshire sales were less than 1% of the magazine's total circulation; the monthly sales in the state ranged from a high of 15,000 copies to a low of 10. Nonetheless, Keeton filed suit in New Hampshire. The lower courts threw the suit out, deciding that New Hampshire's contacts with the case were too paltry and tenuous to support jurisdiction. The courts noted that it was obvious that the only reason Keeton had chosen New Hampshire was that it was the only state with time still left on the statute of limitations clock. To allow this sort of lawsuit would expose a publisher to the risk of covering all damages suffered anywhere as long as the plaintiff could still find one state in which some copies of the publication were sold and the statute of limitations was still alive. The court noted the rule that when a plaintiff sues for libel, he or she is permitted to sue in only one state for all damages incurred in all states. This rule exists to prevent a plaintiff from harrassing a publication by filing separate lawsuits in 50 different states. In Keeton's suit, therefore, New Hampshire courts were being asked to award damages for all of the alleged injuries to Keeton's reputation in every state, even though New Hampshire had imported only a tiny percentage of *Hustler's* circulation.

In a decision with potentially dire implications for the entire media, the United States Supreme Court reversed the lower court rulings, and held that Kathy Keeton could bring her suit against *Hustler* in New Hampshire. In his opinion for the Court, Justice Rehnquist argued that even though neither Kathy Keeton nor *Hustler* had very much to do with New Hampshire, the fact remained that some copies of *Hustler* had been sold there. Even if none of the New Hampshire citizens who read the allegedly offending articles about Kathy Keeton knew who she was or cared, they had nonetheless read material that was allegedly libelous. Justice Rehnquist then shifted his analysis of the problem to an entirely new approach: New Hampshire's libel laws, he reasoned, were not merely designed to protect the direct victims of the media, they were designed to protect New Hampshire's readers and listeners from being exposed to falsehood. This analysis suddenly opened up a whole new notion of what the law of libel is all about—for Justice Rehnquist was maintaining that libel law does not merely safeguard individual reputations, it safeguards the public at large from what is essentially moral and factual "pollution." Justice Rehnquist thus wrote that: "False statements of fact harm both the subject of the falsehood *and* the readers of the statement. New Hampshire may rightly employ its libel laws to discourage the deception of its citizens."

Attorney Roy Grutman's victory over *Hustler* on the jurisdictional question may in the long run do Grutman, Kathy Keeton, Bob Guccione, and *Penthouse* far more harm than good. For most media lawyers quite correctly see the case as a serious setback for all elements of the press. Being banned in Boston is now nothing compared to being sold in New Hampshire, for as a practical matter if one's publication finds it way, even in small numbers, to New Hampshire's bookstores or newstands, one remains exposed to a potential libel suit for six years, an exposure far greater than the one or two year period typical in most states.

In the end, Guccione, *Penthouse*, and Roy Grutman are a maze of contradictions, at times championing the First Amendment and at times chipping at it; at times blasphemously tweaking the culture for its prudish hypocrisy, and at times riding the high horse of moral superiority over the likes of Larry Flynt. And through it all have come the seemingly interminable libel suits. Not all the litigation has been over sexual matters; indeed, *Penthouse* from time to time engages in excellent investigative journalism, and has won awards for some of its efforts. (The same observation, by the way, can be made of *Hustler* and Larry Flynt, who also occasionally display a certain First Amendment seriousness of purpose—when the Defense Department refused to allow United States journalists to accompany the U.S. forces in the invasion of Grenada, Larry Flynt led the way with litigation challenging the policy on First Amendment grounds.) Among the investigative pieces that have led to libel litigation against *Penthouse* have been stories about the use of dolphins for military purposes, an article discussing the distribution and sale of marijuana by successful, upwardly mobile businessmen and attorneys, and an article claiming that a plush California Resort, the Rancho La Costa, "was established and frequented by mobsters." The operators of La Costa sued *Penthouse* for a whopping $522 million. Of all the suits *Penthouse* has been involved in, none has generated more controversy in legal circles than the non-sex-related Rancho La Costa litigation.

If a libel trial itself can develop a bad reputation, no suit has ever generated a worse one than the La Costa case. The case became a circus. After
a pretrial litigation period lasting six and a half years and a trial lasting five
months, (reportedly generating over $4 million in legal fees on each side)
the trial court ultimately ended up ordering a whole new trial. *Penthouse*
was defended by Roy Grutman, and the La Costa resort was represented
by one of the country's most famous trial lawyers, Louis Nizer. Nizer and
Grutman became bitter enemies during the trial, each constantly sniping
at the other both in and out of court. Among the witnesses who testified
were former Nixon White House aide and Watergate co-conspirator John
Erlichman, and ex-Mafia hit man, Aladena ("Jimmy the Weasel") Fratiano.
The *Penthouse* article had claimed that the resort was a hangout for mobsters, and that Nixon White House staff members had used La Costa's
unusually secure grounds for planning the infamous Watergate coverup.
Erlichman said that White House aides, including Presidential Counsel
John Dean, did use the resort, which was located near the Western White
House in San Clemente. But, Erlichman said, the choice was made not for
security reasons, but because of the resort's tennis courts. Similar but
somewhat less elegant amenities would grace the federal detention camps
that many of those White House aides would later visit for more extended
stays.

"Jimmy the Weasel" testified in the case that he visited La Costa in the
1960's and met with three reputed Mafia leaders—Sam ("Momo") Giancana, a reputed Chicago mob boss who was killed in 1975 shortly before
he was supposed to testify before a Senate committee; Johnny Roselli, who
allegedly was hired by the CIA to assassinate Fidel Castro and who turned
up floating in a barrel off of Key Biscayne in 1975; and Frank ("The
Bomp") Bompensiero, an alleged San Diego mob chief who was shot and
killed outside a phone booth in 1976. Fratiano also claimed that he
received orders from Giancana "for the planning of the killing of Desi
Arnez," a remark the judge ruled irrelevant. The whole *Penthouse*/La
Costa legal extravaganza ultimately degenerated into a multi-million dollar
theatre of the absurd, with the hapless trial judge hopelessly overmatched
in trying to keep order. The judge ultimately felt compelled to start all over
and order a new trial. In his ruling he sharply criticized Grutman's trial
tactics, stating in a written opinion that *Penthouse*, under the direction of
Grutman, "flagrantly and deliberately misconducted itself in reprehensible
manners which were calculated to improperly prejudice plaintiffs and
improperly influence the jury against the plaintiffs."[87]

What, in the final analysis, should be made of *Penthouse's* courtroom trib-
ulations? The only candid conclusion is that *Playboy*, *Penthouse*, and *Hustler*

are as often as not penalized in libel and privacy cases because of what they are rather than because of what they say. Some of this persecution comes from the legal and public relations battles they wage against each other; Bob Guccione and Roy Grutman quite clearly view the taste and morality of Larry Flynt and Hugh Hefner as qualitatively different from their own. To much of the American public in the more restrained times of the 1980's, however, what all of these publications are is pornographic.

If there is any type of speech more onerous than libel in the consciousness of most Americans today, it is pornography. So when a pornographic magazine commits a libel, look out: piled on top of the usual aversion to the "factual pollution" created by allegedly inaccurate or biased reporting is the distasteful reality that the defendant routinely engages in "moral pollution" of an even more repugnant variety. The pornography business is under a reinvigorated siege these days. Even among liberals who reflexively rally around the news media, it is increasingly fashionable to disparage pornography, particularly on the grounds that it is degrading to women. In fact, the rejuvenated charge against pornography links elements of the Jerry Falwell right with elements of the feminist left.

In the past year, the cities of Minneapolis and Indianapolis both enacted laws prohibiting pornography on the theory that it discriminates against women. The Indianapolis statute, for example, declares that "pornography is a discriminatory practice based on sex which denies women equal opportunities in society." The ordinance outlaws the production, sale, exhibition, and distribution of pornography. The mayor of Minneapolis vetoed that city's legislation, but the Indianapolis legislation is on the books, with the mayor's strong support. The Indianapolis law is under challenge in the federal courts. (A federal court has since declared the ordinance unconstitutional.) There is every reason to suspect that the Indianapolis and Minneapolis ordinances will be duplicated in many other cities nationwide.

Like it or not, there is an intellectual linkage between attitudes towards libel and pornography. Just as libel is often characterized as outside the protection of the First Amendment because false statements of fact contribute nothing worthwhile to the "marketplace of ideas," pornography is often thought of as unprotected expression because it is "devoid of redeeming social value." The same habits of mind that lead juries in civil cases to free and easy damages awards for libel lead juries in criminal cases to open-and-shut convictions for the publication of obscenity. Like false statements of fact, obscenity has always been thought of as taboo speech, speech that is unrelated to the unfettered interchange of ideas on political and social issues.

In its 1957 decision in *Roth v. United States*, the Supreme Court declared that "obscenity is not within the area of constitutionally protected speech or press." Since that 1957 decision, the Supreme Court has not backed down from its stand that obscene speech does not deserve First Amendment protection. In 1973, Chief Justice Burger wrote that the banning of obscenity was justified by "the interest of the public in the quality of life and the total community environment, the tone of commerce in the great city centers, and, possibly, the public safety itself."

This equation of obscenity with pollution leads easily to the conviction that obscenity can be legitimately banned, for it then becomes a matter of environmental concern, the preservation of the style and quality of life. The government, after all, has always enacted laws based on collective moral sensibilities. Contrary to the cliché that "you can't legislate morality," governments have always been in the business of doing just this, and often very effectively. Much of the criminal law is openly based on morality; laws against incest, adultery, or fornication are direct regulations of sexual behavior, and laws governing prostitution or drug abuse are based not so much on demonstrable harm to others as on collective social judgments of decency. If decency in conduct can be regulated, it is not a great step to further regulate decency in speech, or even in thoughts. Impure thoughts are in fact made sinful by one of the oldest of legal codes: among the commandments on the tablets of Moses was the admonition not to covet thy neighbor's wife. No "overt act" is required to consummate this sin; the coveting alone will suffice. Aristotle wrote that "the legislator ought to banish from the state, as he would any other evil, all unseemly talk. The indecent remark, lightly dropped, results in conduct of a like kind. Especially, therefore, it must forbid pictures or literature of the same kind." And so the Supreme Court, following the wisdom of Aristotle, permits the banning of obscenity, requiring only that to be obscene the material must satisfy three criteria: it must, applying community standards, appeal to the prurient interest of the average person; the material must depict or describe sexual conduct in a patently offensive way; and the work, taken as a whole, must lack serious artistic, literary, political, or scientific value.

The rub in this whole approach, of course, is that someone must define what is or is not "prurient," what is or is not "patently offensive," and what lacks "serious" social value. Someone, in short, must presume to pass judgment that *Playboy*, *Penthouse*, and *Hustler* are trash.

The intellectual anchor to the view that it is constitutionally permissible to ban *Penthouse* is the opinion that expression aimed at sexual arousal for "its own sake" has no redeeming social value. This is simply a more particularized application of the general thesis about speech that has so much currency today, and that has contributed so much to libel litigation—that speech "for its own sake" has no intrinsic value. For a growing number of Americans the "value" of speech is only as good as the "value" of the goals the speech is trying to accomplish. And when the only goal is sexual stimulation, the goal is merely masturbatory, and may be quite legitimately condemned. Under this view the problem with pornography is that it is more physical than mental—it's not really speech, it's arousal. In its first attempt to define the term "prurient interest," the Supreme Court thus described it as: "itching; longing; of persons, having itching, morbid, or lascivious longings; of desire, curiosity or propensity, lewd," drawing from the etymological meaning of "prurient" from the Latin *prusiens*, meaning literally "itch." The description sounded more like a Dessenex commercial than an exercise in constitutional interpretation. The evil seemed to be in the "itch." Under the Supreme Court's definition, if the only message in the speech is sexual arousal, if there is no other fancy window-dressing to give the message a veneer of literary, artistic, political, or scientific value, then the message may be censored.[88]

But why isn't sexual arousal itself a thought, a message that is redeemed in the pleasure, however cheap or evanascent, it gives the speaker and listener, the writer and reader, the poser and voyeur? Most pornographic speech is an aid to fantasizing about sex, an aid that may provoke reactons that are intellectual, emotional, or physical. Isn't the banning of obscenity essentially a social declaration that those fantasies are impure and improper? And if that is what is really going on, doesn't the banning of obscenity put the government in the role of acting as the "thought police?"

There are two approaches to this objection. One is to pretend that books, magazines, and films aimed only at sexual arousal do not communicate actual thoughts, but rather communicate something more animalistic and visceral, something more akin to action, which the state may legitimately regulate. A picture that is aimed only at turning you on is not communication, because the sexual turn on is not an activity of the cognitive side of the brain, but rather an activity of the lesser brain functions, brain functions beneath the concern of the First Amendment. If the only reaction to the *Penthouse* photos of Vanessa Williams (or Madonna) is physical, if it is restricted to "itching" or quickened pulse rates, then the state may ban the photographs, because they do not communicate thoughts, but are mere surrogates for sex. Usually the attempt is made to take this first approach one step further, by arguing that these lustful impulses may lead to overt deviant behavior. Under this view *Penthouse* does not merely reflect sexual promiscuity, it encourages, and yes, it *causes* promiscuity.

The second approach to justifying the banning of pornography is to admit freely that thoughts and attitudes are being regulated, and to further admit that they are being regulated because they are "bad." This is the tactic adopted by the current critique of pornography as sexist. This approach seems more honest; it is certainly truer to the heritage of Aristotle. The feminist critique of pornography sees the "badness" in pornography as its incessant message that women are proper objects for exploitation, dominance, and violence. This feminist critique is largely correct as far as its description goes. In sheer bulk much of the output of the pornography industry does contain a message of degredation against women. (At least some pornography contains counter messages, however, messages of celebration and liberation in newfound female sexual freedom.)

For much of the moral majority the offending messages are much more basic—sex, period, is wrong, outside of the procreative functions of marriage, and even within that function, only certain forms of activity are acceptable. If one is willing to make the jump to the position that society should be free to ban "bad" speech, however, then it makes no difference whether the reasons for banning a particular magazine, movie, or book are feminist or Falwellian. All that matters is that you have enough votes.

Nothing testifies more eloquently to the lack of reverence that Americans have for free expression than the growing popularity of these two approaches to obscenity. Conservatives and liberals, elites and the poorly educated, are in growing numbers and for differing reasons becoming quite comfortable with the idea that the likes of *Playboy*, *Penthouse*, and *Hustler* should all be sent up in flames. A federal judge in Georgia very recently analyzed every article and pictorial in an entire issue of *Penthouse*, and found the magazine as a whole obscene, and completely lacking in any redeeming social value. This is an example of the instinct to persecute feared speech that was identified decades ago in the eloquent Supreme Court opinions of Holmes and Brandeis. Judged by their actions rather than their words, Americans have no more had a long and unwavering attachment to the principles of free speech articulated by the Founding Fathers than Christians have had to the principles of love enunciated by Jesus. Americans today, as they have in the past, routintely tolerate the juxtaposition of an abstract intellectual commitment to free speech with a visceral reflex to supress whatever seems threatening. It is in this rich pure oxygen atmosphere of righteous censorship that magazines aimed at sexual arousal can once again be impounded, ignited, and burned with dispatch. It is in this atmosphere that juries sitting in judgment of these magazines return $26 million libel verdicts for fictional fantasies.

To the poor free speech attorneys left to defend the likes of *Playboy*, *Penthouse*, and *Hustler* (along with Nazis and the Ku Klux Klan), there is in the end only that most basic of all First Amendment values, a value that gets repeated so often that it becomes trivialized to the point of cliché. The value is one that can only be embraced through faith in the open and free exchange of speech, a faith perhaps greater than Jerry Falwell and many feminists are capable of. The faith is that it is more dangerous to try to separate good speech from bad speech than it is to hazard the risks of a government intrusive enough to do the separating.

One either has this faith, or one does not. It is the faith of Supreme Court Justice John Marshall Harlan, who upheld the right of a man to wear a leather jacket with the words "Fuck the Draft" emblazoned on the back, while standing in the corridor of a Los Angeles courthouse. Harlan perceived that even the word "fuck" can have political content, for "one man's vulgarity is another's lyric." It is surely true, Justice Harlan said, that "the state has no right to cleanse public debate to the point where it is grammatically palatable to the most squeamish among us."[89]

The American experience with censorship of the pornographic and the obscene is very clear. Americans know sexual arousal when they see it, and if given the power, they will often persecute it. James Joyce's *Ulysses* at many points is very sexually arousing, and for decades *Ulysses* was banned in the United States. If today you pick up a Random House or Vintage Books edition of *Ulysses* from your bookshelf or library, you will see printed in the forward the opinion of federal Judge John Woolsey lifting the ban on the book, as indelible testimony to the place where the presumption that government may choose between good and bad speech will inevitably lead. There is an air of promiscuity to *Leaves of Grass*, and in our history that poem has been banned. *Tropic of Cancer* is sexually graphic and blunt; it has been censored. *Lady Chatterly's Lover* is a tribute to sensuality, and has in its time been officially pronounced obscene. The persecutions of the Bob Gucciones, Hugh Hefners, Al Goldsteins, and Larry Flynts of our culture can lead to persecutions of the James Joyces, Walt Whitmans, Henry Millers, and D.H. Lawrences of the next generation.

To many feminists and moralists these suggestions are just so much alarmist liberal raving—parades of horribles from a less sophisticated past. Surely, they argue, one can meaningfully differentiate the crude pulp tabloid or violent sado-machistic film from the literature of Joyce or Lawrence. Surely no one today would try to take Walt Whitman or Henry Miller from the shelf. This certitude, however, underestimates the capacity of even a society as robust and open as ours for blind persecution. In the 1980's there are armies of censors waiting for the go-ahead to ban the books of Kurt Vonnegut or the comedy routines of George Carlin.

If it seems beyond reasonable expectation that the willingness of American courts to punish "bad taste" has no serious spillover effect on the freedom of "respectable" journalists and writers; if it seems to many that *Penthouse*, like the *National Enquirer*, simply reaps what it sows, one need not look long to see how the same habits of mind that lead to quick condemnation of the *Enquirer* or *Penthouse* lead to equally precipitous attacks on *Time*, the *Washington Post*, or CBS News. No lawsuit in recent years better reveals the new license that the modern libel jury believes it has been given than the suit of Mobil Oil president William Tavoulareas against the *Washington Post*. In considering that suit in the chapter that follows it is worth reflecting yet again on just how much, in the American public's thinking about the modern media, the *Enquirer*, *Penthouse*, and the *Washington Post* are more alike than different.

9

Mobil Oil Meets the *Washington Post*: Can Investigative Journalism Ever Be Objective?

A single company, in the nation's capital, holds control of the largest newspaper in Washington, D.C., and one of the four major television stations, and an all-news radio station, and one of the three major national news magazines—all grinding out the same editorial line—and this is not a subject that you've seen debated on the editorial pages of the *Washington Post* or the *New York Times*.

Vice President Spiro T. Agnew, in a speech on the media delivered November 20, 1969

Some newspapers are not only reluctant to admit error, but they seem incapable of realizing that the First Amendment which they tout so highly is a two-way street.

William Tavoulareas, President of Mobil Oil Corporation

THE LEAD HEADLINE of the November 30, 1979, edition of the *Washington Post* read "Mexico Will Not Allow Shah's Return." A subheading indicated that "Khomeini Seeks Arab Oil Support." Also on the front page of the *Post* was a story involving the Middle East and oil connections of a different sort. The story's headline read "Mobil Chief Sets Up Son in Venture." Written by *Post* staff writer Patrick Tyler, the 3,500 word story alleged that William P. Tavoulareas, the President and Chief Executive Officer of Mobil Oil Corporation, had used his influence and the assets of Mobil to "set up" and maintain his son, Peter Tavoulareas, in a newly formed shipping business, the Atlas Maritime Corporation, which in turn had lucrative dealings with Mobil. The *Post* story ultimately led to one of the most colorful and revealing libel suits of recent years.[90]

The tone of the *Post* story was established in the lead paragraph, and that paragraph may well have foreordained the lawsuit that would eventually follow.[91] The lead to the story stated that Tavoulareas "set up his son five years ago as a partner in a London based shipping management firm that has since done millions of dollars in business operating Mobil-owned ships under exclusive, no bid contracts." The younger Tavoulareas was only twenty-four when the Atlas firm was started; he had recently graduated from Columbia business school, and was working for $16,500 a year as a trainee-executive with a Greek shipping company run by a long-time shipping executive named George Commas.

Commas was to play a central role in the creation of the Atlas firm, and he would ultimately become a key source in the formulation of the *Washington Post* story. The *Post* was led to Commas through a source who was not necessarily impartial—Dr. Phillip Piro, an eye surgeon who had been divorced (in a less than amicable proceeding) from Tavoulareas's daughter. According to Commas, in 1974 Mobil began to worry that Saudi Arabia might decide to require all oil companies purchasing Saudi crude to transport the oil on Saudi-owned ships. To protect itself against against such a possibility, Mobil decided to enter into shipping company partnerships with a group of Saudis. An enterprise known as Saudi Maritime Company ("Samarco") was established, in which Mobil had a 30% interest. Majority interests were held by powerful members of the Saudi Arabian Alirezas family, and included prominent Saudis, such as Prince Mohamed Bin Fahd, son of King Fahd. Mobil owned a fleet of oil tankers. Using a relatively common admirality device for such a business deal, Mobil agreed to a so-called "bareboat charter" of its ships. Under the "bareboat charter," Mobil chartered its ships empty and unmanned to Samarco, which in turn would "time charter" them (charter them complete with crews and provisions) back to Mobil. Mobil was thus effectively chartering its own ships to itself, obtaining crews and provisions through Samarco, thereby insulating itself from a possible Saudi shipping preference. After Samarco was created, Mobil agreed that a separate company should actually handle the management of these vessels. That separate management company, Atlas, would be a partnership between Commas and young Peter Tavoulareas. Commas agreed to these arrangements and took Peter Tavoulareas in as an equity partner in Atlas, without requiring him to put up any money.

According to Commas, it was Mobil president William Tavoulareas who orchestrated the Mobil-Samarco-Atlas arrangements to his son's benefit, by asking Commas to take Peter in as a partner. Commas further claimed that William Tavoulareas later was instrumental in forcing Commas out of his Atlas position, using Mobil funds to buy out Commas, and then dispatching a top Mobil executive to Atlas' London headquarters to help his son Peter manage Atlas.

If these alleged events were undisputed they would be quite a story. Commas' version of events, however, was vigorously disputed by the Tavoulareases, father and son, and by Mobil. According to Mobil, it was Commas who wanted Peter to join Atlas, not William Tavoulareas who foisted Peter on Commas. According to William Tavoulareas, the arrangements with Samarco and Atlas were not established to aid his son Peter Tavoulareas, but to safeguard Mobil against the possible imposition of a new Saudi-owned vessel rule by Saudi Arabia. When son Peter joined Atlas, Tavoulareas informed Mobil's Conflict of Interest Committee, which found no impropriety in the arrangement. Further, William Tavoulareas told the Mobil board of directors about his son Peter's involvement in Atlas and explained his possible conflict of interest to the directors. Tavoulareas then recused himself from all final decisions involving Atlas and Samarco. William Tavoulareas had nothing to do, Mobil claimed, with the subsequent dismissal of Commas, or with sending a Mobil executive to Atlas to replace Commas. When the Mobil executive was sent to Atlas, his salary became the responsibility of Atlas, not Mobil. The Mobil-Samarco-Atlas relationship, including the Tavoulareas-Atlas connection, was explained to Mobil shareholders in a 1976 letter.

The *Post* article contained *both* the Commas and the Mobil-Tavoulareas versions of the story, but the clear thrust of the article was that Commas was correct, and that Tavoulareas had acted improperly. The *Post* charged, for example, that "United States securities law requires that corporate officials disclose the details of business transactions between companies and relatives of the companies' executives." This charge, later highlighted in the trial, was legally incorrect: the Securities and Exchange Commission did not require such potential conflict-of-interest disclosure unless the relatives were living in the same household, which William and Peter Tavoulareas were not. The *Post's* leanings were further revealed the day after the initial story had run, when the *Post* ran a follow-up item reporting that Michigan Congressman John Dingell, chairman of the House subcommittee that oversees the SEC, had written the Commission to allege that Tavoulareas may have lied to the SEC about the Mobil-Samarco-Atlas relationship. That investigation ultimately ended with no adverse SEC action against Tavoulareas or Mobil.

A few days after the two *Post* stories, William Tavoulareas had a meeting with *Post* editor Ben Bradlee, in which Tavoulareas asked for a retraction. Bradlee refused to retract the story, but did immediately run a story detailing Mobil's denials of wrongdoing. Over the course of the next year (the statute of limitations for libel in the District of Columbia was one year), Tavoulareas tried to get the *Post* to retract, and he quite obviously grew increasingly frustrated and angry. In Tavoulareas' words, "I tried to get them to admit their mistakes. But they're so damn arrogant. I kept telling them I'd sue. But they said I wouldn't because they'd drag me through the mud in discovery. Well, I know my reputation and my integrity, and I knew they'd get nothing on me. I said, 'You don't know me. I'm gonna sue.' " The *Post* should have known to take Tavoulareas seriously, if for no other reason than that two years before the *Post* article, Tavoulareas had sued (and settled with) *Harper's* magazine for libel accusations arising from an article in which editor Lewis Lapham described Tavoulareas as "always loud," "a bad actor," and "a Nixon type."

Almost one year to the day after the *Post* article, William and Peter Tavoulareas filed a $100 million libel suit against the *Post*. William Tavoulareas insisted, "I'm not trying to destroy the press. I know what a free press means to this country. This suit would not have happened if they'd admitted their mistakes." Shortly after the Tavoulareas suit commenced, the story broke that *Post* reporter Janet Cooke's Pulitzer-Prize winning story "Jimmy's World," about an eight-year-old heroin addict, was a fabrication, based entirely on a confidential source that did not exist. For those inclined to believe that Woodward and Bernstein never really had a "Deep Throat" source for their Watergate exposés, the Janet Cooke revelation only served to fuel suspicions about the *Post's* investigative methodology. As in Ariel Sharon's suit against *Time*, the innuendo would be that the media, hungry for a scoop, will sometimes rely on confidential sources that are nothing but phantoms. Picking upon these themes, Tavoulareas' lawyers quoted Bob Woodward's definition of the ideal reporter: "I guess you have to have a compulsive need to succeed. You have to be insecure and want desperately to please your boss." Throughout the trial, Tavoulareas' litigation strategy would be to accentuate the compulsiveness and arrogance that he believed permeated the *Post's* operation.

This strategy produced some effective testimony in favor of Tavoulareas. The *Post* story orignated with a reporter for a small Maryland newspaper, *The Montgomery Journal*, named Sandy Golden. Golden had been told by Philip Piro, the physician who was in the middle of a divorce from Tavoulareas' daughter, that William had used his power to make his son an "overnight millionaire." Golden had been angling for a job at the *Post*, and attempted to get through to *Post* editor Bob Woodward that he had a worthwhile story concerning Tavoulareas. Woodward eventually assigned reporter Patrick Tyler to check out Golden's story. Tyler and Golden then met at the Owl restaurant in Baltimore with Philip Piro. According to the trial testimony, as Tyler left the restaurant, he was obviously pleased with the story's prospects, for he remarked that it's "not every day you knock off one of the seven sisters," referring to Mobil, one of the nation's seven largest oil companies.

Tyler then tracked down Commas, who became the principal source for the story. Tyler wrote the story, with an emphasis on Commas' version of events. To his credit, Tyler included a number of facts favorable to Tav-oulareas to balance the article. To the *Post's* later embarrassment, however, much of the material favorable to Tavoulareas was cut during the editing process, including opinions from people inside and outside of Mobil that the Atlas deal had benefitted Mobil, as well as information indicating that William Tavoulareas was not directly involved with Atlas. For example, one of Mobil's outside directors, Lewis Lapham, told reporter Tyler that the Mobil board had "consistently reviewed the relationship between Mobil and Atlas" and that the board "was completely satisfied with all aspects of it." Lapham told Tyler that he did not believe that Tavoulareas "played a personal role in Atlas" and that at key board meetings Tavoulareas "would leave the room to facilitate the opportunity for more open discussion of the subject." Early drafts of Tyler's article *did include Lapham's information, including his direct quotes.* The edited final draft, however, deleted Lapham's statements, and substituted the following sentence: "Mobil chairman Warner says he assured directors in board meetings that Tav-oulareas does not participate in any decisions regarding Mobil's business with Atlas." The article thus replaced the direct statement of outside direc-tor Lapham with a self-serving "assurance" by inside director and chair-man Warner, a substitution that at once diminished the effectiveness of Lapham's point and underscored the reporter's suspicion of inside influ-ence at Mobil which permeated the entire article.

The jury was also treated to some candid testimony by editor Bob Wood-ward concerning what came to be known in the case as "holy shit" jour-nalism. During the cross examination of Woodward, the following dia-logue ensued:

Question: Did you tell them you were looking for stories that would go on the front page, big, significant stories?

Answer: Not all significant stories go on the front page. I tried to describe the kind of coverage we should have and how we should direct our efforts. Yes, sir.

Question: Did you tell them you were looking for stories with impact?

Answer: Not precisely that word.

Question: In any of these discussions, did you ever use a term such as 'I'm looking for something called a holy shit story?'

Answer: Yes, I did.

Tavoulareas' lawyers also heavily emphasized a piece of evidence that seemed to strongly drive home the allegation that the *Post* acted recklessly. A memorandum, written three days before the *Post* article was published, by a *Post* copy editor, Christine Peterson, to her superior, discussed certain problems Peterson had with the Tavoulareas story:

I've read the Mobil story several times, and while I'm impressed with the amount of work the reporter obviously did, I'm still left with an overwhelming sense of So What? Is there any way to give this story of high-level nepotism a dollars-and-cents angle? Did Mobil's shareholders lose anything? Mobil's customers? Parts of Tyler's case against Tavoulareas seems tenuous, and the whole—a $680,000-a-year plaything for an indulged son, at worst—just seems like a withered peanut in an 84 inch gilded shell.

A far more interesting angle, it seems to me, is Mobil's concern about Saudi preference shipping—a concern so profound that it led to the formation of an entire dummy corporation. It's impossible to believe that Tavoulareas alone could put together such a scheme for the sake of his son's business career, or that he would want to.

This sort of evidence against the *Post* would ultimately play a critical role in the litigation, but what seemed to anger Tavoulareas most was not so much the *Post's* original mistakes (as he saw them) in portraying his actions relative to his son Peter's business ventures, but rather the *Post's* hardheaded refusal to give an inch on its accusations once Tavoulareas pointed out the inaccuracies. The *Post's* refusal to retract was like a matador's twitching cape in front of a wounded bull; the details of the story became secondary to Tavoulareas' perception of the *Post* as arrogant and utterly devoid of conscience or humility. In a letter to this author, Mr. Tavoulareas revealed much of the psychology of his suit, and his view of the explosion of libel litigation generally, in quite powerful and succinct terms:

> What I am suggesting to you is that there is another theory explaining the increase in libel suits. It is the fact that aggressive, irresponsible reporters, engaged in the new fashion of investigative reporting, seek and write sensational angles about public figures without the constraint, as a practical matter, of worry about libel liability. The resulting carelessness with the truth, coupled with the increased use of "reliable sources", has made the resulting libels infinitely more damaging.
>
> It is one thing to laugh off the outrageous fabrication in a *Village Voice*; it is quite another thing to ignore the sophisticated lie in the supposedly reputable *Washington Post*.
>
> Furthermore, the growing tendency of certain of the media to believe in their own omniscience is a contributing factor. Some newspapers are not only reluctant to admit error, but they seem incapable of realizing that the First Amendment which they tout so highly is a two-way street. The corollary of a newspaper's claimed right to publish its version of the facts with impunity ought to be an obligation promptly to give equal space and prominence to the version of the facts of those who are the subject of their attention. Not only do certain newspapers seem unwilling to retract or confess error, but they also seem even more unwilling to print alternate versions of the facts.
>
> In my case, even where a jury has found the article false and libelous, and damaging to me, a finding which is so far undisturbed, the news-

paper persists in asserting that they would not change anything in the article. If newspapers could somehow find the humility to confess error, I suspect there would be less plaintiffs and fewer libel actions.[92]

The Washington D.C. federal court jury appeared to find Tavoulareas' position convincing, for they stunned the media world by returning a verdict against the respected *Washington Post* in the impressive amount of $2.05 million.[93]

In an excellent exercise of investigative journalism, *The American Lawyer*, a monthly magazine for lawyers, set out to discover why the jury in the *Post* case had sided with Tavoulareas.[94] The results, set forth in an outstanding article by *American Lawyer* editor Steven Brill, vindicates the hypothesis that the First Amendment's protective rules for the press often get lost once the jury is ensconced behind closed doors. Five of the six jurors agreed to be interviewed. According to their account, the initial jury vote was 4–2 in favor of the *Post*. One of the two jurors who sided with Tavoulareas, however, was the jury foreman, a young librarian in the Library of Congress law library, who was scheduled to enter Catholic University Law School in the fall. Over the course of more than eighteen hours of deliberation spanning three days, the jury foreman repeatedly hammered in on one theme: "You show me where it proves anywhere else in the articles that Tavoulareas set up his kid."

To this theme, the jurors in favor of the *Post* had two responses: First, "He *did* set him up and we all *know* that;" and second, "What's the big deal? We'd all help our sons." The foreman, however, never backed down. He admitted that William Tavoulareas had probably helped Peter in the deal, but that, he insisted, was beside the point. The *Post's* article had to *prove* that Tavoulareas had set up his son, and it did not.

Adamant in holding to this line of argument, the jury foreman gradually wore away all resistance, and the jury came back with a verdict in favor of William Tavoulareas of $250,000 in compensatory damages, and $1.8 million in punitive damages. The $1.8 million represented exactly the amount Tavoulareas told the jury he had spent in legal fees, and the jury obviously thought that the *Post*, which they were told had a net income for 1981 of $32.7 million, could easily foot Tavoulareas' legal bill. The jury decided not to award Tavoulareas' son Peter any damages against the *Post*, on the theory that whereas the father was a well-known man with a reputation to protect who'd been humiliated, the son was a mere private figure with no substantial reputational stock yet accumulated. Against Dr. Phillip Piro, the eye surgeon and former son-in-law of Tavoulareas who was an initial source for the story, the jury awarded William Tavoulareas $5,000 and Peter $1,000.

The jury's behavior in the Tavoulareas suit has many different shades of meaning. To the First Amendment zealot the jury's conduct is an abomination. The jury foreman convinced the jury to apply a principle exactly the opposite of the legal rule required by the First Amendment. Under the principles of *New York Times v. Sullivan*, it is never the newspaper's burden to prove that its story is true; rather, it is the plaintiff's burden to prove that it is substantially false. The jury thus got the instructions from trial Judge Oliver Gasch exactly backward. The instructions, to Judge Gasch's credit, were perfectly clear: "It is not the defendant's burden to prove that the articles are true. The burden is upon the plaintiffs to prove to you that they are substantially false." The jury, however, turned this instruction upside-down.

The second gigantic legal mistake made by the jury was that it completely ignored the rule under *New York Times* and its progeny that the defendant may be found liable to a public figure like William Tavoulareas only if it knowingly or recklessly disregards the truth. The jury did not seem to zero in on the *Post's* "knowing or reckless disregard of the truth" at all; it was preoccupied instead with the text of the article and the underlying facts of the Tavoulareas dealings. Finally, the decision to give the elder Tavoulareas $2 million against the *Post* and the younger Tavoulareas nothing seems to directly invert the judicial compromise struck by the Supreme Court in the *Gertz* case, which had been designed to give private figures *more* protection against libels by the press than public figures.

But did the jury's apparent failure to obey "the law" as it was instructed really tarnish Tavoulareas' victory, or did it actually reinforce the primary point that Tavoulareas was out to make? Tavoulareas can proudly wear his $2 million verdict as a badge of honor even if the jury perverted "the law" to render it, for Tavoulareas believes the law of libel itself is perverted, and the jury's disregard of the law in his case, like the actions of the overwhelming majority of other juries in other libel cases, is proof to Tavoulareas of exactly how far out of sync the modern law of libel is from the prevailing mores of the American people.

A dissection of the thought process of the Tavoulareas jury demonstrates how deeply the ingrained "psychological burdens of proof" in a libel suit may run, and it highlights how far out of line those natural human habits of mind are from either the formal rules of libel law or the conventions of modern journalism. More than anything else, the jury seemed to be swayed by the discrepancy between the tenor of the words of the *Post's* headline—"Mobil Chief Sets Up Son in Venture"—and the more balanced and less conclusive tenor of the text.

The jury, in short, was reacting to a tactic used with routine bravado by the *National Enquirer*, yet also capable of slipping onto the front page of the *Washington Post*. One of the regular schticks of checkout counter journalism is the headline that reads: "Michael Landon Talks of Secret Love Life," followed by the actual story on page twenty-three, which reveals that what Michael Landon has talked about is that he has no secret love life. Even the most religiously loyal gossip tabloid readers are likely to feel at least mildly offended by this device, not merely out of sympathy for Michael Landon (some readers, after all, were probably hoping the story *would* uncover a secret affair), but out of a sense that the readers themselves were manipulated and cheated. The offense is in the failure to deliver the goods as promised.

On a much more subtle level, that is the offense for which the Tavoulareas jury convicted the *Post*. The headline, and the unmistakeable message communicated between the lines, was that William Tavoulareas had done wrong. The actual text of the *Post* story, however, did not provide the necessary clinchers. Although the text told both sides of the story, and from the literal words alone one could just as well conclude that Tavoulareas's behavior was perfectly above board and legitimate as that it was insidious and dishonest, all the facts and inferences favorable to Tavoulareas were systematically presented so as to diminish their force. The one firm conclusion that the *Post* did venture to draw—that Tavoulareas had failed to make disclosures required by federal securities laws—turned out to be inaccurate.

The jury foreman's insistence that the text of the story did not *prove* the set-up charge thus may have been misguided as a restatement of First Amendment law, but it was right on the money in capturing the prevailing American psychology about fair play in the press. According to the internal ethical systems of most Americans, he who makes the charge *does* have the burden of backing it up. If you don't have the facts, shut up—you don't go around knifing people's reputations on suspicions alone.

The *Washington Post's* shortcomings, as perceived by the jury, were not idiosyncratic. Rather, they reflect prevailing conventions in the world of journalism, conventions that themselves act as unnatural restraints on instinctual patterns of free expression. As writers Walter Karp and Tom Wicker both noted in a recent discussion printed in *Harper's*, there is an unwritten law of journalism that a reporter is not permitted in a news story to offer his own inference regarding a motive from the actions of a public figure; such judgments can only be drawn by another public figure, who can then be duly quoted. Indeed, in other matters as well, the reporter may assemble the facts, but he or she is not permitted to add them together and present a conclusion, at least not as his own. A reporter is bound by the unwritten conventions of journalism to report faithfully a public official's statements. Even if he knows them to be lies he may not in his own voice contradict such statements. A reporter cannot tell the public that the Secretary of State lied about some aspect of the mining of harbors in Nicaragua; all he can do is try to find someone else—the Speaker of the House, perhaps—to quote in order to "balance" the story.

One of the most fascinating aspects of this journalistic practice is that people like William Tavoulareas do not seem to take offense when reporters draw personal conclusions, as long as they make it clear they are drawing them. Nor do they take offense when the "straight" news story neutrally lays out raw facts, leaving all conclusions to the reader.[95] What appeared to irk Tavoulareas and the Washington, D.C. jury was the subtle infiltration of judgmental conclusions by the *Post* in what on its face purported to be neutral reportage. What Tavoulareas lashed out against was advocacy wrapped up in the disguise of neutrality—the news story presented as pure fact that was really a selection of facts to support a predetermined opinion. Tavoulareas' complaint against the *Post* was thus much like Ariel Sharon's complaint against *Time*. Tavoulareas, like Sharon, believes that certain elements of the press use the vehicle of supposedly objective journalism to advance their own political agendas.

The *Washington Post* only just barely crossed this line from objectivity to advocacy, and the jury might well have forgiven the *Post* its transgression, if the *Post* had not, in the process of defending itself, run afoul of a second imposing reality about the psychology of the American jury: American juries get their backs up at the appearance of arrogance and elitism. The people who run the *Washington Post* may not in their routine behavior or daily reportage be arrogant or elitist at all—but when they were challenged for libel that is the image they (perhaps unwittingly) conveyed. Just as *Time* would forever maintain its innocence in the Sharon case, the *Post* would never admit throughout the whole dispute with Tavoulareas that it had done anything wrong. The niceties of the First Amendment notwithstanding, the jury apparently choose not to reward such an attitude.

This is not to say that the jury necessarily bought William Tavoulareas' version of events lock, stock and barrel. The jury clearly thought that Peter Tavoulareas got the partnership interest in Atlas because he was the son of the president of Mobil Oil. How, honestly, could they *not* have reached that conclusion? Does anyone in their heart of hearts really believe that a twenty-four year old named "Peter Sixpack" making $16,500 a year would have been brought in as an equity partner in a lucrative million dollar shipping deal without putting up any front money? *Of course* it made a difference that Peter's last name was Tavoulareas. The significant issue from a social perspective, however, is whether or not society should disapprove of such an arrangement. And on this point, there is ample ground for legitimate disagreement.

The *Post* obviously wanted its readers to conclude that Tavoulareas' assistance to his son was a bad thing. Yet the *Post* didn't have the courage of its own conviction—the courage to make its editorializing explicit, the courage to try to persuade the reader that Tavoulareas simply by allowing the arrangement was guilty of nepotism that, per se, compromised the interests of Mobil stockholders and the public at large. The *Post* slipped into a wimpish middle ground, hinting that Tavoulareas had cheated the public interest, but putting the story in an objective voice. It was as if Dan Rather had quoted Ronald Reagan on the *CBS Evening News* with his eyebrows a mile high and his eyes rolled back to the top of his head. The same *Post* story, packaged more honestly as an inquiry into the complex questions raised by such inter-family dealings, would have been top-notch journalism. Rather than engage in a more searching analysis, however, the *Post* opted to over-simplify, and in the process, to sensationalize.

The internal expression of doubt about the *Post* story expressed in copy editor Christine Peterson's memorandum is one of the most troublesome pieces of evidence in the case. The memorandum did not, standing alone, prove that the *Post* knowingly or recklessly lied about Tavoulareas. For the *Post's* decision to run the story despite this internal criticism could just as well be taken as evidence that the author and editors of the story ultimately concluded that their facts and their conclusions about Tavoulareas were correct. What the memorandum did show, however, was that someone at the *Post* had an insight into the genuine shortcomings of the article—its failure to determine whether Mobil's shareholders or customers were ever really harmed. The jury thought this memorandum particularly damning—the foreman relied on it heavily in his arguments against the *Post*—for it disclosed just how the style of "objective reporting with a wink" made the case against Tavoulareas seem much clearer than it was.

For after all is said and done, it is not obvious that, even if the basic outlines of the facts as the *Post* reported them are true, Tavoulareas necessarily acted improperly. According to Tavoulareas, it was not a question of going out of his way to help his son, but of not going out of his way to hurt him. Most Americans will do what they can to help their kids succeed, short of breaking the rules. If Tavoulareas could make a commercially intelligent deal for Mobil (such as give it a buffer against the machinations of Middle East politics), and at the same time help his son, is that so evil? The entire arrangement was, after all, fully disclosed to the Mobil board of directors.

Tavoulareas has always insisted, "the only test we have in our company is: 'Are these transactions justified from Mobil's point of view?'" Mobil's internal procedures, and Tavoulareas' careful recusals from all decision-making in the area, in his view provided Mobil stockholders and customers with complete protection. Mobil had outside accountants look at all the Atlas-Sumarco deals to insure that they made "commercial sense." If son Peter's career could be given a push on the side, so be it. Peter Tavoulareas, showing some of his father's plucky banter, said in the *Post* trial that "Greeks seem to go into the restaurant business or the shipping business. I happened to go into the shipping business." The elder Tavoulareas noted that "if anything, when my son's involved, [Mobil employees] bend over backwards the other way around, and don't even do things for him they'd do for an outsider," because if they did, "there'll be 14 guys writing about it." And Tavoulareas raised a legitimate question: should top management never deal with relatives or friends to their benefit, even if at arms length with no outsiders damaged? Where can a line be drawn: "Friends, schoolmates, cousins, sister-in-laws? Where do we stop this?"

The *Washington Post*, of course, is perfectly entitled under the First Amendment to express the view that despite Tavoulareas' protestations, American society is better off not permitting these sort of corporate deals, simply because of the possibility of abuse. And if at the time it ran the story the *Post* sincerely believed that Tavoulareas had done wrong, then under the *New York Times* standard it was entitled to victory even if it later was proved wrong. But the *Post* in its defense would not even concede the *possibility* that Tavoulareas' viewpoint might be correct, and that cocksure attitude certainly affected the jury. As Tavoulareas put it, "after nineteen days of trial and five thousand pages of testimony, the *Post's* lawyer was saying, 'We still wouldn't change a line of the articles.' That was the biggest single error he made. All they had to say was, 'At the time, that's what we *believed* was true.'"

The irony of the *Post's* offending certitude is that one of it's own principal witnesses, Bob Woodward, actually described, in a sympathetic way, the *Post's* methodology as much more humanly fallible. During his direct examination he defended the *Post's* "bottom line":

> I guess those stories, both of them, fit fully my definition of what I think our job is: the best obtainable version of the truth. It's a version. It's something particularly Pat Tyler worked as intensely as any reporter can work to get at from both sides.
> I've heard Mr. Tavoulareas testify that he didn't have time for the George Commases of the world. I guess in the newspaper business we listen to . . . the Dr. Philip Piros of the world, we listen to everyone. We listen to Peter Tavoulareas, Mr. Tavoulareas—William Tavoulareas, I mean—we listen to the Mobil public relations apparatus. . . . These stories, rather than being something that should be on trial, are a model of digging, thinking, being fair, balancing the story out, and getting at that time what was the best obtainable version of the truth. And in my my opinion Mr. Tyler got it.

During cross-examination, Woodward conceded some of the subjective judgments that went into the story, and then offered a defense of those subjective judgments based on the inherent subjectivity in the information sorting and reporting process:

Walsh (Tavoulareas' Attorney): Did you ever suggest to Pat Tyler that he ought to mention Samarco in those opening paragraphs?

Woodward: No, sir, I did not, and in fact, as I think I indicated earlier, the problem for us in the story was getting a full, accurate presentation of what was going on in a simple, clear way. I guess everyone who's dealt with this knows it's not very simple and it's complicated.

Walsh: And the best available version of the truth that you gentlemen could put out at that point was to write a story, the lead of which did not mention one of the three companies you were looking at until you got to the sixth paragraph, is that so?

Woodward: No, no.

Walsh: Isn't that a fact? It didn't mention Samarco until the sixth paragraph?

Woodward: That's a fact and there's a reason for this, and that's what this is all about: you people saying, 'Gee, we want you to write a story this way, we want this included, we want this included.' You can write a story a million ways or even more than a million ways. What we do is we process information . . . make it clear. We are trying to be fair and accurate as we were in this story. . . . You're asking a question that hinges on your assumption that you guys dictate how it's done.

Woodward's point here is that there are "judgment calls" required in any investigative story. The reporter does not, in fact *cannot* report *truth*, but only the "best available judgment" as to the truth. Woodward's point parallels the defenses put forward in the two most celebrated "political" libel trials of the 1980's, Ariel Sharon's suit against *Time*, and William Westmoreland's suit against CBS News. Although we would like to think that reporters' and editors' subjective interpretations of events never seep into their ostensibly objective reporting, the reality may be that in any reasonably complex investigative undertaking, subjective judgments by reporters are inevitable. As long as these subjective judgments are "sincere," the First Amendment protects them even when they turn out to be false. That, at least, is the "rule" of the *New York Times* case. The jury in *Sharon v. Time* apparently recognized this rule and was willing to accept it. If the Tavoulareas jury had taken Bob Woodward's argument to heart, the *Post* probably would have won.

But there is evidence that the natural inclination of juries is not to accept this rule, but rather to apply a more primal instinct of "fairness": if subjective judgments infiltrate supposedly neutral reportage, juries will hold the press strictly accountable for conclusions and intimations that turn out to be wrong. Thus, the press is caught by the whipsaw of two powerful psychological realities: serious investigative reporting will always entail subjective judgments, and juries will tend to treat the press harshly whenever these subjective judgments later surface and turn out to have been misguided.

Yet the press, although never able to conquer the problem that some subjectivity inevitably infiltrates even conscientious efforts to objectively report the facts, is not powerless to protect itself against the pinching actions of this dilemma. What the press theoretically can do is disclose in advance when it is engaging in "objective reporting," and when it is really engaging in "commentary," "speculation," or "analysis."

The *Post's* trial lawyer, Irving Younger, famous within the legal world for his writings and lectures on trial tactics and evidence, chose not to emphasize Woodward's "we made the best call we could" line of defense. The Tavoulareas trial, Younger later told *The American Lawyer*, "can kind of be looked at as a criminal case in the sense that the jury's deciding here whether we did something bad. In such a case, where both lawyers are perceived by the jurors to be decent people, the jurors will find a compromise." According to Younger, there are parallels to defending a criminal case. Younger believes that to defend a criminal case on the grounds that there is a "reasonable doubt" about guilt is a mistake. Younger preaches that for a defense lawyer even to use the phrase "beyond a reasonable doubt" is a mistake, because it gives the jury no maneuvering room in which to compromise. "You let the judge give them the middle-ground compromise position," Younger says, "with his charge to the jury about reasonable doubt."

In a libel suit, Younger reasons, the compromise is the "reckless disregard" standard. "So I never mentioned it," Younger stated, "I let the judge do it in his instruction." As much as the abstract outlines of Younger's observations ring true, he and the *Post* may have misjudged the natural compromise that the jury would be inclined to strike. Younger's closing remarks to the jury contain, from the *Post's* perspective, a bitter note of irony:

> I think the law is very wise when it says they, the jury, decide. Because, ladies and gentlemen, jurors can do some things better than lawyers, better even sometimes than judges. Jurors have a wonderful way of being able to put the details to one side, of seeing through the smoke and the fog and getting to what the case is really about.

As it turns out, of course, to the extent that the jury in the *Post* case "saw through the smoke and fog," it did so by applying innate standards of fairness that ignored the First Amendment rules established in *New York Times v. Sullivan*, and that resulted in a $2 million verdict against the *Post*. Despite Younger's professed faith in the jury, the *Post*, like so many other recent press defendants, would ultimately be forced to depend on judges to overturn the jury's verdict.

Exactly what judges will do in the *Post* case remains, at the time of this writing, unresolved. The trial judge in the case first overturned the jury's verdict, but in the spring of 1985 a three-judge panel of the Court of Appeals for the District of Columbia by a 2–1 vote reversed the judge and reinstated the verdict of the jury against the *Post*. The Court of Appeals decision reviewed the evidence from the trial and concluded that the jury could legitimately have found that the *Post* acted with reckless disregard for the truth. (That panel decision by the Court of Appeals is being reconsidered by the entire court at the time of this writing.)

Among the factors that influenced the Court of Appeals decision was the *Post's* emphasis on obtaining the "holy shit" story. The court wrote that "What Woodward meant in exhorting his reporters to come up with the 'holy shit' stories is not exactly clear, but a reasonable inference is that Woodward, as editor, wanted from his reporters the same kind of stories on which he built his own reputation: high-impact investigative stories of wrongdoing." The court then stated that from "Woodward's testimony it was proper for the jurors to infer that the *Post* put some pressure on its reporters to come up with "holy shit" stories—a category into which the Tavoulareas story (described by Peterson as one of 'high-level nepotism' in the corporate context) presumably fit." This policy of the *Post*, the court surmised, could be characterized as conducive either to "hardhitting journalism" or "sophisticated muckraking," but either characterization is relevant to the inquiry of whether a newspaper's employees acted in reckless disregard of whether a statement is false or not."

The Court of Appeals decision in the Tavoulareas case seemed to bend over backward to sustain the jury's verdict, ruling that Tavoulareas was entitled to all reasonable inferences in favor of the jury's decision with regard to the basic facts, and that given the *Post's* conduct in putting together the story, these inferences would support a finding of actual malice. The tone of the Court of Appeals decision, more than any other decision to date, seemed to capture much of the prevailing American suspicion of aggressive investigative journalism, for it held that the *Post's* admitted posture of hardhitting investigation was a factor that could be legitimately taken into account to determine if the *Post* was predisposed to reckless reporting. At the time of this writing, the entire District of Columbia Court of Appeals had agreed to rehear the Tavoulareas case. (Normally, a federal court of appeals, which usually contains between seven and fifteen judges in total, sits in "panels" of three judges to hear cases. In rare circumstances, however, the entire complement of judges on the court may agree to review a three-judge panel decision by the whole court, a procedure known as "rehearing *en banc*.") Whatever the entire District of Columbia Court does with the case, many media lawyers believe that the Supreme Court will ultimately review the decision, meaning that a final judgment may still be years hence.

The irony of all of this appellate review, of course, is that whether or not the evidence would be sufficient to sustain a jury's finding of recklessness as required by *New York Times v. Sullivan* and its progeny, it appears from the post-trial interviews of the jurors that in the actual deliberations of the jurors in the Tavoulareas case they essentially ignored the *New York Times* rules altogether, applying their own version of justice to cut through the smoke and fog of legal rules and lawyer's rhetoric.

If the smoke and fog of the Tavoulareas case would threaten to overwhelm the First Amendment, however, it would be nothing like the smoke and fire of *Westmoreland v. CBS*, a case with issues as complicated as the Vietnam War, and a case in which the jury would in the end turn out to be the American people.

10

Westmoreland v. CBS: Litigating the Symbols and Lessons of Vietnam

Ye shall know the truth, and the truth shall make you free.
John 8:32
Inscribed on the entrance to
CIA headquarters,
in Langley, Virginia

THE STORY BEGINS with a litany of place names that had become all too familiar twenty years ago. Hue, Khesanh, Quangtri, Lang Vei, Ashau, Danang, Hoi An, Kham Duc, Quangngai, Dakto, Kontum, Quinhon, Pleiku, Banmethuot, Nhatrang, Dalat, Bienhoa, Chau Doc, Mytho, Bentre, Vinh Long, Cantho, Camau, Saigon. On the evening of January 31, 1968, cities across the entire length of South Vietnam exploded in a coordinated attack launched by some seventy thousand Communist soldiers. It was Tet, the sacred lunar New Year holiday; for the Vietnamese, a celebration like an American Christmas, New Year's Eve, and Fourth of July rolled into one. Tet in 1968 ushered in the "Year of the Monkey" on the ancient Chinese calendar. For the people of Vietnam, the Year of the Monkey brought with it the largest Communist offensive and the worst bloodshed of the war. For the people of the United States, 1968 brought a cascade of dramatic and numbing television images: North Koreans seizing and humiliating the crew of the *USS Pueblo*; Senator Eugene McCarthy shocking Lyndon Johnson in the New Hampshire primary; Bobby Kennedy announcing the murder of Martin Luther King; Rafer Johnson and Rosy Grier wrestling with the assassin of Bobby Kennedy; Lyndon Johnson declaring that he would not run for re-election; Chicago police beating anti-war demonstrators bloody and unconscious on Balbo Avenue, beneath the hotel view of delegates to the Democratic Convention; a triumphant Richard Nixon nominated for President by the Republican party in Miami; Richard Nixon elected President of the United States.

Punctuating these images on television screens were the ongoing images of frustration and horror from Vietnam. And none of the war footage was more enduring than the portrayal of the Tet offensive. Television screens on the first day of the offensive showed American commandos battling to retain their Saigon stronghold. Stunned Americans watched film footage only hours old of the American Saigon embassy under enemy control, as American soldiers and embassy officials raced chaotically past rubble and dead bodies. For many Americans the pictures on their television sets seemed to crystallize their swelling sense that the Vietnam War was an interminable tunnel of violence, disorder, and futility, a war that America should either win, or stop.

For General William Westmoreland, the Commander of the United States forces in Vietnam, the images had a different meaning. To General Westmoreland the sight of the enemy coming out of the jungles and rice paddies to fight conventional battles in the cities was a welcome one—it was the very type of fight he had been hoping for; it was the type of fight he expected American forces to win. Yet it soon became clear to Westmoreland that Tet, like so much of the Vietnam War, was to be fought not only on the battlefield, but on the television screen. To Westmoreland, the attack on the American embassy in Saigon was a piddling, almost desperate effort, an effort that the Americans quickly crushed. To Westmoreland the entire Tet offensive was a Communist blunder, an ill-fated string of assaults that ultimately emaciated the Communist forces. Yet the press coverage of Tet, particularly the television networks' portrayal of the battles near Saigon, transformed the defeat into a psychological victory for the enemy, by accelerating the unravelling of the American public's support for the war. In General Westmoreland's view, Tet symbolized the pattern of the whole war. Press coverage of the war sapped morale and weakened our effort more than the enemy itself. For Westmoreland, in a sense, the American press became more his enemy than the Viet Cong and the North Vietnamese. American television coverage was warped, lurid, and sensationalist; it was a sophisticated electronic form of yellow journalism. In his memoirs Westmoreland blamed the media for poisoning American opinion about the war, by overplaying atrocities and defeats, and underplaying victories and examples of humanity and courage. A lesson to be learned, he said, "is that young men should never be sent into battle unless the country is going to support them." He might have said, "unless the media is going to support them."

Fifteen years after Tet, in what came to be called by many "The Libel Suit of the Century," General William Westmoreland commenced a $120 million libel suit against the CBS television network, arising from a CBS documentary broadcast in 1982, entitled *The Uncounted Enemy: A Vietnam Deception*. The CBS documentary accused Westmoreland of complicity in a conspiracy to suppress the truth about the actual strength of Communist forces prior to the 1968 Tet offensive.

Westmoreland v. CBS[96] became a battle for the symbols and lessons of Vietnam. As the trial wore interminably on, and as Americans learned more of Vietnam, and more of the media's coverage of it, the symbols and lessons seemed to become increasingly complex and ambiguous.

Federal Judge Pierre Nelson Leval, the very able and creative judge who presided over the trial, constantly attempted to keep the issues in the case focused and restrained.[97] Judge Leval instructed the New York jury of six men and six women that the case was not about their feelings on the military, peace and war, the Vietnam War, freedom of the press, whether press criticism of government was good or bad, or whether they admired or disliked General Westmoreland or CBS. "Those questions," he told the jury, "are completely behind us." But no matter how hard Judge Leval labored to contain the trial within the traditional parameters of libel litigation, the suit could not but spawn a domino-theory dynamic of its own, taking on broader meanings as it moved forward. Westmoreland and CBS entered the litigation with fiercely different subjective colorations about what the "truth" really was, and as the case gathered steam it became a cause célèbre centered on those opposing visions of reality.

The parties came to assume the roles of surrogates for ideological splits within the nation as a whole. For some, Westmoreland was a knight flailing against the liberal eastern establishment press that they believed poisoned the anti-Communist effort in Vietnam, and that they thought continued to warp public perceptions. (In the midst of the trial, conservative Senator Jesse Helms announced a scheme to get conservatives to buy CBS and "become Dan Rather's boss.") For others, CBS was a defender of the First Amendment at a time when solicitude for civil rights was at a low ebb, and the bellicose military establishment was gaining renewed ascendency. But many Americans were not predisposed to feel that either Westmoreland or CBS was particularly evil—they only knew that something somewhere was wrong, and they hoped that the suit would somehow sort it all out.

Yet in the end, the trial came to a termination as cloudy and unresolved as the Vietnam War itself. After eighteen weeks of testimony the case was settled just before it was to go to the jury. In an eerie parallel to the final American pullout from Vietnam, the trial terminated without catharsis, without yielding any answers, without clear victory or vindication. It was a bizarre conclusion to what had always been a bizarre trial, for there was from the very beginning something mildly surreal about the legal system in 1985 inviting a jury of twelve New Yorkers to set their minds back two decades earlier and half a world away, to determine what "really" happened in Vietnam in 1968.

Immediately following the trial, the jurors were interviewed on the major networks as to which way they were leaning. More were leaning to CBS than to Westmoreland, but there were several strongly in the General's camp. There was something objectionable about all of this, however, something that missed the trial's point: these jurors were interviewed as if it were part of the post-game wrap-up to the Super Bowl. The media's insatiable thirst for a simplified bottom line caused it to ignore any more complicated effort to discern what, if anything, the trial had done to deepen our understanding of the media and of Vietnam.[98]

Applying the rules of New York Times v. Sullivan, the jury, had it ever finally been entrusted with the case, would have had two issues to resolve. The first was whether or not the broadcast was false. To prove the broadcast was false Westmoreland did not have to show that the figures on enemy strength that his command was using were correct. He had only to show that he thought they were correct—that the enemy strength estimates were honestly arrived at, and not arbitrarily or consciously shaved for political reasons. If the jury were to find that the broadcast was false, the second issue would have been whether CBS intentionally or recklessly presented a false story. During the trial, CBS and Westmoreland each presented a great deal of oral testimony and documentary evidence on both issues.

What was the evidence CBS had that a conspiracy to doctor the figures had in fact taken place? "We're going to present evidence," Mike Wallace stated at the beginning of the documentary, "of what we have come to believe was a conscious effort—indeed a conspiracy at the highest level of American military intelligence—to suppress and alter critical intelligence on the enemy in the year leading up to the Tet offensive." The thesis was that the continued prosecution of the Vietnam War hinged on the confidence of President Johnson, the Congress, and the American people that the war was winnable, and that it was being won. The American strategy for victory was to vigorously pursue a "war of attrition," draining enemy manpower to the point at which it would be forced to sue for peace on terms favorable to the South Vietnamese regime. Public admission of an enemy build-up in troop strength would have been flatly inconsistent with the optimistic statements from the army in late 1967 that the war of attrition was succeeding, that the enemy was slowly but surely being bled to death.

1968 was also an election year, and it was politically important to Lyndon Johnson to create the impression that there was victorious light visible

at the end of the tunnel. The army command apparently thought it important that Johnson remain in office, or at least that Johnson remain pleased
with the army as long as he was in office. It was therefore important that
figures on enemy troop strength not embarrass the President.

The documentary argued that the method employed to achieve the
deception was to exclude wholesale categories of enemy troop units from
the so-called enemy "Order of Battle," the roster of enemy forces. The
raw totals of Communist forces included "regular" enemy units and more
marginal forces, such as home guards, guerillas, cadres, and other auxil-
iaries, many composed of women, children, and older men. Two of these
more peripheral categories were labeled the "Self-Defense" and "Secret
Self-Defense" forces. The reasoning of the conspiracy theory is that the
army knew that the irregular Communist forces were capable of inflicting
substantial damage, and that no realistic estimate of what the United States
was up against in Vietnam could exclude these forces. But since the army
desperately wanted to create the impression that enemy strength was being
depleted, it was decided arbitrarily to exclude the Self-Defense and Secret
Self-Defense categories, so as to mislead Johnson and the public. Westmoreland in effect created a cap of 300,000 as the maximum number of
enemy troops that the army was prepared to recognize. To fit the intelligence data from the field into this "official reality," it was necessary to
shave the figures of irregular enemy units off the top.

The first consequence of the deception, according to the conspiracy theory, was that American and South Vietnamese forces suffered stunning
defeats during Tet because they were caught unprepared. Thus, as Mike
Wallace put it, "the President of the United States, the American army in
Vietnam, and the American public back home were destined to be caught
totally unprepared for the size of the attack that was coming the following
month."

The eighteen weeks of trial produced a massive array of oral testimony
and documentary evidence, much of it quite technical. To understand the
case, it is useful to begin with the basic framework of CBS's evidence, and
Westmoreland's counterevidence, and then to fill in that framework with
samplings of the critical testimony on the major issues presented by both
sides.

The evidence behind CBS's conspiracy theory basically began with a man
named Sam Adams. Sam Adams worked in the CIA as an intelligence analyst and was assigned to Vietnam in 1965. In analyzing army statistics about
enemy strength levels, Adams testified at the trial, he "began to have this
feeling that something funny was going on." In Adams' view, "The statistics didn't make any sense." Later in 1966, at CIA headquarters, Adams
examined some captured enemy documents from the Binh Dinh province.

He concluded from the documents that the number of guerilla and Self-Defense forces for all of South Vietnam was probably triple the 112,000 listed in the order of battle. The enemy's total force, Adams concluded, was probably twice the 280,000 claimed by Westmoreland's command.

Adams tried to convince his superiors that the offical listings of enemy troop stength were egregiously low, but he was never successful in getting the higher figures accepted, because, in Adams' view, of a conscious decision emanating ultimately from Westmoreland himself that the estimates must be kept below a 300,000 ceiling. Adams spent most of the twenty years following his original "discovery" in 1965 attempting to prove his thesis.

Adams wrote an article for *Harpers* magazine in 1975 that recounted the discrepancies between the enemy troop strength estimates of the army and the "true" troop strength estimates of the CIA; in the *Harpers* piece Adams stated that Westmoreland was ultimately behind the fabrication. Adams' editor at *Harpers* was a man named George Crile. Crile eventually went to work at CBS, and became the producer of *The Uncounted Enemy* documentary. CBS paid Adams $25,000 to be a consultant for the broadcast, and Adams became a major player in shaping the documentary, the man who did the research and assembled the evidence. The basic broadcast was a film documentation of the charges Adams had made in print five years before in *Harpers*. When Westmoreland commenced his suit, he included consultant Sam Adams, producer George Crile, and correspondent Mike Wallace as individual defendants in addition to CBS. The CBS documentary, and the trial that followed it, were both largely the story of what the evidence assembled by Adams does and does not show. Each side presented a parade of witnesses to either support or refute the conspiracy theory.

In CBS's version of events, the entire cover-up arose out of the need of those running the war to make it appear that Westmoreland's "war of attrition" strategy—a strategy built around "search and destroy" missions designed to kill the enemy forces faster then they could replenish themselves—was working. Unlike a more conventional war, with clearly defined fronts and zones of control, the measure of success in the war in Vietnam was not calibrated so much in geographic terms as in statistical terms. The success of the "search and destroy" strategy was not measured by advancing lines on the map, but by declining numbers in the enemy's troop totals. By 1967, a substantial number of Americans were beginning to have doubts about the war of attrition strategy. To give American opinion a morale boost at home, Lyndon Johnson had General Westmoreland undertake the highly unusual step of coming home to do some public relations work for the war. Westmoreland had addressed a joint session of

Congress in April, 1967, stating that the strategy of attrition was "producing results." Although the war's end was not yet in sight, Westmoreland said that we had turned the corner. Congress gave his speech rousing approval.

Westmoreland's sanguineness, CBS implied, was undercut by one of his own intelligence officers when Westmoreland returned from Washington to Saigon. The larger numbers generated by Sam Adams and others had moved their way up the chain of command. The documentary showed General Joseph McChristian, the chief intelligence officer of the Military Assistance Command in Vietnam (known as MAC-V), describing his meeting in Saigon with Westmoreland and stating that Westmoreland was "quite disturbed" by the information that estimates of enemy troop levels were so high; he went on to say, "by the time I left his office I had the definite impression that he felt that if he sent those figures back to Washington at that time it would be a political bombshell." Westmoreland was shown in the documentary stating that he "did not have to accept" McChristian's recommendation. And then, in one of the more damaging passages of the entire program, Westmoreland was shown as stating:

> I did not accept it. And I didn't accept it because of political reasons.
> That was a—I may have mentioned this; I guess I did—that was not
> the fundamental thing. I just didn't accept it.

On November 21, 1967, in a very upbeat "progress report" in front of the National Press Club in Washington, Westmoreland stated that "I see progress as I travel all over Vietnam," and that success "lies within our grasp—the enemy's hopes are bankrupt." General Westmoreland knew, CBS claimed, when he made these statements that his actual intelligence from the field showed quite the opposite.

According to CBS, not long after his fateful meeting with Westmoreland, General McChristian ended his tour in Vietnam. He was replaced by General Phillip Davidson, and it was during Davidson's term as chief intelligence officer of MAC-V, in 1967–68, that the alleged cover-up occurred. This McChristian-Westmoreland episode was one of the most damning segments of the documentary, made all the more damning by CBS's editing. When General Westmoreland said on the program that "people in Washington were not sophisticated enough to understand and evaluate this thing, and neither was the public," Mike Wallace said: "We underscore what General Westmoreland just said about his decision. He chose not to inform the Congress, the President, not even the Joint Chiefs of Staff, of the evidence collected by his intelligence chief, evidence which indicated a far larger enemy."

At the trial, two points surfaced with regard to the Westmoreland-McChristian interlude. The first was that CBS had disingenuously edited Westmoreland's interview with Mike Wallace, by never showing on the air any of Westmoreland's qualifying statements about his "political" motivations. Three times in the interview, Westmoreland said that "politics . . . was a non-issue." Three more times he emphasized that he was looking for "an accurate appraisal," "something realistic," and "accuracy," and that he did not consider McChristian's figures accurate. At the trial, Westmoreland testifed that of course he was concerned with politics and with the media, "we'd have been dumb oxes if we weren't," but that his primary motivation was accuracy, and McChristian's figures were not accurate, because they did not separate the enemy's "fighters" from its "non-fighters."

The second point that emerged was that CBS had spliced McChristian's interview to create the false implication that he was forced to leave Vietman because "he would not keep the numbers down." In the unedited transcript, the producer of the show, George Crile, asked McChristian if he had to leave "because you would not keep the numbers down." McChristian responded: "No, because nobody ever asked me that, because I reported it as I saw it and evidently people didn't like my reporting because I was constantly showing that enemy strength was increasing." On the documentary, Crile's remarks to McChristian were substituted by a statement by Mike Wallace: "Consider General Westmoreland's dilemma. If he accepted his intelligence chief's findings, he would have to take the bad news to the President. If he didn't, well, there was only General McChristian to deal with." And General McChristian's answer was edited to begin with the word "evidently."

The "bottom line" from the evidence on this point, however, was that the trial produced a stand-off, Westmoreland's word against McChristian's. Westmoreland stood by the position that his motivation was not political, while McChristian told the jury, "When I presented the cable to General Westmoreland, he read it, he looked up—looked at me—and said 'If I send this cable to Washington, it will create a political bombshell.' He said: 'No leave it with me, I want to go over it'." McChristian steadfastly insisted that "the only concern he expressed to me was a political concern."

The next critical evidentiary dispute in the case was over the competing enemy strength figures that were being proposed in 1967 by the CIA and by MAC-V. CBS attempted to create the impression that the CIA knew the real strength of the enemy, which was around 500,000, and that MAC-V, under Westmoreland's pressure, arbitrarily kept the totals below a ceiling of 300,000. This simplistic presentation by CBS, however, was highly misleading. Both MAC-V and the CIA recognized a series of gradations in the fighting capabilities of different categories of enemy forces. The CIA and MAC-V were in agreement over the numbers of conventional "regular" enemy forces, which both listed at below 200,000. MAC-V also recognized as part of its total two other categories, the so-called "Self-Defense" forces, which were basically less organized and more rag-tag guerilla units, and "Political Cadre" forces, persons serving as administrative support who would assist in quasi-military functions once an area was taken over by the communists. In the MAC-V totals, these two other categories had a total strength in the 100,000 range, bringing the total enemy "Order of Battle" up to around 300,000. The CIA totals differed in three basic respects. The CIA believed that the Political Cadre was in the range of 85,000, about double MAC-V's estimate. The CIA also thought that the "Self-Defense" forces were at least double MAC-V's totals, and that a third category of forces, the "Secret Self-Defense" forces, should also be included. The Secret Self-Defense forces included old men, women, and children who actively aided the enemy. MAC-V did not list them at all. *All* of the extra 200,000 forces in the CIA listings that were above MAC-V's 300,000 total consisted of higher estimates for these lower grade forces, Self-Defense, Secret Self-Defense, and Political Cadre.

In order to straighten out the conflict between MAC-V and the CIA, a series of meetings were held in Saigon. At the heart of CBS's conspiracy theory there is the premise that at these meetings the CIA caved in to pressure from Westmoreland and agreed to the lower totals, which then had to be justified by going back and "cooking the numbers." That CBS accusation, however, turned out at the trial to be grossly over-simplistic.

The MAC-V representatives at the meetings included General Davidson (McChristian's replacement), Colonel Gaines Hawkins, and General George Godding. The CIA contingent was headed by a senior analyst named George Carver. There was disagreement among Hawkins, Godding, and Davidson in their testimony as to what their mandate from Westmoreland was. Hawkins seemed to see his mission as keeping the numbers down. Godding and Davidson, however, testifed in support of Westmoreland's position that no such orders, explicit or implicit, existed. George Carver's testimony turned out to be the key, and it was very damaging to CBS. For Carver had not only his memory, but CIA documents, to back up his version of what happened at the MAC-V and CIA meetings. What the CIA documents revealed were the perceptions of George Carver, the primary negotiator for the CIA. Carver cabled summaries of the meetings to his boss in Washington, CIA Director Richard Helms. These cables were important evidence, because they were contemporaneous written accounts of Carver's impressions, and were thus somewhat less susceptible to the vicissitudes of waning memories, after-the-fact rationalizations, or outright fabrications that are always possibly present in undocumented oral testimony.

The first cable, dated September 10, 1967, stated that "so far our mission frustratingly unproductive, since MAC-V stonewalling, obviously under orders." It continued, "unless or until I can persuade Westmoreland to amend these orders serious discussion of evidence or substantive issues will be impossible." The first Carver cable concluded with the statement that his bottom-line assessment of the negotiations was "that General Westmoreland . . . has given instruction tantamount to direct order that VC strength total will not exceed 300,000 ceiling."

In the next two cables, both dated September 12, Carver continued to convey frustration, reporting that although MAC-V was willing to make upward adjustments in some categories—the figures for enemy guerillas, for example, were "appreciably raised"—the army still kept a "weather-eye on the total." Carver further noted that Davidson had angrily stated to Carver that "he had no predetermined total."

The fourth and fifth cables, dated September 13 and 14, were of a dramatically different tenor. The September 13 cable began with the euphoric exclamation "circle now squared." Carver had arranged a face-to-face meeting with Westmoreland, Davidson, Creighton Abrams, and several others. Prior to the meeting, Carver was not optimistic, because "General Davidson advised Westmoreland meeting would do nothing but formalize our impasse since Westmoreland would not accept our position." But at the face-to-face meeting the chemistry of the negotiations changed. Davidson presented his case to the group, and Carver then presented his. To Carver's surprise, Westmoreland was "most cordial and receptive." Westmoreland, Carver wrote, "said he agrees with most of my observations and could see the clear logic behind both sets of figures, which were really not that far apart." The negotiations concluded with a set of figures that Carver reported the CIA could "live quite comfortably with."

Were the figures that emerged from this meeting a cave-in? The answer is that virtually all of the forces in the CIA's total of 500,000 were included in the compromise, it was simply a matter of their "packaging." The new Order of Battle would list as "fighting forces" a total of 225,000 to 250,000. Listed separately, under "Political Cadre," would be forces totaling 75,000 to 85,000. The Self-Defense and Secret Self-Defense forces would then be noted with a verbal statement, describing the types of enemy functions they served, and noting that in the past they had been estimated as high as 150,000. Those figures add up to just about 500,000. The "compromise" was, arguably, now more accurate than either MAC-V's or the CIA's original positions. MAC-V's original total of 300,000 may have understated the significance of the peripheral forces that helped the enemy. The CIA's original total of 500,000 may also have been misleading, for it created the impression that the enemy had a real army of that size, when in fact a huge percentage of its totals had little effective fighting power.

Westmoreland thus put forward a reasonably strong case that the whole Order of Battle debate was no sinister ploy concocted out of base political or war-mongering motives by the generals in control of the war; it was instead a bona-fide dispute among professional military intelligence officers acting in good faith to estimate the real fighting capability of an elusive enemy. The debate was a matter of public record; the main issue in the debate was known to any reasonably well-informed American: how does one identify an enemy that often materializes in the form of peasant children, women, and old men? The army did not count the many non-uniformed citizens of South Vietnam who actively *aided* the South Vietnamese government (and the South Vietnamese and American forces) as part of the official total of allied military strength, so why should it have counted those same sorts of persons loyal to the opposition as part of the enemy's official troop totals? Westmoreland's case was that he did not arbitrarily order that enemy troop levels be capped at less than 300,000, but in fact was open-minded about the Order of the Battle debate and accepted as accurate many of the CIA's central premises and did nothing to squelch information about them.

The next major conflict in the trial evidence concerned the nuts-and-bolts of shaving the enemy figures. Much of Westmoreland's argument that no conspiracy existed seemed highly plausible, and was supported by an impressive array of witnesses—eighteen in all—including names as illustrious as Robert McNamara, Paul Nitze, and Walt Rostow. During his witness parade, Westmoreland seemed to make a convincing case that CBS had just gotten the "cook the books" story wrong.

At one point in the broadcast, Mike Wallace said: "CBS Reports has learned that during the five months preceding the Tet offensive, Westmoreland's infiltration analysts had actually been reporting not seven or eight thousand but more than 25,000 North Vietnamese coming down the Ho Chi Minh Trail each month, and that amounted to a near invasion. But those reports of a dramatically increased infiltration were systematically blocked." CBS then made it appear that part of this "systematic blocking" was accomplished by squelching the information being supplied by Lt. Colonel Everette S. Parkins. CBS presented a witness on camera, Major Russell Cooley, who said that Parkins' 25,000 infiltration rate figures were blocked higher up the chain of command by Colonel Daniel Graham. Further, Cooley asserted that Parkins was fired from his position by his superior, Colonel Charles Morris, "for trying to get this report through."

At the trial, Morris testified that he did relieve Parkins of his command, but not for the reasons suggested by CBS. Instead, Morris "fired" Parkins because he "refused to carry out a legal order" to devise a better method for estimating enemy losses—a dispute unrelated to infiltration rates. Parkins himself testifed that he "disliked intensely" his superior Charles Morris, who "more than reciprocated" the hatred, but their conflict had nothing to do with infiltration rates, and that as far as Parkins knew the actual infiltration rates were no more than the 6,000 to 8,000 that were offically reported. Westmoreland's lawyer asked Parkins whether he ever submitted an infiltration rate of 25,000, and the following exchange ensued:

A. No, I did not.

Q. Is Mr. Wallace's statement true or false?

A. I believe that statement is false.

A. . . . When you were in Vietnam, was there ever a limit placed on the figures you could report?

A. There was not.

Q. Were you ever asked to falsify figures?

A. I was not.

At the trial, Daniel Graham (who had since been promoted to General) ridiculed CBS's suppression theory as "preposterous," saying that the CIA wanted to include as part of the enemy even civilians "who washed socks for the Viet Cong or carried rice for them." In the documentary, CBS had shown Graham for only 21 seconds, simply summarizing his position and stating "I'm not that dumb." In portions of CBS's interview that CBS left out of the show, Graham also explained precisely why a charge that he had ordered others to "tamper with the computers" after Tet as part of a cover-up "doesn't make any sense." His superior, Graham said, would have "hanged me from the nearest yardarm for trying to screw up the computers." On an issue involving the North Vietnamese forces massing for an attack on Khesahn, Graham ridiculed the idea that MAC-V had suppressed the data about the build-up, saying, "Hell, everybody in the world knew."

General Westmoreland's own testimony, which lasted nine days, was universally regarded by observers as powerful and convincing for the first few days. Under relentless cross-examination, however, Westmoreland seemed to tire in the latter stages of his testimony, and also to get caught in a number of embarrassing contradictions. The jury's reaction to his testimony, like the reaction of press observers, seemed mixed. Westmoreland came across as a man with a powerful presence, a man of dignity, honesty, and polite South Carolina charm, but also a man who tended to get things mixed up and confused under constant pressure. To some, his contradictions gave the impression of someone who would lie to serve what he saw as the truth; to others it simply made the CBS lawyer look badgering and oppressive, imitating the tactics of Mike Wallace: crossing up and intimidating an old soldier whose memory was understandably fuzzy about details from seventeen years before.

Whatever the merits of Westmoreland's performance, however, CBS had a very impressive parade of witnesses of its own, many of whom testified toward the end of the trial. They relentlessly hammered home the accusations that in fact the books were being doctored. Many of those CBS witnesses were men who had actually done the doctoring. Sam Adams reiterated his charges in detail. Westmoreland's witnesses tried to paint Adams as a nut, who had made a career profiting from his vendetta against Westmoreland. CBS in turn presented witnesses who bolstered Adams' integrity, saying that Adams' only problem was that he did not know how to salute and shut up. George Allen, the highest ranking CIA analyst in Vietnam, who had 17 years' experience in the country and was regarded as the "dean" by his fellow analysts (one testifed that he'd been in Vietnam "almost as long as Ho Chi Minh"), supported the conspiracy theory as he had in the broadcast.

CBS's evidence even included deposition testimony read to the jury of Nguyen Cao Ky, Prime Minister of South Vietnam from 1965 to 1967, and titular vice-president until 1971. According to Ky, "Tet had all the horrors of another Pearl Harbor." In his 1978 book *How We Lost the Vietnam War*, Ky endorsed the conspiracy theory of Tet bag and baggage. "Westmoreland must have known all along about the strength of the impending attack," wrote Ky, but "I am convinced that the White House did not." Ky believed that "American leaders in Saigon deliberately issued a string of lies to the White House, in an effort to maintain the impression that the Americans were getting on top of the Viet Cong." Ky concluded that this "squalid deception" resulted in fooling not only the American press, public, and Congress, but the allied troops in the field. (That the South Vietnamese, at least, were unready for Tet is supported by the actions of the man who squeezed Ky out of power in 1967, South Vietnamese President Nguyen Van Thieu. Thieu furloughed the bulk of his South Vietnamese troops for the Tet holiday, and retreated for the holiday with his wife to her family's home in the town of Mytho, in the Mekong delta.)

Without doubt, however, the witness who did the most damage to Westmoreland was Colonel Gaines Hawkins. Colonel Hawkins, known in Vietnam as "The Hawk," was a crusty 25-year career soldier who was actually in charge of the day-to-day intelligence estimates for the order of battle. Hawkins testifed that in a briefing with Westmoreland the General expressed concern about the "public relations" problem and said he wanted Hawkins to separate out the "non-fighters." According to Hawkins, Westmoreland said: "What will I tell the President? What will I tell the Congress? What will be the reaction of the press to the high figures?"

Hawkins said that his two superior officers, Philip Davidson and Charles Morris (both of whom testified that no alteration of figures took place) repeatedly returned figures to Hawkins to have him look at them again. Eventually Hawkins just told them: "If you don't like these figures, you just make up your own rules, and I'll carry out your orders."

Hawkins then proceeded to order his subordinates to cut the figures. In an emotional exchange at the trial CBS's lawyer questioned Hawkins:

Q. Was there any intelligence or evidence that you were aware of that justified those orders that you gave?

A. There were none sir.

Q. Did you believe those were proper orders, sir?

A. They were not sir.

Hawkins' subordinates reinforced his testimony with chilling detail. Major Michael F. Dilley, for example, said that the figures were reduced "arbitrarily," hamlet by hamlet. If the enemy numbers for a hamlet said 4, they would be cut to 3, creating the new raw data that would be aggregated to conform to a pre-determined bottom line.

Because General Westmoreland and CBS ultimately chose to leave the final verdict to the judgment of history, it is appropriate at this stage to ask how, given what we now know, that historical judgment is likely to shape up. History is not confined to the rules of evidence that govern a libel trial, nor is it forced to channel its inquiry within the banks of the issues as they were defined by the judge and lawyers in the case. The most significant judgments that Americans will make about "what it all means," in fact, will tend to go well beyond the technical issues that dominated the trial. Like the Vietnam War itself, the trial tended to get bogged down in the "technology" of the process; as everyone was caught up in infiltration rates and Secret Self-Defense force estimates, the broader perspective on the lessons of Vietnam and the media's treatment of those lessons tended to get lost.

In factoring in the evidence produced at the Westmoreland trial as part of the "judgment of history" about Tet and Vietnam, there are at least two major observations worth making about the evidentiary pattern that emerged from the case. The first is that the testimony of the army officers and the CIA analysts did not yield any clear-cut conclusion about what really happened. There were witnesses for the conspiracy theory, and witnesses against it. Within the command hierarchy, the pattern was for the officials at the high end of the chain of command to deny that any conspiracy existed, and for officials farther down in the pyramid to support it.

For some jurors and observers, this pattern probably leads to the conclusion that a conspiracy at the highest levels did exist, that subordinates
such as MacArthur and Gaines Hawkins caught glimpses of it, and that
quite expectedly, their superiors, such as Westmoreland, Godding, and
Davidson, now attempt to cover their tracks by denying it. For others, the
pattern of testimony carries a very different implication. Perhaps the
higher officers were not part of a conspiracy, but were merely the arbiters
of a dispute between two subordinate groups. The army command may
have listened to both sides of the argument, made their own judgments as
to credibility and plausibility, and opted for lower totals.

Based on the conflicting testimony of the army officers, either of these
versions of events is *possible*. Witnesses like William Westmoreland, Robert
McNamara, and Walt Rostow may be deliberately lying to protect themselves. Persons such as Joseph McChristian, Gaines Hawkins, or Sam
Adams, the paid CBS consultant who started it all, may also be lying, grinding axes of their own. Perhaps they believe that their superiors were
myopic or negligent and deserve the sort of censure that accusations of
"conspiracy" bring.

But recalling the whole problem of libel suits as forums for litigating
ideology, the subjective world views of the various witnesses in the case
may have so colored their perceptions of reality that it is also possible that
none of the parties were consciously lying. The "Order of Battle" debate
was a bitter bureaucratic dispute that became even more emotionally
charged after Tet. Ideology may have forever shaded the participants' perceptions: "orders" may have been softened in the memories of those who
made them to mere "judgment calls" on the significance of the raw data
at hand; good-faith "judgment calls" may become hardened in the memories of those who opposed them to devious, self-serving manipulations by
superiors.

Hearing the testimony in the role of jurors, reasonable persons might
differ, with the balance likely to be tipped by unconscious biases. Some are
reflexively skeptical of any set of facts recounted by authority figures, and
the authority figures involved in Vietnam may be especially suspect. Others
may naturally question the credibility of apparently disgruntled subordinates in any institutional hierarchy, and may feel particularly wary of persons "who lost their perspective" in Vietnam.

The second observation about the evidence is that at each sharp evidentiary dispute in the trial in which *documents* from the period immediately
prior to and after Tet were introduced, the documents often yielded conclusions no more certain than the oral evidence based on witnesses' memories. Take, as an example, the cables from CIA negotiator George Carver
to CIA director Richard Helms. Though they surely did lend support to

Westmoreland, even those cables must be treated with caution. The meetings between MAC-V and the CIA were obviously acrimonious at times—witness Carver's September 12 cable relating that "General Davidson angrily accused me of impugning his integrity." All through that acrimony Carver was quite obviously convinced that senior army officers, beginning with Westmoreland, had ordered that enemy totals be kept beneath 300,000. Westmoreland then agreed to a face to face meeting, and suddenly the mood became "cordial and receptive." Perhaps Westmoreland's gracious open mindedness at the meeting was indicative of his open minded attitude all along. Perhaps Westmoreland's subordinates misread him, and Carver misread Westmoreland's subordinates, with everyone finally set straight at the meeting.

But it is also possible to speculate—and of course it is *only* speculation—that Westmoreland had originally issued an explicit or "implicit" order to keep the numbers below 300,000. (CBS now apparently believes, it should be noted, that it may be more likely that the order may have been issued "between the lines.") Faced with the possibility that the meetings with the CIA might get out of hand and cause a major schism within the administration—or even worse, public embarrassment at the hands of the embittered CIA analysts—Westmoreland may have decided to feign basic agreement with the CIA position to temporarily defuse a crisis.

Again, however, the problem is that either alternative is possible. The statement by Davidson to Carver that Westmoreland would do nothing at the meeting other than reaffirm the army's prior position, for example, is consistent either with the view that Davidson misread Westmoreland, or that Davidson had read Westmoreland perfectly, but that Westmoreland had flip-flopped. Once again, one's views of the significance of the Carver cables are as much a matter of predisposition as of their inherent plausibility. Some, for example, believe that the CIA itself may have been part of the cover-up, and advance the theory that Richard Helms may have ordered his own negotiator Carver to cave in at the negotiations. A biography of Helms written by Thomas Powers, entitled *The Man Who Kept the Secrets*, puts forth this cave-in theory. No documentation has surfaced, however, to support this account, and Helms denies it.

Americans have learned enough about the machinations of the CIA to realize that such a tangled web *could* have been woven. There have even been suggestions—again suggestions that are not impossible to entertain seriously—that the chief conspirator was Lyndon Johnson. Perhaps a besieged President ordered the CIA and the Army to get together on a set of figures that would not appear ridiculously low but that would nonetheless avoid embarrassment. But again, there is the problem—perhaps, perhaps, perhaps. We do not know for sure how Order of Battle estimates were actually assembled, and cannot, in the very nature of things, ever know. Paranoia, from either the right or the left, is no substitute for proof, nor is blind confidence. The trial evidence, such as it was, supplied no definitive answer—to be confident in either scenario requires a certain ideological leap of faith.

Even if Westmoreland's command was as evil as CBS painted it to be in the documentary, could it really have had any impact on either Vietnamese or American history? If one is willing to accept the CBS view that there was a deception by Westmoreland's command and that the deception led to defeat at Tet, the broader historical consequences implicit in the conspiracy theory at first seem to spread outward like concentric shock blasts from an exploded bomb. The stunning defeat at Tet, the story goes, gave new impetus to the peace movement and allowed Eugene McCarthy to come within 300 votes of defeating Lyndon Johnson in the New Hampshire primary. Buoyed by McCarthy's "stalking horse" victory, Bobby Kennedy entered the presidential race in a defiant challenge to Johnson. Walter Cronkite, in the aftermath of Tet, rejected official forecasts of victory, stating in a February 27 broadcast after returning from a trip to Saigon that it was now "more certain then ever that the bloody experience of Vietnam is to end in a stalemate." Cronkite's broadcast, fourteen years before the 1982 documentary that would ultimately trigger the acrimonious legal contest between CBS and General Westmoreland, seems to have foreshadowed much of that later dispute. The broadcast began with a portrait of Tet's impact on Saigon:

> These ruins are in Saigon, capital and largest city of South Vietnam. They were left here by an act of war, Vietnamese against Vietnamese. Hundreds died here. Here in these ruins can be seen physical evidence of the Viet Cong's Tet offensive, but far less tangible is what those ruins mean, and like everything else in this burned and blasted and weary land, they mean success or setback, victory or defeat, depending upon whom you talk to.

In the middle of the broadcast Cronkite raised the specter of an "intelligence failure."

> Intelligence people, American and Vietnamese, agree on the same story. They figured the enemy might launch a big attack on Saigon or another South Vietnamese city, but they admit they grossly underestimated the enemy's ability to plan, to provision, to coordinate, to launch such a widespread full-scale attack as this. There are some odd stories about this intelligence failure. High American sources, for instance, say that they warned the Vietnamese, but they let their troops go on Tet leave anyway, until some units were down to just 10% of normal strength.

From the perspective of William Westmoreland and Lyndon Johnson, however, it was Cronkite's personal closing evaluation that was the most stinging:

> We have been too often disappointed by the optimism of the American leaders both in Vietnam and Washington, to have faith any longer in the silver linings they find in the darkest clouds. They may be right, that Hanoi's winter-spring offensive has been forced by the Communist realization that they could not win the longer war of attrition, and that the Communists hope that any success in the offensive will improve their position for eventual negotiations. It would improve their position, and it would also require our realization, that we should have had all along, that any negotiations must be that—negotiations, not the dictation of peace terms. For it seems now more certain than ever that the bloody experience of Vietnam is to end in a stalemate. This summer's almost certain stand-off will either end in real give-and-take negotiations or terrible escalation; and for every means we have to escalate, the enemy can match us, and that applies to invasion of the North, the use of nuclear weapons, or the mere commitment of 100, or 200, or 300,000 more American troops to the battle. And with each escalation, the world comes closer to the brink of cosmic disaster.
>
> To say that we are closer to victory today is to believe, in the face of the evidence, the optimists who have been wrong in the past. To suggest we are on the edge of defeat is to yield to unreasonable pessimism. To say that we are mired in stalemate seems the only realistic, yet unsatisfactory, conclusion. On the off chance that military and political analysts are right, in the next few months we must test the enemy's intentions, in case this is indeed his last gasp before negotiations. But it is increasingly clear to this reporter that the only rational way out then will be to negotiate, not as victors, but as an honorable people who lived up to their pledge to defend democracy, and did the best they could. This is Walter Cronkite. Good night.

Lyndon Johnson viewed Cronkite as having enormous influence on American attitudes, and he was profoundly depressed by Cronkite's evaluation. After Cronkite's pessimistic assessment Johnson began to feel that he had no hope of rekindling confidence in his war effort. Deceptive intelligence had unraveled the American army at Tet, and Tet would now unravel the Johnson presidency. On March 31, 1968, Johnson spoke to the nation on television, announcing, "I have concluded that I should not permit the presidency to become involved in the partisan divisions that are developing in this political year. . . . Accordingly, I shall not seek, and I will not accept, the nomination of my party for another term as your president."

Under this theory, the consequences radiating from the alleged intelligence deception may even include the final outcome of the war. Tet alone may not have been enough to defeat the United States on the ground in Vietnam, but it was enough to infect domestic debate about the war. After

Tet the government's credibility never returned, and public opposition to the war, crystallized by Tet, prevented future success on the battlefield. In their efforts to win the war or to obtain an honorable peace, Henry Kissinger and Richard Nixon were hamstrung by vitriolic dissent at home, dissent that would never have gained serious momentum if the war of attrition had not suffered the Tet setback.

This view of the consequences of the alleged Tet deception, however, is riddled with oversimplifications and inconsistencies. Westmoreland, for example, can marshal a reasonably impressive array of outside historical evidence to support his position that Lyndon Johnson was never in any way misled. There were warnings, it is clear, of an enemy build-up and impending attack prior to Tet. Lyndon Johnson in his memoirs (which, admittedly, were bound to be apologetic), wrote that prior to Tet a mammoth build-up of enemy men and material was observed, and that the American intelligence apparatus had spoken unequivocally that an all-out assault was pending. In December of 1967, weeks prior to Tet, Johnson shared his information with the Austrialian Cabinet, warning of "dark days ahead," and stating that he foresaw "the North Vietnamese using Kamikaze tactics in the weeks ahead." The existence of these warnings has been confirmed from many different sources. Walt Rostow, who was Johnson's National Security Advisor from 1966 to 1968, and a partisan exponent of an aggressive stance in Vietnam, stated that intelligence sources were supplying reliable information on the infiltration of enemy units into the south, down the Ho Chi Minh trail. "They didn't come marching down the Ho Chi Minh Trail with flags flying and a band playing," said Rostow, "but they were still plainly observable," to the point that "we knew the regiments and the battalion numbers."

For his part, Westmoreland on December 20, 1967 warned Washington that a "maximum effort" by the Communists was imminent. In a cable to General Earle Wheeler, Chairman of the Joint Chiefs of Staff and the principal military figure in Washington overseeing the war, Westmoreland stated that the enemy had "already made a crucial decision concerning the conduct of the war." The cable continued that "the enemy decided that prolongation of his past policies for conducting the war would lead to his defeat, and that he would have to make a major effort to reverse this downward trend." The enemy commander, North Vietnamese General Vo Nguyen Giap, would, Westmoreland predicted, "make a maximum effort on all fronts (political and military) in order to achieve victory in a short period of time," or to gain "an apparent position of strength" from which to initiate peace negotiations.

Moreover, the dispute over enemy strength levels in South Vietnam was not contained to bureaucratic infights; it was a matter of general public debate, and it was a controversy of which the decisionmakers in Washington, including Lyndon Johnson, were well aware. The Joint United States Public Affairs office publicly released a North Vietnamese document on January 5, 1968, three weeks prior to Tet, that had been captured by the 101st Airborne Division in November 1967, which described plans for an impending assault:

> Use very strong military attacks in coordination with the uprisings of the local population to take over towns and cities. Troops should flood the lowlands. They should move toward liberating the capital city, take power and try to rally enemy brigades and regiments to our side one by one. Propaganda should be broadly disseminated among the population in general, and leaflets should be used to reach enemy officers and enlisted personnel.

Prior to Tet there were many newspaper and magazine stories debating the strength of the Communist forces in South Vietnam, stories that focused on the same issues that were being disputed within the intelligence apparatus itself, such as how to quantify the strength of the many irregular non-uniformed guerillas, saboteurs, and "fellow travelers" of the Viet Cong. That debate, in fact, became part of American folklore about the war; anyone with a friend or relative in Vietnam, or who read or heard contemporaneous accounts about the experience of the American combat troops, knew that the inability to identify the enemy was one of the great frustrations and sources of horror of the whole war. Massacres like My Lai, and the brutal, frenzied, and irrational assassinations of suspected Viet Cong sympathizers, of the sort captured by Phil Caputo in his book *Rumors of War*, were partly the product of this very phenomenon; American soldiers lost the ability to distinguish between enemy soldier and civilian, in a war in which the distinctions were continuously blurred. Lyndon Johnson knew of this problem as well as anyone.

Johnson was not merely apprised of the enemy buildup, and aware generally of the problem of characterizing the strength of enemy sources, he was aware of the actual details of the bureaucratic dispute with regard to enemy strength levels. Johnson's biographers, and the more objective accounts of the war, uniformly agree that Johnson, like many Presidents, drew his information from multiple sources. Johnson was as able an infighter and as knowledgeable a manager of the machinations of rival government agencies as any President in history; he was well aware of the fact that different government agencies routinely disagreed on what was going on in Vietnam and selectively reported data back to Washington to support their own parochial interests.

A second major problem with CBS's historical scenario is that it does not jibe with the actual military picture on the ground after Tet. Did the

Communist forces actually attack with more troops than even our most deflated intelligence estimates said they would? Was Tet really a defeat? From Westmoreland's viewpoint, CBS was examining the wrong tempest in the wrong teapot. The real cover-up in Vietnam in 1968 from his view was not the army's, but the media's, and the CBS documentary was in a sense more of the same. Estimates of how many troops the Communists actually used at Tet range from 70,000 to 90,000. Yet even the lowest nominees from among the army's range of estimates placed the enemy's capability at well above 100,000 troops. This means that there was arguably no causal connection whatsoever between pre-invasion quantitative estimates of potential enemy strength (even if they were too low), and the effectiveness of the assault, because the actual troops used were below the estimates anyway.

But most important of all to the Westmoreland side is that from a military perspective, the Tet offensive was a colossal failure for the Communists. By February 2, only days after the offensive began, the Communist forces had been routed on almost all battlefronts. On February 5, significant fighting was continuing only at Hue and Khesanh (and the siege of Khesanh had actually begun prior to Tet, on January 20), though sporadic rocket attacks in scores of cities did last into late February.

The Communists at Tet suffered horrendous losses, with between 45,000 and 50,000 troops killed. The Communists lost many of their key operatives in the South, and after the war many of the Communist leaders who had been in power at the time of Tet would frankly concede that Tet was largely a military failure. In Stanley Karnow's recent history of the Vietnam War, he writes "Revisiting Vietnam after the war, I was astonished by the number of Communist veterans who retained bad memories of the Tet episode." Many of the Viet Cong and North Vietnamese soldiers were deeply discouraged that their momentous assault had resulted in such carnage, and were even more depressed at the failure of their extreme sacrifices to rally large numbers of the South Vietnamese population to their cause.

One Viet Cong leader, Truong Nu Tang, recently wrote: "The Tet Offensive proved catastrophic to our plans. It's a major irony of the Vietnamese War that our propaganda transformed this military debacle into a brilliant victory." Truong Van Tang said that Tet cost the Communists half of their forces. Another senior Communist leader stationed in South Vietnam during Tet, Tran Van Tra, wrote of the Tet offensive in a history of the war published in 1982 in Hanoi, "we did not correctly evaluate the specific balance of forces between ourselves and the enemy, did not fully realize that the enemy still had considerable capabilities and that our capabilities were limited." According to Tran Van Tra, the Communists had set objectives that were unrealistically ambitious, "in part on an illusion based on our subjective desires." To him the offensive was crippling to his forces; "we suffered large losses in material and manpower," he wrote, "especially cadres at various echelons, which clearly weakened us . . . we were not only unable to retain the gains we had made but had to overcome a myriad of difficulties in 1969 and 1970 so that the Revolution could stand firm in the storm."

In the context of *Westmoreland v. CBS* these historical assessments of Tet by the Communist leaders from the period are stunning: they portray Tet as the diametric opposite of the orthodox version according to CBS. The Communist leaders accuse *themselves* of not correctly evaluating the strength of their American opponents, not the other way around; the Communists accuse *themselves* of "illusion based on subjective desires." And all talk of illusions and perceptions aside, the rawest physical facts of Tet were that the Communists did little lasting physical damage to their opponents; American and South Vietnamese casualties were miniscule compared to the Communists'. The Communist forces captured no significant territory, and they suffered crushing human losses.

From this perspective, only the media's distortions in reporting Tet turned military victory into psychological defeat. Peter Braestrup, in a 1977 book *The Big Story*, concluded that "rarely has contemporary crisis journalism turned out, in retrospect, to have veered so widely from reality." The dominant tones of the film and words from Vietnam, Braestrup argued, "added up to a portrait of defeat for the allies," while historians "have concluded that the Tet offensive resulted in a severe military-political setback for Hanoi in the South." Braestrup concluded that "to have portrayed such a setback for one side as a defeat for the other—in a major crisis abroad—cannot be counted as a triumph for American journalism."

Braestrup's conclusions are shared by Major General Winant Sidle, who served as General Westmoreland's chief of information in Saigon from 1967 through 1969. Sidle uses the epithet "conspiracy" against the media itself. After Tet, Sidle wrote, "many, probably most, of the Saigon press corps seemed to go into shock—at least for a few days—with the result that reporters seemed to have a desire to believe the worst, and this produced disaster-type reporting." Sidle continued that the "initial shock to America of the offensive itself was compounded and continued beyond reason by the reporting. The calm, professional, factual reports that should have followed the first few days never materialized. In retrospect, there appeared to be a conspiracy never to admit that the original coverage was greatly overblown."

For his part, General Westmoreland quite clearly blames the press for a large part of what went wrong in Vietnam. In his memoirs Westmoreland particularly indicted the broadcast media:

> Television presented special problems. Even more than the telegraph during the Crimean War and the radio in World War II, television brought war into the American home, but in the process television's unique requirements contributed to a distorted view of the war. The news had to be compressed and visually dramatic. Thus the war that Americans saw was almost exclusively violent, miserable, or controversial: guns firing, men falling, helicopters crashing, buildings toppling, huts burning, refugees fleeing, women wailing. A shot of a single building in ruins could give an impression of an entire town destroyed. The propensity of cameramen at Khesanh to pose their commentators before a wrecked C-130 and deliver reports in a tone of voice suggesting doomsday was all too common. Only scant attention was paid to pacification, civic action, medical assistance, the way life went on in a generally normal way for most of the people much of the time.[99]

But Westmoreland's discontent with the press was over more than the distortions of television; he wrote of Vietnam as the first war lost in the columns of the *New York Times*:

> Reflecting the view of the war held by many in the United States and often contributing to it, the general tone of press and television comment was critical, particularly following the Tet offensive of 1968. As a respected Australian journalist, Dennis Warner, has noted, there are those who say it was the first war in history lost in the columns of the *New York Times*. Lacking all but the most limited access to the enemy, reporters often focused on the death and destruction inevitably produced by American and South Vietnamese operations. I sometimes wondered that if the same uncensored comment had been coming out of occupied France during the years 1942–44 when the Allies were bombing French railroads in preparation for the invasion of Normandy, whether Allied public opinion would have supported Allied armies going ashore on D-Day.

Westmoreland's version of events in Vietnam thus could not be more at odds with both the spirit and the detail of CBS's documentary; for Westmoreland, it was the accuser who deserved to be the accused.

The debate over the conduct of CBS in putting the documentary together turned out to be every bit as divisive as the questions surrounding the Tet offensive. In its May 29, 1982 issue, *TV Guide* magazine ran a major cover story on the CBS broadcast, provocatively entitled "Anatomy of a Smear—How CBS News Broke the Rules and 'Got' General Westmoreland." The article was written by two *TV Guide* reporters, Don Kowett and Sally Bedell, who relied on inside sources at CBS to construct their story. Kowett has since written a book, *A Matter of Honor*, that is a detailed elaboration of the charges in the *TV Guide* article.[100] The *TV Guide* piece and the subsequent book by Kowett were unmercifully critical of CBS's honesty and professionalism in putting together the documentary. During the trial, Westmoreland's attorneys attempted to convince the jury that CBS indeed had intentionally or recklessly distorted the evidence to "smear" General Westmoreland.

The raw statistics on CBS's behavior in putting the documentary together did not look good for CBS. The network interviewed about eighty witnesses, many of whom denied the premise of the CBS broadcast. But CBS only actually showed eleven witnesses in the broadcast. Two of them were Sam Adams, the accuser, and Westmoreland, the accused. Of the remaining nine witnesses, eight supported CBS's theory. The one who did not was given 21 seconds worth of lame and conclusory denials.

Although it acknowledged that some of its journalistic practices in putting together *The Uncounted Enemy* were below the standards that CBS sets for itself, CBS's official position remained vigorously supportive of the broadcast before, during, and after the trial. In an internal report on the broadcast written by CBS employee Burton Benjamin before the trial, for example, numerous errors were recounted, and the emphasis on the word "conspiracy" was criticized. Benjamin took the position that although a conspiracy may well have existed, the evidence was not conclusive. The Benjamin report nonetheless did state (though among the strong supporters of the broadcast, the statement was thought to be damning with faint praise), that "to get a group of high-ranking military men and former Central Intelligence Agents to say that this is what happened was an achievement of no small dimension. These were not fringe people but rather prototypical Americans." CBS News president Van Gordon Sauter took a stronger position in endorsing the broadcast. Although Sauter also noted that there were a number of poor practices in putting together the documentary, and that within CBS itself there was "debate regarding editorial decisions," the bottom line was that "CBS News stands by this broadcast."

At the trial Westmoreland presented a long line of witnesses supporting his position that no conspiracy existed. Westmoreland's witnesses basically fell into three categories according to how CBS treated them in putting together the documentary: (1) witnesses that CBS never bothered to interview; (2) witnesses that CBS did interview, but ignored for the documentary; and (3) witnesses that CBS did interview and did use on the broadcast, but only after editing the interview tape to distort or undercut the witnesses' positions.

Among those that CBS did not interview were a number of crucial figures from the Vietnam era: Ellsworth Bunker, U.S. Ambassador to South

Vietnam, Admiral Ulysses S. Grant Sharp, the Commander of American forces in the Pacific and Westmoreland's immediate superior, and Robert Komer, who held the rank of Ambassador and was in charge of the "pacification" program in South Vietnam. These were the very people who reported to Lyndon Johnson, and whom Westmoreland allegedly deceived—yet none of them were interviewed. The two most glaring examples of key witnesses CBS failed to interview, however, were General Phillip Davidson and CIA analyst George Carver.

Phillip Davidson was one of the pivotal players in the drama CBS was describing. As head of MAC-V intelligence during the alleged conspiracy period, and as one of the main actors in the negotiations with Carver, Davidson's testimony should have been in the documentary. CBS claimed that it was under the impression that Davidson was a terminal cancer patient, and that it would not be possible to interview him. CBS also claimed that it made a number of efforts to contact Davidson, but could not. Davidson, who had recovered from cancer in 1974, claimed that in the 15 months during which the broadcast was being prepared, he had remarried and was playing golf every day. Davidson claimed that to his knowledge no one at CBS attempted to contact him.

CBS's failure to interview Davidson was, ironically, subject to the same sorts of divergent interpretations as the Vietnam story itself. Cast in its most sinister light, CBS was guilty of deliberately avoiding a witness who would have upset the preconceived story-line that a conspiracy existed. If, according to CBS, Westmoreland had established a cap of 300,000 enemy forces and had ordered that there be no dissent from that position, had not CBS producer George Crile in effect imposed a similar order—that there be no dissent about the story line?

Recast in a more innocent light, however, CBS simply had gotten bad information about Davidson's health, had made some cursory efforts to contact him, and, not having succeeded in doing so, just let the pursuit of Davidson fall between the cracks. CBS may also have been convinced that Davidson, at the top end of the pyramid, would naturally support Westmoreland, and that Westmoreland's perspective had already been represented. CBS, however, cannot avoid the bottom line that whether out of dark or pure motives, the failure to interview Davidson or verify the seriousness of his illness was sloppy journalism. CBS's own internal investigation by Burton Benjamin listed the lack of journalistic enterprise in pursuing Davidson as a principal flaw in the broadcast.

CBS also failed to interview Davidson's counterpart in the Saigon negotiations, George Carver. CBS producer George Crile took the position that Carver had nothing to say that would have changed the overall picture of events concerning the Tet conspiracy. Carver's version of events, however, would have been consistent with the "non-sinister" version of the CIA negotiations with MAC-V that later seemed to be supported by Carver's cables to Helms. Carver's overall view of the controversy was that the CIA and MAC-V ultimately hit upon a sensible compromise, and that the entire controversy was an open book within the administration, all the way up to the White House. Again, Carver may be wrong, he may be lying. And then again he may be telling the truth. In judging the journalistic quality of CBS's broadcast, the essential point is that viewers were not permitted to make the judgment for themselves.

CBS was also guilty of completely ignoring the testimony of many powerful witnesses who were interviewed and who supported Westmoreland. One of those witnesses was Robert McNamara. During the discovery process Westmoreland's attorneys learned that producer George Crile had conducted a number of telephone interviews. Crile tape-recorded his telephone interview with McNamara, but did not tell McNamara he was being taped, a violation of CBS News guidelines. When asked to produce the tapes, CBS was caught in the embarrassing position of having to admit that the tapes had either been lost or erased. CBS tried to put the best light on the matter, claiming that the tapes had probably been erased in the normal course of business so that they could be reused. The other side, of course, charged that CBS had surreptitiously destroyed the tapes, raising the specter of a Watergate-style seventeen-minute gap. George Crile eventually did locate a cassette containing a portion of his McNamara interview, as well as telephone interviews with George Ball, former Undersecretary of State, Arthur Goldberg, former United States Supreme Court Justice and U.S. Ambassador to the United Nations, and Matthew Ridgeway, former Army Chief of Staff. It turned out that none of these interviewees knew he was being taped.

None of these key historical figures in the Vietnam saga whom Crile secretly taped supported the conspiracy theory of the broadcast. Robert McNamara testified that he told Crile that the debate between the CIA and MAC-V intelligence had not been about numbers (which had always been a preoccupation of McNamara's during the war), but about which categories of enemy units should be counted in the former Order of Battle. McNamara found the conspiracy theory inconceivable, and resoundingly supported Westmoreland as an honorable man of the highest integrity who in Vietnam had served his President and his country honorably and honestly.

Another inexplicable example of CBS totally ignoring unfavorable testimony was its failure to mention or show any of the information filmed in its interview with Walt Rostow, the National Security Advisor to Lyndon Johnson. Rostow's filmed interview lasted three hours, and he made it very clear that no conspiracy existed and that Lyndon Johnson was well acquainted with all the competing intelligence information from Vietnam. At one point in the interview, Rostow bluntly warned Mike Wallace that he was in danger of getting his facts wrong about this "rather complex war" and was "going to do great damage to the country." CBS did not use one second of Rostow's filmed interview.

Perhaps the most devastating indication of CBS's bias in the broadcast was the stark difference between how it handled General Westmoreland's interview and the interviews of favorable witnesses. Mike Wallace was unrelenting in his adversarial cross-examination of Westmoreland. The General seemed to dissemble under Wallace's pressure, getting caught in contradictions, falling back on hollow denials. Most of Westmoreland's clarifications, qualifications, and denials were edited out of the interview. The interview with Westmoreland was chopped up and interspersed with other "testimony" from Sam Adams, as well as with long soliloquies by Mike Wallace himself. This last technique, in fact, was one of CBS's most effective and unfair weapons. Mike Wallace at times was the inquisitor, and at times he was essentially a "witness" himself, delivering speeches that devastated Westmoreland's testimony. During one exchange with West-moreland, for example, Wallace basically took over the role of Sam Adams, the principal accuser:

> I put that to Sam Adams, the young man from the CIA. I said, "General Westmoreland had told me this. He (Westmoreland) said that not only was Tet a great military victory, but it proved that (the military) had been overestimating enemy strength all along. How do you answer that? He still thinks you're nuts, Adams. He still thinks that you're dead wrong. Were and remain dead wrong."
> Forgive me sir, for what I'm about to say. Adams said, "He's a liar. I know so much about what General Westmoreland has done behind the scenes that I know General Westmoreland is lying." I say, "What do you mean, what do you know?" I know about all that he said to his Order of Battle subordinates." "What did he say?" "He told them, for example, to keep a ceiling on the Order of Battle, to count as many Viet Cong as you want to, but just don't count anymore than three hundred thousand. He told them . . . he was behind that little slip of paper which says, yeah, I'll give you fifteen thousand extra guerillas if you allow us to march the Self-Defense militia out of the Order of Battle. He wrote the cable which says: The reason we want to have an Order of Battle that is under three hundred thousand is . . . a desire to keep our image of success."

One of the most misleading elements of this passage by Wallace is that it gave the viewer the impression that an enterprising Mike Wallace had gone back and forth from Adams to Westmoreland, spontaneously chal-

lenging each to try to ferret out the "truth." In fact, Adams was the archi-
tect of the whole story, a paid consultant for CBS, and it was only Westmoreland who had been ambushed and challenged. After his interview,
General Westmoreland went back over his files and notes from fifteen
years earlier to refresh his memory on many of the issues on which Wallace
had examined him. Westmoreland then sent Wallace and Crile a detailed
letter clarifying and correcting a number of the points in the interview,
and supporting his overall position. Wallace and Crile never used Westmoreland's letter.

From the beginning, Crile appeared to have seen that his documentary
would hinge on Mike Wallace blowing Westmoreland out of the water. In
a note introduced at the trial, Crile wrote to Mike Wallace prior to the
interview that: "all you have to do is break Westmoreland and we have this
whole thing aced."

In contrast to its treatment of Westmoreland, CBS blatantly coddled its
own witnesses. One of its key accusers would be Joseph McChristian. Crile
and Sam Adams both sent letters to McChristian in advance of his interview, describing the documentary's story line and containing a specific
sequence of events to be included in the documentary. The night before
the interview, Crile and Adams had dinner with McChristian and supplied
him with data they had gathered from other intelligence officers. Needless
to say, neither Crile nor Adams ever prepared or dined with Westmoreland. Perhaps nothing more strongly points to how the interviews were
orchestrated by George Crile than a note he gave to Mike Wallace concerning the linkage between the McChristian and Westmoreland interviews. Crile knew that he would not be interviewing Philip Davidson,
McChristian's replacement, and he knew that McChristian would be accusing Westmoreland of a political cover-up. So he wanted Wallace to set up
Westmoreland by getting him to say good things about McChristian, writing to Wallace: "We want to get Westmoreland to say McChristian was
great stuff. We don't give a goddamn about Davidson."

A similarly suspicious sequence surrounded Crile's interview of CIA
analyst George Allen, the "dean" of the CIA witnesses who was supposed
to lend needed support to Sam Adams' story. In Crile's first interview with
Allen, Allen basically seemed to contradict the conspiracy theory, emphasizing that the CIA and MAC-V compromise had basically included all the
CIA figures, but put them in a new "presentation":

Mr. Crile: But in—but—but please, in November of—in September of
1967 when we are moving towards a war with 500,000 troops in Vietnam
to—consciously in a national intelligence estimate say that the enemy is
much, much smaller than you believed to be the case, isn't that an extreme
position for the Central Intelligence Agency to take?

Mr. Allen: But that is not what the estimate said. Mind you! The numbers were in there.

Mr. Crile: But my view—Mr. Allen—

Mr. Allen: The presentation was different.

Unsatisfied with this interview, Crile took an extraordinary step, a step that violated CBS's internal rules. Crile showed Allen video-tapes of interviews with other witnesses, and then interviewed Allen a second time. In Allen's second interview, used on the broadcast, Allen dropped his equivocations and supported the conspiracy theory. On cross-examination about this procedure, Crile told the jury that in the first interview Allen felt awkward about saying anything critical of the CIA and was looking for "an intellectually defensible fig leaf to put over the position that had been taken" by the CIA in 1967. Crile told Westmoreland's lawyer, "I would not have wanted to put in the broadcast a line which Mr. Allen would not have felt comfortable with, nor would I have felt comfortable with it if I thought it did not reflect his views." Again, Crile's apparent duplicity was striking: he never seemed much worried about whether General Westmoreland would be "comfortable" with Crile's editing of the General's interview.

Mike Wallace never got to testify in the trial; he was one of the few remaining witnesses scheduled when it ended. In his 1984 book *Close Encounters* (co-authored with Gary Paul Gates), and in statements after the trial, however, Wallace's position was made quite clear.[101] Wallace vigorously defends CBS's position in the Westmoreland case, essentially arguing that any mistakes CBS made were trivial, and that whatever they might have been, they were not enough to impugn the credibility of the broadcast. Wallace, like CBS, stands by the story. Wallace proudly asserts that "seldom has a major figure in American history been put so squarely on the spot in a network television interview." Wallace describes his interview of Westmoreland as the "key element, the *pièce de résistance*" of the broadcast.

According to Wallace, one of the factors that convinced him that the story was correct was that "most whistle-blowers speak out of anger. These men spoke in sorrow, or in shame that some of them had participated in a fraud. There is nothing in it for them to go on the record so long after the fact. It was painful and it showed." On the decision to emphasize the conspiracy element of the story, Wallace notes that CBS thought very deliberately about the choice of the word "conspiracy." One of the CBS officials, Roger Colloff, later explained "we recognized that use of the word 'conspiracy' was an issue that needed to be discussed given the strength of the word." Nevertheless, stated Colloff, "we agreed that use of the word 'conspiracy,' while tough, was warranted by the facts presented by the broadcast and the underlying research." Wallace similarly defended George Crile:

> As to some of the journalistic calls made in the course of the pro-
> duction, there is no doubt another producer might have gone about it
> differently. Some other characters might indeed have made the piece
> more varied, more a puzzle than a polemic, in the sense that the evi-
> dence we adduced pointed unmistakably at "cooking" by the [military]
> command. But there are surely other journalists who wound up with
> the same conclusion that CBS News did, most noticeably Thomas Pow-
> ers of *The Man Who Kept the Secrets*. I don't think I've often seen a piece
> on *60 Minutes* that I didn't believe might have benefited from a slightly
> different emphasis here, a nuance there, some cutting here, some add-
> ing there (all of this in retrospect, mind you), including some of my
> own. But that's a judgment call, not a failure of integrity or honest
> reporting. . . .
> There were lapses in technique, standards violated in spirit, if not in
> fact. But I'm persuaded they were not venal in nature. I don't think
> the truth was violated.

One of the ironies of Mike Wallace's and CBS's position is that much of Westmoreland's defense of his own conduct in Vietnam was *identical to CBS's defense of its conduct*: there may have been lapses, but they were not venal, and the truth was not violated. Nothing could more squarely pose the question that undergrids the contemporary American ambivalence towards freedom of speech. Why should society give CBS a benefit of the doubt that CBS was unwilling to give Westmoreland?

This point was placed in relief by CBS's handling of two of Westmore-land's most powerful arguments concerning the CBS conspiracy theory. Both invoke the same thought process that CBS relied on in its defense. Westmoreland noted that the Communists actually used between 70,000 and 90,000 troops at Tet, numbers well within the force levels projected by even the lowest (300,000 or lower) enemy troop strength estimates. Sec-ond, Westmoreland pointed to the overwhelming evidence (much of it from Communist leaders themselves) that Tet was a serious military defeat for the Communists. Westmoreland's defense is thus *identical to Mike Wal-lace's*. Whatever intelligence mistakes Westmoreland or his subordinates made, the General asserts, were venal, and were ultimately irrelevant, because the end result on the battlefield proved the army correct. West-moreland can say exactly what CBS said: we were groping for the truth, and we essentially got it.

Had the case gone to the jury box, would there have been enough evi-dence to permit the jury to decide that Westmoreland made a "clear and convincing" case that CBS acted with knowing or reckless disregard of the truth? The jury's call would depend largely on judgments of credibility, and on the weight it gave to key circumstantial evidence. The worst possible conduct that CBS could have engaged in would be deliberate lying. If key decisionmaking personnel within CBS's "chain of command" *consciously* distorted the story, believing that the story they were telling was false, but proceeded anyway, then the legal consequences are certain— CBS would be liable.

Some of producer Crile's behavior *could* be interpreted as circumstantial evidence of outright falsification, such as splicing interview footage, ignoring unfavorable witnesses, rehearsing friendly witnesses, and surreptitiously taping and then misplacing tapes, including the interview of Robert McNamara. One has to stretch this circumstantial evidence to its limit, however, to accept the view that Crile deliberately set out to assassinate Westmoreland's reputation and falsified the story to do it. Dan Burt, Westmoreland's lawyer, claimed that Crile did deliberately mislead viewers, because he needed a big, sensational story to become "famous" like Mike Wallace.

If the scenario that CBS deliberately lied seems too sinister to be plausible, however, CBS could still have lost the case if the jury found that Crile made a conscious decision to avoid discovering the truth. Imagine, for example, that Crile said to himself one day, "the conspiracy theory may be false, or the conspiracy theory may be true—I do not know—I have doubts. Nonetheless, I am going to present a documentary that portrays the story as true. I am going to avoid uncovering any evidence that would tend to disprove the conspiracy theory, and all the evidence that we do gather will be presented in a light most favorable to the conspiracy assumption."

This type of conduct would not be knowing misstatement of the truth, because Crile would not be aware of the actual truth. The combination of his subjective doubt, and his conscious decision to close his eyes to evidence that might confirm his doubts and disprove his premise, however, would qualify as recklessness under the *New York Times* rules. Once again, CBS's behavior *could* be given this interpretation, particularly the repeated failure to pursue interviews with persons who would have supported Westmoreland's view of events. The decision to permit CIA analyst Allen to see tapes of other interviews before giving his own repeat performance also might be construed as evidence of a desire to short-circuit any counterevidence. One of the witnesses at the trial, Ira Klein, who had worked as a film editor on the broadcast, claimed that after the show was put together, Sam Adams told him "we have to come clean, we have to make a statement, the premise of the show is inaccurate." Klein also said that he once said to Crile, "you realize that Mr. Adams seems obsessed. Can you trust the information, the accuracy that Sam is providing you?" Klein said that Crile replied: "I know." Klein also claimed that he warned Crile that the failure to give Westmoreland sufficient opportunity to reply to the charges was "destroying our credibility." CBS's lawyers vigorously attacked Klein's testimony, claiming it was false and motivated by Klein's intense dislike of Crile. Adams and Crile denied Klein's charges. But the jury might have chosen to believe Klein, and if they had, CBS could have been found liable.

The third possible type of behavior would be subconscious bias on CBS's part. Imagine that Crile, for example, latched on to Sam Adam's conspiracy theory the first time he heard it. Imagine that Crile never sought to independently verify the story; he simply accepted it as true from the beginning. Imagine that all his editorial judgments from then on were colored by his heartfelt belief that the conspiracy story was true. He may have thought he was being objective, while in fact he was presenting a one-sided story designed only to reinforce his preconceptions. This sort of behavior, though unreasonable, careless, negligent journalism, *would not be reckless*, and CBS would not be liable to Westmoreland if this were the case. As long as one subjectively believes that a story is accurate, the publication or broadcast of the story cannot be reckless. This example will be troublesome to many, who will perceive that it puts a premium on ignorance. The criticism is true, as far as it goes—ignorance is bliss under the *New York Times* standard—but the jury must still find the ignorance plausible. The jury must believe that CBS never doubted its story, and the jury need *not* believe CBS personnel who proclaim their genuine belief just because they say so. Although this benign blindness (as distinguished from the intentional blindness in the second example) would insulate CBS from liability, the line between conscious and unconscious averting of the eyes is very thin, and the mere admission that eyes were averted at all is likely to tempt a jury to make the finding one of genuine recklessness.

We will never know what the jury would have decided in judging this fine line between a "sincerely prejudiced" broadcast and a "dishonestly prejudiced" broadcast. From the perspective of history, however, two assessments seem justified. The first is that in one limited sense, CBS did lie to the American public. CBS deliberately created the impression that an ambiguous case, filled with contradictory evidence, was in fact unambiguous and straightforward.[102] CBS did intentionally mislead the viewer as to what the evidence *was*, even if it innocently and sincerely thought that it was telling the truth about what the evidence *meant*. No viewer that watched the broadcast could have guessed that CBS had reams of evidence that did not support its conspiracy theory. Viewers were deceitfully robbed of the chance to make their own judgments of its credibility.

The second assessment is that for all the wrong reasons, as much by accident as design, CBS's documentary in the end told the "truth." One of the mystifying intrigues of the *Westmoreland* lawsuit is that it appears very likely that in a certain sense, the CBS documentary inadvertently got the story right, but in a way totally different from what CBS thought. There *was* an intelligence failure prior to Tet, it just wasn't quite the intelligence failure CBS reported. General Westmoreland should probably bear part of the responsibility for it, but assigning responsibility to him is justified by reasons other than those implied by CBS. Tet was the watershed military event of the war—historians agree on that much—but not for the simplistic reasons assigned by CBS. Tet did precipitate Lyndon Johnson's decision to abdicate the presidency, but the links between cause and effect were not as clear and direct as CBS implied.

At the same time, however, General Westmoreland's counter-conspiracy theory of what went wrong in Vietnam is also correct. Tet did, in a sense, lead to the defeat of the United States in Vietnam, but the ultimate irony of the whole *Westmoreland* lawsuit is that this most important consequence of Tet probably was, as Westmoreland has always maintained, caused not so much by the actions of Westmoreland or the army, as by the actions of the American media, particularly CBS. Westmoreland's demonology, however, is also oversimplified, and (quite sadly), Westmoreland's oversimplifications, when combined with those of the media and the Johnson administration itself, guaranteed that Vietnam would end as an American tragedy.

A West Point textbook on Vietnam published after the war appraised Tet as a "complete surprise" and as an "intelligence failure ranking with Pearl Harbor." In his first public reaction to Tet, hours after the attack began, General Westmoreland himself seemed caught off balance, stating lamely that "very deceitfully" the Communists had launched their attack "to create maximum consternation," though he added that their "well-laid plans went afoul." But the intelligence failure of Tet was not, as the CBS documentary assumed, a matter of manipulated numbers. It was instead a clash of cultures which jarred American psychology about the war in complex, oblique ways that we still may not completely understand. Looking back at the Tet offensive, the American intelligence failure clearly was not in the assessment of the numerical strength of the enemy, but in the failure of American leaders, including Johnson and Westmoreland, to appreciate with any real insight the history and culture of Vietnam. Unhappily, the mainstream media as of 1968 also did little to genuinely enlighten us.

The Communists in the north and the south saw the reunification of Vietnam under their control as a continuation of two thousand years of resistance to Chinese, and later, French rule. Ho Chi Minh stated in the 1940's, in reference to the French, that, "You can kill ten of my men for every one I kill of yours, but even at those odds, you will lose and I will win." The deeper truth in Ho's calculations never changed, only his enemy.

Whether the Tet offensive was a "victory" or "defeat" for the United States depends upon whether one sees the war from the patient, long view of the North Vietnamese, or the narrower statistical perspective of Westmoreland. In fairness to General Westmoreland, he quite clearly *did* see that "quantitative" assessments of the situation in Vietnam were likely to be misleading, and he often said so, before and after Tet. The "narrow statistical perspective" that I speak of, however, is the perspective that comes through so strongly in his memoirs, a perspective that never rings with any sense of a true feel for the will and motivation of the enemy. To this day Westmoreland does not seem to genuinely accept the possibility that the war was never winnable. Perhaps it is beyond the world-view of a great military commander to entertain the possibility that however much America punished the bodies and the land of the enemy, America would never conquer the enemy's mind and spirit. To this day Westmoreland seems preoccupied with the "statistical reality" of Vietnam, with the fact that the Communists suffered enormous casualties from Tet. Westmoreland appears to believe today what he believed all along, that the war could have been won by attrition, killing the North Vietnamese "to the point of national disaster for generations." To Westmoreland, Tet was a disgrace not for himself, but for the Commander of the Communist forces, General Vo Nguyen Giap.

Giap said after the war that "for us, you know there is no such thing as a single strategy. Ours is always a synthesis, simultaneously military, political, and diplomatic—which is why, quite clearly, the Tet offensive had multiple objectives." Giap did not calibrate suffering on the same temporal or moral scales as Westmoreland. "Every minute," Giap stated, "hundreds of thousands of people die on this earth." He was willing to accept the deaths of tens of thousands of his compatriots, or wait "ten, fifteen, twenty, fifty years" for ultimate victory. A secondary, but nonetheless important strategy of Giap's was to divide the South Vietnamese from the United States. Part of the genius of the Tet assault on the American embassy in Saigon was its demonstration to the South Vietnamese that the United States' very center of control and prestige remained vulnerable despite America's overwhelming power. Yet for Westmoreland, only the body counts seemed significant: "Any American commander who took the same vast losses as General Giap would have been sacked overnight."

Maybe Westmoreland was right, and Giap wrong. Maybe Westmoreland was right and Dr. Spock, Abbie Hoffman, and Walter Cronkite were wrong. And maybe not. But whoever was right, isn't it clear that this is the stuff of history, of politics, of ideology, and not the stuff of a jury trial?

That asking a jury to arbitrate controversies over this sort of disputed "truth" is a meaningless exercise becomes more apparent the further one takes the alleged consequences of either the CBS conspiracy theory or the Westmoreland counter-conspiracy theory. The idea that the media hounded Lyndon Johnson from office and lost the Vietnam War, for example, is misguided in its simplicity. Media reportage of the Tet offensive does not appear to have significantly altered public opinion about the war. Public opinion surveys indicate that support for the war began to gradually but steadily decline two years before Tet. In the immediate aftermath of Tet, public support actually increased briefly, out of reflexive patriotism, but the ripple of support then dissipated and support for the war resumed its downward trend. Opposition to the war, however, was not primarily dovish. As both Peter Braestrup and Stanley Karnow in their writing about Tet point out, a large percentage of those who came to oppose the war were actually hawkish; what they were against was not the war in Vietnam as such, but rather the Johnson administration's unwillingness to "do what was necessary" to win it.

In the New Hampshire primary, for example, the majority of Democrats who voted for Senator Eugene McCarthy were hawks—outnumbering doves by three to two. Political science studies have since revealed that some New Hampshire voters actually thought they were voting for *Joe* McCarthy, not Gene. As Karnow points out, in November 1967, prior to Tet, polls showed that 44% of Americans favored withdrawal from the war, while 55% favored a get-tough policy. In February 1968, in the immediate aftermath of Tet, 53% favored more aggressiveness in Vietnam even if it would trigger the intervention of China or the Soviet Union, while those favoring withdrawal had dropped to 24%.

Even long after the war, it appears that the majority of Americans may have remained modestly hawkish about Vietnam; a 1980 survey indicated that 65% of the nation believed that we did not do what was necessary to win. The unanimity among American troops who fought in Vietnam is even more striking, and runs to some degree counter to popular mythology. The Veteran's Administration conducted a survey in 1980 of former soldiers who had engaged in heavy combat in Vietnam, and found that 82% believed that the war was lost because they were not allowed to win. The staying power of this hawkish perception of Vietnam, and the continuing currrency of the view that the media distorted the war, is attested to by the interpretation President Ronald Reagan holds.

Ronald Reagan believes that Vietnam proves that the domino theory was correct all along. In 1978 he stated: "Remember when antiwar protesters and some well-known public figures ridiculed the 'domino theory,' the idea that if South Vietnam fell to the Communists other southeast Asia nations would follow? Well South Vietnam fell in 1975 and Laos shortly thereafter. Now Cambodia (already Communist) is faced with attack by the North Vietnamese Communists . . . . after all the ridicule, it seems the dominoes are really falling." Reagan, speaking in 1980 before the Veterans of Foreign Wars convention in Chicago, stated, "For too long, we have lived with the 'Vietnam syndrome' . . . . It is time we recognized that ours was, in truth, a noble cause." Reagan said in 1976 that the United States "will no longer tolerate wars of the Vietnam type, because they no longer feel a threat, thanks to the liberal press, from communism, and they cannot interpret those wars as being really in the defense of freedom and our own country." Reagan in 1978 made a statement that sounded as if it had come from William Westmoreland's memoirs almost verbatim. The wrong of the Vietnam War came "when a government asked its young men to fight and die in a war the government was afraid to let them win." And in 1978 Reagan quoted Alexander Solzhenitsyn on the lesson of Vietnam, saying that "members of the U.S. anti-war movement wound up being involved in the betrayal of eastern nations in genocide and in suffering imposed on 30 million people."

If the view that the media trumped up and distorted Tet and thus swayed public opinion is thus too simplistic, too colored by ideology, so is the view that media coverage of Tet misled and ultimately destroyed Lyndon Johnson. Johnson, after all, knew the military facts about Tet; he knew of the heavy enemy casualties; he knew that most of the cities and military installations that were assaulted were quickly returned to American control. There is a contradiction in the biographical accounts of Johnson's reaction to Tet, for the evidence seems clear that Johnson was well prepared in advance for the invasion, and well briefed on American success in mopping it up after it occurred. Yet Johnson also remained fixated on the ongoing battles at Hue and Khesahn (particularly Khesahn) and seemed destroyed by Walter Cronkite's post-Tet-broadcast predicting an interminable stalemate. Most accounts seem to agree that Tet precipitated the unraveling of the Johnson presidency, but they also seem to agree that the evidence in front of Johnson about Tet supported Westmoreland's war of attrition.

Johnson was a complex man responding to a complex event. Any pat interpretation of his reaction to Tet is likely to be misleading. In describing Johnson's changing attitudes toward Vietnam, David Halberstam used a phrase in *The Best and the Brightest* that rings with a sort of novelist's truth: "Johnson *knew increasingly in his gut that it had gone all wrong*, that the other side had not folded." But until Tet, the other side's tenacity was never visible on the television screen. The hit and run tactics of the North Vietnamese and Viet Cong prevented their petty nagging victories from ever materializing visually; they were evanescent and intangible, dissolving into the landscape by the time that television cameras arrived at the scene of the already concluded battle. Westmoreland's attrition figures were the *only* evidence prior to Tet. Before Tet there were no tangible symbols to contradict the army's conclusion that the war was being won. In the words of Bobby Kennedy, words shown to the jury during the Westmoreland trial, Tet "finally shattered the mask of official illusion with which we have concealed our true circumstances, even from ourselves."

And so ironically, even though Tet added to the level of enemy attrition, it simultaneously eroded the public relations strength of the attrition tables. For the first time, television saw the enemy, saw that it was not an anemic, dissipated band of rabble. For the first time, the cold statistics of the war of attrition were offset by the sight of the enemy fighting out in the open, on multiple fronts across the whole of South Vietnam, in the cities (within immediate camera range), instead of the paddies and jungles.

Johnson and Westmoreland lost the *appearance* of credibility with Tet, even though their actual credibility arguably ought to have been enhanced. In the immediate aftermath of Tet the administration launched a public relations campaign, characterizing the offensive as a failure that had devestated enemy ranks, and claiming that the army had been well prepared for it in advance. It was a case of protesting too much; the more the administration sought to save face, the worse its image became. Other than the Cronkite broadcast, perhaps nothing did more to deflate the administration's efforts than a biting satire in a February 6 column by Art Buchwald: "General George Armstrong Custer said today in an exclusive interview with this correspondent that the battle of Little Big Horn had just turned the corner and he could now see the light at the end of the tunnel. 'We have the Sioux on the run,' General Custer told me. 'Of course we will have some cleaning up to do, but the Redskins are hurting badly and it will only be a matter of time before they cave in'."

The army's continuing reliance on cold mathematics after Tet did not, of course, do much to help its case, even within the administration. During the Westmoreland trial the jury was told about the meeting of the celebrated "Wise Men," the special advisory group chaired by Clark Clifford that Johnson convened after Tet to study future options in the war. The army spokesman told the group that the enemy had suffered 45,000 casualties during Tet. Arthur Goldberg, former Supreme Court Justice and Ambassador to the United Nations, asked what the enemy's estimated strength prior to Tet was. The officer estimated that it was between 160,000 and 175,000. Goldberg then asked what the "killed-to-wounded-ratio" was, the usual number of expected wounded for every enemy soldier killed. The army officer stated that the Army used a conservative assumption of three-and-a-half to one. Contrasted with the known Amer-

ican killed-to-wounded ratio of seven to one, this was an extremely conservative assumption, since the superior American medical facilities and
evacuation capability surely made the Americans' ability to rescue
wounded men greater than the Communists', rather than two times worse,
as the three-and-a-half to one ratio assumed. Yet even with that conservative estimate, the Army's figures were internally nonsensical. For, as
Goldberg immediately observed, if there were 175,000 enemy troops prior
to Tet, and 45,000 were dead, and some 157,000 (3.5 $\times$ 45,000) more
were wounded, then there were no more effective enemy forces in the
field. According to the statistics, the war was over, and the United States
had won.

One can go around and around and around again in searching for the
truth about Tet. In Frances Fitzgerald's 1972 book *Fire in the Lake*, Fitzgerald quotes from a *Washington Post* report by *Post* correspondent Ward
Just, who reported on the American military command's morale just after
Tet, finding it almost euphorically optimistic:

> One had forgotten how thoroughly caught up one had been, how thor-
> oughly a part of the war's odd, mad logic. So when you asked about
> the effect here of the Tet offensive, you were not prepared for the
> bizarre analysis. The feeling is almost universal that the attacks were a
> good thing, almost beneficial, because they made clear to both the
> Vietnamese and the Americans in the cities that the war was real; the
> Saigonese could not longer fiddle while Rome burned. The analysis
> offered by most Americans in Saigon was turned on its head, topsy-
> turvy: the effect of Tet was something of a psychological triumph for
> the reason that it woke up the Americans and badly frightened the
> Vietnamese and their fragile government.
> "We had people here after Tet who actually volunteered to go into
> ARVN," said one official. "And if that isn't progress, I don't know
> what is."
> Baffled, one tried to explain that if a single moment could be marked
> as a turning point in the support of the war in America it was the
> moment that the Viet Cong occupied the American Embassy, and later
> the pictures in *Life* magazine of George Jacobson leaning out of his
> bedroom window with an automatic pistol in his hand. The Commu-
> nists have occupied the Embassy! Well, that may be the way it looks to
> you in Washington, they say here, but it is not the reality in South
> Vietnam.

This optimism, "bizarre" in the mind of Ward Just, may have simply
captured the total divorce between the three world-views that surfaced in
Vietnam after Tet: the views of the Communists, the American military,
and the American media. As Don Oberdorfer in his book *Tet!* concluded,
"the United States failed abysmally to understand the setting into which it
was intruding." We did not lack knowledge, but wisdom. Oberdorfer

writes that Tet "was an intelligence failure not so much for lack of information as for lack of understanding and belief. Had the traditions and theories of the Vietnamese Communists been taken seriously—to say nothing of their psychology and strategy—the Tet offensive would have been no surprise. The United States never understood its foe."

And if American leaders never understood their foe, the media never understood American leaders, and the CBS documentary did not understand Westmoreland. In a *New York Times* piece after the war, James Reston wrote that "maybe the historians will agree that the reporters and the cameras were decisive in the end. They brought the war to the people, before the Congress and the courts, and forced the withdrawal of American power from Vietnam." As right as Reston is in his judgment that "the cameras were decisive in the end," it remains equally true that the cameras were incapable of enlarging our understanding, and as late as the 1982 CBS documentary, the insights of the cameras had not improved. Don Oberdorfer's conclusions describing the media's response to Tet could well have been written about CBS's behavior fifteen years later:

> For the American press, the combination of high drama and low national understanding created a monumental challenge in Vietnam— and the press, like the government, was ill-equipped to meet it. Newsmen sensed that something in the official Vietnam picture was terribly wrong but were unable to put a finger on just what. Without a broad mosaic of knowledge, individual actions and attitudes often seemed to make little sense. Convinced that officials had been lying about conditions and prospects in the war zone, unable to trust the information gathered by the government or the judgments dispensed by it, unrestrained by censorship and goaded by competition, much of the press leaped to stark conclusions when sudden events in the previously untouched cities seemed to prove its theories right. The electronics revolution, which took the battlefield into the American living room via satellite, increased the power and velocity of fragments of experience, with no increase in the power or velocity of reasoned judgment.

What is the final "truth" about *Westmoreland v. CBS*, about Tet, and about Vietnam? In the midst of the Westmoreland trial, the second of the Vietnam war memorials was unveiled in Washington, D.C. Many of the witnesses in the trial spoke of their own pilgrimages to the Vietnam memorials. The long dark wall, with the names of 46,000 Americans dead, is for Americans an emotional time tunnel. The wall is today the most visited site in the capital. Americans walk up to the wall, and they touch it, and they cry. In his 1984 song, "Born in the U.S.A.," Bruce Springsteen writes: "Had a brother at Khesahn, fighting off the Viet Cong. They're still there, he's all gone." The line distills as efficiently as any statement has the American experience in Vietnam. The seige of Khesahn, part of the Tet offensive that began early and that lingered on the longest, was one of the bloodiest battles of the war, but it was fought over terrain of no military significance. The Communist forces suffered huge losses, far worse than the Americans, but the media treated Khesahn as a defeat paralleling the French debacle two decades earlier at Dienbienphu. And in the end, like the lawsuit *Westmoreland v. CBS*, the battle just stopped, as arbitrarily as it had begun, when, after General William Westmoreland ended his tour of Vietnam duty, the United States forces simply packed up and left. "They're still there, and we're all gone."[103]

11

"I'm Okay but You're Sued": Closing Reflections and Suggestions for Reform

> First, if any opinion is compelled to silence, that opinion may, for aught we can certainly know, be true. To deny this is to assume our own infallibility. Secondly, though the silenced opinion be in error, it may, and very commonly does, contain a portion of the truth; and since the general or prevailing opinion on any subject is rarely or never the whole truth, it is only by the collision of adverse opinions that the remainder of the truth has any chance of being supplied. Thirdly, even if the received opinion be not only true, but the whole truth; unless it is suffered to be, and actually is, vigorously and earnestly contested, it will, by most of those who receive it, be held in the manner of a prejudice, with little comprehension or feeling of its rational grounds. And not only this, but fourthly, the meaning of the doctrine itself will be in danger of being lost, or enfeebled.
>
> John Stuart Mill, *On Liberty*

ALMOST EVERYONE these days seems dissatisfied with the current state of the American law of libel.[104] Public officials and public figures complain about the difficulties they face in trying to prevail against the press. The media complains about the chilling effect on free expression of the litigation aimed against it. One fact seems clear: American society is not about to do away with the libel suit. The law of libel serves a vital individual interest in providing a civilized method for resurrecting wrongfully damaged reputations, and it serves a vital social interest in providing a check and balance on media power by opening up the media's news-gathering and decision-making processes to public scrutiny and accountability. At the same time, however, though Americans' valuation of the importance of freedom of speech has over history had its peaks and valleys, we remain an essentially vigorous, wide-open, robust culture, and our society is not likely to ever completely abandon the notion that First Amendment

values should provide at least some limitations on the ability of plaintiffs
to successfully sue the press.[105]

If it is thus certain that the law of libel, and the related invasion of privacy torts, are with us to stay, it seems equally certain that they will not
retain their current form. There is simply too much discontent in all quarters with the current system to make it plausible that the current ferment
will not end in significant change. What sorts of reforms are possible?
What follows is a list and discussion of some of the adjustments to the
current system that have been suggested in recent years, followed by a
prognosis of what changes, if any, will be brought about in the future by
the most influential institutional force in this area, the Supreme Court,
and a final commentary on what is perhaps the most intriguing aspect of
this entire debate, the interplay between the evolution of the legal system
and the shifting patterns of American culture.

The following is a non-exhaustive list of suggestions for reforms in the
operation of the law of libel, which have come from judges, lawyers, journalists, and concerned citizens, some of whom are media defenders, others
media critics, with brief discussions of some of the merits and demerits of
these suggestions.

1. *Require the losing side to pay the opponent's legal fees.* Unlike the English
litigation system, in which the losing side normally must pay the winning
side's legal fees, the American civil litigation system normally requires each
side to pay its own legal costs, win or lose. Strong arguments can be made
that the law of libel in America could be made much fairer and saner if
the English practice were adopted for libel suits, because of two factors
relatively unique to libel litigation.

The first is economic. Unlike any other form of modern civil litigation,
the litigation costs for libel cases tend to dwarf the actual damages
involved. As previously noted, 80 percent of the money spent by the media
in defending libel suits goes to attorneys' fees, with only 20 percent
actually devoted to compensation through settlements or awards. To force
the media to incur huge legal costs to defend what ultimately turns out to
be the truth creates an obvious chill on free expression. The current system, however, also chills the plaintiff's right to vindicate his or her reputation when the media is in the wrong. Viewed from the plaintiff's perspective, it seems unfair that much or all of the money recovered in a
successful suit will often be gobbled up in legal expenses. The bulk of William Tavoulareas' jury award against the *Washington Post*, for example, was
consumed by Tavoulareas' legal fees.

The second reason for adopting a loser-pays-the-winner's-lawyer
approach to libel cases involves the peculiar psychology of libel suits. More

than any other form of modern civil litigation, libel suits are often surrounded by an aura of anger and frustration that tends to encourage ill-advised litigation, often because both the plaintiff and the defendant act out of less then perfect rationality.

Lawyers who frequently handle libel litigation know that it is fairly common for a libel suit to arise after months, or even years, of growing tensions between the plaintiff and the defendant. Although some libel suits literally arise out of the blue, that is often not the pattern. A media outlet may focus in on a particular historical event, dispute, or scandal over time, coming out with a series of stories that portray an individual (the eventual plantiff) in an unfavorable light, bit by bit stretching that individual's patience. It may be the check-out counter gossip sheet that week after week claims exclusive inside information on the love life of the celebrity; it may be the local newspaper that day after day blasts the mayor in its editorials. Any one story alone may seem innocuous, but as the train of petty abuses continues, deep grudges may form by slow accretion, until finally one story that goes a bit too far precipitates a lawsuit. When this "straw that broke the camel's back" pattern exists, the attorneys for both sides will often come quite quickly to the realization that they were not retained by their clients to effectuate a settlement. Libel suits tend to be fueled by acrimonious grudges that make cold economic judgments about the costs and benefits of litigation irrelevant.

A by-product of this grudge match overtone to many libel suits is that the parties to the litigation often come to the litigation with radically different perceptions of the truth. Disputes over the truth are, of course, part of any trial. But in a typical, run-of-the-mill civil case, such disputes usually come down to relatively mundane and narrow issues of "raw fact." Was the other driver drunk? Had the light changed from green to red? The parties may dispute these issues, but they are not the sorts of disagreements that put the essential character, the fundamental good or evil, of the competing litigants at issue. In a sharply contested libel suit, however, the courtroom contest can expand to issues that generate profound bitterness. Is Oscar Wilde homosexual? Is it Whittaker Chambers or Alger Hiss that is the compulsive liar and consummate actor? Is William Westmoreland an honorable man? As a juror, or even an observer, one's judgment on these issues may be colored by one's views on everything from sexual mores to communism to Richard Nixon. If one can be emotionally moved by these disputes as an observer, imagine how wrenching it can be to be a participant. In the bitterest of libel suits, the parties are likely to sincerely and emphatically entertain versions of reality that could not be more at odds. Committed to the causes of their clients, the lawyers involved in the suit will often come to substantively embrace, without serious critique, their own clients' perceptions of the truth. When both sides think they're right, both sides think that they will win, and neither side will settle.

Given this peculiar psychology, the legal system should employ whatever devices it has available to try to inject more sober rationality into the thinking of both sides. If both plaintiffs and defendants know in advance that they will bear the other side's legal costs if they lose, there is a greater probability of flexibility and cool-headed judgment in negotiating a solution that does not involve going to court.

2. *Put a greater emphasis on retraction and equal time remedies, using restorative speech to cure damaging speech.* Many libel suits could be avoided if the media outlet that first broadcast or published the alleged libel would be immunized from suit if they printed or broadcast a timely retraction, or if they offered the victim equal time or equal space to present his or her side of the story. Such retraction statutes are in existence in a number of states, but they are often filled with loopholes or given uneven judicial interpretation (as in the Carol Burnett case, in which the *National Enquirer* was held not to qualify under California's retraction statute). Many editors and reporters do not like the idea of retraction statutes, because they don't want to be forced to retract a story they basically believe in, just to avoid a libel suit. That is why, as an alternative to a retraction, the victim could be offered equal space or time, in a similarly conspicuous place in the publication or time in the broadcast day. If the media outlet refuses the request, then a libel suit could be commenced, but if the request is granted, the victim's opportunity to present his or her side of the story would be deemed sufficient remedy, and no suit could be brought. (A possible variation of this proposal would be to permit a suit after a retraction, but to limit recover to "special damages"—actual pecuniary losses.)

3. *Punitive damages should be eliminated, and absolute caps on all non-pecuniary losses should be employed.* Another often suggested reform is to eliminate punitive damages as a way to hold down ludicrously large mega-verdicts. Nobody's reputation, the argument goes, is truly worth $20 million—such jury awards make the system a farce, and serve primarily to encourage the use of libel suits to persecute disfavored ideology, or fringe publications. The counterpoint to this suggestion is that punitive damages are a necessary form of leverage if the media is to be kept in line—punitive damages, it is argued, are for certain media outlets "the only language they understand."

Gigantic mega-verdicts do seem out of touch with reality, but the elimination of punitive damages as such will not necessarily bring them under control. For as noted in the discussion of damages in the Carol Burnett case, the law of libel has always struggled with the problem of valuing in any intelligent or comprehensible way the notion of damage to reputation. Tort law has similar problems in valuing damage from invasion of privacy, infliction of emotional distress, and "pain and suffering" compensation. Today, in cases that do not involve matters of public interest, the Supreme Court, after a 1985 decision (discussed later in this chapter) apparently now imposes no First Amendment restriction on the award of either punitive or compensatory damages. In cases that are subject to First Amendment restraints, punitive damages are still constitutionally permissible when actual malice is demonstrated, and compensatory damages are not limited to real pecuniary loss. The current First Amendment rules therefore restrain punitive damages only in a limited number of cases, and they permit juries to award huge verdicts under the rubric of compensatory damages, in form awarding no punitive damages at all, though in fact including punitive damages as a disguised component of the compensatory damages award.

To restrict all damages in libel suits to actual pecuniary loss would go too far to insulate the media from accountability, and would deny the psychological truth that defamatory speech does in fact injure the victim, even though it is usually difficult to place a price tag on the injury. The following two-part compromise appears fair to both sides: First, in cases in which the media defendant issues a prompt and complete retraction in a manner calculated to reach the same audience with the same impact, only pecuniary losses should be recoverable. This would normally mean printing a retraction in the same space on the printed page as the defamatory speech, or broadcasting a retraction during the same time periods as the offending broadcast. As an alternative, the plaintiff could opt for equal time or equal space to present his or her side of the story.[106]

Second, in all cases in which the defendant refuses to retract, or to offer equal time or space, damages should not be limited to pecuniary loss. However, no punitive damages should be permitted, and a ceiling on all "general" damages not supported by evidence of real pecuniary loss should be set, such as a ceiling of $500,000. This would prevent a jury from sneaking punitive damages into the verdict as disguised compensatory damages. Such arbitrary ceilings are not uncommon in American law; they have been routine in many states for decades in "wrongful death" lawsuits, and have been employed in medical malpractice cases. They are particularly sensible when the injury involved cannot be measured quantitatively. Several states, including Massachusetts, Oregon, and Washington,[107] have already eliminated punitive damages in libel cases, and there is no indication that the media is especially reckless or rides roughshod over the interests of citizens in those states.[108]

4. *Eliminate entirely libel suits by high-ranking policy-making public officials for matters arising from their public duties.* The ACLU has proposed barring libel suits by public officials altogether, for any libel arising from the performance of their official duties, on the theory that to criticize the official is to criticize the government, and such criticism should be absolutely protected. The counterpoint to this argument is that it is already hard enough to attract quality people to public office, and if public office becomes a libel free-fire zone, good people in office will be even harder to find. Perhaps the most sensible compromise would be to continue to permit public officials to recover upon a showing of actual malice (continue, that is, the rule of *New York Times v. Sullivan*), but to recognize, as the Supreme Court in the *New York Times* case recognized, that courts should be extremely wary of public officials attempting to turn speech critical of governmental policy into speech that is personally defamatory. Seldom do Americans criticize the "presidency" or the "Speaker of the House" as impersonal institutions; instead we criticize Ronald Reagan or Tip O'Neill by name. Nevertheless, such criticism, no matter how violent, is often aimed essentially at policy. The law of libel already has a device for eliminating such suits: the distinction between fact and opinion. As an alternative to the ACLU proposal, it may be preferable to adopt the following device: in any lawsuit brought by a high public official with policy-making responsibility arising from matters relating to his or her performance of public duties, there should be (in addition to the *New York Times* actual malice requirement) a heavy presumption that the speech involved is non-actionable opinion. In short, in distinguishing between fact and opinion when public officials are involved, courts in close cases should err on the side of characterizing the speech as opinion. This approach would dovetail with the next suggestion for a broader definition of the term "opinion."

5. *Adopt an approach to the fact/opinion distinction that discourages the use of libel suits as ideological forums.* As explained in Chapter Three, under both the common law and the Constitution, only misstatements of fact are actionable in a libel suit; opinions are absolutely protected. Nevertheless, a great deal of modern anti-media litigation involves issues in the gray area between pure fact and pure opinion, in which the parties seem to be litigating the merits of competing ideologies rather than competing versions of the hard-core facts. The American law of libel needs to adopt a broader definition of "opinion" that takes into account a very special American trait: our cultural tendency to view the lawsuit as the answer to every conflict, including our political and philosophical differences.

Alexis de Tocqueville wrote over a century ago that "scarcely any political question arises in the United States that is not resolved, sooner or later, into a judicial question." Tocqueville was remarkably prescient; in modern American life the lawsuit has come to be thought of as the solution to virtually every problem. Much of today's libel litigation seems to be brought to "solve social problems," or at least to publicly debate social issues, rather than to protect reputation.

Libel suits today are subject to abuse as forums for doing ideological battle. From the struggles of Martin Luther King, to the literary sensibilities of Lillian Hellman, to the fortunes of war of Generals Sharon and Westmoreland, American libel litigation seems inseparable from political, philosophical, and artistic debate.

In this milieu it makes perfect sense, for example, that Ralph Nader, America's great lawyer-crusader, would adopt the libel and invasion of privacy suit as one of his weapons. Nader resorted to both invasion of privacy and libel theories in two separate lawsuits arising from his consumerist efforts against the Corvair. The first of those lawsuits—a case brought by Nader against General Motors for invasion of privacy—illustrates the perfectly legitimate use of litigation to simultaneously serve Nader's individual interest in personal privacy and dignity, and a larger social interest in corporate accountability and honesty. His second lawsuit, however, against a conservative columnist, Ralph de Toledano, for libel, illustrates the use of the law of libel as an ideological weapon, a use that serves less as a means of redressing reputational damage than as a means of punishing an ideological adversary for alleged misstatements made in the heat of virulent debate.

In the first example, Ralph Nader sued General Motors, alleging that General Motors, having learned that Nader was about to publish a book critical of the General Motors Corvair, *Unsafe at Any Speed*, initiated a series of efforts to intimidate him and suppress his critique. Nader alleged that General Motors made inquiries into his political, social, racial, and religious opinions; kept him under surveillance; hired women to attempt to seduce him into illicit sexual relationships; made harassing and obnoxious phone calls; and tapped his phone and eavesdropped on his private conversations. The New York Court of Appeals held that although "the law does not provide a remedy for every annoyance that occurs in everyday life," several of Nader's allegations against General Motors, if true, would constitute an invasion of privacy. After the court's ruling General Motors settled the suit, though still denying any wrongdoing. Nader had sought $7 million in punitive damages and $2 million in compensatory damages. The settlement reportedly was for $425,000—nowhere near the figures sought, but a handsome amount nonetheless.

In the second example, Nader sued conservative columnist Ralph de Toledano for libel, for statements de Toledano made that were critical of certain congressional testimony by Nader concerning the Corvair. As part

of a protracted effort by Nader against the Corvair, Nader submitted a
mass of material to a Senate subcommittee chaired by Abraham Ribicoff.
Ribicoff's subcommittee issued a report that addressed each of Nader's
allegations concerning General Motor's conduct toward Nader, and
Nader's allegations that General Motors had misled the subcommittee
about the Corvair's safety. The subcommittee's conclusion was that the evidence did not substantiate Nader's claims. The central finding of the subcommittee was summarized at the beginning of the report:

> Although we have not upheld Mr. Nader's charges against the Cor-
> vair and General Motors, we believe they were made in good faith
> based on the information available to him. After gathering all the evi-
> dence concerning them, we can understand how he reached the posi-
> tions stated in his letters. The documents he cites provide some sup-
> port for his views. However, we believe the clear preponderance of the
> evidence, much of which was unavailable to Mr. Nader, is on the other
> side.

Columnist de Toledano had criticized Nader's efforts in prior columns,
and he was only too happy to seize the occasion of Nader's defeat in the
subcommittee report as an opportunity to make hay against Nader. In a
column dealing with a completely different topic, nuclear power (but a
topic also associated with Nader and Senator Ribicoff), de Toledano went
after both Nader and Ribicoff with an acid pen:

> Ralph Nader and his cohorts are at it again, working overtime to
> sabotage American efforts to achieve energy independence and eco-
> nomic balance. Their target is nuclear power, a subject about which—
> as any reputable scientist will tell you—the sum total of Nader's knowl-
> edge could be comfortably stuffed in a frog's ear.
> In this endeavor, Nader is being aided and abetted by Sen. Abraham
> Ribicoff, D-Conn., who not too long ago devoted some 250 devastating
> columns of Congressional Record to demonstrate conclusively that
> Nader falsified and distorted evidence to make his case against the
> automobile.
> In recent articles for the New York Times, Ribicoff displayed an
> amazing ignorance of the facts when he called for "breaking the
> nuclear habit."
> Now Nader and his eco-freaks know what they are about to this
> extent. They want to shut down most of this country's industrial plants
> and send us back to the spinning wheel.

Nader filed a suit against de Toledano for libel because of this column,
seeking $5,000 in compensatory damages and $1 million in punitive damages. Like his suit against General Motors, this suit also was settled, but
not without first extracting its toll from de Toledano, a toll he was obviously less able to absorb than General Motors.

There is a subtle but important difference between these two suits by Nader, a difference that goes well beyond the distinction between suing General Motors and suing a single writer. General Motors stood accused of harrassment; de Toledano, however, stood accused only of making statements that were critical of Nader, statements obviously imbued with a world-view that happened to be quite different from Nader's. And in that difference lurks the greatest danger of the lawsuit-as-the-solution-to-everything syndrome: that it will be twisted (often unconsciously) into a device for punishing those who espouse ideological positions different from one's own. Nader believed, of course, that de Toledano had *lied* about him, and that no First Amendment values are served by letting the lie go unchallenged. But the "lie," if it existed, was the product of a virulent political clash; it was hyperbole born of heated debate.

After all, it is not as if Ralph Nader himself has never resorted to powerful language to make a political point. The masterful orchestration of publicity for his group's causes is one of the principal ingredients in Nader's success, and these propaganda efforts ("propaganda," here, used merely in its descriptive sense) quite naturally lend themselves from time to time to certain rhetorical flourishes. (A Nader publication, for example, once condemned the "misguided leadership" of the Federal Trade Commission as the "malignant cancer" that "is silently destroying" the FTC and spreading "its contagion on the growing crisis of the American consumer.") Nader and his disciples might think of everything he says as nothing but the purest truth. But his ideological enemies might just as sincerely characterize his statements as bold-faced lies.

To live by the sword is to die by the sword; if lawsuits could be used as ideological weapons for the left, they could be used as ideological weapons for the right. It took a while for conservatives to catch on, but caught on they have. For every liberal public interest group renting office space in Washington, D.C. today, there are conservative counterparts, just as adept at using the courtroom as one of the forums for waging ideological battle. Conservative public interest groups have become vendors in the emerging libel industry. The conservatives' recent brandishing of the libel suit as a political weapon has been made possible to some degree by a habit of mind created by liberals themselves, a habit of mind that perhaps takes a bit too much in earnest Tocqueville's observation that most significant American issues ultimately become judicial.

If the political right and big business feel they have never been able to get the respect they deserve from the "eastern liberal press," they have never had any trouble attracting the attention of lawyers. In an innovative development, the Mobil Oil Corporation, in the aftermath of the Tavoulareas suit, has offered top executives "libel insurance," designed to pay for the costs of suing the press if an executive is defamed.

Another example of an ideologically conservative use of libel litigation (and one with racial overtones) is a suit by physicist William Shockley against the *Atlanta Constitution*. Shockley shared the Nobel Prize for Physics in 1956 for his part in inventing the transistor. In recent years, however, Shockley has become more well known for his belief that human intelligence is largely genetically determined, and that blacks have lower I.Q.'s than whites because blacks are genetically inferior. Shockley believes that the "selected multiplication of less gifted members of society through extremely large families or higher rate of illegitimacy" is harming society, because those with lower intelligence generally tend to have larger numbers of offspring than those of higher intelligence. In Shockley's view this threatens to turn upside down the law of survival of the fittest. To meet this perceived peril, Shockley proposed a voluntary sterilization plan in which bonuses would be offered to all people of childbearing age if they become sterilized, with the amount of the bonus varying, and geared toward discouraging reproduction by those of lowest intelligence who were most likely to transmit unfavorable characteristics. For example, Shockley would increase the bonus by $1,000 for every I.Q. point below 100; the bonus would also be based upon the "best scientific estimates of any genetically carried disabilities such as hemophilia, sickle cell anemia, epilepsy, Huntington's and so on."

In an article by *Atlanta Constitution* writer Roger Witherspoon on Shockley's theory, Witherspoon stated that "the Shockley program was tried out in Germany during World War II, when scientists under the direction of the government experimented on Jews and defectives in an effort to study genetic development." Shockley regarded the comparison of his theory to Nazi genetic experiments as libelous and sued Witherspoon and the *Constitution* for $1.25 million. The trial judge told the jury that the trial was not over the validity of Shockley's genetic or racial theories, but after retiring for three and a half hours to consider the evidence against Witherspoon, who is black, an Atlanta jury of five whites and one black returned a verdict in favor of Shockley, but for the paltry sum of one dollar. Like it or not, the jury transparently acted as an arbiter of an ideological clash; Witherspoon and the *Constitution* may have technically violated the law of libel, and technically they lost the case. But the real trial, despite the judge's admonitions, was over Shockley's theory, and his theory lost.

Libel suits are simply not the proper social forum for these sorts of ideological battles, and judges should begin to interpret the distinction between fact and opinion with a greater willingness to label ostensibly factual statements as opinions, when the underlying sting of the offending

speech involves matters of interpretation of facts, even when those interpretations are patently unfair, when they are made in an obviously ideological context.

We should remember that individuals and institutions alike largely
define themselves by the enemies they choose, and those enemies are often
ideas. The urge to harass opposing viewpoints, from the theories of William Shockley to the media's view of the Vietnam War, is a natural tendency, which is endemic to social organization. Oliver Wendell Holmes
described this persecution instinct in his famous dissenting opinion in
Abrams v. United States:

> Persecution for the expression of opinions seems to me perfectly log-
> ical. If you have no doubt of your premises or your power and want a
> certain result with all your heart you naturally express your wishes in
> law and sweep away all opposition. To allow opposition by speech
> seems to indicate that you think the speech impotent, as when a man
> says that he has squared the circle, or that you do not care whole-heart-
> edly for the result, or that you doubt either your power or your
> premises.

In recent years Americans have seemed increasingly willing to give this
instinct free rein, through the vehicle of libel litigation. Those who relish
the reinvigoration of the American law of libel place at the cornerstone of
their defense of it one elemental premise: that the essential mission of the
law of libel ought to be the punishment of "bad" speech, speech that is
"false" and injurious to reputation. If libel law has a "chilling effect" on
the media, so be it; for the only speech that will be chilled is speech which
deserves to be chilled. This view is dependent on a high level of confidence
that such terms as "fact," "opinion," "idea," and "truth" are capable of
being meaningfully defined for the purposes of the libel litigation process.

One of the great clichés of the legal process is that the real truth often
lies somewhere in between the plaintiff's story and the defendant's story,
and that twelve persons "good and true," applying their common sense
and the values of the community, will ferret that truth out. The problem
with this cliché is that it assumes that the truth is knowable at all; it assumes
that a "truth" exists in the first place. The litigation process itself can lead
to a spurious sense of scientific certainty about the truth; after spending
ten million dollars investigating the truth, it is hard to accept the possibility
that the whole quest was quixotic from its inception. But perhaps some
litigation quests are misconceived from the start; perhaps in *some* litigation,
to use Gertrude Stein's phrase, there's no there there.

In ordinary litigation, of course, it is possible to meaningfully say that
"truth" exists. The defendant either murdered his wife or he did not. The
driver was either drunk or he was sober. This is not to say that the jury will

necessarily get the right answer. Obviously it may not—all of the law is an assessment of probabilities—but at least we have confidence that the process itself is not ridiculous, that even if only God could know with omniscient certainty what really happened, a jury can take a fair and intelligent stab. But not all factual disputes are reducible to the pluses and minuses of the usual litigation process. When we move away from litigation over relatively confined arenas of fact and into litigation over the unbounded causes and effects of history, the normal "fact-finding" function of the jury may break down. At some point on the continuum from raw factual detail to the larger themes of history we move from fact to ideology; we turn jurors into historians and political scientists. This problem of the "ideological fact" has always plagued the conceptual underpinnings of libel law, and the constitutionalization of libel rules that began with the 1964 decision in *New York Times v. Sullivan* has still not solved the problem. Rather than face the issue of ideological fact squarely, the stock response of the legal system has been to paper the conflict over. If we look at what plaintiffs in libel litigation really do, rather than at idealized visions of what the law is supposed to permit them to do, the conclusion is inescapable that the law of libel is routinely used to punish ideas.

6. *Greater attention should be paid to the context in which the defamatory speech is disseminated.* The modern law of libel has paid insufficient attention to the context in which defamatory speech is spoken, largely because the most celebrated and controversial libel cases, the cases that set trends and establish legal doctrine, too often involve issues of national attention, thus slighting the significance of more "everyday" speech. For most people, speech concerning the neighborhoods, workplaces, schools, or churches in which they function daily is more immediately vital than the speech that appears in the *CBS Evening News*, the *Washington Post*, or *Harper's*. The First Amendment is not intended only to protect the speech of Dan Rather. There are national marketplaces of ideas and local marketplaces of ideas, and for most citizens the local marketplaces are usually where wide-open, robust, and uninhibited dicussion is most relevant. Few people purposefully inject themselves into arenas of national attention, but many people involve themselves actively in events and controversies in their neighborhoods, their children's schools, and their workplaces. An obscure professor at a law school, for example, is not likely to be a public figure as defined in *Gertz*, and an article in *Newsweek* about that professor not connected to any significant public controversy should probably not be protected by the actual malice standard. Within the law school community, however, even the obscure professor is a "public figure." Statements in a student newspaper attacking the professor for poor teaching, bad scholarship, lack of public service, or arbitrary grading deserve the special pro-

tection of the actual malice standard, just as statements made within the faculty committee reviewing the professor's application for tenure and promotion should be actionable only upon a showing of actual malice.

7. *General streamlining and simplification should be a dominant feature of any comprehensive effort at reform.* The truth of the following theorem is close to intuitively obvious: "the tendency of juries to nullify the law increases in proportion to the level of complexity of the law they are instructed to apply." If juries are inclined for cultural reasons to be hostile to the media, giving them legal standards too complicated to understand only invites them to take the law into their own hands. The problem of nullification by the jury can never be totally eliminated, but it can be brought under greater control, primarily by simplifying and streamlining the law.

Similarly, the following corollary seems self-evident: the more complicated the law, the more expensive the legal fees. Since the high cost of libel litigation hurts both plaintiffs and defendants, simplifying the libel rules we apply would provide at least some benefit for both sides.

In the last two decades, the most dramatic changes in the direction of the law of libel have come from the Supreme Court. Given the current national debate over the law of libel, what sorts of changes is the Supreme Court likely to make in the future? A revealing glimpse of what the future may have in store came from a decision handed down by the Court in the summer of 1985.

In an important libel decision decided in June of 1985 entitled *Dun & Bradstreet v. Greenmoss Builders, Inc.*, the Supreme Court appeared to cut back yet again on the scope of First Amendment protection that applies to defamatory speech, with some Justices going even so far as to suggest the overruling of *New York Times v. Sullivan.* The case involved the credit reporting agency Dun & Bradstreet, which had sent a report to five of its subscribers indicating that a construction company known as Greenmoss Builders had filed for bankruptcy. The report was false—an agent of Dun & Bradstreet had mixed up a bankruptcy petition filed by an employee of Greenmoss with Greenmoss itself. The construction company sued Dun & Bradstreet for libel and won, recovering $50,000 in compensatory and $300,000 in punitive damages. Those punitive damages were awarded despite the fact that Dun & Bradstreet was not found to have acted with actual malice as defined in *New York Times.* The case reached the United States Supreme Court, which was asked to decide whether or not the rule ennunciated in the 1974 *Gertz v. Robert Welch* decision, which appeared to prohibit punitive damages in all cases unless actual malice was established, should apply in this sort of circumstance. Ever since the *Gertz* decision, lower courts and scholars had debated whether it was meant to apply to

defendants that were not part of the media. In *Dun & Bradstreet*, the
Supreme Court appeared to lay that debate to rest, ruling that no distinction should exist between media and nonmedia defendants. In a dramatic
alteration of *Gertz*, however, the Court ruled that henceforth the *Gertz* case
should not be deemed to apply to speech not involving "matters of public
concern." Holding that a credit report did not come within the definition
of speech involving issues of "public concern," the Court held that the
punitive damages against Dun & Bradstreet should be upheld, because
there "is simply no credible argument that this type of credit reporting
requires special protection to ensure that 'debate on public issues [will] be
uninhibited, robust, and wide open,'" invoking the famous phrase from
the *Times* case.

Just as dramatic as this new curtailment on *Gertz*, were suggestions in
concurring opinions by Chief Justice Burger and Justice White that *Gertz*,
and perhaps even *New York Times v. Sullivan*, be overruled. Chief Justice
Burger stated that the *Times* case should be "reexamined," noting that the
"great rights guaranteed by the First Amendment carry with them certain
responsibilities as well." In an almost flippant dig at the press, Chief Justice
Burger ended his opinion with the statement: "Consideration of these
issues inevitably recalls the aphorism of journalism attributed to the late
Roy Howard that 'too much checking on the facts has ruined many a good
news story'."

Justice White, going substantially beyond Chief Justice Burger, wrote an
extensive and aggressive attack on the *Times* case, stating that the "*New
York Times* rule thus countenances two evils: first, the stream of information about public officials and public affairs is polluted and often remains
polluted by false information; and second, the reputation and professional
life of the defeated plaintiff may be destroyed by falsehoods that might
have been avoided with a reasonable effort to investigate the facts." Justice
White concluded that in terms of the First Amendment and reputational
interests at stake, "these seem grossly perverse results."

The ramifications of the shift in legal doctrine created by the *Dun &
Bradstreet* decision will take years to play out, for although the case seems
in part a response to a general cultural uneasiness about the media's
increasing role as the superintendent of the national agenda, the Court's
cut-back on the coverage of *Gertz* was achieved through the resurrection
of the methodology of the very pro-media case that *Gertz* overruled, *Rosenbloom v. Metromedia*. Once again, the constitutional focus has been placed
on the phrase "matters of public concern." The "public concern"
approach was originally abandoned in *Gertz* largely because it was becoming virtually impossible for courts to resist applying the actual malice standard in almost all suits against the media, *since the very fact that the media*

252   Suing the Press

had chosen to publish the story could raise a presumption that the story was some-
thing that some segment of the public would be interested in. Once "matters of
public interest" becomes synonomous with "what the public is interested
in," the media can instantly bootstrap itself into a favored First Amendment position, because the media has the power to create public interest
in a story by choosing to focus on it. *Gertz* responded to these concerns by
holding that private figures need show only negligence to recover against
the media, even if the matter involved an issue of public interest. The *Dun
& Bradstreet* decision goes even further, by seeming to say that the First
Amendment rules of *Gertz* will not apply at all for speech that does not
involve issues of public interest.

The future implications of the *Dun & Bradstreet* opinion will thus turn
to a large degree on how narrowly or expansively the term "public interest" is defined. One need not have any paranoid visions of the media as a
monolithic manipulator of reality to accept the point that there is no objective definition possible for what is "a matter of public interest." In the
parlance of Oliver Wendell Holmes, the definition does not have any
"brooding omnipresence in the sky." Is a muckraking segment on *60 Minutes* about an auto insurance scheme newsworthy before *60 Minutes* moves
in with cameras rolling, or do the rolling cameras make it so? The answer
must be some of both: in its function as the intermediary between raw
events and the public consumers of information about those events, the
media acts at times as a passive conduit that merely responds to market
forces, and at times as a conscious agent deciding what to market. Investigative reporting does not merely uncover pre-existing reality, it creates
new reality. In the media coverage of Vietnam and Watergate, the power
of the press to shape events rather than merely record them was obvious,
and the press reveled in a golden moment of national praise. But whereas
the manipulation and destructive interventions of the yellow journalism
practiced by the Hearsts and Pulitzers are thought of with a sort of amusing admiration for the enterprising pluck of bygone entrepreneurs, the
more muted and responsible modern press that exposed the evils of Watergate and Vietnam is curiously less trusted. As a culture we enjoy watching
60 Minutes and *Nightline*—witness their ratings—but we are unwilling to
assign to those orthodox corporate repositories of news the power to
decide for themselves the level of legal protection that will be extended
to their efforts.

The Supreme Court, for all its seeming judicial remove, is still a collection of politically sensitive persons who rose to prominence in political and
legal circles where image was a precious commodity, and it appears very
probable that the Court will further cut back on First Amendment protection for the press, by giving the term "public interest" an extremely nar-

row definition. Justices of the Supreme Court do not lose their natural concern for public relations merely by donning their robes, and the Supreme Court as a political institution has obviously been as suspicious as beleaguered presidents and members of Congress of the power of the press to establish the tone of national life and influence perceptions of governmental institutions. The Justices, after all, were themselves the unwitting targets of the investigative reportage of Bob Woodward and Scott Armstrong in *The Brethren,* and even the most dispassionate legal mind is not likely to be immune from the natural (and perhaps unconscious) shadings of world-view that came from being the victim of an unflattering public portrait. In the last five years Burger Court decisions in the defamation area have grown increasingly hostile to the media. In a sort of judicial version of the multiplier effect, the Burger Court has used relatively small adjustments in legal doctrine to give substantial impetus to the pursuit of vindication against the media through litigation.

On the whole, the media has not fared well in the last decade. Several of the media's Supreme Court defeats have involved plaintiffs on the borderline between public figure and private figure status, in which the Court has held that they should be classified as private figures, and thus able to recover without meeting the rigorous *New York Times* standards. The Court, for example, held that Mary Alice Firestone, wife of Russell Firestone, a scion of the wealthy Firestone family, was a private figure in a suit she brought against *Time* magazine. In 1964 the Firestones became embroiled in a vigorously contested divorce proceeding in Palm Beach County, Florida. Mary Alice Firestone had filed a complaint seeking separate maintenance, and Russell Firestone had counterclaimed for divorce, on grounds of "extreme cruelty and adultery." The Florida circuit court granted the divorce, and included, in the final judgment, the statement that: "According to certain testimony in behalf of the defendant, extramarital escapades of the plaintiff were bizarre and of an amatory nature which would have made Dr. Freud's hair curl. Other testimony, in plaintiff's behalf, would indicate that the defendant was guilty of bounding from one bedpartner to another with the erotic zest of a satyr." *Time's* editorial staff composed an item which appeared in the magazine's "Milestones" section the following week, stating that the divorce was "on grounds of extreme cruelty and adultery" and noting that the "trial produced enough testimony of extramarital adventures on both sides, said the judge, 'to make Dr. Freud's hair curl'."

Mary Alice Firestone sued *Time* for defamation and won a jury verdict of $100,000, a decision that ultimately was affirmed by the United States Supreme Court. *Time* argued that the *New York Times* standard should have applied because the Firestone divorce was a "cause célèbre," and Mary

Alice Firestone was a "public figure" with regard to the divorce proceedings. *Time* emphasized that Ms. Firestone subscribed to a press clipping service that chronicled her media exposure and that she held several press conferences during the divorce proceeding in which she answered questions regarding the case. The United States Supreme Court held, however, that despite Mary Alice Firestone's prominence in "the sporting set," she did not qualify as a person of "especial prominence in the affairs of society."

The Firestone case set the tone for a number of other media defeats in the Supreme Court in the late 1970's and early 1980's. The Court held, for example, that a man wrongly accused of being a Soviet spy, who had been subpoenaed as part of a grand jury investigation into Soviet espionage, was a private figure in a suit arising from a book by John Barron on the KGB. The Court also held that a university professor who sued Senator William Proxmire for being ridiculed for allegedly wasteful research in one of Proxmire's "Golden Fleece Awards" was also a private figure. The same Justices who voted to vindicate reputational interests at the expense of free expression in this line of cases, however, voted in precisely the opposite way when the value of reputation was at issue in a different legal context. In *Paul v. Davis*, a 1976 case, Justice Rehnquist wrote for the Court about reputation in a manner that directly contradicted the sentiments of the Court when the media was being sued. *Paul* was an action brought by Edward Davis, a Louisville newspaper reporter, against two local police chiefs, because the reporter's name and picture had been circulated on a police flyer purporting to identify "active shoplifters." Davis had been arrested for shoplifting, but at the time the materials were circulated the charge had not yet been tried, and it was subsequently dismissed. Davis brought suit in federal court claiming that the police flyer branded him as a criminal without the benefit of trial, thereby damaging his reputation and depriving him of "liberty or property" without due process of law. In an Iago-like reversal, the same six Justices who treated reputation as legally hallowed when the media was the defendant in the *Firestone* case (decided the same year as Davis' case was) found that Davis' reputation was not the type of legal interest encompassed by the words "life, liberty, or property" in the due process clause. Just as Iago admonished Cassius, "I thought you had received some bodily wound," for "there is more sense in that than in reputation," the Supreme Court conveniently abandoned its view of reputation as "a basic of our constitutional system," and held that "the words 'liberty' and 'property' as used in the Fourteenth Amendment do not in terms single out reputation as a candidate for special protection over and above other interests. The Court stated that "the frequently drastic effect of the 'stigma' which may result from defamation by the government in a variety of contexts, does not establish the proposition that reputation alone, apart from some more tangible interests such as employment, is . . . by itself sufficient to invoke the procedural protection of the Due Process Clause."

The contrast between the treatment of the importance of reputation in the defamation cases and the *Paul* case accents the Court's willingness to manipulate its treatment of "reputation" to fit its purposes. On the Burger Court today reputation is a "basic to our constitution system" when measured against the competition of freedom of expression, but it is not "a candidate for special protection" when it faces off with the Court's generally conservative deference to the actions of government officials. The Supreme Court freely manipulates the valve of reputation, either enhancing or diminishing its importance as it sees fit. Perplexingly, the unifying principle appears to be that reputation will be given whatever level of importance is necessary to undermine other constitutional guarantees. The importance of reputation is built up by the Court when such a build-up helps decrease the coverage of the First Amendment's free speech guarantees; the importance of reputation is dismantled when the dismantling serves to constrict the scope of the due process clause. In charting the long-term movement of the Burger Court, however, the direction of the Court in reconciling First Amendment claims with reputational claims is unmistakable: protection of reputation is ascending, and protection of the media is falling fast.[109]

In the end, perhaps the most significant lessons to be drawn from the recent libel explosion are cultural. As a society we may have a reflexive reverence for the notion of "checks and balances" implicit in our Constitution, a notion that has been part of the American philosophical tradition since *The Federalist Papers*. We are a society wary of any institution, governmental or private, whose power appears to be emerging unhindered by significant restraints or counterbalances. In response to the "liberal activism" of the Supreme Court under Earl Warren, American presidents began to appoint more conservative Justices. In response to the "imperial presidency" that grew from Franklin Roosevelt to Richard Nixon, the Congress and the press gradually increased scrutiny and asserted greater control. And in response to the growing American perception that the press is enormously powerful and sometimes out of control, the legal system seems to have reasserted its own methods of insuring accountability.

We are also a society in which ideology often seems intimately linked to personality. It is not surprising that so many ideological battles should be fought out in the context of libel suits brought by persons of prominence. In a world that trades on what people appear to be, reputation becomes the most precious of currency. As self-image becomes inextricably wrapped up in public image, it is no wonder that many who now strike out at the media are the very persons who have profited by the media attention they were able to command. It is understandable that Ralph Nader should feel the need to sue Ralph de Toledano for de Toledano's critical statements concerning Nader's crusade against the Corvair, for Nader's image as a consumerist crusader is an essential element of his stock in trade, an invaluable asset to be tenaciously defended. If the public image of Nader as David the slayer of corporate and bureaucratic Goliaths is important to him, image is no less critical to the heads of the corporations and government agencies that Nader pursues. Why should William Tavoulareas, president of Mobil Oil, really give a damn about an article in the *Washington Post* claiming that he had used his influence to set up his son in business? Surely there was a time when presidents of giant corporations would not have given a minute's worry to such a story (how many shares has the *Post?*) but in a world in which effectiveness as a consumer advocate or corporate executive depends on the precious commodity of a good media reputation, Nader and Tavoulareas find themselves in litigation kinship. (Tavoulareas has noted the transforming power of bringing a lawsuit for libel. After the *Post* ran its story, Tavoulareas said, "You walk into the halls and people you've known for years feel sort of sorry for you. And some are saying, 'Hey, maybe he did something wrong.' But the moment I sued, the attitude of everybody changed—suddenly people started to believe you. My days changed the day I started the suit.")

And in an era in which political campaigns are dominated by public relations consultants instead of crusty political power brokers, an era in which one president is hounded from office largely because of a personality that exuded malaise, to be replaced by a president who has parlayed acting and style into the label the Great Communicator, who can be surprised that so many politicians and public officials sue to protect their reputations? For example, Jimmy Carter's outraged threats of suit over a gossip column item in the *Washington Post* that relayed rumors that Blair House had been bugged during Ronald and Nancy Reagan's stay there forced a retraction from the *Post* and a published letter of apology. The Carter threats took on an almost sad too-little-too-late quality; his indignation seemed an almost poignant attempt to rejuvenate reputational stock that was hopelessly depleted. Yet it could also be said that for public officials lawsuits brought after their moment in history has passed are critical to their long-term success in accomplishing their ideological goals. A former president's or army general's image remains forever intertwined with the historical gloss that accretes over their moments in the limelight: long after the Vietnam War is over General Westmoreland was essentially fighting to correct the historical record that CBS allegedly marred; the former United States ambassador to Chile had invited a jury of New Yorkers to decide the extent to which the American embassy was connected with the killing of an American freelance writer during the coup d'état in Chile ten years earlier; and Ariel Sharon was trying to repair the damage done to his reputation by the massacres in Lebanon, to help rescue a political life that may have as many rebounds as Richard Nixon's.

Despite all of these cultural forces fueling litigation against the media, however, we also remain a society with a wonderful, idealistic commitment to the value of free speech. The libel explosion does chill the courage of the press, and in that chill all of us suffer, for it threatens to make the press slavishly safe, pouring out a centrist, spiceless paste of consensus thought. All of us lose if we permit the trivialization of free speech.

What the libel explosion does to the free expression interests of the media, however, may in the end be less significant than what it does to the free expression interests of ordinary private citizens. For if we take the libel suit too seriously, we are in danger of raising our collective cultural sensitivity to reputation to unhealthy levels. We are in danger of surrendering a wonderful part of our national identity—our strapping, scrambling, free-wheeling individualism, in danger of becoming less American, less robust, wild-eyed, pluralistic and free, and more decorous, image-conscious, and narcissistic. The media is itself partly to blame for this direction, and it would be dangerous to release it totally from the important check and balance that the libel laws provide. But in the United States, the balance that must be struck between reputation and expression should never be tilted too far against expression, for the right to defiantly, robustly, and irreverently speak one's mind just because it is one's mind is quintessentially what it means to be an American.

Notes

Chapter 1

1. The Carol Burnett case, *Burnett v. National Enquirer, Inc.*, is reported at 144 Cal. App. 3d 991, 193 Cal. Rptr. 206 (1983).

2. The Westmoreland case, *Westmoreland v. CBS,* is reported at 596 F. Supp. 1170 (S.D.N.Y. 1984).

3. For further background on General Westmoreland's decision to sue CBS, see Don Kowett, *A Matter of Honor* (MacMillan, 1984).

4. The Tavoulareas case, *Tavoulareas v. Washington Post,* is reported at 11 Med. L. Rep. (BNA) 1777 (D.C. Cir. 1985), rehearing en banc granted, 11 Med. L. Rept. (BNA) 2017 (June 18, 1985 "News Notes").

5. For a collection of citations to recent libel cases involving well-known cultural figures, see Smolla, *Let the Author Beware: The Rejuvenation of the American Law of Libel,* 132 U. Pa. L. Rev. 1 (1983). See also Jenkins, "Chilly Days for the Press," *Student Lawyer,* Apr. 1983, pp. 23–25.

6. For an excellent essay on the current state of the law of libel in America, see Anthony Lewis, "Annals of Law, The *Sullivan* Case," *The New Yorker,* Nov. 5, 1984.

7. The Ariel Sharon case, *Sharon v. Time, Inc.,* is reported at 559 F. Supp. 538 (S.D.N.Y. 1984).

8. For statistical data concerning current libel litigation trends, see information published periodically by the Libel Defense Resource Center (LDRC), a New York based information clearing house organized by media groups to monitor developments in libel law. A summary of recent LDRC data is reported in James Goodale, *Survey of Recent Media Verdicts, Their Disposition on Appeal, and Media Defense Costs,* in *Media Insurance and Risk Management,* J. Lankeneau, ed. (New York: The Practicing Law Institute, 1985).

9. Two excellent scholarly articles analyzing statistical data in the libel area are Marc Franklin's *Winners and Losers and Why: A Study of Defamation Litigation,* Am. Bar. Found. Research J. 795 (1980), and *Suing the Media for Libel: A Litigation Study,* Am. Bar. Found. Research J. 455 (1981).

10. For discussions of the nature of the reputational interests protected by modern defamation law, see David Anderson, *Reputation, Compensation, and Proof,* 25 Wm. & Mary L. Rev. 747 (1984); Stanley Ingbar, *Defamation: A Conflict Between Reason and Decency,* 65 Va. L. Rev. 785 (1979); Probert, *Defamation, A Camouflage of Psychic Interests: The Beginning of a Behavioral Analysis,* 15 Vand. L. Rev. 1173 (1962); Rodney A. Smolla, "Self-Love and Libel," *The Washington Monthly,* Nov. 1983; and Smolla, *supra* note 5.

11. The narcissistic trends in American culture are discussed in Marin, "The New Narcissism," *Harper's,* Oct. 1975, p. 45; Lasch, "The New Narcissist Society," *New York Review of Books,* Sept. 30, 1976, p. 5, col. 1; and Tom Wolfe, "The "Me" Decade and the Third Great Awakening," *New York,* Aug. 23, 1976.

12. Public opinion poll evidence on attitudes towards the media is reported in "The Media on Trial," *Newsweek,* Oct. 22, 1984.

13. For a discussion of media errors such as the Janet Cooke and Hitler's diaries episodes, see David Johnston, "The Wrong Stuff; How Errors Get to the Printed Page," *Washington Journalism Review*, June 1984, p. 24.

14. For an excellent essay on CBS's *60 Minutes*, see John Weisman, "60 Minutes: A Look at Whether the Show's Success Has Affected the Quality and Zeal of its Reporting," *T.V. Guide*, Apr. 16, 1983.

15. Judge Friendly's suggestion in the Buckley case concerning the media's obligation to "pay the freight" is from *Buckley v. New York Post Corp.*, 373 F.2d 175 (2d Cir. 1967).

16. An interesting discussion of the cross-current between strict liability trends in tort law and defamation is contained in Weiler, *Defamation, Enterprise Liability, and Freedom of Speech*, 17 U. Toronto L. J. 278 (1967).

17. Professor David Anderson has attached the analogy between liability for defamation and other business enterprises. See David Anderson, *Libel and Press Self-Censorship*, 53 Texas L. Rev. 422, 432 n.52 (1975).

18. The changes in the corporate roles of editors are discussed in Alex Jones, "Newspaper Editors on Business Role," *New York Times*, Apr. 14, 1985, p. 11, cols. 1–6.

19. For examples of litigation arising from ABC's *20/20*, see *Cantrell v. ABC*, 529 F. Supp. 746 (N.D. Ill. 1981) (arson for profit story); *New York Times*, May 11, 1982, p. A13, col. 2 (reporting ABC jury victory in Cleveland suit arising from plaintiff's alleged relations with a judge); *Wall Street Journal*, Feb. 23, 1983, p. 31, col. 3 (reporting on litigation from story on Justice Department's witness program).

20. On the Nixon administration's relationship with the press, see E. Porter, *Assault on the Media, The Nixon Years* (University of Michigan Press, 1976).

21. Zechariah Chafee's observations on American libel law are from Zechariah Chafee, *Government and Mass Communications*, 106–07 (1947).

22. David Reisman's observations on the role of libel in American culture are from David Reisman, *Democracy and Defamation: Control of Group Libel*, 42 Colum. L. Rev. 727 (1942).

23. For discussions of the role of tort law in compensating for infliction of emotional distress, see Magruder, *Mental and Emotional Disturbance in the Law of Torts*, 49 Harv. L. Rev. 1033 (1936); Wade, *Defamation and the Right of Privacy*, 15 Vand. L. Rev. 1093 (1962); Ingber, *supra* note 10; Probert, *supra* note 10; Anderson, *supra* note 10; Smolla, *supra* note 5; Delgado, *Words that Wound: A Tort Action for Racial Insults, Epithets and Name-Calling*, 17 Har. Civ. Rts-Civ. Lib. L. Rev. 133 (1982).

Chapter 2

24. The *Times* case is reported at *New York Times Co. v. Sullivan*, 376 U.S. 254 (1964).

25. For two outstanding historical essays on the events surrounding the *Times* case, see Samuel R. Pierce, Jr., *Anatomy of an Historic Decision:* New York Times Co. v. Sullivan, 43 N. Carolina L. Rev. 315 (1965); and Anthony Lewis, *supra* note 6.

26. The scholarly commentary on the *Times* case is extensive. The classic treatment in linking the civil rights and free speech themes of the case is by Harry Kalven, Jr. See Harry Kalven, Jr., *The Negro and the First Amendment* (1966), and *The* New York Times *Case: A Note on the Central Meaning of the First Amendment*, Sup. Ct. Rev. 191 (1964).

27. For other insightful commentary on the *Times* case see Arthur L. Berney, *Libel and the First Amendment—A New Constitutional Privilege*, 51 Va. L. Rev. 1 (1965); William O. Bertelsman, *The First Amendment and Protection of Reputation and Privacy*—New York Times Co. v. Sullivan *and How it Grew*, 56 Ky. L. J. 718 (1967); Anthony Lewis, New York Times v. Sullivan *Reconsidered: Time to Return to "The Central Meaning of the First Amendment"*, 83 Colum. L. Rev. 603 (1983); Willard H. Pedrick, *Freedom of the Press and the Law of Libel: The Modern Revised Translation*, 49 Cornell L.Q. 581 (1964).

28. The school desegregation cases are reported at *Brown v. Board of Education*, 347 U.S. 483 (1954).

29. On the *Brown* case, see generally Richard Kluger, *Simple Justice* (1975); J. Harvey Wilkinson III, *From Brown to Bakke* (Oxford University Press, 1979).

30. For an outstanding intellectual history of the evolution of tort law in the United States, see G. Edward White, *Tort Law in America* (Oxford University Press, 1980).

31. The Eugene Debs case is reported at *Debs v. United States*, 249 U.S. 211 (1919).

32. The Abrams case, containing Justice Holmes' famous dissent, is reported at *Abrams v. United States*, 250 U.S. 616 (1919).

33. Justice Brandeis' equally famous words on free expression are from his concurring opinion in *Whitney v. California*, 274 U.S. 357 (1927).

Chapter 3

34. The Walker and Butts decisions, decided by the Court as companion cases, are reported at *Curtis Pub. Co. v. Butts*, 388 U.S. 130 (1967); *Associated Press v. Walker*, 388 U.S. 130 (1967).

35. The Hill case is reported at *Time, Inc. v. Hill*, 385 U.S. 374 (1967).

36. For commentary on the Hill, Butts, and Walker decisions, see Mellville B. Nimmer, *The Right to Speak from Times to Time: First Amendment Theory Applied to Libel and Misapplied to Privacy*, 56 Cal. L. Rev. 935 (1968); Harry Kalven, Jr., *The Reasonable Man and the First Amendment: Hill, Butts, and Walker*, 1967 Sup. Ct. Rev. 267 (1967).

37. The Rosenbloom case is reported at *Rosenbloom v. Metromedia, Inc.*, 403 U.S. 29 (1971).

38. The Gertz case is reported at *Gertz v. Robert Welch, Inc.*, 418 U.S. 323 (1974).

39. For commentary on *Gertz* see Gerald Ashdown, *Gertz and Firestone: A Study in Constitutional Policy-Making*, 61 Minn. L. Rev. 645 (1977); David W. Robertson, *Defamation and the First Amendment: In Praise of* Gertz v. Robert Welch, Inc., 54 Texas L. Rev. 199 (1976); Victor A. Kovner, *Disturbing Trends in the Law of Defamation: A Publishing Attorney's Opinion*, 3 Hastings Constitutional L.Q. 363 (1976); Marc Franklin, *Good Names and Bad Law: A Critique of Libel Law and a Proposal*, 18 U.S.F.L. Rev. 1 (1983); George Christie, *Defamatory Opinoins and the Restatement (Second) of Torts*, 75 Mich. L. Rev. 1621 (1977); David Anderson, *Libel and Press Self-Censorship*, 53 Tex. L. Rev. 422 (1975); David Anderson, *A Response to Professor Robertson: The Issue is Control of Press Power*, 54 Tex. L. Rev. 271 (1976); David Anderson, *Reputation, Compensation, and Proof*, 25 Wm. & Mary L. Rev. 747 (1984); Joel Eaton, *The American Law of Defamation Through* Gertz v. Robert Welch, Inc. *and Beyond: An Analytical Primer*, 61 Va. L. Rev. 1349 (1975); LaRue; *Living with Gertz: A Practical Look at Constitutional Libel Standards*, 67 Va. L. Rev. 287 (1981); Rosen, *Media Cament—The Rise and Fall of Involuntary Public Figures*, 54 St. John's L. Rev. 487 (1980).

40. Professor John J. Watkins and Charles W. Schwartz authored an insightful review of the issues left open by the *Gertz* case, anticipating the issues that the Supreme Court would be facing in the 1985 *Dun & Bradstreet* decision: John J. Watkins and Charles W. Schwartz, *Gertz and the Common Law of Defamation: Of Fault, Nonmedia Defendants, and Conditional Privileges*, 15 Tex. Tech. L. Rev. 823 (1984).

41. For an excellent series of recent discussions of the fact/opinion distinction in the context of an ideologically charged case, see the various opinions of the judges of the District of Columbia Court of Appeals in *Ollman v. Evans*, 750 F.2d 970 (D.C. Cir. 1984) (en banc). Of particular note is the scholarly opinion of Judge Robert Bork.

42. The quotation from Oliver Wendell Holmes that a word is "the skin of a living thought" comes from *Towne v. Eisner*, 245 U.S. 418, 425 (1918).

43. The fact/opinion distinction is discussed in: Titus, *Statement of Fact Versus Statement of Opinion—A Spurious Dispute in Fair Comment*, 15 Vand. L. Rev. 1203 (1962); Marc Franklin and Daniel Bussel, *The Plaintiff's Burden in Defamation: Awareness and Falsity*, 25 Wm. & Mary L. Rev. 825 (1984).

44. The Lillian Hellman/Mary McCarthy suit is reported at *Hellman v. McCarthy*, 10 Med. L. Rep. (BNA) 1789 (N.Y. Sup. Ct. 1984).

45. For commentary on the *Hellman* case see Robert Kaus, "The Plaintiff's Hour," *Harper's*, March 1983; Goodman, "Literary Incentive," *New York Times*, June 19, 1983, p. 35.

46. Libel suits by writers are not an entirely modern phenomenon: James Fenimore Cooper, for example, sued Horace Greeley for libel. See *Cooper v. Greeley*, 1 Denio 347 (N.Y. Sup. Ct. 1845).

47. For general background on Lillian Hellman and Mary McCarthy, including past literary reviews of each other's work, see McCarthy, "Theatre: The Reform of Dr. Pangloss," *New Republic*, Vol. 135, December 17, 1956, pp. 30–31; McCarthy, "Theatre Chronicle: Dry Ice," *Partisan Review*, Vol. 13, November–December 1946, pp. 577–79; Katherine Lederer, *Lillian Hellman* (Twayne, 1979); Doris Grumbach, *The Company She Kept* (Coward-McCann, 1967); Barbara McKenzie, *Mary McCarthy* (Twayne, 1966).

48. Norman Mailer's open letter to Hellman and McCarthy, "Appeal to Lillian Hellman and Mary McCarthy," was printed in the *New York Times Book Review*, May 11, 1980, p. 3.

49. The Supreme Court decision in the Herbert case is reported in *Herbert v. Lando*, 441 U.S. 153 (1979).

50. The latest round in the lower court in the Herbert litigation is *Herbert v. Lando*, 596 F. Supp. 1178 (S.D.N.Y. 1984) (decision granting CBS partial summary judgment but finding certain statements actionable).

51. CBS correspondent Mike Wallace's commentary on *Herbert v. Lando* is contained in Mike Wallace and Gary Paul Gates, *Close Encounters* (Morrow, 1984).

52. The Rhinehart case is reported at *Seattle Times v. Rhinehart*, 104 S.Ct. 2199 (1984).

53. The protective order dispute in the Tavoulareas litigation is discussed at *Tavoulareas v. Washington Post*, 724 F.2d 1010, and 737 F.2d 1170 (D.C. Cir. 1984).

54. The *Alton Telegraph* case is reported at *Green v. Alton Telegraph Co.*, No. 77-66 (Madison County, Ill. 1980), appellate decision reported at 107 Ill. App. 3d 755, 438 N.E.2d 203 (1982).

55. For a commentary on the impact of cases such as the *Alton Telegraph* litigation on media resources, see John Curley, "'Chilling Effect,' How Libel Suit Sapped the Crusading Spirit of a Small Newspaper," *Wall Street Journal*, Sept. 29, 1983, p. 1, col. 1. See also Fred W. Friendly, "Is Our Libel Law a Threat to Free Speech?," *Washington Post*, January 15, 1984, p. Dl, col. 1; Martin Garbus, "New Challenge to Press Freedom," *New York Times Magazine*, Jan. 29, 1984, p. 34.

56. For data on the costs and plaintiff success rates of modern libel litigation see LDRC data, *supra* note 8; Goodale, *supra* note 8; Franklin, *Winners and Losers*, *supra* note 9; Franklin, *Suing the Media for Libel*, *supra* note 9; Smolla, *supra* note 5.

57. For a fuller explanation of the argument that society should consider the value of free speech in the context of the value of the other social "goods," such as food, shelter, and productivity, see Frederick Schauer, *Public Figures*, 25 Wm. & Mary L. Rev. 905 (1984).

Chapter 4

58. The Sharon case is reported at *Sharon v. Time, Inc.*, 599 F. Supp. 538 (S.D.N.Y. 1984) (opinion denying defendant's motion for summary judgment).

59. For an exhaustive and excellent scholarly review of the issue of responsibility for the Sabra and Shattilla massacres under principles of international law, see Linda Malone, *The Kahan Report, Ariel Sharon, and the Sabra/Shatilla Massacres in Lebanon: Responsibility Under International Law for Massacres of Civilian Populations*, 1985 Utah L. Rev. 373.

60. For a particularly critical and insightful analysis of *Time*'s conduct in putting together the Sharon story, see Steven Brill, "Say it Ain't So, Henry," *The American Lawyer*, Feb. 1985.

61. For a review of the debate concerning *Time*'s editorial standards, see Alex S. Jones, "Editing and Libel; *Time*'s Methods in Sharon Case Spur Debate About Journalism Standards," *New York Times*, Jan. 8, 1985, p. B4, cols. 1–2.

62. For a comparison of the editing techniques of *Time* and *CBS*, see Alex S. Jones, "Libel Suits Show Differing News Approaches of Papers, TV and Magazines," *New York Times*, Jan. 31, 1985, p. B9, cols. 1–6.

63. The Sharon jury instructions are reprinted in *Libel on Trial: The Westmoreland and Sharon Cases,* BNA Special Report, Appendix 4 (Bureau of National Affairs, 1985).

64. For background on the Sharon trial, including a bibliography of the *New York Times'* daily coverage (most of it by *Times* reporter Arnold Lubasch) see generally: David A. Kaplan, "The Judge's Postmortem on the Sharon Libel Trial," *The National Law Journal,* Mar. 18, 1985, p. 1; "Sharon v. *Time,* Inc., The Absence of Malice," *Newsweek,* Feb. 4, 1985, p. 52; Arnold H. Lubasch, "*Time* Magazine Asks U.S. Judge to Dismiss Libel Suit by Sharon, *New York Times,* Oct. 21, 1984, p. 16, cols. 4–5; Lubasch, "Sharon Testifies He Came to U.S. to Defend Truth," *New York Times,* Nov. 15, 1984, p. B1, col. 6; Lubasch, "Sharon Tells of High Moral Values," *New York Times,* Nov. 16, 1984, p. B4, cols. 3–5; Lubasch, "Sharon, Completing His Testimony Says *Time* Article Created Hatred," *New York Times,* Nov. 28, 1984, p. B6, cols. 1–6; Lubasch, "Writer Says He Didn't See Key Part of Sharon Report," *New York Times,* Nov. 30, 1984, p. B4, cols. 4–6; "Israel to Allow Review of Files in Sharon Case," *New York Times,* Dec. 1, 1984, p. 26, col. 1; Lubasch, "Reporter Criticizes Sharon for Staying with Government," *New York Times,* Dec. 4, 1984, p. B2, cols. 5–6; Amos Perlmutter, "Sharon's 'Blood Libel'," *New York Times,* Dec. 5, 1984, p. A31, cols. 1–3; Lubasch, "*Time* Writer, at Libel Trial, Describes Gemayel Slaying," *New York Times,* Dec. 5, 1984, p. B4, cols. 5–6; Lubasch, "Correspondent's Memo on Sharon is Described," *New York Times,* Dec. 7, 1984, p. B21, cols. 1–2; Lubasch, "*Time* Employee Tells How He Wrote Sharon Article," *New York Times,* Dec. 11, 1984, p. B10, cols. 2–6; Lubasch, "*Time* Writer Terms Sharon a Victim of an Obsession," *New York Times,* Dec. 12, 1984, p. B4, cols. 5–6; Lubasch, "Judge Rules Out Israeli Proposal for Trial Data," *New York Times,* Dec. 13, 1984, p. B5, col. 1; Lubasch, "Sharon Lawyer Attacks Career of a Journalist," *New York Times,* Dec. 14, 1984, p. B4, col. 1; Lubasch, "Reporter Was Warned to Stay out of Politics, Sharon Jury Is Told," *New York Times,* Dec. 18, 1984, p. B12, cols. 3–6; Lubasch, "*Time's* Chief Praises Sharon Article," *New York Times,* Dec. 12, 1984, p. B4, cols. 2–4; "Lawyers in Sharon Case To See Secret Appendix," *New York Times,* Jan. 1, 1985, p. 31, cols. 5–6; Lubasch, "Report by Israeli Supports Sharon," *New York Times,* Jan. 8, 1985, p. B4, cols. 5–6; Lubasch, "Sharon Judge Weighing Ruling on Israeli's Report," *New York Times,* Jan. 9, 1985, p. B8, cols. 4–6; Lubasch, "*Time* Denies It Libeled Sharon Despite Error," *New York Times,* Jan. 11, 1985, p. B4, cols. 1–2; Lubasch, "Sharon's Lawyer Gives Final Statement at Trial," *New York Times,* Jan. 12, 1985, p. 24, cols. 1–2; Lubasch, "Sharon Jury Begins Its Deliberations," *New York Times,* Jan. 15, 1985, p. B2, cols. 1–6; Lubasch, "Jurors Back Sharon on 2d Key Point in Libel Trial," *New York Times,* Jan. 19, 1985, p. A1, cols. 5–6; Lubasch, "A Reporter's Notebook: Awaiting Sharon Verdict," *New York Times,* Jan. 20, 1985, p. 20, cols. 3–6.

65. For a portrait of Judge Abraham Sofaer, see: James Brooke, "Accomplished Judge in Sharon Case," *New York Times,* Jan. 15, 1985, p. B2, cols. 1–4.

66. The text of the statement by *Time* acknowledging its error in the Sharon story appeared in the January 21, 1985 issue of *Time,* and was reprinted in the *New York Times,* Jan. 15, 1985, p. B2, cols. 5–6.

67. For discussions of how the Sharon case "played" in Israel, see Thomas L. Friedman, "In Israel, Even Sharon's Worst Enemies Aren't Friends of *Time,*" *New York Times,* Jan. 14, 1984, p. B9, cols. 2–5; Friedman, "Sharon Returns to Fray in Israel," *New York Times,* Jan. 31, 1985, p. A3, col. 1.

68. For a review of the "victory" claims of each side in the Sharon case, see companion articles by Edward Walsh and Herbert Denton, in "Jury Clears *Time* of Malice, Ending Libel Case," *Washington Post,* Jan. 25, 1985, p. A1.

69. In the aftermath of the Sharon case the *New York Times* in an editorial criticized the costly and lengthy libel trial process. See "After Sharon, Improving a Flawed Process," *New York Times,* Jan. 31, 1985, p. A23, cols. 1–3.

Chapter 5

70. The trial court opinion in the Burnett case is reported at *Burnett v. National Enquirer,* 7 Med. L. Rep. (BNA) 1321 (Cal. Super. Ct. 1981).

71. The appellate decision in the Burnett case is reported at *Burnett v. National Enquirer,* 144 Cal. App. 3d 991, 193 Cal. Rptr. 206 (1983).

72. The California retraction statute is codified at Cal. Civ. Code Section 48a.

73. The most significant prior California decisions involving the applicability of the retraction statute to magazines and other publication formats besides straight newspaper stories were *Briscoe v. Reader's Digest, Ass'n,* 4 Cal. 3d 529, 483 P.2d 34, 93 Cal. Rptr. 866 (1971); *Maidman v. Jewish Publications,* 54 Cal. 2d 643 (1969); *Werner v. Southern Cal. Newspapers,* 35 Cal. 2d 121 (1950); *Field Research Corp. v. Superior Court,* 71 Cal.2d 110 (1969); *Kapellas v. Koffman,* 1 Cal. 3d 20 (1969).

74. To support its position that the *Enquirer* could not avail itself of the retraction statute, the court relied primarily upon *Montandon v. Triangle Publications, Inc.,* 45 Cal. App. 3d 938 (1975); *Morris v. National Federation of the Blind,* 192 Cal. App. 2d 162 (1961).

75. The California Court of Appeals' quoted explication of the various meanings of malice was largely taken directly from *Davis v. Hearst,* 160 Cal. 140 (1911).

Chapter 6

76. The Onassis/Dior litigation is reported at *Onassis v. Christian Dior,* 10 Media L. Rep. 1859 (N.Y. Sup. Ct. 1984).

77. The Galella/Onassis case is reported at *Galella v. Onassis,* 487 F.2d 986 (2d Cir. 1973), 533 F. Supp. 1076 (S.D.N.Y. 1982).

78. On the evolution of the rights of privacy and publicity, see generally Samuel Warren and Louis Brandeis, *The Right to Privacy,* 4 Harv. L. Rev. 193 (1980); William Prosser, *Privacy,* 48 Calif. L. Rev. 383 (1960); Peter Felcher and Edward Rubin, *Privacy, Publicity, and the Portrayal of Real People in the Media,* 88 Yale L. J. 1577 (1979).

79. Other cases discussed in the chapter are reported at *Estate of Presley v. Russen,* 513 F. Supp. 1339 (D.N.J. 1981); *Groucho Marx Prods. Inc. v. Day & Night Co.,* 523 F. Supp. 485 (S.D.N.Y. 1981), 689 F.2d 317 (2d Cir. 1982); *Zacchini v. Scripps-Howard Broadcasting Co.,* 433 U.S. 562 (1977); *Grant v. Esquire, Inc.,* 367 F. Supp. 876 (S.D.N.Y. 1973); *Namath v. Sports Illustrated,* 39 N.Y.2d 897, 352 N.E.2d 584, 386 N.Y.2d 397 (1976); *Cher v. Forum International Ltd.,* 692 F.2d 634 (9th Cir. 1982); *Eastwood v. Superior Court,* 149 Cal. App.3d 409, 198 Cal. Rptr. 342, 10 Media L. Rptr. 1073 (1983); *Ali v. Playgirl, Inc.,* 447 F. Supp. 723 (S.D.N.Y. 1978).

Chapter 7

80. The Bindrim case is reported at *Bindrim v. Mitchell,* 92 Cal. App. 3d 61, 155 Cal. Rptr. 29 (1979).

81. For commentary on *Bindrim,* and on the general problem of libel in fiction, see Vivian Deborah Wilson, *The Law of Libel and the Art of Fiction,* 44 Law & Contemp. Problems 29 (1981); Isidore Silver, *Libel, The "Higher Truths" of Art, and The First Amendment,* 126 U. Pennsylvania L. Rev. 1065 (1978); Peter Felcher & Edward Rubin, *Privacy, Publicity, and The Portrayal of Real People by the Media,* 88 Yale L. J. 1577 (1979); Smolla, *supra* note 5.

82. The *Missing* litigation is reported at *Davis v. Costa-Gavras,* 580 F. Supp. 1082 (S.D.N.Y. 1984).

83. For an excellent review of Costa-Gavras' techniques, see the reviews of his films reprinted in Pauline Kael, *When the Lights Go Down* (Holt, Rinehart, & Winston, 1975).

84. The Kissinger and Nixon accounts of events in Chile are recounted in Henry Kissinger, *Years of Upheavel* (Little Brown, 1982); Richard Nixon, *RN: The Memoirs of Richard Nixon* (Grosset & Dunlap, 1978).

85. Seymour Hersh's account of the Nixon administration's actions in Chile is described in Seymour Hersh, *The Price of Power* (Summit, 1983).

86. For two interesting essays revealing the ideological overtones of the *Missing* litigation, see Andrew Kopkind, "Missing: Cultural Battlefield," *The Nation,* Apr. 17, 1982; Jose Yglesias, "WNET, the *Times* and Some History," *The Nation,* May 15, 1982.

Chapter 8

87. Cases discussed in the text are reported at *Pring v. Penthouse Int'l, Ltd.,* 695 F.2d 438 2409 (10th Cir. 1982); *Miss America Pagaent v. Penthouse,* 524 F. Supp. 128 (D. N.J. 1981); *Falwell v. Penthouse,* 7 Med. L. Rep. (BNA) 1891 (D. W.Va. 1981); *Rancho La Costa v. Penthouse,* 8 Med. L. Rep. (BNA) 1865 (1982); *Guccione v. Hustler,* 7 Med. L. Rep. (BNA) 2077 (Ohio Ct. App. Franklin City, 1981); *Keeton v. Hustler Magazine,* 104 S.Ct. 1473 (1984); *Lerman v. Flynt,* 10 Med. L. Rep. (BNA) 2497 (2d Cir. 1984); *Falwell v. Hustler* (Dist. Ct. Roanoke, Va. 1984) (unreported decision).

88. One of the most prolific modern commentators on obscenity problems, Frederick Schauer, has heavily emphasized the purported distinction between speech that causes a mental stimulus, and speech, like pornography, designed to produce a physical effect. See Frederick Schauer, *Speech and 'Speech'—Obscenity and 'Obscenity': An Exercise in Interpretation of Constitutional Language,* 67 Geo. L.J. 899 (1979); Schauer, *Response: Pornography and the First Amendment,* 40 U. Pitt. L. Rev. 605 (1979).

89. The landmark Supreme Court cases on obscenity include *Roth v. United States,* 354 U.S. 476 (1957); *Kingsley International Pictures Corp. v. Regents,* 360 U.S. 684 (1959) (involving film *Lady Chatterley's Lover*); *Stanley v. Georgia,* 394 U.S. 557 (1969); *Miller v. California,* 413 U.S. 15 (1973); *Paris Adult Theatre I v. Slaton,* 413 U.S. 49 (1973); *Jenkins v. Georgia,* 418 U.S. 153 (1974) (involving film *Carnal Knowledge*).

Chapter 9

90. The panel Court of Appeals decision in Tavoulareas is reported at *Tavoulareas v. Washington Post,* 11 Med. L. Rep. (BNA) 1777 (D.C. Cir. 1985), rehearing en banc granted, 11 Med. L. Rep. (BNA) 2017 (June 18, 1985 "News Notes").

91. The District Court opinion in the Tavoulareas case, reversing the jury verdict, is printed at 567 F. Supp. 651 (D. D.C. 1983).

92. Letter from William P. Tavoulareas to Rodney A. Smolla, Dec. 1, 1983, on file with author.

93. For an early review of the impact of the Tavoulareas decision, see James Goodale, *supra* note 9.

94. Steven Brill's excellent investigative article into the jury's behavior in the case is published in Steven Brill, "Inside the Jury Room at the *Washington Post* Libel Trial," *The American Lawyer,* Nov. 1982. See also James J. Cramer, "Cadwalader Goes After the *Washington Post,*" *The American Lawyer,* Sept. 1981.

95. For an intriguing collection of viewpoints on the problem of subjectivity and objectivity in modern journalism, see "Can the Press Tell the Truth?," *Harpers,* Jan. 1985 (Symposium with Lewis H. Lapham, Tom Wicker, Walter Karp, Herbert Schmertz, Sidney Zion, Frances Fitzgerald, and Charles Rembar).

Chapter 10

96. The Westmoreland case is reported at *Westmoreland v. CBS,* 10 Med. L. Rep. (BNA) 2417 (S.D.N.Y. 1984).

97. The trial procedures and proposed jury instructions in the Westmoreland case are reprinted in *Libel on Trial, The Westmoreland and Sharon Cases,* BNA Special Report 1985.

98. For background on the Tet offensive and the American reaction to it, see Don Oberdorfer, *Tet!* (Da Capo, 1971); Peter Braestrup, *The Big Story: How the American Press and the Television Reported and Interpreted the Crisis of Tet 1968* (Westview, 1977); Stanley Karnow, *Vietnam, A History* (Viking, 1983); Frances Fitzgerald, *Fire in the Lake* (Vintage, 1972); Seymour Hersh, *The Price of Power* (Summit, 1983); Nguyen Cao Ky, *How We Lost the Vietnam War* (Stein & Day, 1976); Harrison Salisbury (ed.) *Vietnam Reconsidered, Lessons From a War* (Harper & Row, 1983); David Halberstam, *The Best and the Brightest* (Random House, 1972).

99. General Westmoreland's memoirs are entitled *A Soldier Reports* (Doubleday, 1976).

100. For a discussion of the background of the Westmoreland case, see Don Kowet, *supra* note 3.

101. Mike Wallace's views on the Westmoreland case appear in Wallace and Gates, *supra* note 51.

102. Hodding Carter's PBS series *Inside Story* was highly critical of the CBS broadcast. See *Inside Story* (Hodding Carter, Chief Correspondent), "Uncounted Enemy: Unproven Conspiracy" (broadcast April 21, 1983).

103. For background on the Westmoreland trial, including a bibliography of *New York Times* daily coverage (most of it by *Times* reporter M.A. Farber) see generally Connie Bruck, "The Soldier Takes the Stand," *The American Lawyer*, Jan./Feb. 1985, p. 113; *Newsweek*, "Westmoreland v. CBS: The Media on Trial," Oct. 22, 1984, p. 60; M.A. Farber, "Westmoreland Suit Against CBS Begins Today With Jury Selection," *New York Times*, Oct. 9, 1984, p. A1, cols. 5–6; Farber, "Westmoreland's Lawyer Accuses CBS of Twisting the Truth," *New York Times*, Oct. 12, 1984, p. B3, cols. 1–5; Farber, "Ex-Colonel Denies an Assertion in CBS Show on Aide's Dismissal," *New York Times*, Oct. 23, 1984, p. 19, cols. 1–4; Farber, "U.S. Intelligence Chief Says He Wasn't Asked to Falsify Reports in Vietnam," *New York Times*, Oct. 25, 1984, p. 17, cols. 1–6; Farber, "No 'Ceiling' on Figures, CBS Case Witness Says," *New York Times*, Oct. 26, 1984, p. 13, cols. 1–4; Farber, "A Reporter's Notebook: The Jargon of CBS Trial," *New York Times*, Oct. 29, 1984, p. A21, cols. 2–3; Farber, "Colonel Disputes CBS Documentary at Libel Trial," Oct. 31, 1984, p. A28, cols. 1–4; Farber, "CBS Jury Hears Doubt on Ability of Vietcong's Self-Defense Forces," *New York Times*, Nov. 8, 1984, p. B2, cols. 5–6; Farber, "C.I.A. Aide in Saigon Says Data Was 'Enormous'," *New York Times*, Nov. 9, 1984, p. 9, col. 2; Farber, "Ex-CIA Aide Cites Westmoreland's Help on Troop Figures," *New York Times*, Nov. 10, 1984, p. 9, cols. 1–5; Farber, "'68 Memo by C.I.A. Aide Read at CBS Libel Trial," *New York Times*, Nov. 15, 1984, p. B9, cols. 1–4; Farber, "Westmoreland Rebuts CBS Program at Libel Trial," *New York Times*, Nov. 16, 1984, p. A1, cols. 3; Charles Mohr, "Brilliant Commander of a U.S. Defeat," *New York Times*, Nov. 16, 1984, p. B4, cols. 1–3; Farber, "Westmoreland—CBS Trial, A Running Battle Over Statistics and Credibility," *New York Times*, Nov. 28, 1984, p. B6, cols. 1–6; Farber, "General Disputes Quote in CBS Trial," *New York Times*, Nov. 30, 1984, p. B4, cols. 1–3; Farber, "Westmoreland Testifies Johnson Wanted Data," *New York Times*, Dec. 4, 1984, p. B2, cols. 1–4; Farber, "Paul Nitze Takes Stand in CBS Trial," *New York Times*, Dec. 5, 1984, p. B4, cols. 1–4; Farber, "McNamara Discusses War at CBS Libel Trial," *New York Times*, Dec. 7, 1984, p. B12, cols. 2–3; Farber, "Producer Tells CBS Jurors of Rationale on Interviews," *New York Times*, Dec. 11, 1984, p. B10, cols. 2–5; Farber, "Crile Testifies on Program's Accuracy," Dec. 12, 1984, p. B4, cols. 1–4; Farber, "Crile on Stand, Accused of Subverting the Truth," *New York Times*, Dec. 13, 1984, p. B20, cols. 5–6; Peter W. Kaplan, "Judge Rules CBS Study Not Admissible in Trial," *New York Times*, Dec. 14, 1984, p. B11, cols. 1–2; Nan Robertson, "At Westmoreland Trial, A Judge in Firm Control," *New York Times*, Dec. 18, 1984, p. B14, cols. 1–3; Farber, "Crile's Note Introduced in CBS Trial," *New York Times*, Dec. 18, 1984, p. B14, cols. 4–6; Farber, "CBS Producer Says General Played 'Shell Game'," *New York Times*, Dec. 19, 1984, p. B7, cols. 1–4; Peter W. Kaplan, "For Mike Wallace, A Pause in Trial," *New York Times*, Dec. 21, 1984, p. A32, cols. 3–5; Farber, "CBS—Westmoreland Trial: A Reprise," *New York Times*, Dec. 21, 1984, p. 27, cols. 1–5; Farber, "CBS Jury Is Told of Officer's Letters Citing 'Lies' About Enemy Strength," *New York Times*, Jan. 4, 1985, p. B5, cols. 1–6; Farber, "At CBS Trial, Film Editor Cites His Complaints Concerning Documentary," *New York Times*, Jan. 8, 1985, p. B4, cols. 1–6; Farber, "CBS Opens Libel Trial Defense, Asserts Vietnam Documentary Was True," *New York Times*, Jan. 9, 1985, p. B8, cols. 1–6; Farber, "Ex-C.I.A. Analyst Takes Stand for CBS," *New York Times*, Jan. 11, 1985, p. B4, cols. 4–6; Farber, "Ex-C.I.A. Analyst Says Westmoreland's Actions Cost Thousands of Lives," *New York Times*, Jan. 15, 1985, p. B2, cols. 1–6; Farber, "CBS Assertion Based on 'Guesses,' Witness Says," *New York Times*, Jan. 18, 1985, p. A8, cols. 1–3; Farber, "CBS Witness Denies Profiting From Troop Dispute," *New York Times*, Jan. 22, 1985, p. A12, cols. 1–3; Farber, "CBS Witness Links U.S. Losses to Vietnam Self-Defense Force," *New York Times*, Jan. 23, 1985, p. B28,

cols. 1–6; Farber, "CBS Jury Told of C.I.A. 'Sellout' in '67," *New York Times*, Jan. 24, 1985, p. B5, cols. 1–4; Farber, "CBS Witness Says General Used 'Political Power'," *New York Times*, Jan. 30, 1985, p. B12, cols. 3–6; Farber, "Ex-C.I.A. Witness for CBS Supports Adams Testimony," *New York Times*, Jan. 31, 1985, cols. 1–2; Farber, "Jurors in CBS Case Get Preview of Summations," *New York Times*, Feb. 1, 1985, p. B4, cols. 1–2; Farber, "CBS Witness Says General Set Ceiling," *New York Times*, Feb. 6, 1985, p. B4, cols. 1–6; Farber, "Ex-Intelligence Aide Says Westmoreland Delayed a Key Cable," *New York Times*, Feb. 7, 1985, p. A1, col. 6; Farber, "CBS Producer Reasserts Politics Led to Low Estimates of Enemy Strength," *New York Times*, Feb. 8, 1985, p. B4, cols. 1–6; Farber, "Kennedy Speech Is Shown to Jury in Trial for Libel," *New York Times*, Feb. 9, 1985, p. 46, cols. 1–4; Farber, "Jury Told of Order to Cut Troop Count," *New York Times*, Feb. 12, 1985, p. 27, cols. 1–3; Farber, "CBS and General Seek Settlement in Libel Lawsuit," *New York Times*, Feb. 18, 1985, p. A1, col. 1; Farber, "The Westmoreland Case: A Broken West Point Tie," *New York Times*, Feb. 24, 1985, p. 1, cols. 3–4.

Chapter 11

104. For a discussion of some of the reform suggestions prompted by the Sharon and Westmoreland suits, see Stuart Taylor, Jr., "Cost of Libel Suits Prompts Calls to Alter System," *New York Times*, Feb. 25, 1985, p. A11, cols. 1–6.

105. A collection of suggestions on libel reform was recently compiled in a special pullout section of *The American Lawyer*, edited by Steven Brill (July/August 1985), including the viewpoints of Brill, Floyd Abrams, Harold Evans, Marc Franklin, John Kuhns, Jonathan Lubell, William Rusher, Thomas Shields, William Tavoulareas, William Thomas, Mike Wallace and Bob Woodward.

106. For a discussion of possible constitutional barriers to so-called "right of reply" remedies, see *Miami Herald Publishing Co. v. Tornillo*, 418 U.S. 241 (1974).

107. For examples of decisions outlawing punitive damages awards in libel cases, see *Stone v. Essex County Newspapers*, 367 Mass. 849, 330 N.E.2d 161 (1975); *Wheeler v. Green*, 286 Ore. 99, 593 P.2d 777 (1978); *Tasket v. King Broadcasting*, 86 Wash. 2d 439, 447 546 P.2d 81 (1976).

108. For an excellent discussion of the possible First Amendment arguments that might be garnered to support reforms aimed at ending punitive damages and tying jury awards more directly to compensation, see William W. Van Alstyne, *First Amendment Limitations on Recovery From the Press—An Extended Comment on the "Anderson Solution"*, 24 Wm. & Mary L. Rev. 793 (1984).

109. Cases cited in the chapter are reported at *Dun & Bradstreet, Inc. v. Greenmoss Builders, Inc.*, No. 83-18, (U.S. Sup. Ct., June 26, 1985); *Nader v. General Motors Corp.*, 25 N.Y.2d 560, 30 N.Y.S.2d 647, 255 N.E.2d 765 (1970); *Nader v. De Toledano*, 408 A.2d 31 (D.C. Ct. App. 1978); *Time, Inc. v. Firestone*, 424 U.S. 448 (1976); *Wolston v. Reader's Digest Ass'n*, 443 U.S. 157 (1979); *Hutchinson v. Proxmire*, 443 U.S. 111 (1979) *Paul v. Davis*, 424 U.S. 693 (1976).

Index

269

Index   275

Piro, Dr. Philip, 183, 185, 188, 193
Playboy, 161–162, 177, 179
Playgirl, 136–137
Pope, Generoso, 108
Pornography and First Amendment, 162–181
Powers, Thomas, 227
Presley, Elvis, 124–127
Press. *See* Media
Price of Power, The, 155
Pring, Kimerli Jane, 6, 163–164
Privacy
  invasion of, 7, 239
  protection of, 8, 18, 118–137
  right of, 118–137
  suits, growing numbers, 6–7
Private figures as libel plaintiffs, 57–60
Private property of public figures, 118–137
Protective orders, 72
Proxmire, Sen. William, 254
Prurient interest, 178
Psychic injury, 24–25
Public figures as libel plaintiffs, 53–54, 58–60, 118–137, 254
"Public interest," as standard in libel litigation, 55–56, 251–254
Public officials as libel plaintiffs, 50, 58–60, 243
Public personality, 53–54, 58–60, 118–137, 243, 254
Publicity, right of, 124, 135, 170. *See also* Privacy, right of
Punitive damages awards, 74, 108, 111–112, 116, 250
  limiting, 241–242
Purdy, Frederick D., 151

Rancho LaCosta resort, 6, 174–175
Rather, Dan, 11, 12, 21
Reagan, Ronald, 20, 57, 112, 120, 166, 232–233
Reasoner, Harry, 11
Reckless disregard standard, 50–51, 54, 55–56, 58, 67, 91–92, 195–197
Reforms for the law of libel, 238–257
Regents of the University of California v. Bakke, 27
Rehnquist, Justice, 173–174, 254
Reisman, David, 17
Reporters, changing image of, 10–11
Reporting, investigative. *See* Journalism, investigative
Reputation
  attitudes toward, 17–19, 24, 254–257

protection of, 8, 17–19, 58
value of, 107, 254–257
Reston, James, 236
Retractions
  in Burnett case, 107, 109
  equal time remedies, 241
  in *New York Times v. Sullivan* case, 30
  refusal, 242
  in *Sharon v. Time, Inc.*, 92
  statutes, 107–111, 241
  Washington Post's refusal, 187–188
Reynolds, Barbara, 119–120, 122
Rhinehart, Keith Milton, 72–73
Ribicoff, Abraham, 245
Ridgeway, Matthew, 223
Right to Privacy, The, 123
Rivera, Geraldo, 14
Roe v. Wade, 27
Ron Smith Celebrity Look-Alikes, 119–120, 122
Roosevelt, Franklin, 255
Roselli, Johnny, 175
Rosenbloom, George, 56
Rosenbloom v. Metromedia, Inc., 56, 57, 251
Rosenblum, Ken, 69–70
Rosenthal, A. M., 10
Rostow, Walter, 208, 212, 216, 223–224
Roth v. United States, 177
Rumors of War, 217
Rustin, Bayard, 34

Sacramento Bee, 5
Sadat, Anwar, 83
Safer, Morely, 11
St. Amant v. Thompson, 67
Salisbury, Harrison E., 34
San Francisco Examiner, 74
Saturday Evening Post, 54
Saudi Maritime Company (Samarco), 183–184, 193, 194
Sauter, Van Gordon, 221
Sawyer, Diane, 11
Seattle Times, 72
Seay, Rev. S. S., Sr., 31, 33
Sedition Act (1798), 45–46, 50
Self-censorship, 58, 66, 76. *See also* Freedom of speech, chilling of
"Selling of Colonel Herbert, The," 69
Sharon, Ariel, 5, 67, 80–99, 108, 185, 191, 194, 244, 257
Sharon v. Time, Inc., 80–99, 194
Sharp, Admiral Ulysses S. Grant, 222
Shockley, William, 247–248
Shuttlesworth, Rev. Fred, 31, 33